— The New —
Twelve Month Gardener
A West Coast Guide

The New Twelve Month Gardener

A West Coast Guide

Elaine Stevens ❧ Jane Mitchell ❧ Ann Buffam
Dagmar Hungerford ❧ Doris Fancourt-Smith

WHITECAP BOOKS

VANCOUVER/TORONTO

Whitecap Books
Vancouver / Toronto

Edited by Elaine Jones
Proofread by Elizabeth McLean
Cover design by Warren Clark
Interior design and typesetting by Warren Clark
Front cover photograph by Paddy Wales
Interior photographs by Paddy Wales except where noted
Interior decorative graphics by Jennifer Rogers
Interior illustrations by Doris Fancourt-Smith

Printed and bound in Canada

Canadian Cataloguing in Publication Data

Main entry under title:
    The new twelve-month gardener

    Includes bibliographical references and index.
    ISBN 1-55285-063-3

    1. Garden—British Columbia—Vancouver Island.
2. Gardening—British Columbia—Lower Mainland.
I. Stevens, Elaine.
SB453.3.C2N48 2000   635'.09711'2   C00-911182-4

The publisher acknowledges the support of the Canada Council and the Cultural Services
Branch of the Government of British Columbia in making this publication possible. We
acknowledge the financial support of the Government of Canada through the Book
Publishing Industry Development Program for our publishing activities.

To the next generation of gardeners,

especially to Alison, Caroline,

Jessica, Jonathan, Mark, Nicholas,

Richard, Robert, Rory, Sarah,

Suzanne and Tara.

Contents

Foreword

S ome years ago, when visiting a rather old garden, I saw a carved inscription:
"If thou has two loaves of bread, sell one to buy flowers—for one will nourish thy body, the other one, thy soul."

How true, especially in my case; however, while buying flowers is always satisfying, my experience tells me that a better way is to "grow" them. Growing them, for me, starts with sowing seeds (after the joy of reading seed catalogues while being curled up in a reclining chair by the fire on a cold winter's night), transplanting and watering them, and savouring the exquisitely wonderful feeling that one is giving life.

The care and loving attention that follows have taught me patience and an appreciation for the magnificence of nature and creation, from which I have derived peace of mind and tranquillity. Need I say more?

To fully enjoy a garden, one needs to make as few mistakes as possible. To put it another way, one has to take full advantage of the expert knowledge others are willing to share with you.

The Twelve-Month Gardener, compiled by five exceptionally knowledgeable and experienced gardeners, is an excellent guide, specifically created for gardeners in our West Coast region. This book is an answer to my prayers. I started reading the draft and could not put it down; but, alas, my volunteer gardeners, who helped me rebuild several gardens in Government House, found it so useful that they borrowed it often and almost refused to return it!

I will treasure this book as interesting reading as well as a valuable guide.

David C. Lam
Lieutenant-Governor of British Columbia
1988–1995

Acknowledgements

The inspiration for this book grew out of our involvement with the VanDusen Master Gardener's Program; our thanks to the many lecturers and experienced Master Gardeners who have shared their knowledge and ideas with us over the years.

Thanks are due to the following people: to our editor Elaine Jones who ironed out the kinks with unfailing humour and patience; technical editor Carolyn Jones who caught our technical goofs; and illustrator Jennifer Rogers, for the delightful decorative graphics.

To Carol Dale, Louise Hager and Allan MacDougall who shared their professional advice on books, helping to bring this one to print; to Claire Bennett who advised on rhododendrons; and to Nenagh McCutcheon for her help on water gardens.

To Robert Hungerford, Peter Fancourt-Smith, Erle Mitchell and Frank Buffam for their patience, support and understanding; to Larry Chan for his help and support; to Terri Clark for her warm enthusiasm; and to Karin O'Connor for being our cheering section in Victoria.

Last, but not least, our heartfelt thanks to friends and family who responded positively and enthusiastically as the book developed, even when we ignored or neglected them. We're free now, and look forward to meeting again for lunch or dinner . . . .

Introduction

I knew nothing whatever last year about gardening and this year know very little more, but I have dawnings of what may be done. . . .

Elizabeth von Arnim,
from *Elizabeth and her German Garden*

Writing this book has brought together five distinct individuals with one common bond: gardening. We wrote it because we believe there is a need for a practical handbook for local gardeners, a book that applies specifically to our region and climate, that will help people to garden creatively and enjoyably in this wonderful area.

The main body of the book is divided into monthly chapters, each with a list of garden highlights, a checklist of things to do, and selected topics of interest to local gardeners. This information is linked to the month that seems most appropriate, but in many cases it is readily applied to several different months. We have cross-referenced information where applicable, and the index at the back will help readers find multiple references.

The sections at the end of the book provide general gardening information, including a list of monthly gardening special events. Specific information on parks and gardens, nurseries and various other local resources can be found in the Resources section.

The monthly highlights identify blooming times, but these times can vary considerably in our area, even from one garden to the next, depending upon location and exposure. As a general rule, the Victoria area is the most advanced, and the Fraser Valley is the furthest behind. We give times that are somewhere in the middle. Plant hardiness can also vary considerably, depending upon the severity of the winter, the protection afforded by the site, and any extra protection given to the plant by its owner. Check carefully before you buy a plant to make sure it will survive in your garden.

The chapters contain extensive plant lists, selected for our particular gardening area and including annuals and perennials, flowering shrubs and trees, and plants suitable for sunny or shady sites. Some plants are not available in every gardening store, but are included because they are interesting and worth the search. The lists of specialty nurseries and mail-order gardening in the Resources section should help you to locate the plants you are seeking. By including unusual as well as more common plants, we hope this book will be of help and interest to both beginners and expert gardeners.

Recommended reading lists relating to specific topics are provided at the end of every chapter, as well as a general reading list at the back of the book. Some of the books are no longer available for purchase but are available either through the public library or the libraries at the various botanical gardens and garden societies.

Geographically, we live in an extremely rich plant-growing area, with gardens and gardeners who represent the many diverse gardening traditions of the world. We hope this book will help you to draw on these rich traditions, and that you will visit the gardens we describe and use the ideas and knowledge you gain in your own garden.

Your garden is your refuge from the world. It should be a place that meets the needs of the whole family, and is a safe environment for children and animals, enjoyed by everyone. For this reason we recommend only organic care, and organic pest and disease control. It is important that home gardeners take the initiative to move away from chemical controls and return the earth to a more natural, healthy state.

Gardening is a very humbling experience. Plants cannot be controlled, but grow as and when they want to. Working in the garden is an exercise in patience and understanding. If you let it, gardening can teach you a lot, not just about plants but also about life. The garden is one of the best places for creative thinking, for meditating as you pull the weeds, dig the earth or watch the flowers grow.

We don't pretend to be expert gardeners but, like Elizabeth von Arnim, we have "dawnings of what may be done" and look forward to many more years of learning in the garden.

January

January is so unpredictable. Our area can be covered in a blanket of snow, or basking in the warmth of springlike days. Some years the weather changes so quickly that buds start to open, only to be stopped in midstride by a freezing cold snap that kills the tender blossoms.

The key words for January are "be prepared." You might need to dash out in the middle of the night to cover a tender shrub, protecting it from sudden ice and frost. Heavy snow can break branches and deform plants very quickly, unless you keep on clearing it away.

January offers more colour than we may imagine at first glance. The delicate autumn-flowering cherry (*Prunus subhirtella* 'Autumnalis') is still in bloom, and fragrant *Viburnum* x *bodnantense* continues to open its pink flowers. At this time, winter aconites begin to flower and the first snowdrops make a welcome appearance. Conifers and evergreens are particularly valuable, giving shape and structure to the garden, and variegated leaves can create an impression of sunshine even on the greyest days.

There are many trees and shrubs with coloured and patterned bark and stems, excellent for flower arranging. Take time to admire the furry buds of magnolias, the twisted silhouette of the corkscrew hazel (*Corylus avellana* 'Contorta'), and the silvery-grey branches of the pink dogwood (*Cornus florida* 'Rubra'). There's beauty all around us if we just look.

This is a great time to catch up on indoor gardening activities such as planning a new garden or redesigning an old one. Garden design is the main topic this month, followed by simple instructions on how to train an apple or pear tree against a wall or fence.

Perusing seed and mail-order catalogues is another indoor activity that is uplifting at this often dismal time of year. To quote from the *Globe and Mail*, "some people get erotic pleasure out of reading seed catalogues, with such descriptions as 'good in a bed, but better still up against a wall!'" For more information on mail-order gardening, refer to the Resources section.

If the weather cooperates, January is also a good time for outdoor construction, such as building fences and laying a patio. Shrubs, trees, and even bare-root roses can be planted if the ground is workable enough.

Garden Highlights

*indicates fragrance

Bulbs

Crocus spp.,* *Cyclamen coum, Eranthis hyemalis* (winter aconite), *Galanthus* spp. (snowdrop), *Iris reticulata.**

Perennials

Arum italicum 'Pictum', *Helleborus* x *foetidus*, *H.* x *hybridus, H. niger* (Christmas rose), *Iris unguicularis* (Algerian iris).*

Climbers

Jasminum nudiflorum (winter jasmine).

Shrubs

Camellia sasanqua, Chimonanthus praecox (wintersweet),* *Cornus alba* 'Elegantissima' (Tatarian dogwood), *C. a.* 'Sibirica' (Siberian dogwood), *C. sericea* 'Flaviramea' (gold-twig dogwood), *Corylus avellana* 'Contorta' (Harry Lauder's walking stick, corkscrew hazel), *Daphne mezereum* (February daphne),* *Erica carnea* (winter heath), *Garrya elliptica* (tassel bush), *G. elliptica* 'James Roof', *Hamamelis mollis* (Chinese witch hazel),* *H.* x *intermedia* 'Arnold Promise', 'Diane' and 'Copper Beauty', *Mahonia* x 'Charity',* *Rhododendron dauricum, R. mucronulatum, Viburnum* x *bodnantense,** *V. fragrans.**

Trees

Prunus subhirtella 'Autumnalis' (autumn-flowering cherry).

January Checklist

Annuals, perennials and bulbs

- Order annual seeds from catalogues and plan flower garden.
- Check stored gladioli corms and dahlia and begonia tubers for rot, disease or insect problems. Order new bulbs now for spring planting.
- Check overwintered geranium (*Pelargonium* spp.) cuttings, and throw out failures.
- Plant lily bulbs in well-drained soil if weather permits.
- Protect crowns of tender perennials if frost is expected, and firm down roots of plants lifted by frost.
- Start cleaning up flower beds, removing leaves and other debris.

Trees, shrubs and climbers

- After a snowfall, carefully shake snow from evergreens to lessen the chance of branches breaking.

- Ensure that stakes and ties are secure on climbers and trees, and that ties are not too tight.
- On a mild day, cut a few branches of early-flowering shrubs, such as forsythia, Chinese witch hazel (*Hamamelis mollis*) or camellia for forcing indoors.
- Spray deciduous trees and shrubs with dormant oil and lime sulphur to kill overwintering eggs of insect pests and spores of plant diseases.
- Continue to plant bare-root roses if ground is not frozen or waterlogged.

Fruits, vegetables and herbs

- Plan the vegetable and herb garden, listing the vegetables you want to grow and when they should be planted (see the July chapter for planting and planning information). Order seeds from catalogues.
- Prune fruit trees and bushes and spray with dormant oil and lime sulphur towards the end of the month if the weather is mild.
- Plant fruit trees and bushes if the weather permits.
- Mulch or cover tender herbs if it gets too cold.
- Start lettuce and early greens in cold frame (see the July chapter) towards the end of the month.

General garden activities

- Study garden layout and plan changes for next season.
- Sharpen, clean and oil garden tools and clean and service power equipment.
- Turn compost if weather permits.
- Remove any accumulated leaves or other debris from the lawn and try not to walk on frozen grass.

- Create a beautiful basket for your front door or porch, filled with primulas, cyclamen or other spring flowers.

Garden Design and Colour

January is a good time to analyze the strengths and weaknesses of a garden. Leaves are off the trees, perennials have died back, the earth looks barren and forlorn. What is left behind—shrubs and trees, paths and walkways, walls and trellises—are the "bones" of the garden, its basic structure and form. How these features look in midwinter can tell you a lot about the changes you may want to make.

Public gardens provide ideas

Our area has a fascinating variety of different types of gardens, reflecting the diversity of cultural groups with strong gardening traditions that have made this area their home. The Japanese Nitobe Garden at the University of British Columbia, Dr. Sun Yat-Sen Classical Chinese Garden in Vancouver's Chinatown, and the Japanese Garden in Butchart Gardens are excellent examples of traditional Oriental gardens, where each element of the garden has a specific and often symbolic meaning. On the other hand, some gardens follow European traditions, such as most of Butchart Gardens and VanDusen Garden, with lawns, wide annual and perennial beds, formal areas reminiscent of Italy and France, and many colourful summer displays.

Looking at these and other public gardens is useful, because the first thing to think about when planning your own garden is how you want it to feel. After all, it is an extension of the interior of your house, and both are reflections of your interests and personality. The age and style of your house is also a factor: the garden should enhance the look of the house, rather than fight with it. Do you prefer the cool elegance of a Japanese garden, or the robust colour and energy of a traditional English perennial border? Are you particularly interested in growing roses, or hostas, or rhododendrons? Do you need lots of room in the garden for children and dogs to play, or can you plant fragile, delicate things without worrying that they will be trampled underfoot?

When they are first designed, public gardens are planned in some detail. Major plants are chosen carefully, sited appropriately and combined with other materials, including paving, paths, walls and fences, to create the desired result. In large gardens, such as VanDusen Botanical Garden, there are many different gardens-within-the-garden, including a wide Rhododendron Walk with a large collection of species rhododendrons, a tiny, secluded Meditation Garden, and a Heritage Garden of native plants.

Planning on a small scale

In a private garden the scale is different, but the possibilities are just as exciting: check out the back lanes in your area and you will be amazed at the diversity and variety of gardens created from the same-sized lot. Your final design will depend upon your individual taste, needs and priorities, helping you to create a pleasant, functional and personal environment.

Where to begin? First, there are some important questions to ask yourself. They will help you establish some of the design criteria for your plan.

Privacy: How much, or little, would you like in your garden?

Some people like to be able to chat with their neighbours across an open expanse of lawn, while others need to surround their property with a tall hedge before they can feel at home. Chainlink fences, wooden fences, hedging trees and shrubs offer different amounts of privacy. Barriers between one property and another can cause tension between neighbours so, whatever you decide to do, it is an excellent idea to discuss it with the neighbours first.

Comfort: Do you need protection from street noise, or wind, or strong summer sun?

If your house fronts onto a busy street, you may need a high hedge to keep out the noise, and a secure garden to keep children and animals safe. Although the Lower Mainland is rarely affected by strong winds, residents of exposed shoreline areas, such as southern Vancouver Island and Howe Sound, may need some protection. Too much sun is not usually a problem here, but long, hot, dry spells during the summer can make it uncomfortable to sit out in the garden unless you have created a shady, sheltered spot somewhere.

Beauty: Do you look out at a neighbour's beautiful tree—or an ugly garage wall? Is your garden full of colour in summer, but dull and uninteresting in winter?

It's not hard to camouflage visual eyesores. Ugly walls can be covered with ivy, roses, clematis and other climbers. A pretty tree in one corner of the garden can hide a telephone pole and suspended wires. If your garden consists mainly of annuals and summer-flowering perennials, you may want to consider adding trees, shrubs and winter-flowering perennials for year-round interest.

Convenience and safety: *Are your walks and pathways well located and free of overhanging shrubs and other obstacles? Are steps well lit?*

Siting of pathways and walkways and good garden lighting are important aspects of garden design. Paths should lead easily from one area of the garden to another and be well lit for maximum safety, even on dark winter nights. Materials for paths and walkways are discussed briefly below, and lighting is discussed in the November chapter.

Ease of maintenance: *How many hours a week are you prepared to spend on your garden, cutting lawns, weeding beds, pruning bushes? Are you away a lot and unable to water during dry summer months?*

Many people have unrealistic expectations about the time it takes to garden. There's really no shortcut to keeping a garden in good shape, unless you can afford to pay someone to do it for you. However, as any keen gardener will tell you, gardening is its own reward, calming for the soul and soothing to the spirit. If you are away a lot in the summer, it's best to concentrate on spring-, fall- and winter-blooming plants, and install a sprinkler system for the dry, hot months.

Flexibility: *How many different uses will you have for each area? Can you alter the garden easily as needs change?*

If you plan to stay in one house for many years, your outdoor needs will change over time. A well-fenced lot with a minimum of plants to wreck is best for small children and dogs. As they grow, they will learn to respect the garden and may even want a little area of their own to plant, and you can become more adventurous. Your garden can be divided into a series of "rooms," each with a different function. It can also be specially prepared to provide proper environments for different kinds of plants with widely differing soil requirements, such as acid-loving and lime-loving plants.

Bearing the above questions in mind, the first step is to look at your lot carefully, from viewpoints inside and outside the house. What do you like? What don't you like? How much sun do you get in winter, and in summer? What do others in the family think about the garden? What would they like to see changed?

Go and look at other gardens, both public and private. Every year garden tours are offered through various organizations (see Monthly Special Events), and these are great opportunities to see other people's ideas. How do they use walls, pathways, fences, trellises and different planting materials to create various effects? If you see something you like, you can always adapt the idea for your own garden. You may also find inspiration from illustrated gardening books and photos.

Preparing the plan

As you make your plan, the first rule is to trust your own judgement; after all, it's your garden. Wander around it whenever you can and try to imagine how different ideas, plants, colours and designs might work. This kind of creative leisure activity takes time but will probably generate some of your best ideas. Next, take pictures of your garden from every angle, including views from the house. Paste the pictures together to create a collage of the garden as it looks presently, and you're ready to experiment. Lay tracing paper over the top and, by adding structures and plantings, see if you can create your desired effect.

Using graph paper, make scale drawings of the garden. Use tracing paper in the same way as you did with the photo collage to try out different landscaping ideas. The more you experiment beforehand, the less chance there is of making a major mistake. Begin planning in the abstract, concentrating on the broad characteristics of shape, texture and colour, rather than on specific details. For example, a tall screen structure could be a brick wall, a wooden fence, an evergreen hedge or a row of lilacs, depending upon adjacent garden features. In planning, try to relate the garden to the house. You can create a sense of intrigue by having distinct spaces that lead cleverly to the next point of interest. Or you may decide upon a water feature, which brings a sense of tranquillity to the garden.

Keep all elements of the design to scale. One of the most common errors people make is to select shrubs and trees that will grow too large: a Douglas fir looks magnificent in the forest, but is completely out of place on a 33-foot (10-metre) city lot.

The garden framework

Before you decide upon the placement of plants, the first things to locate on the plan are major structural elements: paths, walkways, patios, decks and fences. These will give you a framework for the plantings. There are many materials in use today for paths, walkways and patios, including poured concrete, exposed aggregate, patio slabs of concrete squares and rounds, red and grey interlocking pavers, old bricks, granite off-cuts and slabs, slate, mica pieces and many others. It's worth visiting stone suppliers and lumber yards to look at the range of possibilities. Some materials are extremely expensive, others quite reasonable; you'll need to look around.

Decks and fences are usually made of local lumber, such as cedar. If you are looking for a softer look than a fence will give, check out hedging plants, which can be either evergreen or deciduous. Evergreen will give you the best screen if privacy is desired. In many situations informal floral hedges can be used to beautiful effect as boundary hedges; in other cases, boundaries demand something solid and uncompromising, such as English laurel (*Prunus laurocerasus*), western red cedar (*Thuja plicata*) and the less commonly seen yew (*Taxus baccata*). These are perfectly suitable and in scale with the larger garden. In the smaller garden there is an opportunity to use flowering and berried shrubs, such as forsythia (*Forsythia* x *intermedia*), Mexican orange (*Choisya ternata*), spirea (*Spiraea thunbergii*), escallonia (*Escallonia* spp.) and roses (*Rosa* spp.).

Focal points: pergolas, arbours, trellises, bird baths and statues

These romantic and stylistic garden structures can make an enormous difference to the look of a garden. Try to imagine an archway over your walkway covered with roses, an arbour of clematis, a bird bath in the middle of the rose bed, or a statue rising out of the rhododendron bushes. Non-essential structural elements add a lot to the character of your garden. Each major area should have some sort of focal point, whether it is a specimen shrub or tree, a piece of sculpture, a bench or a bed of hostas. Be careful, however, to avoid having too many focal points, as they will tend to cause visual confusion and cancel one another out.

Simplicity works best

It is usually best to keep things simple. Once the major structural elements are established, choose and combine plant materials carefully, paying attention to their shapes, textures, colours and blooming times, so that they will provide ever-changing interest throughout the seasons. Too great a variety of plants is distracting, while some massed plantings of similar shapes, textures and colours tend to be pleasing and harmonious.

Consider selecting plants purely for the different shapes and textures of their foliage. After all, unlike flowers, foliage is with us from spring to winter. Also, look at the different shapes of flower heads, such as umbels, spires, plumes and buttons, and keep in mind plants that produce interesting seed heads that remain long after the flowers themselves have faded.

You may want to develop specific themes in your garden, especially if you are particularly fond of a certain kind of plant. Ideas might include a rose garden, herb garden, fragrant garden, heather garden, thyme lawn and a rhododendron walk. Colour is also a critical element in design, because it has such a strong effect upon the feeling of a garden. An all-white garden, for instance, makes even the smallest area feel more spacious and serene, whereas hot pinks and oranges will give the illusion of tropical warmth. Deciding what colours to have in your garden is as important as deciding what colours to paint the rooms in your house. However, garden colours are more flexible; you can have different colours in the same area at different times of the year.

Professional help: do you need it?

Maybe, maybe not. It all depends upon the complexity of your project, how much money

Tip of the Month: Lawns

If you've been wondering whether you should give up having a lawn because it requires too much maintenance or too many chemicals, have a look at these tips before you make your decision. If you still feel that grass is too much work, attractive alternatives include a moss or thyme lawn or wildflower meadow.

De-thatching. Some lawns have a dense layer of dead grass that forms into a thick mat and stops the penetration of water to grass roots. It is usually a result of poor drainage, overfertilization and overwatering. Routine raking may keep it in check, but a spring or early fall scarification with a rented machine is better. The dead grass should be removed.

Aeration. Soil compaction is usually the greatest threat to lawns, reducing the movement of air, water and nutrients to grass roots, making it vulnerable to weeds, disease, moss and thatch buildup. It is worth aerating the soil twice a year, spring and fall, with a plug remover. Grass plugs may be left on the lawn or raked up.

Top-dressing. After aerating the lawn, top-dress with a layer of topsoil, sand or compost, or a mixture of loam, sand and organic matter. Successful lawns depend on a nutrient-rich, physically aerated, 6-inch (15-cm) layer of topsoil. Sifted compost makes the best all-round soil conditioner.

Liming the soil. In our rainy climate, salts leach quickly out of the soil, leaving it too acidic for healthy grass. Spring and fall dusting with dolomite lime will rebalance the soil. Use a spreader set to appropriate density, following product directions.

Seeding. Bare patches should be reseeded with seed mixes appropriate to your area. Plant new lawn in late summer or early fall, when warm days, light rains and cool nights provide the best growing conditions.

Mowing. Grass is much healthier if it is left a bit long. Longer grass shades any bare patches, making it difficult for weed seeds to germinate, and causes less stress to grass plants. Keep your mower blades sharp and about 3 inches (7 cm) high. Allow the grass to grow about an inch (2.5 cm) high before cutting it again. Grass clippings can be left on the lawn.

Watering. Water long enough to give the lawn a deep soaking to the roots to a depth of 4 to 6 inches (10 to 15 cm). Deep roots aid survival through dry summers. Frequent, shallow watering simply encourages the roots to grow at a shallow level, and does more harm than good.

you have to spend, and whether you are looking at minor changes or major revisions. There are many experts you can call, including landscape architects, designers, contractors, design-build contractors and gardeners. They each have their own areas of expertise and training, but the differences aren't always clear.

Representatives of the various professional groups, garden store owners, landscape supply companies, and private individuals who have used professional help agree that there is a big difference between commercial and residential landscaping: the landscape architect whose downtown work you admire may not be the best one to help you with a small city lot.

All landscape architects have to be registered and licensed by the British Columbia Society of Landscape Architects (B.C.S.L.A.), and pass the B.C.S.L.A. exam before they can practise. There are no prerequisite qualifications for any of the other groups, but this does not mean they can't do the job. There are some excellent and very capable designers and contractors, just as there are also some excellent residential landscape architects.

The best way to find the right person for your garden is to ask around, especially among your friends and supply people at the local garden store. If you decide to consult with an expert, ask to see their portfolio, with examples of their work, and obtain references from previous clients. Make sure you are satisfied with all the details of the project and put the contract in writing before work begins.

What services do the different professionals offer?

Landscape architects. Landscape architects do for landscape what architects do for buildings: that is, they study the form and function of the site, plan structures to frame it, create separate areas within the frame, and then decorate these areas. They have received many years of training in structural site problems such as drainage, irrigation, retaining walls and complex structures. They can follow a project through from conceptual drawings to supervision of final construction.

Only licensed members of the B.C.S.L.A. may use the title of landscape architect in this province. In order to be licensed, they must have a degree from a recognized university program in landscape architecture, work experience and successful completion of professional licensing examinations. For the most current listing of landscape architects willing to work on small-scale residential projects, contact the B.C.S.L.A.

Landscape designers. Vancouver has an abundance of landscape designers. Many hold a degree and have years of experience in the field, but they do not have to be licensed, and their qualifications and abilities vary. Some of the most successful small gardens in the city were designed by landscape designers. Some knowledgeable nursery people and garden store owners may be able to help with recommendations.

Landscape contractors. These contractors are generally called in to execute landscaping plans. They should know a lot about installation of materials and plants, and be able to obtain items you want from their sources of supply. However, here again, you should make sure anyone hired to work on your garden is well recommended. If you are subcontracting the installation yourself, you'll want to get several quotes; the cheapest is not always the best.

Design-build contractors. This is another very useful group. These people can take care of the whole project for you, from conceptual plan to final installation. If they know what they are doing in all aspects of this work, they may be just what you need. Again, it's very important to check their portfolio and references.

General gardeners. This group needs little introduction. Our area is well supplied with professional gardening services. If you are simply moving plants around and installing a few new ones, the help of a good gardener could be all you need, but make sure of their credentials before you hire them.

Whether you go ahead on your own or seek help, there are many excellent books you may want to consult as you plan your garden. Even if you need professional advice, it does not have to be expensive, since many landscape designers and architects are willing to consult on an hour-by-hour basis. This may help you avoid making costly mistakes.

The most important thing to remember when planning changes to your garden is to have patience; make changes slowly, carefully and thoughtfully and your garden will be a source of pleasure for years to come.

Training an Apple or Pear Tree

The gnarled old apple tree, so long a feature of home gardens, is becoming a thing of the past. Gardeners with less room to spare are growing dwarf and semidwarf fruit trees that can produce more fruit in less space than older varieties and are much easier to manage, prune and harvest.

Training or espaliering a fruit tree against a wall is a practice that started with the Romans and reached a state of high art in medieval monastery gardens. Garden centres today are carrying an increasing variety of dwarf, semidwarf and espaliered trees; it is a decorative way to display the tree, and increases its fruit yield.

There are many different ways to train fruit trees, and you can see several of them in the Food Garden at UBC Botanical Garden. The garden regularly offers a course on how to espalier fruit trees (see "Education and Information" in the Resources section). The method described here is called horizontal T espalier. Dwarf varieties are recommended; there are some excellent varieties that show good disease resistance and can be grown organically.

1. Run horizontal wires at intervals of 18 inches (45 cm) across the wall or fence. Plastic-covered clothesline wire works well.
2. Plant a bare-root "whip" (a one-year-old unbranched tree), then cut it off at 18 inches (45 cm), just below the first wire. This cut will activate the buds just below it.
3. At the end of the growing season, the branches that have sprouted from the buds can be lowered and tied carefully to the first wire with twine or plastic ties. Rub off all the growth from the trunk. (Fig. 1)

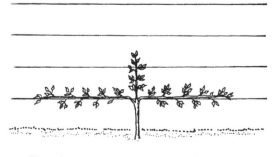

Figure 1

4. As the main leader grows, cut it off 1/4 inch (.6 cm) above a set of buds, a little below the second wire, at a height of 36 inches (90 cm). This will activate these buds. (Fig. 2)

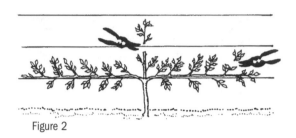

Figure 2

5. Cut the laterals of the branches on the first wire back to three buds. These will develop into fruiting spurs.
6. Continue training with ties until the four wires, or as many as you wish, are covered

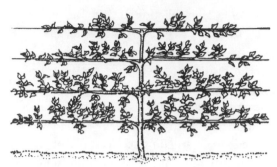

Figure 3

with branches. On the top wire there will be no trunk extension, just the two side branches. (Fig. 3)

Espaliers need tie support and close attention for at least three years. After the desired pattern is formed, maintenance consists of checking and retying supports and cutting out unwanted buds before they develop into extra branches.

Recommended Reading

Design

Brookes, John. *The Garden Book: Designing, Creating and Maintaining Your Garden.* Crown Publishers, New York, 1984.

Brookes, John. *The Country Garden: A Seasonal Guide to Designing and Planting Gardens with Natural Style.* Crown Publishers, New York, 1987.

Damrosch, Barbara. *Theme Gardens.* Workman Publishing, New York, 1982.

Hobhouse, Penelope. *Colour in Your Garden.* Little, Brown and Co., Toronto, 1985.

Johnson, Hugh. *The Principles of Gardening.* Simon and Schuster, New York, 1979.

Keswick, Maggie; Judy Oberlander; and Joe Wai. *In a Chinese Garden: The Art and Architecture of the Dr. Sun Yat-Sen Classical Chinese Garden.* The Dr. Sun Yat-Sen Garden Society, Vancouver, 1990.

Oudolf, Piet with Noel Kingsbury. *Designing with Plants.* Timber Press, Portland, Oregon, 1999.

Page, Russell. *The Education of a Gardener.* Penguin Books, London, 1985.

Patrick, John. *Designing the Small Garden.* Lansdowne Publishing, Sydney, Australia, 1994.

Rose, Graham. *The Romantic Garden.* Penguin Books, Toronto, 1988.

Stevens, David. *Simple Garden Projects.* Octopus Publishing Group, London, 1992.

Verey, Rosemary. *Rosemary Verey's Making of a Garden.* Henry Holt and Company, New York, 1995.

Williams, Robin. *The Garden Planner.* Barrons, New York, 1990.

Pruning and espaliering

All About Pruning. Ortho Books, San Francisco, 1978.

Chamberlin, Susan. *Hedges, Screens and Espaliers: How to Select, Grow and Enjoy.* HPBooks, Tucson, Arizona, 1983.

Hill, Lewis. *Pruning Simplified.* Garden Way Publishing, Pownal, Vermont, 1986.

Illustrated Guide to Gardening in Canada. Reader's Digest, Toronto, 1978.

February

Why do we live in Canada's southern Pacific coastal region? February is one reason. While the rest of the country is covered in winter snow, we watch green tips of early bulbs emerge from the softening ground. Bright yellow, fragrant flowers of the Chinese witch hazel (*Hamamelis mollis*) shine like luminous stars on a sunny day, and waxen heads of the Christmas rose (*Helleborus niger*) open creamy white and pink petals above crisp, green foliage.

The weather can still bring us snow one day and mild, sunny weather the next, but there comes a day when we know for certain that spring is on its way. Early crocuses make their cheerful appearance, and our gardens display some of the more than seventy species and countless varieties of this hardy little plant.

Snowdrops are at their peak, and there is a surprisingly wide variety of them in addition to the common snowdrop (*Galanthus nivalis*). Snowdrops take a while to become established but, once they do, they spread easily. If you wish to divide overcrowded clumps, the best time to do so is immediately after they have finished flowering.

The fragrance of many winter-flowering shrubs is an extra bonus. Many of those grown in gardens today were originally native to China. In addition to *Hamamelis mollis*, they include the spicy-scented wintersweet (*Chimonanthus praecox*), lily-of-the-valley–scented *Mahonia japonica*, and the dwarf evergreen sweet box (*Sarcococca hookeriana* var. *humilis*). As February is still a little cool for lingering in the garden, it's worth placing these plants near doors or walkways so you can enjoy their sweet scent every day.

This month we discuss shade gardens, native plants and wildflowers, and show you how to make a garden of native plants in your own backyard. These topics are particularly relevant to our region, in part because we live so close to the wilderness, and in part because so many gardens are shaded by tall and spreading trees.

The January calendar of garden chores applies equally well to February, but there are a few additional tasks to be done towards the end of the month, weather permitting. For instance, many clematis can be pruned back now (see the March chapter for discussion of these climbers). Last season's debris can be cleared from flower beds, and the beds can be lightly cultivated, ready for a top-dressing of compost or mushroom manure in March. When spring arrives, you'll be ready.

Garden Highlights

* indicates fragrance

Bulbs

Anemone blanda (windflower), *Chionodoxa* spp. (glory-of-the-snow), *Crocus sieberi*,* *C. chrysanthus*,* *Cyclamen coum*, *Eranthis hyemalis* (winter aconite), *Galanthus* spp. (snowdrop), *Iris reticulata*,* *Leucojum ver-* *num* (spring snowflake), *Narcissus jonquilla* (jonquil),* *N. cyclamineus*,* *Scilla sibirica* (Siberian squill).

Perennials

Arum italicum 'Pictum', *Bergenia* 'Bressingham Ruby', *Hacquetia epipactis*, *Helleborus niger* (Christmas rose), *Helleborus* x *foetidus*, *H.* x *hybridus*, *H.* x *sternii*, *Hepatica nobilis*, *Iris unguicularis* (Algerian iris),* *Primula* spp. (primroses,* primulas and polyanthus).

Climbers

Clematis balearica, *Jasminum nudiflorum* (winter jasmine).

Shrubs

Camellia sasanqua, *Chimonanthus praecox* (wintersweet),* *Cornus mas* (Cornelian cherry), *Corylopsis pauciflora* (buttercup winter hazel),* *Daphne odora*,* *Erica carnea* (winter heath), *Hamamelis japonica* (Japanese witch hazel), *H. mollis* (Chinese witch hazel),* *Mahonia japonica*, *Rhododendron dauricum*, *R. moupinense*,* *R. mucronulatum*, *R.* 'Olive', *Sarcococca hookeriana* var. *humilis* (sweet box),* *S. ruscifolia*,* *Viburnum* x *bodnantense*.*

Trees

Prunus subhirtella 'Autumnalis' (autumn-flowering cherry), *Prunus* 'Pissardii Nigra' (flowering plum).

February Checklist

Annuals, perennials and bulbs

• If you haven't already done so, order seeds and start seed flats under glass. Sweet peas can be sown outside.

- Pot up cuttings taken from overwintered geraniums (*Pelargonium* spp.) and water sparingly.
- Clean up flower beds and put debris in the compost pile, except for leaves from diseased plants, such as rose leaves with black spot.
- Cultivate the soil and weed thoroughly.
- Lift and divide perennials, taking care not to damage new shoots.
- Plant lily bulbs if not already done.
- Deadhead early-flowering bulbs after blooming. Snowdrops can be moved or divided after flowering.

Trees, shrubs and climbers

- Finish pruning ornamental trees and spray with dormant oil if not already done.
- Prune summer-flowering shrubs that flower on this year's wood, such as hardy fuchsia (*Fuchsia magellanica*) and butterfly bush (*Buddleia davidii*).
- Prune summer-flowering clematis (see the March chapter), and make sure lattice and supports are in good order before growth commences.
- Feed hydrangeas with well-rotted compost or manure.
- Plant trees and shrubs in good weather. Lightly fork soil under established hedges and give a light dressing of a general organic fertilizer, bone meal or well-rotted compost or manure.
- Continue planting bare-root roses and prune die-back on established roses in preparation for final pruning next month (see the June chapter). Remove the old leaves and destroy them, since they may contain diseases.

Fruits, vegetables and herbs

- Complete pruning of fruit trees and spray with dormant oil and lime sulphur if not done already.
- Plant new bush and cane fruits and prune existing ones. Feed with well-rotted compost or manure.
- Sow annual herbs in seed flats, and sow parsley outdoors.
- Prepare vegetable beds by working in plenty of compost or manure (see the July chapter). Lime two weeks later.
- Early salad crops can be sown under glass in a cold frame, and broad beans, leeks, radishes and shallots can be sown outside at the end of the month. Dates for planting can be advanced by two weeks if a cold frame is used (see the July chapter).

General garden activities

- Power-rake lawns to remove thatch and moss, or hand-rake with a wire leaf rake. Aerate with fork or aerator. Fill in dips and hollows in existing lawns with a mixture of topsoil and coarse sand.
- Apply dolomite lime to lawn at the end of the month.
- Prepare the ground now if new lawns are to be sown in the next few months.
- Turn compost and keep it moist.
- Check for slugs and snails before they damage emerging bulbs and new shoots.

Shade Gardens, Native Plants and Wildflowers

One of the loveliest shade gardens in British Columbia is the Nitobe Memorial Garden, situated at the University of British Columbia campus. Its varied and interesting landscaping is an inspiration for anyone who thinks that having a shade garden is boring. Carefully designed landscaping is harmonized with a well-chosen selection of plants to create a serene and tranquil setting that changes with the seasons.

Fortunately, there is a wide variety of plants that love the shade. Their colours tend to be softer and more subtle than their sun-loving relatives and, given the right conditions, many are easy and rewarding to grow in our moist climate.

The concept of layering begins in nature

Shade gardens lend themselves well to the concept of layering. In the forest, small woodland plants, such as bunchberry (*Cornus canadensis*), woodland violets and trout lilies (*Erythronium revolutum*), are first to poke their heads through the bare earth; by the time they have finished flowering, ferns of many shapes and sizes unfurl their new fronds, covering the dying foliage of early bloomers. Leaves and flowers of huckleberries and salmonberries come next, providing delicious fruits in the fall, covered by a protective canopy of forest evergreens.

Similarly, shade plants can be layered in a domestic garden to provide continuous interest and variety throughout the seasons. For example, early bulbs, violets and primulas can be followed by hostas and ferns, which grow well under a protective covering of rhododendrons, azaleas and flowering trees.

Shade has its advantages

There are many advantages to growing plants in the shade. Flowers tend to last longer and keep their colour better than those exposed to full sun, and the various textures and greens of shade plants create a feeling of tranquillity and harmony. Plants with variegated foliage lighten dark areas, giving an impression of brightness and sunlight.

There are two different approaches to successful shade and wildflower gardening: you can either create the soil, water and light conditions that the plants you have chosen will like, or you can choose plants that like the existing conditions in your garden. For instance, some plants thrive in dry, poor soil conditions, while others require a lot of moisture to do well.

Before buying anything, plan your shade selection. By varying the shapes, colours and textures of your plants you can create illusions of space, mass and depth. This principle works well for any small garden, not just for shade gardens. Don't be afraid to experiment; if what you try doesn't work, you can always move the plants around next year.

In praise of hostas

Hostas are some of the loveliest and most versatile of the cultivated shade plants, and the growing appreciation and popularity of this genus is fully warranted. They are robust, fully hardy, long-lived herbaceous perennials, prized for their sculptural foliage and wide range of colour and variegation. Hostas look marvellous as groundcovers, in borders, as individual specimens or in mixed plantings in association with perennials such as astilbe, corydalis, ferns, lilies and meconopsis. They look lovely by water and can be used to very good effect in containers beside a shaded door. The leaves make a dramatic addition to a flower arrangement.

Hostas are adaptable plants that generally grow best in deep, humus-enriched soil in partial shade. Some hostas, especially the gold-leaved varieties, will thrive in sun, providing there is some relief during the day and the soil does not get too dry. They may be left alone for several years to develop. If necessary, cultivars should be propagated by division in the spring. Hostas come into their own in late spring and summer, so plant them in association with evergreen ferns, hellebores and spring bulbs.

The following are particularly garden-worthy cultivars.

'Abiqua Drinking Gourd'. Height: 24 inches (60 cm). Spread 32 inches (80 cm). A specimen hosta with huge, cup-shaped leaves of a distinctive frosty blue.

'Blue Angel'. Height: 36 inches (95 cm). Spread: 44 inches (110 cm). Very wide, pointed and deeply veined blue leaves, ideal as a groundcover.

'Frances Williams'. Height: 30 inches (75 cm). Spread: 36 inches (90 cm). One of the best specimen hostas for the shade garden and very good in a container. Blue-green leaves have a yellow edge. Try planting with *Corydalis lutea,* whose colour and fernlike foliage contrast well with the broad leaf of the hosta.

'Ginko Craig'. Height: 6 inches (15 cm). Spread: 18 inches (45 cm). Low-growing variety, ideal for edging a pathway or border. Its straplike leaves are grass green with a wide white margin.

'Gold Medallion'. Height: 14 inches (35 cm). Spread: 20 inches (50 cm). A highly recommended specimen hosta with heavily textured, cup-shaped foliage. Yellow with copper highlights.

'Golden Tiara'. Height: 14 inches (35 cm). Spread: 24 inches (60 cm). Light green leaves with a yellow edge. Very good as a small groundcover and in mass plantings.

'Hadspen Blue'. Height: 12 inches (30 cm). Spread: 20 inches (50 cm). Valuable for its smaller size and very blue leaves. Slow to mature.

'Halcyon'. Height: 14 inches (35 cm). Spread: 28 inches (70 cm). An award-winning hosta ideal for the smaller garden. Blue leaves form a dense compact mound. Good as a groundcover or in a container.

'June'. Height: 12 inches (30 cm). Spread: 16 inches (40 cm). A sport of 'Halcyon'. Lovely variegation with pale chartreuse centre and a blue-green margin.

'Love Pat'. Height: 20 inches (50 cm). Spread: 24 inches (60 cm). Cupped, very puckered, frosty blue leaves make this an outstanding specimen hosta.

'Patriot'. Height: 18 inches (45 cm). Spread: 24 inches (60 cm). An outstanding variety, with clear white border variegation and bright green marbling. The best white-edged hosta available at present.

'Shade Fanfare'. Height: 16 inches (40 cm). Spread: 24 inches (60 cm). Golden foliage with a creamy white margin in spring, turning to chartreuse and white by summer. Very nice in a heavily shaded area.

'Sum and Substance'. Height: 30 inches (75 cm). Spread: 72 inches (1.8 m). This is possibly the largest-leaved of all, and a most spectacular plant when established. With smooth, deeply veined chartreuse leaves, it is tolerant of a fair amount of sun.

Turning to nature for inspiration

In our climate, there is a natural connection between shade gardens, native plants and wildflowers. Surrounding Pacific rain forests provide natural protection and shade for British Columbia's wide variety of native plants, and can give us many excellent ideas for shady areas of our own gardens. Ferns, mosses and lichens are just as beautiful in the garden as they are in the wild; given the right conditions, they will thrive with little or no care, just as they do in the forest.

In Vancouver there are several excellent

places to see native plants, including the Museum of Anthropology and the Botanical Gardens at the University of British Columbia, the Canadian Heritage Garden at VanDusen Garden, and Stanley Park. In Victoria good places to visit are Beacon Hill Park, the Native Garden at the Provincial Museum, and Saxe Point Park. A special treat is to visit Beaconhill Park in May when the blue camas (*Camassia quamash*) blooms. (See "Public Parks and Gardens" in the Resources section.)

Endangered species need protection

Sadly, many native plants and wildflowers are beginning to disappear from around the world, in part because of the quest of gardeners for unusual plants for their gardens. It is very important, therefore, not to buy plants whose origin you cannot determine: some endangered plants are being smuggled out of their countries of origin and sold for large profits overseas, in spite of international legislation which makes this practice illegal. Some plants are advertised as "nursery-grown" when in fact they are collected from the wild, potted up, and then sold. Make sure any native or rare plants you buy come from a reputable nursery that is propagating the plants from established nursery stock.

The only time you should consider gathering native plants is for reasons of conservation. Thanks to the efforts of concerned people, there is an increased awareness of the need to save plants threatened by encroaching "civilization." This same need for conservation exists anywhere where plants, whether domestic or wild, are endangered by new construction and development.

In British Columbia there are perhaps two dozen species of plants that could be considered endangered. Many of these are endemic,

and most are very rare or very local in their occurrence. The degree to which they are threatened varies, as some are found in remote and presently undeveloped parts of the province and are not in immediate danger of extinction.

Several plant species are legally protected in British Columbia, including the western flowering dogwood (*Cornus nuttalli*), the western white trillium (*Trillium ovatum*), the Pacific white rhododendron (*Rhododendron albiflorum*), and the pink or California rhododendron (*Rhododendron macrophyllum*).

Plants for a shady garden

When planning a shady garden, don't forget the bulbs. Most spring-flowering bulbs do well in the shade of deciduous trees. Bulbs such as bluebells and snowdrops are native to woodland but many others adapt well.

Perennials

Many of these are described in greater detail in the May chapter.

Aconitum spp. (**monkshood**). Hardy perennials with tall spires of helmet-shaped blue flowers. Grow best in moist soil. All parts of this plant are poisonous, so handle with care. Blooms in June and July. Good cultivars for light shade include 'Ivorine' and 'Bressingham Spire'.

Alchemilla mollis (**lady's mantle**). A beautiful and useful plant that forms a clump of soft green leaves about 12 inches (30 cm) high. Sprays of greenish-yellow flowers are produced from early June to August. *A. erythropoda* (dwarf lady's mantle) has chartreuse flowers and small, silver-edged foliage. Growing 6 to 8 inches (15 to 20 cm) in height, it's ideal for the smaller garden and shaded rockery.

Anemone x *hybrida* (**Japanese anemone**). Very free-flowering plants once they are established. They grow 2 to 4 feet (.6 to 1.2 m) tall, and produce beautiful single or semidouble white, silvery-pink or rose flowers from August to October. Can be a bit invasive, so choose the site carefully. Look for 'Hadspen Abundance', single, deep pink flowers with a golden centre; 'Honorine Jobert', pure white flowers with prominent golden stamens; 'September Charm', single, soft pink flowers with darker reverse.

Aquilegia spp. (**columbine**). Lovely old-fashioned cottage plants with lacy foliage and pretty, bonnet-shaped flowers that seed themselves freely in a half-shady garden. Many self-coloured or bicoloured cultivars, including *A. alpina* (large, clear blue flowers above finely divided foliage and *A. canadensis* (scarlet petals with a lemon spur). Very attractive to hummingbirds.

Arum italicum. Valuable for its winter foliage, the large, shiny, dark green leaves start to unfold in autumn and grow larger all through winter and spring. The pale green, somewhat inconspicuous spathes emerge in spring. By midsummer, flowers and leaves disappear underground, but in early autumn spikes of bright red, poisonous berries shoot up before the leaf cycle starts afresh. Look for 'Pictum', which has outstanding glossy green leaves with prominent, silvery-green marbling.

Aruncus dioicus (**goatsbeard**). Very handsome plants growing 4 to 6 feet (1.2 to 1.8 m) tall, ideal for a shady woodland setting. Long narrow plumes of creamy white flowers are produced in late May to June and last for several weeks. 'Kneiffi' is a dwarf cultivar which only grows to 2 feet (60 cm).

Asarum caudatum (**wild ginger**). This British Columbia native is an excellent groundcover plant for deep shade. Grown primarily for its glossy green, heart-shaped foliage, the leaf and root give off a ginger odour.

Asarum europeum. A much sought-after plant for the shade garden, it is valued for its lovely, green, kidney-shaped foliage. It is rather slow to establish.

Asplenium scolopendrium (**hart's tongue fern**). Distinctive, evergreen, straplike leaves up to 15 inches (38 cm) in height. Prefers alkaline soil.

Astilbe spp. (**false spirea**). A beautiful genus of densely clump-forming perennials, with attractive fernlike leaves, often tinged with purple or bronze, especially when young. The long-lasting, tapering plumes of tiny flowers appear in midsummer in shades of white, pink to purple and red. It combines beautifully with other moisture-loving perennials such as primula, hosta, meconopsis and iris. It thrives in rich, moisture-retentive soil, and is best left undisturbed for periods of 4 to 5 years before dividing. There are many outstanding cultivars to choose from. 'White Gloria' has dense white blooms produced mid- to late season. 'Bressingham Beauty' bears dusty rose flowers mid- to late season. *A. chinensis* 'Pumila', a late bloomer, has lavender flowers with bright pink highlights.

Tip of the Month: Hellebores

Try picking the flowers of hellebores and floating them in a simple glass bowl to truly appreciate the subtle beauty of the cup-shaped flowers, normally hidden by the plant's nodding habit.

Astrantia major (**masterwort**). Tiny white flowers surrounded by green and white bracts are carried in midsummer. Very attractive plants growing to about 3 feet (90 cm). 'Shaggy', also called 'Margery Fish', produces large white flowers with long pointed bracts tinged with green all summer long. 'Sunningdale Variegated' is valuable for its striking variegated foliage; flowers are white to green with a slight flush of pink. May be hard to find, but it's well worth the effort.

Athyrium niponicum 'Pictum' (**Japanese painted fern**). A beautiful fern with distinctive, metallic-grey foliage and burgundy stems and overtones. A slow developer, it grows to a height of 18 inches (45 cm).

Carex morrowii 'Aureo-variegata' (**variegated Japanese sedge**). One of the few grasses that will thrive in shade. Long, narrow, evergreen leaves have creamy yellow stripes. 'Valley Gold' has bright golden leaves. Both make 12-inch (30-cm) mounds and are useful edging plants.

Cimicifuga spp. (**bugbane**). Tall graceful plants with wandlike spires of cream or white flowers and finely divided, fernlike leaves. They grow to a height of 3 to 5 feet (1 to 1.5 m) and bloom in July and August. *C. simplex* 'Brunette' has beautiful dark burgundy foliage and pure white, fragrant blossoms in late summer. *C. simplex* 'White Pearl' bears spikes of white flowers that arise from lacy green foliage in late summer.

Corydalis spp. A large and important genus for the shade gardener. It is easily grown in humus-enriched soil in partial shade. The fernlike foliage looks its best when planted with other shade-loving perennials, such as hostas, primulas and ferns. *C. flexuosa* 'Père David' has intensely blue flowers and goes dormant in the summer. *C. flexuosa* 'Purple Leaf' has reddish stems and a purple tinge to the leaves; flowers are a clear blue. *C. lutea*, which has finely cut leaves and bears its spikes of bright yellow flowers over a long period, seeds very freely. *C. ochroleuca* is a white-flowered form with a tiny dash of yellow on the lip. It blooms over a long period and seeds itself with gay abandon!

Dicentra spp. (**bleeding heart**). Dainty, heart-shaped flowers hang on arching stems. The foliage is attractive and finely dissected. They are ideal plants for a shady border or woodland setting. 'Langtrees' has silvery-grey foliage and creamy white flowers with pink tips. *D. spectabilis* has fernlike green leaves and nodding, rose-pink flowers with a white tip on stems to 2 feet (60 cm). The pure white form 'Alba' is exquisite in a woodland setting. *D. spectabilis* 'Goldheart' is valuable for its golden foliage.

Digitalis spp. (**foxglove**). Foxgloves are a familiar sight in woodlands and wild gardens, with their tall spires of white, pink or purple tubular flowers. Many are variable and can be biennial or perennial, but fortunately they often reseed themselves. *D. grandiflora* has creamy yellow flowers lightly veined with brown inside. 'Temple Bells' is a larger-flowered cultivar. *D. x mertonensis* is perennial and has flowers of a crushed strawberry colour. *D. purpurea* 'Apricot' flowers are a lovely shade of apricot-pink.

Dryopteris filix-mas (**male fern**). Does best in moist woodland soil. Grows to a height and spread of 2 to 4 feet (.6 to 1.2 m).

Epimedium spp. (**barrenwort**). A lovely groundcover for shade, it is also valued for its dainty flowers. Rather leathery, wing-shaped leaves develop a lovely autumn colour in many of the species. Cut them back in winter to expose the delicate flowers. *E. x perralchicum* 'Fröhnleiten' has glossy green foliage edged with bronze in the spring; bright yellow flowers grow to 12 inches (30 cm). *E. youngianum* 'Niveum' has rounded, lightly bronzed foliage and pure white flowers.

***Filipendula* spp. (meadowsweet).** Attractive plants that produce large fluffy heads of tiny, white, red or pink flowers in June and July. They thrive in moist soil and reach a height of 3 to 4 feet (1 to 1.2 m). *F. ulmaria* 'Aurea' has outstanding golden yellow foliage and produces creamy white flowers in early summer.

***Gentiana asclepiadea* (willow gentian).** A spectacular plant, blooming in late summer. Upright arching stems to 2 feet (60 cm) carry brilliant blue trumpet-shaped flowers. Thrives in rich, moist soil, in part or full shade. Plant where it is to remain, as it resents being moved.

***Geranium* spp. (hardy geranium, cranesbill).** A very useful group of perennial plants that thrive in partial shade. Saucer-shaped flowers in white, pink, blue and purple are produced over a long period in the summer. Not to be confused with the tender perennial bedding plants, commonly called geraniums, which are actually pelargoniums. Many bloom off and on all summer. Refer to the May chapter for more details.

Hacquetia epipactis. This small, clump-forming perennial blooms over a long period in late winter or earliest spring. The clusters of small, yellow and green, daisy-like flowers are borne on 4-inch (10-cm) stems. Look for 'Thor'; this stunning new introduction is a creamy white variegated form.

***Helleborus* spp. (Christmas and lenten roses).** These lovely plants are described in detail in the December chapter. They thrive in shade and flower from late winter to early spring. A great addition to any garden.

***Hemerocallis* spp. (daylily).** Large, trumpet-shaped flowers in a wide range of colours are produced from June to August. Most forms reach a height of 3 feet (90 cm), and form large clumps of arching, straplike leaves. Refer to the May chapter for more details.

Hosta. Grown for their striking leaves, which provide interest for many months. The tall spikes of usually pale flowers are sometimes fragrant, but are often somewhat insignificant. See "In praise of hostas," earlier this chapter, for more information.

***Kirengeshoma* spp.** An elegant addition to the shade garden, thriving in rich, moist soil in semishade. *K. palmata* has maple-like leaves and branching stems up to 4 1/2 feet (1.4 m), from which dangle creamy yellow flowers. Blooms in late summer. *K. koreana* has less deeply incised leaves, and the waxy yellow flowers are more upright-facing, with wider-spreading petals. Grows to 3 feet (90 cm).

***Liriope muscari* (lily turf).** This species forms a clump of graceful, curving, grasslike evergreen leaves, with spikes of lilac flowers in late summer. 'Variegata' has yellow-edged leaves.

***Matteuccia struthiopteris* (ostrich fern).** An upright-growing fern whose emerging green fronds are the edible fiddleheads. Unfurled, they resemble ostrich plumes. It must not be allowed to dry out. Grows to 4 to 5 feet (1.2 to 1.5 m).

***Osmunda regalis* (royal fern).** A moisture-loving fern that can reach a height of 4 to

5 feet (1.2 to 1.5 m). The copper-coloured spores that appear at the end of the fronds give the impression that it is flowering. Slow to mature.

Polygonatum x *hybridum* (**Solomon's seal**). Very elegant perennial with arching stems decorated with rows of creamy white bell flowers in early spring. Reaches a height of 2 to 3 feet (60 to 90 cm). *P. odoratum* 'Variegatum' is a lovely form with a fine white edging to the leaf.

Primula **spp. (primulas, cowslips and prim-roses).** Ideal plants for the woodland garden or shady border. Primulas are discussed in detail in the March chapter.

Scrophularia aquatica '**Variegata**' (**figwort**). Also known as *S. auriculata* 'Variegata', this is an outstanding specimen plant. Grows to 2 to 3 feet (60 to 90 cm) with magnificent, creamy yellow variegation along the edges of the leaves. Flowers are insignificant.

Thalictrum **spp. (meadow rue).** Grown as much for the delicately divided foliage as for the flowers, these pretty plants range in height from 2 to 4 feet (.6 to 1.2 m), and produce clusters of tiny white, yellow, pink or purple flowers. *T. aquilegifolium* 'Album' has plumes of delicate white flowers. *T. flavum* var. *glaucum* has attractive bluish-grey foliage and yellow flowers.

Tiarella **spp. (foamflower).** Perfect for the woodland garden, these are low-growing plants with lobed leaves and attractive, bottlebrush-shaped flowers. They are easily grown and suitable for moist shade, among shrubs or at the front of a border. *T. cordifolia* is a native species with dense, spiky white flowers and leaves that colour well in the fall. *T. wherryi* has sharply toothed, pointed leaves tinged with purple and white flowers tinged with pink.

Shrubs

The shrub lists for April, June and November have more detailed information on plants listed below, and are organized according to their flowering time: spring-flowering shrubs are listed in April, summer-flowering in June, and fall- and winter-flowering in November.

Aucuba japonica. A useful evergreen shrub that performs well in deep shade and grows at a moderate rate to about 5 feet (1.5 m). There are green and variegated cultivars to choose from. 'Picturata' has striking yellow leaves with green margins. Plant male and female plants to get red berries.

Buxus sempervirens (**box**). A slow-growing shrub that can be grown as a specimen or as a hedge. Very easy to grow, succeeding in any soil, in sun or shade. 'Aureovariegata' is one of several variegated forms.

Camellia **spp.** These beautiful evergreen shrubs do well in shade, and the glossy, dark green leaves are a delight all year round. Single, semidouble or double flowers come in white, pink or red.

Choisya ternata (**Mexican orange**). A rounded evergreen shrub reaching a height of 4 to 5 feet (1.2 to 1.5 m) with trifoliate glossy green leaves. The sweet-scented flowers, which resemble orange blossoms, are produced in April and May.

Corylopsis pauciflora and C. spicata (**winter hazel**). Deciduous, with pale yellow, fragrant, bell-shaped flowers in February and March on bare branches. Slow growing to 5 to 10 feet (1.5 to 3 m), depending on the species.

"Sunny" plants for a shady border

fence

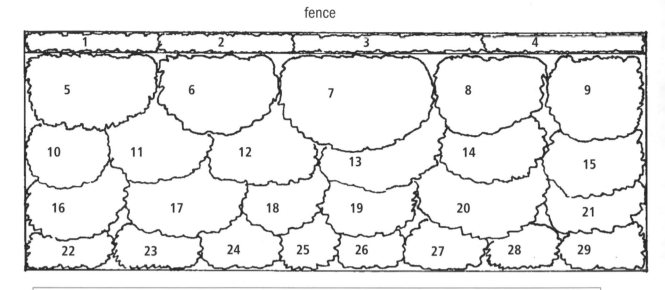

This planting plan has been specially designed to brighten up a shady corner. All the plants are described in this section. The plant selection is based on a yellow, green and white colour scheme.

1. *Jasminum nudiflorum* (winter jasmine)
2. *Hedera helix* 'Gold Heart' (ivy)
3. *Hydrangea anomala* ssp. *petiolaris* (climbing hydrangea)
4. *Lonicera* x *tellmanniana* (honeysuckle)
5. *Rhododendron* 'Mrs. Betty Robertson'
6. *Aucuba japonica* 'Picturata'
7. *Hamamelis mollis* (Chinese witch hazel)
8. *Mahonia* 'Charity'
9. *Euonymus japonica* 'Silver King'
10. *Buxus sempervirens* 'Aureovariegata' (box)
11. *Digitalis grandiflora* (foxglove)
12. *Hemerocallis flava* (lemon daylily)
13. *Aruncus dioicus* 'Kneiffi' (goatsbeard)
14. *Sarcococca hookeriana* var. *humilis* (sweet box)
15. *Dryopteris filix-mas* (male fern)
16. *Phyllitis scolopendrium* (hart's-tongue fern)
17. *Polygonatum* x *hybridum* (Solomon's seal)
18. *Helleborus lividus* ssp. *corsicus* (Corsican hellebore)
19. *Astrantia major* (masterwort)
20. *Athyrium filix-femina* (lady fern)
21. *Helleborus foetidus* (stinking hellebore)
22. *Carex morrowii* 'Aureo-variegata' (Japanese sedge)
23. *Alchemilla mollis* (lady's mantle)
24. *Hosta* 'Piedmont Gold'
25. *Primula vulgaris* (English primrose)
26. *Erythronium* 'Pagoda'
27. *Hosta fortunei* 'Green Gold'
28. *Carex morrowii* 'Valley Gold' (Japanese sedge)
29. *Liriope muscari* 'Variegata' (lily turf)

***Daphne* spp.** A group of deciduous and evergreen shrubs with sweetly scented flowers. *D. mezereum* (February daphne) produces dense clusters of white, pink or purple-red flowers as early as December on bare branches. *D. odora* (winter daphne) is evergreen and blooms from January to April.

***Euonymus japonica* (Japanese spindle tree).** Dense, evergreen shrub with bushy upright branches. It can be grown as a specimen or a hedge. 'Silver King' is a variegated cultivar with soft green leaves and silvery-white edges.

***Hamamelis mollis* (Chinese witch hazel).** A beautiful deciduous shrub or small tree eventually growing to about 25 feet (7.6 m). Fragrant yellow flowers cover the branches in January and February.

***Hydrangea* spp.** These shrubs thrive in partial shade in rich, moisture-retentive soil. Try growing the lacecap varieties, which are much daintier than the large, round-flowered Hortensia Group most commonly grown.

***Kalmia latifolia* (mountain laurel).** A beautiful evergreen shrub suited to semishaded woodland conditions. It associates well with rhododendrons. Saucer-shaped white, pink or red flowers are carried in large clusters in May and early June.

Kerria japonica. A slender-stemmed deciduous shrub with bright green leaves and branches. The cultivar 'Pleniflora' is the best known, with double, pompomlike, orange-yellow flowers. It reaches a height of up to 10 feet (3 m). 'Variegata' is smaller and has white-edged leaves and single yellow flowers.

***Leucothoe* spp.** An evergreen shrub with elliptical green or variegated leaves that grows to about 5 feet (1.5 m) with an equal spread. It is a graceful shrub with arching branches, rather like Solomon's seal. *L. fontanesiana* 'Rainbow' is a lovely variegated cultivar growing to 3 to 4 feet (.9 to 1.2 m).

***Lonicera nitida* 'Baggesen's Gold'.** An evergreen shrub with striking, golden yellow foliage that lights up the winter garden and associates well with other shade-loving plants. Grows to a height of 6 feet (1.8 m), but it may be pruned to maintain it at any height.

***Mahonia* spp.** Evergreen shrubs, some of which are native to this area. Glossy, dark green, hollylike leaves and clusters of bell-shaped flowers make these useful shrubs for a shady place. *Mahonia* 'Charity' produces long clusters of fragrant, deep yellow flowers from November to January.

***Nandina domestica* (heavenly bamboo).** A lovely evergreen shrub for shade, with slender upright canes to a height of 4 to 6 feet (1.2 to 1.8 m). White flowers are produced in July, followed by red fruits.

***Osmanthus* spp.** Slow-growing evergreen shrubs with small, but very fragrant, white flowers produced in early spring. Two good species are *O. x burkwoodii* and *O. delavayi*.

***Pieris* spp. (lily-of-the-valley shrub).** Hardy evergreen shrubs that produce lily-of-the-valley–like flowers. The leaves of 'Forest Flame' are bright red when young, turning green later. A very eye-catching shrub.

***Rhododendron* spp. (rhododendrons and azaleas).** What roses are to gardening in the sun, rhododendrons and azaleas are to gardening in the shade. There are over a thousand species, and many times more that number of hybrids. Grow them in filtered shade and rich, cool, moist soil. For more information see the April chapter.

Sarcococca **spp. (sweet box).** Evergreen shrubs with glossy, dark green, narrow oval leaves. Tiny, fragrant white flowers are carried in early spring. *S. humilis* rarely grows more than 18 inches (45 cm) high, while *S. ruscifolia* reaches 4 to 6 feet (1.2 to 1.8 m).

Skimmia japonica. A shade garden standby, with glossy evergreen leaves, a compact habit and white flowers in spring. When planting *S. japonica*, plant one male to a group of female plants to ensure red berries in late summer. *S. reevesiana* is self-fertile.

Climbers

Hedera **(ivy).** Evergreen climbers with green or variegated leaves. A very attractive variety is *H. helix* 'Gold Heart', which has small green leaves splashed in the middle with yellow. It will clamber up a fence or wall to 5 feet (1.5 m) or more. An evergreen, the colours remain true all year round. *H. helix* 'Pedata' is a shade-loving ivy with finely dissected leaves; it will climb to a height of 12 feet (3.7 m).

Hydrangea anomala **ssp.** *petiolaris* **(climbing hydrangea).** Deciduous climber that climbs by way of ivylike aerial roots. Creamy white clusters are carried in June.

Jasminum nudiflorum **(winter jasmine).** Not strictly a climber, but a deciduous shrub which can be trained loosely against a fence or wall. It produces sunny yellow flowers from December to March on bare slender branches.

Lonicera **spp. (honeysuckle).** All do well in partial shade, but *L.* x *tellmanniana* will grow in deep shade. Unfortunately it has no scent, but makes up for it by having masses of coppery-yellow flowers in June and July.

Creating a Native Garden

If you can, set aside an area of your garden to grow plants native to the Pacific Northwest. A bank, rockery, space between rhododendrons or flat, semishady spot will do. Even a half-barrel planted with natural growth layers can give a woodland effect. Whether your area is large or small, be sure to include a succession of layers from the ground upwards. Dappled sunlight filtering through differing textures of shrubs and trees will introduce the spirit of our native woodlands to your garden, and you can use full-grown evergreen or deciduous trees as a starting point. Most city dwellers, however, will have to rely on planting lower-growing trees and associated shrubs to create a woodland feeling.

The best examples of native gardens are the woods themselves. A walk in a nearby forest will teach you a great deal about texture, colour and natural layering. Compare the growing conditions to those in your own garden. Our native plants grow in a variety of conditions and they will be happy in your garden if you select the plants to match the conditions of your site. Try to visit one of our botanical display gardens where native plants are labelled. Jot down the names of your favourites and you won't have to ask your garden centre for "a little shrub with edible red berries."

Start your native garden by choosing a focal point, such as an evergreen, vine maple or dogwood. Shrubs to plant around the tree may include huckleberry, red-flowering currant, snowberry bush, Oregon grape and salal. Perennials come next, including ferns, foxgloves, bleeding hearts, lupines, columbines and gentians. Bulbs might include camas, wild tiger lily and dog-tooth violet. Groundcover choices might include kinnikinnik, violets, alpine strawberries and bunchberry.

For added interest, add a peat-moss path if you have room, or a moss-covered rock, a cedar sculpture or a bird house. For privacy you could build a hand-hewn timber arbour and cover it with ivy, wild honeysuckle or a wild rose. Let your imagination carry you away.

Pacific Northwest native plants adaptable to home gardens

Thanks to the efforts of UBC Botanical Garden researchers and members of the BC Nursery Trades Association, an increasing number of native plants are being selected and bred for good performance in the garden. Some of these cultivars are included here, marked with an asterisk if they have been developed under the UBC Botanical Garden's Plant Introduction Scheme (see the October chapter). In 1995, the BCNTA published a list of "Optimum Ornamental" Pacific Northwest native plants, divided into an "A" list (readily available) and a "B" list (limited availability). The selection of plants given below includes selected "A" list plants and some of the "B" list plants that are or could easily be available without harming wild stocks.

Good sources for native plants include specialty nurseries (see "Specialty Nurseries, General Nurseries and Garden Centres" in the Resources section), botanical gardens' plant sales, garden club sales and a limited selection in garden centres. Please remember to respect our native plants; do not remove any from the wild unless they are in immediate danger of destruction. It is also worth noting that large specimens of some plants you find in garden centres, especially native ferns, may have been wild-harvested rather than grown from seeds or spores, or tissue cultured.

Trees and shrubs

Acer circinatum (**vine maple**). A large, many-trunked deciduous shrub or small tree, the vine maple can grow up to 20 feet (6 m) and looks quite dramatic in mid-spring when the wine-coloured sepals and white petals emerge before the leaves. In the fall, leaves turn brilliant shades of orange and red. It even grows well in deep shade.

Amelanchier alnifolia (**Saskatoon**). This deciduous native grows to a height of 6 to 12 feet (1.8 to 3.7 m) and bears drooping clusters of fragrant white flowers in March and April. The edible berries are produced in May and June, and the grey-green leaves take on good autumn colour.

Andromeda polifolia (**bog rosemary**). An attractive, low-spreading, evergreen shrub with white to pinkish urn-shaped flowers and leathery, lance-shaped leaves. The plant grows to a height of 2 feet (60 cm) and is an excellent garden plant. As its name implies, it likes boggy ground and will thrive in full sun or part shade. 'Blue Ice' is a particularly desirable cultivar with blue-green leaves.

Arctostaphylos uva-ursi '**Vancouver Jade**' (**bearberry or kinnikinnik**). A vigorous, low-growing evergreen groundcover with rich green leaves, fragrant clusters of pink flowers in spring, and bright red berries in the fall. It grows well in sun or light shade, in well-drained or sandy soil.

Cornus '**Eddie's White Wonder**' (**dogwood**). 'Eddie's White Wonder' is a very successful and lovely hybrid of the B.C. native *C. nuttallii* and the eastern *C. florida*. The tree grows to about 25 feet (7.6 m) and bears large white blooms in early spring and often again in September, with striking fall foliage. *C. nuttallii* is not recom-

mended for planting since it is very susceptible to blight.

Cornus stolonifera (**red-osier dogwood**). A
beautiful shrub with brilliant, bright red
winter twigs. It grows rapidly to a large
multistemmed shrub. Small, creamy white
flowers appear among the leaves in summer. It likes moisture and shade.

Gaultheria shallon (**salal**). Salal is found
throughout coastal regions, spreading by
suckers to form thickets of upright plants
with bright green leaves, excellent for
flower arranging. It grows to about
3 feet (90 cm) and prefers a moist, shady
location.

Juniperus horizontalis (**common juniper**).
Common, easy to grow, hardy and
drought tolerant, these prickly, low-growing conifers make excellent groundcover
for rocky, well-drained areas. They grow to
a height of 1 foot (30 cm) with a much
greater spread and must be grown in full
sun. Numerous cultivars are available.

Mahonia x *media* '**Charity**' (**Oregon grape**).
This evergreen, upright shrub is perhaps
more desirable for the garden than its
species relative, *M. aquifolium*. It has dark
green, spiny foliage and grows to 6 feet
(1.8 m) with a spread of 3 feet (90 cm).
It bears long spikes of fragrant, lemony
yellow flowers from late fall to early
spring and prefers semishade and a
moist, fertile soil.

Philadelphus lewisii (**mock orange**). A wild
ancestor of the prized garden hybrids, this
mock orange deserves to be better known.
It was introduced to European gardeners
by the 19th-century botanist-explorer
David Douglas. It is a medium to large,
many-stemmed and -branched shrub with
a height and spread of 6 to 9 feet (1.8 to
2.7 m) and broadly ovate leaves. It bears

large, snow-white, fragrant flowers in late
June and likes sun and fertile soil.

Rhododendron **spp.** All three native species,
R. albiflorum, *R. lapponicum*, and *R.
macrophyllum*, are rare and not marketed
commercially; therefore you should use
substitutes (see plant list in the April
chapter).

Ribes sanguineum **and** *R. s.* '**White Icicle**'
(**red- and white-flowering currants**).
The species plant is a deciduous flowering
shrub with drooping clusters of red flowers in spring; the flowers are great for
attracting hummingbirds. Flowering currant grows to a height and spread of 6 feet
(1.8 m) and tolerates both sun and shade.
The UBC cultivar 'White Icicle' bears pure
white flower clusters about two weeks earlier than the red forms.

Symphoricarpos albus (**waxberry or snowberry**). A thin-stemmed shrub that grows
to about 3 feet (90 cm) high and bears
pinkish, bell-like flowers in late spring. In
the fall clumps of waxy white berries cling
to the bare stems and persist throughout
the winter.

Vaccinium ovatum '**Thunderbird**' (**evergreen huckleberry**). An upright shrub
with intense red-bronze spring foliage, the
evergreen huckleberry produces clusters of
pink flowers from early to late spring and
bears shiny, black, edible berries in the fall.
It grows to a height of 6 feet (1.8 m), with
half that spread, tolerates sun or part
shade, and likes moist, well-drained,
acid soil.

Vaccinium vitis-idaea (**mountain cranberry**). This is an excellent evergreen groundcover for boggy areas; a small shrub with
glossy leaves, pink flowers in the spring,
and edible red fruits in the fall. It only
grows to a height of 8 inches (20 cm),

Native garden planting plan

back

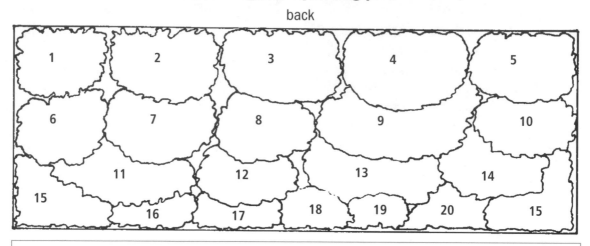

1. *Aruncus dioicus* (goatsbeard)
2. *Amelanchier alnifolia* (service berry)
3. *Cornus stolonifera* (red-osier dogwood)
4. *Mahonia* x *media* 'Charity' (Oregon grape)
5. *Ribes sanguineum* 'White Icicle' (white-flowering currant)
6. *Polystichum munitum* (western sword fern)
7. *Smilacina racemosa* (false Solomon's seal)
8. *Camassia quamash* (camas)
9. *Symphoricarpos albus* (snowberry or waxberry)
10. *Adiantum pedatum* (maidenhair fern)
11. *Dicentra formosa* (bleeding heart)
12. *Aquilegia formosa* (wild columbine)
13. *Cryptogramma crispa* var. *acrostichoides* (parsley fern)
14. *Trillium ovatum* (western white trillium)
15. *Cornus canadensis* (bunchberry)
16. *Lilium columbianum* (wild tiger lily)
17. *Anemone oregana* (wood anemone)
18. *Erythronium oregonum* (fawn lily)
19. *Dodecatheon pulchellum* (shooting star)
20. *Erythronium revolutum* (trout lily)

likes part shade to full sun, and does not tolerate drought.

Flowering perennials, ferns and bulbs

Adiantum pedatum (**maidenhair fern**). One of the loveliest and most delicate of our native ferns with bright green, toothed leaflets on black stems. It is deciduous, prefers partial shade and a rich, dense soil, and grows from 1 to 2 feet (30 to 60 cm).

Allium cernuum (**nodding onion**). Produces lovely little pink flowers in June to August and thrives on the edge of woodlands. Grows to a height of 12 inches (30 cm) and multiplies quickly.

Anemone oregana, A. piperi, A. lyallii (**wood anemones**). Delicate, shade-loving, deciduous perennials that come up year after year and resemble the anemones you can buy for flower-arranging, only smaller and more fragile. They grow well from seed to a height of 6 inches (15 cm), and come in soft shades of pink, white and mauve.

Aquilegia flavescens (**yellow columbine**). This very lovely species has nodding flowers of the clearest yellow and grows to a height of 8 to 12 inches (20 to 30 cm). It resents winter wet, so plant it in a well-drained location.

Aquilegia formosa (**wild columbine**). This lovely wild relative of the garden columbine is the most common of its genus in the Pacific Northwest. Its nodding red flowers with short spurs are easy to spot in the wild. Hummingbirds love it. It thrives in moist spots, prefers some sun and grows to a height of 8 to 12 inches (20 to 30 cm).

Aruncus dioicus (**goatsbeard**). A large, imposing plant that can reach up to 5 feet (1.5 m) tall and prefers partial shade. Its large, creamy white flowers, produced in May and June, resemble astilbe blossoms.

Asarum caudatum (**wild ginger**). This lovely perennial evergreen has deep green, heart-shaped, scented leaves and funny little brownish-purple, thimblelike flowers that hide in the leafy rosette. It is easily grown from seed or rhizome pieces and likes moist, shady places.

Camassia quamash (**camas**). Beacon Hill Park in Victoria would not be the same in the spring without its carpet of bluish-purple camas lilies. Growing up to 2 feet (60 cm) in height, these bulbs naturalize well with narcissi. Although they are not readily available yet, they should be.

Campanula rotundifolia (**Scotch bellflower or lady's thimble**). One of the many harebells that grow in this area, its nodding blue bells are each about the size of a thimble and hang down from strong but slender stalks. It likes some sun and grows to 6 to 8 inches (15 to 20 cm).

Cornus canadensis (**bunchberry, dwarf dogwood**). With flowers just like those of the dogwood tree, these tiny plants are 6 inches (15 cm) high and grow underneath woodland trees and shrubs in moist, shady conditions. In the fall their seeds mature into a bunch of red berries.

Cryptogramma crispa var. *acrostichoides* (**parsley fern**). This is an ideal fern for the rockery. It is deciduous, with parsleylike fronds that grow from 6 to 9 inches (15 to 23 cm) tall. It will tolerate drier conditions than many ferns and prefers shade.

Dicentra formosa (**bleeding heart**). This charming little plant grows 6 to 8 inches (15 to 20 cm) tall, with heartlike pink or deep rose flowers that hang from drooping stems. It likes moist, shady places. Many fine cultivars are available in white, pink and red.

Disporum hookeri (**Hooker's fairy bell**). A shade-loving plant growing to 2 to 3 feet (60 to 90 cm). Bell-shaped ivory flowers hang from the tips of branched stems in late spring, followed by stunning, orange-red berries.

Dodecatheon spp. (**shooting star**). Blooming in spring, these beautiful little plants resemble small cyclamen, and about six species are native to British Columbia. They have a rosette of basal leaves and rose-purple flowers that look like tiny, jet-propelled missiles, complete with nose cone. Colours are white, pink, lavender and magenta. It can be hard to find.

Erythronium spp. (**glacier, fawn and trout lilies, dog's-tooth violet**). Looking a bit like small lilies, the nodding, open, trumpetlike flowers of these bulbs are yellow, white or pink, depending upon the species. Truly a lovely sight when in bloom, they like moist, shady places and come up happily year after year, growing to a height and spread of 5 to 8 inches (12.5 to 20 cm).

Fragaria chiloensis (**sand strawberry**). Sand strawberry is easy to cultivate and makes an excellent groundcover in the sunshine, quickly forming a carpet of interconnected plants. It produces delicately perfumed little berries throughout the summer and prefers a sunny, dry location.

***Lilium columbianum* (wild tiger lily).** This is the most common of the many native lilies found in our area. Its smallish flowers are orange and spotted red, their petals furled backwards, and they hang down from 2- to 4-foot (60-cm to 1.2-m) stems. They usually grow best in an open, sunny position but will take some shade. Not that common yet, but becoming more available.

***Linnaea borealis* (twinflower).** A charming groundcover to 4 inches (10 cm), with round, glossy, evergreen leaves. Rosy-pink, bell-shaped flowers grow from each side of the stem and have a sweet fragrance.

***Maianthenum dilitatum* (Pacific or false lily-of-the-valley).** An attractive perennial with heart-shaped leaves and small, white, delicately perfumed flowers that grow in terminal clusters on 4- to 16-inch (10- to 40-cm) stalks. This makes a good groundcover for moist, shady places.

***Mimulus guttatus* (yellow monkey flower).** The glossy green leaves hug the ground, rooting along the stems to form a dense mat. Bright yellow tubular flowers with burgundy spotting in the throat are produced all summer. Prefers moist soil in semishade, and grows to 8 inches (20 cm).

***Penstemon fruticosus* 'Purple Haze'.** An introduction from the University of British Columbia, this evergreen or partially evergreen shrub grows up to 8 inches (20 cm) tall and 2 feet (60 cm) wide. The plants are covered with mauve to purple tubular flowers in late spring, forming a solid mound of colour for several weeks.

***Polemonium carneum* (Jacob's ladder).** Paired leaves that resemble the steps of a ladder grow on arching stems. The soft pink flowers tinged with blue are produced in late spring to midsummer. Plant in full sun to light shade.

***Polystichum munitum* (western sword fern).** Probably the best known of all the west coast ferns, the sword fern produces a massive clump of 3- to 5-foot (90- to 120-cm) arching fronds. Easy to grow, especially in coastal areas, in woodland conditions, underneath large evergreens and rhododendrons.

***Sedum* spp. (stonecrops).** Members of the stonecrop family are found throughout our area in rocky, sunny places. These succulents have fleshy leaves that retain moisture, and the broad-leaved species make excellent, drought-resistant rockery plants, easy to grow and propagate. One of the best is *S. spathulifolium*, which bears clusters of yellow flowers above tight leafy rosettes. 'Capo Blanca' is a good cultivar.

***Sisyrinchium douglasii* (satin-flower).** This delicate, grasslike perennial has very narrow tufted leaves that grow to 6 to 8 inches (15 to 20 cm); its bell-shaped mauve flowers are produced on stalks slightly above the foliage in March or April. It grows in sun to semishade in well-drained soil.

***Smilacina racemosa* (false Solomon's seal).** This woodland plant reaches a height of about 3 feet (90 cm) and has arching stems topped by fluffy, conical clusters of small, fragrant, creamy white flowers in late spring, followed by red berries in the fall. Its smaller relative, *S. stellata*, is more delicate and only grows to a height of 10 inches (25 cm). Both can be propagated easily from their rhizomes and grow well in wet, shady places.

***Trillium ovatum* (western white trillium).** Enthusiastic gardeners and encroaching civilization have endangered native stocks of trilliums, and they are very fussy about their habitat if they are to do well. To see trilliums at their finest, visit our botanical gardens in the spring where you will find these unmistakable plants in clumps, each single stalk bearing three large leaves arranged at the top of the stem around a single white, green or purple flower. The white-flowered *T. ovatum* is the most common of our western trilliums. A lovely addition to the garden, but please make sure any plants you get have not been taken from the wild.

***Viola glabella* (yellow wood violet).**
Thriving in open woodland, this lovely violet has heart-shaped, serrated leaves and canary-yellow flowers with purple veining on the lower three petals. It blooms in early spring.

Recommended Reading

Shade gardens

Aden, Paul. *The Hosta Book*. Timber Press, Portland, Oregon, 1988.

Bird, Richard and David Tarrant, *Hostas and Other Shade Loving Plants*. Whitecap Books, Vancouver/Toronto, 1999.

Case, Frederick W. Case, Jr. and Roberta B. Case, *Trilliums*. Timber Press, Portland, Oregon, 1987.

Fish, Margery. *Gardening in the Shade*. Faber and Faber, London, 1983.

Gardening in the Shade: Plants and Gardens. Brooklyn Botanic Garden, Brooklyn, New York, 1989.

Schenk, George. *The Complete Shade Gardener*. Houghton Mifflin, Boston, 1984.

Native gardens

Foster, F. Gordon. *Ferns to Know and Grow*. Timber Press, Portland, Oregon, 1984.

Johnson, Lorraine. *100 Easy to Grow Native Plants*. Random House, Toronto, 1999.

Kruckeberg, Arthur R. *Gardening with Native Plants of the Pacific Northwest*. Douglas & McIntyre, Vancouver/Toronto, 1996.

Martin, Laura. *The Wildflower Meadow Book: A Gardener's Guide*. Thomas Allen and Son, New York, 1990.

Natural History Handbook Series. British Columbia Provincial Museum's guides to the flora and fauna of B.C.

Scholefield, Janice J. *Discovering Wild Plants: Alaska, Western Canada, the Northwest*. Alaska Northwest Books, Anchorage, Alaska, 1989.

Tenenbaum, Frances. *Gardening with Wild Flowers*. Ballantine Books, New York, 1986.

March

The arrival of spring and the beginning of the garden year coincide in the month of March. Suddenly the days are longer, the nights are warmer, and the garden is bursting with green shoots and colourful spring bulbs and flowers. After a few sunny days the garden seems to grow by the minute as trees and shrubs unfurl new buds and leaves. Red, pink and white camellias and yellow forsythias are especially cheerful, providing welcome patches of colour among the tender green foliage.

Among the highlights of the month are displays of spring bulbs, visible everywhere in city gardens, open fields and local parks, even in front of downtown highrise buildings. As the early crocuses and snowdrops fade, they are replaced by an amazing variety of shapes, colours and sizes of bulbs, including scillas, iris, anemones, hyacinths, daffodils and tulips, giving us some of the most beautiful displays of bulbs to be seen anywhere in the world.

Don't forget to look at our native species; a delightful bulb that flowers this month is the Easter lily or dog-tooth violet (*Erythronium oreganum*), a plant that can be incorporated easily into a woodland area of your garden.

The flowering of native salmonberry and red-flowering currant shrubs about the third week in March marks the annual spring return of the rufous hummingbird to our area. The best way to attract these lovely little birds to your garden is to provide plants that are covered profusely with sweet nectar flowers, such as beauty bush (*Kolkwitzia amabilis*) and weigela.

Primulas are also making an appearance this month, and we feature them in this chapter. We also discuss some of the climbers you can use to soften and adorn your walls and fences, with special emphasis on the many lovely and varied clematis that grow so well in our area.

This is also a good time to review some basic, common-sense garden practices and organic gardening ways. The points we make may be simple and, perhaps, self-evident, but it cannot be overemphasized that, just like us, the garden that thrives best is the one that is loved and cared for, kept clean, tidy, well fed and well watered. It's easy to do, and an ounce of organic prevention will save you a pound of unpleasant chemical cure.

Garden Highlights

* indicates fragrance

Bulbs

Anemone blanda (windflower), *Chionodoxa* spp. (glory-of-the-snow), *Crocus* spp.,* *Cyclamen coum*, *Erythronium oreganum* (Easter lily, dog-tooth violet), *Fritillaria meleagris*, *Hyacinthus* spp. (hyacinth),* *Iris reticulata*,* *Leucojum vernum* (spring snowflake), *Narcissus* spp. (daffodils and narcissus), *Scilla* spp. (squill), *Tulipa* spp. (tulips).

Perennials

Alyssum montanum (perennial alyssum), *Anemone sylvestris* (snowdrop windflower), *Aurinia saxatilis* (formerly *Alyssum saxatilis*), *Aubrieta deltoidea* (aubretia), *Bergenia* spp. (bergenia), *Doronicum* spp. (leopard's bane), *Primula* spp. (primroses), *P. vulgaris* (English primrose),* *Pulmonaria* spp. (lungwort), *Viola odorata* (sweet violet).*

Climbers

Clematis armandii (evergreen clematis).*

Shrubs

Camellia japonica (camellia), *Cornus mas* (Cornelian cherry), *Corylopsis pauciflora*, *Daphne odora* (winter daphne),* *Forsythia* spp., *Magnolia stellata* (star magnolia),* *Pieris* spp. (lily-of-the-valley shrub), *Rhododendron* 'Cilipinense', *R.* 'Christmas Cheer'.

Trees

Prunus x *blireana* (flowering plum), *P.* 'Pissardii Nigra' (flowering plum), *P.* 'Accolade' (flowering cherry), *P. subhirtella* 'Pendula' (flowering cherry), *P.* x *yedoensis* (flowering cherry).*

March Checklist

Annuals, perennials and bulbs

- Continue to clear and weed flower beds, and mulch with well-rotted compost.
- Plant summer bulbs of lilies, acidanthera, montbretia and nerines, and corms of gladioli.
- Continue to lift and divide perennials and plant new ones.
- Cut down ornamental grasses.

- Deadhead and feed spring bulbs when they have finished flowering. Now is the time to move and plant snowdrops (*Galanthus* spp.).
- Harden off hardy annual seedlings in a cold frame or sow in the ground.
- Sow tender annuals indoors.
- Pot up rooted cuttings if not already done, and pot up overwintered tuberous begonias in potting soil.

Trees, shrubs and climbers

- Shop now for flowering trees while they are in bloom.
- Prune early-blooming deciduous shrubs, such as forsythia, after flowering.
- Prune grey-leafed plants such as lavender, lavender-cotton and senecio.
- After the middle of the month, prune hybrid tea and floribunda roses (see the June chapter). Apply a handful of organic rose food to soil (see "Making Organic Fertilizer" later in this chapter) and carefully hoe in.
- If shrubs or trees are to be moved, this is a good month to do so. Alternatively, shrubs or trees can be root-pruned in readiness for moving in the fall.
- Evergreens, including hedges, should be planted now and mulched with well-rotted compost or manure. Prune out any winter-damaged hedging.

Fruits, vegetables and herbs

- Complete pruning of tree and bush fruits by the end of the month.
- Train berry bushes to wire or fence supports with string.
- March 1 to 15, begin to sow radish, garlic and broad beans.
- March 16 to 31, begin successive sowings of peas, spinach, leaf lettuce, Chinese vegetables, onion sets, turnips and shallots.

- Sow tomatoes indoors.
- Plant new strawberry plants and feed established plants.
- Feed rhubarb well with rich organic material.
- Sow seeds of annual herbs, and prune established herbs such as sage, rue and thyme if they have become leggy.

General garden activities

- Seed or sod new lawns and repair worn patches on existing ones.
- Edge lawns and begin mowing when grass is 3 inches (8 cm) high. Aerate and apply dolomite lime if not already done.
- Remove winter mulches and compost them.
- Check for slugs and snails; remove and destroy.
- Take soil samples for testing if necessary.

Common-sense Gardening

There's no great secret to having a healthy, productive garden. All it takes is common sense, a basic knowledge of good gardening practices, and consistent effort. This means keeping the garden clean, enriching the soil regularly and treating insects and diseases in an environmentally responsible way, so that you can maintain the health and ecological balance of your garden.

The harmful side effects of many pesticides and herbicides are now generally acknowledged, and each year the number of people allergic to chemicals increases. All of us need to be aware of the dangers posed by garden chemicals to our own lives, and those of our chidren, pets, birds and beneficial insects. A common-sense approach to gardening can eliminate the need for toxic chemicals by creating a healthy balance in our own gardens. March, when the garden is at the beginning of its growing season, is the ideal time to start, beginning with a spring-cleaning.

Keep it clean

Old leaves, bits of wood, weeds and general garden debris provide excellent hiding places for snails, slugs, cutworms and other garden pests. Although you will have cleaned up your garden in the fall, there always seems to be more garden waste by the following spring. Start to clean up as soon as the weather allows, which may be as early as mid-February.

Watch for tiny, round, pearly white eggs, looking rather like fish eggs. These are slug eggs, and you should destroy them before the slug population takes off in your garden. However, don't hurt the large, shiny-backed, slow-moving black ground beetles. They will eat many times their weight in pests.

Don't add the end-of-winter garden debris to the compost heap. Fallen leaves may have mildew, black spot or other diseases, which will spread to other parts of the garden if they are composted and reused. It's much better to bag this debris and remove it from the garden.

Know your soil: pH and nutrients

Once the garden is clean and tidy, it's time to take a critical look at your soil. The state of health of your plants and the species and varieties that grow well will tell you a lot. If plants look puny and weak, grow poorly and are susceptible to disease, then your soil is probably lacking in some essential nutrients. If rhododendrons and azaleas grow well, but you have difficulty with peonies and sweet peas, then your soil is more acid than alkaline.

In our climate, where heavy rains are constantly dissolving water-soluble compounds out of the topsoil, the soil tends to lose nutrients rapidly and is relatively acidic, making it easier for us to grow acid-loving plants. The relative acidity or alkalinity of soil is called its pH. The pH is measured on a scale of 14; 7 is neutral. As the number drops, the relative acidity increases; as it rises, the relative alkalinity increases. Since our soil tends to be acidic, we need to add an alkaline compound, such as dolomite lime, if we want to increase the pH and make the soil more alkaline.

It is probably fair to assume that if your garden has not been receiving regular additions of organic matter, your soil is depleted in some way. Before you make any assumptions, however, have the soil tested. Home-test kits are readily available and easy to use, or you can send your sample to a laboratory for more accurate and detailed testing. Soil-testing will measure the pH of the soil and the levels of the three major soil nutrients, nitrogen, phosphorus and potassium. Samples can also be tested for valuable trace minerals, which are often depleted or lacking. For information on soil-testing, see "Soil: Testing and Supplies" in the Resources section.

Know your soil: the look and the feel

It's also important to check the look and feel of your soil. Good soil holds moisture well and is rich and crumbly. If you squeeze it tightly in your hand, it will hold together and then crumble evenly when you let it go. Sandy soil, which won't form a ball, does not hold moisture; and clay soil holds too much, forming a compact hard ball when squeezed. Even soil in good condition can benefit from the addition of organic matter to improve the texture. Feed the soil and not the plant.

Feed the earth: fertilizers and amendments

Once you have determined the needs of your soil, you will know which organic fertilizers and amendments to add. Make sure to follow directions for the correct amount to use, and spread it evenly and carefully.

Soil pH. If your soil is too acid, add dolomite lime (this should be added each year to the lawn; see monthly checklists).

Nitrogen. Blood meal, fish meal, alfalfa meal, soybean meal and canola seed meal are all good sources of organic nitrogen, and their effects will last from four to eight months. Avoid overuse of nitrogen, since most insects are attracted to nitrogen-rich plants.

Phosphorus. Bone meal and rock phosphate are good sources of organic phosphorus and their effects will last at least twelve months.

Potassium. Kelp meal, liquid seaweed, granite meal, greensand and wood ashes are all excellent sources of potassium, and they will last from six to twelve months.

Magnesium. Epsom salts, chelates and borax are good sources of magnesium.

Calcium. Gypsum, calcitic lime and oyster shells provide calcium.

Boron. Borax is a good source of boron.

Other natural amendments should be added, depending upon the needs of your soil, in order to balance different elements and add trace minerals. If a laboratory makes recommendations, ask them for organic sources of amendments. Later in this chapter, we give a recipe for making your own all-purpose organic fertilizer.

Well-rotted animal manures. As the season progresses, the manure and soil will blend, enriching the earth. One of the very best things you can do for your garden is to add a generous layer of well-rotted manure to every bed in the spring and/or fall. Just make sure the manure you buy is properly decomposed and weed-free. There's nothing quite so satisfying as looking at your garden covered in a healthy layer of manure. It will smother any weeds that are on their way up, and its nutrients will gradually leach down into the soil. As the season progresses, the manure and soil will blend, enriching the earth. Be careful, though, to keep manure away from stems and trunks of plants, shrubs and trees as it could burn them if it is too fresh. Manure tea (that is, manure steeped in water that is then used to water the garden) is less likely to burn plant roots when applied directly to the garden.

Manures most commonly used are chicken, cow, duck, horse, pig, rabbit, sheep and steer. There is a growing market for zoo and circus animal manures. Local llama breeders have made llama manures available to gardeners. Dog and cat feces, however, should not be used. Cow manure is moister and less concentrated than that of other farm animals; because of their complex digestive systems, cows, sheep and goats produce manure that is rich in beneficial microorganisms.

Mushroom manure is the used-up bedding from commercial mushroom production. We do not recommend using it unless the seller can give you a laboratory analysis showing it is free from pesticide residues. Mushroom manure should not be put around acid-loving plants, such as rhododendrons, since it contains some lime.

Peat moss. We now consider it an environmentally endangered substance and no longer recommend its use in the garden.

Seaweed. Seaweed is a good source of potassium and trace elements. If you collect your own, make sure it is free of oil and any other pollutants, and wash it thoroughly to remove excess salt. Water-soluble seaweed fertilizer

solution is readily available and inexpensive.
Leaf mulch compost. The leaves of deciduous trees can be gathered in autumn, stacked in a corner of the garden and returned to the soil after they have decomposed to a crumbly, dark brown form. The mulch is valued for its ability to improve soil structure, rather than for the nutrients it provides. An alternative to storing the leaves is to spread them out on your lawn or boulevard on a dry day and run the lawn mower over them. Once they're shredded this way, you can rake them on top of your beds and borders. They will decompose over the winter months and add a bit of protection for your plants. It is also possible to buy composted leaves from the City of Vancouver and from VanDusen Botanical Garden. (See "Soil amendments" in the Resources section.)

Making Organic Fertilizer

We recommend the use of organic fertilizers whenever possible. Since they release nutrients into the soil more slowly than do chemical fertilizers, they usually only need to be spread once, at sowing or transplanting time. They should be spread evenly around a plant, mixed in with the soil directly below a transplanted seedling, or buried a few inches below seeds that are being sown. This will give you the most economical, most effective use of your fertilizer. Most garden stores now carry organic fertilizers and other organic products.

It is easy to make your own all-purpose organic fertilizer.

Materials

- 4 parts seed meal, such as canola seed meal or fish meal, which add nitrogen.
- 1 part dolomite lime, finely ground (*not* quick lime or slaked lime); it sweetens the soil, making it more alkaline.

- 1 part rock phosphate or 1/2 part bone meal; this adds phosphate.
- 1/2 part kelp meal, to add potassium and trace elements.

Method

Mix all ingredients together and use as outlined above.

For rhododendrons and other acid-loving plants, leave out the lime, since these plants prefer acid soils.

For roses, add to the above mix 1 part blood meal, 2 parts more rock phosphate or bone meal, 1 part sulphate of potash, and 1/2 part magnesium sulphate.

Compost: the true meaning of recycling

Making compost is the ultimate recycling experience. It is an excellent way to return organic matter and nutrients to the soil and reduce the amount of organic supplements you will need. Compost renews and conditions the soil, helps to retain moisture and feeds the plants. Making compost makes sense.

Compost is easy to make from just about any kind of organic material, including coffee grounds, eggshells, vegetable and fruit peelings, grass clippings and decaying leaves. Carbon-rich organic matter (leaves, hay and straw) are mixed with nitrogen-rich materials (grass clippings, fresh manure, vegetable and fruit scraps). To achieve the desired carbon to nitrogen ratio, add a thin layer of nitrogen-rich material to several inches of carbon-rich material. A good balance of high carbon and high nitrogen with moisture will provide all the right conditions for the microbes to break down the organic matter and create a rich humus. If the organic material does not break down, if there is a bad odor or if your pile

Compost problems and solutions

Most compost problems are easily solved by adjusting the mixture of ingredients, adding more moisture and aerating regularly.

Problem	Remedy
Wet, foul smelling.	Add high-carbon material, such as dry leaves, newspaper, straw, hay or cut-up burlap bags. Turn pile and cover with a lid.
Centre of compost pile is dry and not decomposing.	Water thoroughly, cover to retain moisture.
Pile is damp but not heating up.	Add material high in nitrogen, such as grass clippings and fresh manure, and turn pile.
Layers of matted leaves or grass clippings not decomposing.	Use a garden fork to break up layers; mix in carbon-rich straw, hay or dry leaves.
Large and undecomposed material.	Screen it and use it as a base for the new compost pile.

does not heat up, it is easily resolved by adjusting your mixture of ingredients.

Do not add meat, bones, grease, pet waste, diseased plant material or lawn clippings if the lawn has been sprayed with weed killers. Sticks, branches and large pieces should be shredded or cut into smaller pieces to help speed the decomposition. A layer of soil on top of the carbon and nitrogen layers will also add earthworms and soil microbes to the compost. They will help break down the organic matter.

Aerate the pile regularly and make sure the middle does not dry out. As the organic matter begins to decompose and break down, the pile heats up. In a matter of months, your kitchen and garden wastes become rich, dark compost, a wonderful conditioner for your garden.

You can make compost simply by piling all the composting material into a heap and poking it with a long pole occasionally to keep it aerated. Eventually the pile will decompose. However, if you live in an urban environment it is best to use a compost bin to ensure faster decomposition. More importantly, an unprotected compost pile will attract rats and mice looking for food and shelter. There are many locally manufactured, rodent-proof compost bins available. It is a good idea to visit the compost demonstration gardens in your area, where you can look at various kinds of bins in action (see "Compost Education and Demonstration Gardens" in the Resources section).

Outdoor worm composter

Cut out the bottom of a plastic garbage can and bury the can up to 2 feet (60 cm) deep in a shady, unused area of the garden. Drill some ventilation holes in the plastic that remains above ground. Layer compost material as you would a normal compost (see above) until the can is full, cover with the plastic cover and leave it for a year. The worms will invade the compost from below and increase in numbers. In the winter they will go below ground, and you will have a rich compost with lots of nutrient-rich castings left by the worms.

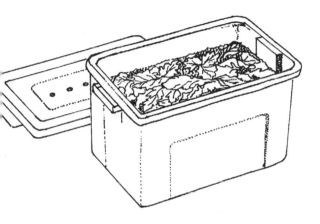

Making a Worm Bin

A worm bin is just the thing for apartment dwellers. It is not smelly and can easily be tucked into a corner of your apartment or balcony just so long as air can get into the holes on the top. This size of worm bin will handle kitchen scraps for the average household, and provide you with fresh, rich humus for your apartment or patio.

Materials

- One heavy plastic storage box with lid, about 2 feet (60 cm) long, 18 inches (45 cm) wide, and 9 inches (23 cm) deep.
- About 1/2 pound (225 g) of garden worms. If you don't have a garden, try bait shops or a friend's garden.
- Some soil, either from the garden or bagged from a garden store.

Method

Drill the lid of the box full of holes. Fill the box about two-thirds full of soil and add the worms. Chop vegetable scraps, the finer the better, and bury them several inches (8 or 10 cm) deep in the soil. Worms don't like onions and garlic, but just about any other fruit and vegetable scraps, coffee grounds, eggshells, etc. are fine. After a while the compost material compacts and becomes very heavy and dense. At this point, place the box, with the lid off, in the sun. The worms will tend to go towards the bottom of the box and the soil they have made can be taken off the top. The rest of the soil/worm mix is ready to use again.

Water

Once the garden is fed, you should make sure it is also properly watered. Long dry spells can occur any time during the growing season, especially in late summer and early fall. Plants can suffer serious damage if they are not watered adequately and regularly. Watering is especially important for newly planted trees and shrubs and flowering and fruiting plants. Morning is an ideal time for watering, as the foliage can dry off during the day. Water restrictions are now in effect in many areas during the growing season and this does mean we are limited to watering only on certain days and times. It is important to water deeply so that the roots reach down into the soil to obtain nutrients and water. Flower beds and shrub borders close to the house are often lacking in organic matter and are heavily planted, so they are prone to drying out very quickly. The same applies to soil under large trees and along hedges. Add organic matter, water deeply and thoroughly, and mulch to help retain moisture in the soil.

Controlling weeds: know your weeds

Some weeds seem to grow, flower, set seed and scatter their offspring throughout the garden before your very eyes, especially in springtime. These "ephemerals" of the garden can become a big nuisance if you let them go to seed, and some of them also provide excellent hosts for unwanted garden pests. The best way to control weeds is to pull them up whenever you see them. You'll be amazed at how successful you can be just by spending a few minutes each day on weed patrol.

Make a list of weeds you have in your garden and find out as much as you can about them. For example, determine what kind of root system they have, whether they are annual or perennial, when they flower and go to seed, how they spread through the garden, and what soil conditions they flourish in. The knowledge you have will help you eliminate your weed problem. In lawns the most troublesome weeds are the creepers—clover, daisies, plaintain and creeping veronica. These weeds do not seem to mind being cut down every week by a lawn mower; if anything they seem to thrive with this regular treatment. To eliminate these weeds without adding poisonous chemicals to the garden, aerate and power rake the lawn in the spring, spread a layer of fine sand on top of it and fertilize with an organic lawn fertilizer. Dig up any obvious, large weed clumps and fill the gap with grass seed. Bad soil drainage, excessive shade, lack of aeration and mowing too closely will result in unhealthy lawns, and this in turn will result in a weed-infested lawn.

To keep the weed population in control in flower borders and along hedges, try mulching with well-aged manure, compost, leaf mould, shredded newspaper, small rocks or gravel.

Start with healthy plants

It sounds obvious, but it is very important to make sure that the plants you introduce into your garden are as healthy as possible. Buy strong plants with healthy foliage and make sure there are no signs of disease or pests. Many varieties of plants, especially vegetables, are bred for their ability to resist disease, and it is worth looking for them.

Make sure that you buy varieties suitable to your garden. Plant your purchases in the right spot, with the right exposure and soil conditions, and provide the right amount of food and water. These simple precautions will save you a lot of trouble later on. If, in spite of all your efforts, a plant does not thrive, don't be afraid to get rid of it. If the problem is the site, you may be able to move it to another place in your garden, or give it to someone with a more appropriate spot for it.

Pests and diseases

It is a challenge to keep to organic gardening practices when a favourite plant is chewed to the ground by slugs, rosebuds are deformed by aphids, or bedding plants are covered with mildew. But wait before you reach for the chemicals. For centuries, before modern chemicals were developed, nature maintained its delicate balance without help from us.

However, you will need to be patient and tolerant. You will also have to plan your garden properly and rotate vegetable crops to prevent a large-scale pest or disease infestation, and watch carefully for signs of problems. When they occur, act quickly, identify the cause accurately, and treat it correctly (see the "Common Pests and Diseases" section). If you do your part, and provide the right conditions for natural predators to do their job, you should be able to sit back and watch nature take care of itself.

Physical pest barriers and simple insect removal methods

There are two excellent products on the market that every gardener will want to have on hand: Tanglefoot and Reemay. Tanglefoot is a sticky substance that is spread on tape and placed around the base of the plant as a collar. As the insects crawl up the plant, they are trapped on the sticky tape. This is especially useful to prevent root weevils from attacking rhododendrons, and to stop the wingless female winter moth from climbing into fruit trees and infesting them.

Reemay is a spun-polyester fabric that allows sunlight, air and water through but is fine enough to exclude insect pests. Reemay is ideal as a temporary cover for plants such as carrots, which are subject to infestation by tiny rust flies at certain times during the growing season.

Aphids and other soft-bodied insects that eat leaves and fruits can be destroyed with organic sprays made from pure soaps or from some of the aromatic herbs, such as garlic, chili peppers and thyme. Dried horsetail (*Equisetum*), which contains lots of rough, gritty silica, or diatomaceous earth (fossilized sea shells) can be spread around tender plants, acting as a barrier for slugs and snails.

Invaluable aids for any gardener are a magnifying glass and a book about diseases and harmful and beneficial pests. These will help you identify problems in your garden—the first step towards accurate treatment.

There are some excellent organic books dealing in depth with this topic. If you still cannot identify the source of your problem, take a sample to your local garden store, or contact one of the garden experts listed under "Plant and garden information lines" in the Resources section.

Above all, don't panic. Healthy plants can tolerate a certain amount of insect damage. If you identify the problem early enough, you'll have time to get the situation under control before it gets out of hand.

Clematis and Other Ornamental Climbers

Ornamental climbers are the great softeners in a garden. They can hide an ugly wall, decorate an aging tree, cover a post or enhance a trellis. One of the most important and popular of all the climbers is clematis, which comes in many shapes, sizes and colours.

Most clematis are climbing perennials, but a few are herbaceous perennials and make free-standing border plants. Most are deciduous, but there are a few exceptions, including the lovely *C. armandii*, which produces fragrant white flowers in April. Clematis flowers vary in size and shape, from small, nodding pitcher-, bell-, or star-shaped flowers to large, flat, circular blooms of popular hybrids. The larger-flowered clematis are the ones most commonly seen.

Where to plant

Clematis need support of some kind, whether it is a lattice, a post, hooks on a wall, a shrub or a tree. They are sociable plants and combine well with others, gently twisting their leaf stalks around the nearest support. The one exception in this gentle-mannered group is the overvigorous *C. montana*, which will smother everything in its path and, if allowed to climb freely on a house, will lift gutters, down-pipes and roof shingles. *C. montana* is best grown up a very large tree, at least 30 feet (9 m), where its pale pink flowers will form an aerial carpet of colour. You can see a lovely example of this in the Meditation Garden at VanDusen Gardens.

Clematis are quite fussy about their growing conditions. They like to have their roots in the shade and their heads in the sun. If their base is in a sunny position, it is a good idea to cover the area over the roots with stones, or protect it with a bushy groundcover.

When to plant

The best times to plant are in the spring, from late March until the end of May, and in the fall, from the end of August until mid-November. However, container-grown specimens can be planted any time, providing they are fed and watered well.

How to plant

Before planting, give the clematis plenty of water by soaking the rootball in a bucket of water for 10 minutes. Dig a hole about 6 inches (15 cm) larger in diameter than the rootball, break up the bottom of the hole with a garden fork, add two or three handfuls of bone meal, and cover this with some well-rotted compost or manure.

Carefully remove the well-soaked clematis from the pot by turning it upside down and tapping gently. Place it so that the top of the plant is a couple of inches (5 cm) below soil level. Fill the hole with garden soil mixed with well-soaked peat moss and tread the soil down carefully but firmly around the rootball.

Care and protection

Clematis have a reputation for being difficult, but they are really easy to grow in our climate provided they have the right conditions and are given an ample supply of food and water. They benefit from a mulching of well-rotted manure in the spring, but care must be taken not to place manure on the main stem, since it will burn the delicate tissues of the plant. Instead, leave a space of at least 6 inches (15 cm) around its base.

Pruning

This is not nearly as difficult or complicated as it is often made out to be. Clematis can be divided into three groups, with three basic pruning methods.

Group 1. These are the earliest spring-flowering species, the ones that flower on old wood. They do not require any pruning.

Group 2. These are the early-summer, large-flowered hybrids, including the doubles. They also flower on old wood and should be pruned lightly, back to a strong set of buds, in February or March.

Group 3. This group are the later-flowering clematis that flower on new wood. They should be pruned hard at the end of February to about 30 inches (75 cm) above soil level.

Oddities

Just to be confusing, there are clematis that produce double flowers on old wood in early spring and single flowers on new wood in early fall. This habit generates lots of calls to garden centres from customers who think that something has gone terribly wrong with their clematis. If you find this happens with your clematis, then it should receive only a light pruning, as if it falls into group 2.

Problems

The large-flowered hybrids are susceptible to a problem called "wilt," where a plant that is healthy and vigorous one day will suddenly collapse. The cause is believed to be a fungus. There is no cure for wilt, nor can preventative measures be taken before a plant is affected. If it strikes your plant, the stems should be cut off below ground level, and all the affected material disposed of (do not put it into the compost bin). This is why it is important to plant the clematis extra-deep to start off with (see "How to plant" above). This drastic treatment should result in your clematis sprouting again, although some take three years or longer to make a reappearance.

Clematis for north-facing walls

The best clematis for these conditions are the alpina, macropetala and montana species and their cultivars, but there are a number of large-flowered hybrids that do well too. The popular 'Nelly Moser' is a good example of a clematis that becomes totally "washed out" in full sun. The petals, however, will retain their vibrant colour for much longer when grown in shade. Some others for a shady area are 'Alice Fisk', 'Barbara Dibley', 'Hagley Hybrid', *C.* x *jackmanii*, 'Marie Boisselot', 'Silver Moon', 'Victoria', 'Vyvyan Pennell' and 'William Kennet'.

Clematis, according to their pruning requirements

Group 1: No pruning required

Name	Colour	Flower size	Flowering times
C. alpina	Satiny blue	Small nodding	April-May
'Columbine'	Pale blue	Small nodding	April-May
'Frances Rivis'	Deep blue	Small nodding	April-May
'Pamela Jackman'	Mid-blue	Small nodding	April-May
'Ruby'	Purple-pink	Small nodding	April-May
'White Moth'	White	Small nodding	April-May
'Willy'	Mauve-pink	Small nodding	April-May
C. armandii	Creamy white	Small	March-April
'Apple Blossom'	Pale pink	Small	March-April
'Snowdrift'	Pure white	Small	March-April
C. balearica syn. calycina	Creamy yellow	Small nodding	January-March
C. chrysocoma	Soft pink	Small	May
C. columbiana	Violet-blue	Small nodding	May
C. macropetala	Blue semidouble	Small nodding	April-May
'Bluebird'	Blue semidouble	Small nodding	April-May
'Jan Lindmark'	Dark pink	Small nodding	May
'Maidwell Hall'	Deeper blue	Small nodding	April-May
'Markham's Pink'	Lavender-pink	Small nodding	April-May
'White Swan'	White	Small nodding	May
C. montana	White	Small	May-June
'Elizabeth'	Pale pink	Small	May-June
'Picton's Variety'	Deep pink	Small	May-June
'Pink Perfection'	Pale pink	Small	May-June
'Tetrarose'	Deep rosy-mauve	Medium	May-June
var. rubens	Purplish-pink	Small	May-June
var. wilsonii	White	Small	May-June

Clematis, according to their pruning requirements

Group 2: Prune lightly in February and March

Name	Colour	Flower size	Flowering times
'Alice Fisk'	Wisteria blue	Large	May-June and August
'Barbara Dibley'	Petunia red	Large	May-June and August
'Bee's Jubilee'	Deep pink, carmine bar	Large	May-June and August
'Belle of Woking'	Silvery-mauve	Large double	May-June and August
'Blue Light'	Violet-blue	Large double	May-June and August
'Capitan Thuilleaux'	Rosy-mauve, carmine bar	Large	May-June
'C.W. Dowman'	Lavender-pink	Large	May-June and August
'Countess of Lovelace'	Pale lilac blue	Large double	May-June and August
'Dr. Ruppel'	Rose, carmine bar	Large	May-June
'Duchess of Edinburgh'	White	Large double	May-June and August
'Gillian Blades'	White	Large	May-June
'Gladys Picard'	Pale mauve	Large	May-June
'Guernsey Cream'	Creamy yellow	Large	May-June
'Haku-okan'	Purple	Large	May-June and August
'Henryi'	Creamy white	Large	June-August
'H.F. Young'	Wedgewood blue	Large	May-June and August
'Horn of Plenty'	Deep rosy-mauve	Large	May-June and August
'Joan Picton'	Rosy-lilac	Large	May-June and August
'Kathleen Dunford'	Rosy-purple	Large, semidouble	May-June and August
'Lady Londesborough'	Pale mauve-blue	Large	June-August
'Lady Northcliffe'	Wedgewood blue	Large	June-August
'Lasurstern'	Deep rich blue	Large	May-June and August
'Lawsonia'	Lavender-blue	Large	June-August
'Marie Boisselot', also called 'Madame le Coultre'	White	Large	June-August
'Miss Bateman'	Creamy white	Large	May-June
'Nelly Moser'	Pale pink, carmine bar	Large	May-June and August
'Niobe'	Ruby-red	Large	June-August
'Ramona'	Lavender-blue	Large	June-August
'Sealand Gem'	Rosy-mauve, carmine bar	Large	June-August
'Silver Moon'	Mother of pearl	Large	June-August
'The President'	Deep purple-blue	Large	June-August
'Vyvyan Pennell'	Violet-blue	Large double	May-June and August
'William Kennett'	Deep lavender-blue	Large	June-August
'Xerxes', also called 'Elsa Spath'	Deep violet-blue	Large	June-August

Clematis, according to their pruning requirements

Group 3: Hard pruning in February and March

Name	Colour	Flower size	Flowering times
C. campaniflora	Soft lavender	Small nodding	July-August
C. chiisanensis	Bright yellow	Small nodding	July-September
'Comtesse de Bouchaud'	Mauve-pink	Large	July-September
C. connata	Pale yellow	Small nodding	September-October
C. crispa	Lilac-blue	Small nodding	June-September
'Ernest Markham'	Magenta	Large	July-September
'Etoile Violette'	Deep purple	Medium	July-September
C. fargesii var. souliei	White	Small	July-September
C. flammula	White	Small	August-October
'Gipsy Queen'	Violet-purple	Large	July-September
'Hagley Hybrid'	Rosy-mauve	Medium	June-September
'Huldine'	Pearly white	Medium	July-September
C. x jackmanii	Deep purple	Large	June-September
'Alba'	White	Large	June-September
'Superba'	Dark purple	Large	June-September
'Lady Betty Balfour'	Violet-blue	Large	August-September
'Margaret Hunt'	Dusty pink	Large	July-September
'Margot Koster'	Mauve-pink	Large	July and August
'My Angel'	Orange-yellow	Small nodding	August-September
C. orientalis	Yellow	Small nodding	July-September
'Perle d'Azur'	Azure	Medium	July-September
C. tangutica	Yellow	Small nodding	July-September
C. terniflora	White	Small	September-October
C. texensis			
'Duchess of Albany'	Pink	Small nodding	August-October
'Etoile Rose'	Pink	Small nodding	July-September
'Gravetye Beauty'	Ruby-red	Small nodding	August-October
'Pagoda'	Pink	Small nodding	July-September
C. x triternata			
'Rubromarginata'	Pink	Small nodding	July-September
'Victoria'	Rosy-purple	Medium	July-September
C. vitalba	Creamy white	Small star	July-September
C. viticella			
'Abundance'	Mauve-red	Small	June-September
'Alba Luxurians'	White	Small	June-September
'Betty Corning'	Pale blue	Small nodding	June-September
'Minuet'	Mauve-red	Small nodding	June-September
'Polish Spirit'	Deep purple	Medium	June-September
'Purpurea plena Elegans'	Burgundy	Small nodding	June-September
'Royal Velours'	Reddish-purple	Small	June-September
'Rubra'	Wine-red	Small	July-September
'Venosa Violacea'	Purple	Small nodding	June-September

10 special clematis

The pruning list, while useful, leaves little room for plant descriptions. The following is an in-depth look at 10 clematis that merit more attention. Some are tender, some need special care, some are wonderfully easy to grow, while others may be hard to find. Whatever the reason, these are all worthy of special mention. With only space for 10, it should be said that all the alpina, macropetala, montana and texensis species—in fact, all the small-flowered species—are special and well worth growing.

'Blue Light'. This double-flowered clematis is an offspring of 'Mrs. Cholmondeley', whose name, for those who have not read Christopher Lloyd's chapter on pronunciation, is pronounced Chumley. Lloyd goes on to say of Mrs. Cholmondeley that "The blowsy old girl makes a splendid show." Catalogues continue in this vein, saying that 'Blue Light' is a "sport of the otherwise respectable Mrs. Cholmondeley." With a mother like that, who could resist? It has lovely, double violet-blue flowers in June and then single flowers in August on new wood. It grows to a height of about 6 feet (1.8 m) and would do equally well in a container or the garden. Pruning group 2.

C. campaniflora (**harebell clematis**). A vigorous climber with tiny, bell-shaped, violet-blue flowers that are very freely produced in July and August. Grow it in a place where you can appreciate the small delicate flowers. Once established it can grow to a height of more than 15 feet (4.5 m). It can be hard-pruned in February or left unpruned if space allows.

C. x *cartmanii* '**Joe**'. This is an exquisite but tender clematis from New Zealand. It came from the garden of Joe Cartman and

it is a natural cross between *C. marmoria* and *C. paniculata*. The white flowers, greenish at the centre, are beautifully formed and set off to perfection by the evergreen foliage. It is very showy and blooms prolifically. As it needs protection from the cold, it is best grown in a container and brought inside to a frost-free place in winter. It can grow to a height of 6 feet (1.8 m). Pruning group 3.

C. florida sieboldii (*C. f. bicolor, C. f.* '**Sieboldiana**'). Pale green petals open to creamy white with a large purple central boss. It is so exotic-looking that it is sometimes confused with a passion flower. It flowers from June to September, and can grow to a height of between 6 and 10 feet (1.8 to 3 m). The drawback is that it is not an easy clematis to get started, nor is it reliably hardy in our climate. Having said that, if you have a warm sunny wall to give it warmth and protection, it is well worth trying. If not, then it is a good candidate for growing in a container that can be overwintered in a frost-free place. Pruning group 2.

'**My Angel**'. This stunning clematis is a *C. orientalis* hybrid. Similar in form to its parent, the reflexed, bell-shaped flowers are yellow on the inside and orange-red on the outside, with the petals outlined in

Tip of the Month: Pruning Clematis

To help you remember when to prune your clematis, put a colour-coded tie that indicates its pruning group around the base of each plant. For example, use a red tie for group 1 (no pruning), a blue tie for group 2 (lightly prune in February and March) and a yellow tie for group 3 (hard-prune in February and March). Just don't forget your code!

cream. It blooms in August through October, and grows to a height of 8 feet (2.4 m). It is certainly one to look out for to add a touch of drama to the late summer and fall garden. Pruning group 3.

'Perle d'Azur'. It is an almost impossible task to pick out only one of the large-flowered hybrids, but having said that, 'Perle d'Azur' would be near the top of any list. It is not the easiest clematis to grow in this region, and can often turn up its toes for no discernible reason, but it is worth persevering with. The large flowers with deeply lined midribs are a light clear blue with small green stamens, and given the right conditions, it will bloom profusely from June through September. It has been in cultivation for over a hundred years, and for those who have seen it growing at Sissinghurst, it is a "must have." It grows to a height of 10 to 16 feet (3 to 5 m). Pruning group 3.

C. rehderiana **(nodding virgin's bower).** Small primrose-yellow bell-shaped flowers that are deliciously scented cover this climber from August to October. It is a very vigorous and easy-to-grow plant that will reach 10 to 20 feet (3 to 6 m). It can be left unpruned if there is plenty of room, or pruned hard in winter if space is at a premium. It flowers best in full sun.

C. terniflora **(syn.** *C. paniculata, C. maximow icziana***) (sweet autumn clematis).** When we need it most, this lovely deciduous or semievergreen clematis produces masses of small, white, sweetly scented, star-shaped flowers. It blooms in September, October and often much later, depending on weather conditions. Very vigorous to a height of 20 feet (6 m) or more, so think carefully what to grow it on. It can be left unpruned or pruned hard in February, depending on location.

C. x *triternata* **'Rubromarginata'.** A vigorous and very pretty climber that is a cross between *C. flammula* and *C. viticella*. The tiny flowers with four narrow petals are cruciform, and purple-red shading to white at the centre. They are sweetly fragrant and bloom from August to September. A very easy-to-grow and trouble-free plant, equally suited to growing through shrubs and trees or on an arbour. It reaches a height of 15 to 20 feet (4.6 to 6 m). Pruning group 3.

C. viticella **'Etoile Violette'.** It is hard to say enough good things about this plant or, in fact, any of the viticella group. They are much easier to care for than the large-flowered hybrids, with the biggest advantage being that they are free from wilt. The flowers of the viticellas are generally very much smaller, but they make up for it in sheer numbers. 'Etoile Violette' is similar in colour to the popular 'Jackmanii' but the flowers are smaller, daintier and slightly recurved at the tips. It is very vigorous, growing to a height of 10 to 12 feet (3 to 3.7 m) and is probably one of the most free-flowering hybrids. From July to September the foliage is obscured with deep purple velvety blooms. Pruning group 3.

The non-climbing clematis

People assume that all clematis are climbers, but there are a number that aren't. These can be grown as groundcovers, or left to scramble through other perennials or shrubs in the border.

C. x **'Durandii'.** A wonderful border plant with stems up to 6 feet (1.8 m) that drape over and through other plants. Large indigo-blue flowers with off-white stamens. It is a cross between *C. integrifolia* and *C.* 'Jackmanii'.

C. x *eriostemon* 'Hendersonii'. A semiwoody subshrub with small, nodding, lantern-shaped purple flowers. A cross between *C. integrifolia* and *C. viticella*, it scrambles happily through neighbouring shrubs, growing to a height of 6 to 8 feet (1.8 to 2.4 m). It flowers over a long season, from July to September.

C. heracleifolia var. *davidiana.* A semi-herbaceous perennial with small, hyacinthlike flowers, which are a clear lavender-blue and highly scented. Very attractive, deeply lobed leaves enhance the tiny flowers. It grows to a height of about 3 feet (90 cm) and forms a largish clump from underground shoots. It does not die down completely but forms a woody base. It should be pruned back to the wood in early spring or in the fall cleanup. Cultivars to look out for are 'Wyevale' and 'Campanile'.

C. integrifolia. Another herbaceous perennial forming a clump of thin stems that intertwine beautifully with neighbouring plants. It grows to a height of about 3 feet (90 cm). Some cultivars to look for are 'Blue Boy' (sky-blue flowers), 'Caerulea' (deep blue flowers) and 'Pangbourne Pink' (mauve-pink bells on wiry stems).

C. x *jouiniana* 'Praecox'. Ideal for the perennial border, producing numerous, tiny, mauve-blue flowers throughout the summer. It forms a woody framework, and it is better pruned back to the woody growth than down to the ground. It is an ideal candidate for sprawling on a bank, where it can grow up to 10 feet (3 m). The attractive, deeply lobed leaves turn yellow in autumn.

C. recta. A herbaceous perennial that grows to a height of between 3 and 6 feet (90 cm to 1.8 m). It can be left to flop over its neighbours or can be tied to a support. With masses of small, white, starry, scented flowers, we have seen it intermingling with old roses to great effect. Attractive, deep green, pinnate leaves are the perfect foil to the flowers. Some forms are scented but others are not, so it is best to buy it in bloom. Look for 'Atropurpurea', which has lovely foliage tinged with purple when young.

C. stans. A herbaceous perennial growing to a height of about 3 feet (90 cm) with terminal panicles of tiny, bluish-white flowers in May to July. The large midgreen leaves are coarsely toothed. It thrives in full sun or part shade, and although not showy it associates well with other plants in the border.

Other ornamental climbers

The following is a list of favourite annual and perennial climbers. Planting and care instructions for clematis apply equally well to the climbers listed here.

Actinidia kolomikta. An eye-catching climber belonging to the same family as the kiwi fruit. It grows to about 30 feet (9 m), producing heart-shaped green leaves tinged with purple in spring. As the season progresses, the leaves variegate with splashes of white and pink. It produces the best variegation when grown in full sun. Train it on strong wall supports when young, and prune it to shape in early spring.

Akebia quinata (five-leaf akebia). A deciduous or semievergreen climber that can grow to a height of 30 feet (9 m). It is grown more for its foliage than for its maroon/chocolate flowers which, although they have a vanilla fragrance, are fairly insignificant. It is a fast grower and will cover a trellis, arbour or pergola easily.

After flowering, prune out weak shoots and, if space is restricted, cut back hard.

Campsis radicans (**Chinese trumpet vine**). A deciduous vine that clings to wood, brick or stucco by means of aerial roots, similar to ivy. It produces arching sprays of brilliant orange, trumpet-shaped flowers in late summer. It climbs to about 30 feet (9 m) and requires full sun. Prune back all shoots to within a few inches (8 to 10 cm) of the ground in February. *C.* x *tagliabuana* 'Madame Galen' is also commonly available here, with salmon-red flowers.

Cobaea scandens (**cup and saucer plant, cathedral bell**). Rapid-growing annual climber, planted in May, which will reach a height of 12 feet (3.7 m) by the end of the season. Its bell-shaped flowers sit in green saucerlike cups and are very freely produced. The display lasts until the first hard frost. Does best in full sun, but will tolerate light shade. The lovely white form 'Alba' is even more vigorous and has larger flowers. Provide support for the plant's tendrils, using trellis or netting.

Codonopsis convolvulacea. This herbaceous summer-flowering climber bears soft, blue-violet flowers 1 to 2 inches (2.5 to 5 cm) across and is a good climber for a semishaded woodland setting. It will grow to a height of 6 feet (1.8 m). The fragile, slender stems are easily damaged and should be protected. It makes its appearance quite late—in early summer—so its planting spot should be marked.

Dicentra scandens. This climber is native to the Himalayas and closely related to *Dicentra spectabilis* (the red and white bleeding heart). It produces the same flower shape but the flowers grow in clusters and are a lemon-greenish colour. It is not readily available but is easily propa-

gated from cuttings taken in autumn. The seeds are difficult to germinate.

Dolichos lablab. This annual vine is native to the tropics where it is grown as a perennial. Plant from seed after the last frost. It will quickly grow up to 10 feet (3 m), making a fine temporary summer screen. The sweet pea–like flowers are purple or white, about 1 inch (2.5 cm) long, and edible. In the fall the large, dark purple and brown seed pods make an interesting display until the plant is dug up after the first frost.

Eccremocarpus scaber (**Chilean glory flower**). A fast-growing climber that is grown as an annual in colder climates, it scrambles up to 10 feet (3 m) over trellises, arches and pergolas. The brilliant orange-red tubular flowers grow in clusters through summer into autumn.

Hedera **spp.** (**ivy**). A very useful group of hardy evergreen woody vines, climbing any vertical surface by aerial roots, in sun or shade. Prune back close to their support during February or March, if desired. *H. canariensis* 'Gloire de Marengo' has wide leaves with silvery margins. It requires a sunny position to colour well. *H. colchica* 'Dentata' has the largest leaves of all the readily available ivies. The leaves are faintly toothed and the variegated variety 'Dentata-variegata' has grey-green leaves with broad, pale yellow edges. *H. colchica* 'Sulphur Heart' has large heart-shaped dark green leaves suffused with a creamy yellow; as they grow older the creamy yellow becomes more evenly distributed throughout the leaf. This ivy will quickly cover a shady wall. *H. helix* 'Glacier' is a small-leafed cultivar with elegantly elongated central lobes. It has soft, grey-green leaves with white edging. *H.*

helix 'Gold Heart' has bright, variegated leaves and is ideal for brightening up a shady wall. It associates well with other climbers.

Humulus lupulus 'Aureus' (golden hop). This hop is grown for its bright, golden yellow foliage. The conelike flowers are papery green and yellowish and hang in clusters. They appear in late summer and are a nice addition to the foliage. The flowers dry well and can be used in wreaths and garlands. Train the vine over a fence, trellis or into a small tree. It should be planted in full sun to obtain the best leaf colour. Cut dead growth back in early spring.

Hydrangea anomala ssp. petiolaris (climbing hydrangea). A tough and vigorous deciduous climber that clings to support by means of aerial roots. It likes sun or shade, even a north wall. Clusters of lacecap-type, creamy white flowers are carried in June. It usually takes some time to become established, and it may need some initial support until its aerial roots become active. If necessary to maintain shape and size, prune in February.

Ipomoea alba (also known as Calonyction aculeatum)(moonflower, belle de nuit). Grown as an annual where the temperature drops below freezing. The fragrant white flowers open only at night and close before midday. In one growing season it can reach a height of 16 feet (5 m). Chip or soak seeds before planting.

Ipomoea purpurea (morning glory). Best grown in full sun, this morning glory bears deep blue or purple flowers continuously throughout the summer. It grows to a height of 16 feet (5 m) in one season. 'Scarlet O'Hara' is a new variety bearing scarlet blooms with a pure white throat. Chip or soak seeds before planting.

Ipomoea tricolor (morning glory). A showy annual, entirely different from the troublesome weed with the same common name. It grows from seed to 8 feet (2.4 m) by the end of the season. It has trumpet-shaped, single or double flowers in blue, lavender, pink or red, with some striped or bicoloured varieties. 'Heavenly Blue' has beautiful, sky-blue flowers. Like most morning glories, its flowers are at their best in the morning and fade in the afternoon. Grow against a sunny fence or other support.

Ipomoea versicolor (also known as Mina lobata) (Spanish flag). Only on close inspection does this plant look like a morning glory. The flowers grow on long spikes and open from the bottom to the tip. They open red and fade to orange and then cream. A single stem will contain all the varying stages of flower. The plant blooms non-stop all summer and is wonderful in containers where it can climb up bamboo stakes. It is an annual vine easily grown from seed.

Jasminum spp. (jasmine). We tend to think of the richly fragrant *Jasminum officinale* when we think of jasmine, but not all of the jasmines are fragrant. *J. nudiflorum* (winter jasmine) is not scented, but from late November to March it carries sprays of golden, starry flowers on bare twigs. It's not strictly a climber, but can be trained against a support and grows to 10 feet (3 m). After flowering, prune out old and weak wood, and tie in new shoots. *J. officinale* (common white jasmine) is a vigorous twining climber with a rich, heavy scent from clusters of small white flowers borne from June to October. It grows in sun or partial shade. Thin out shoots after flowering.

J. polyanthum is also available here but

is not reliably hardy in our climate. It grows to about 20 feet (6 m) and has dense clusters of very fragrant flowers that are pink opening to white. If grown in a container, it can be brought inside in the winter for use as a house plant.

Lathyrus latifolius (everlasting sweet pea). A herbaceous perennial and vigorous climber, it is a common sight growing wild in sand and near salt water. In summer it produces vivid magenta, pink and purplish unscented flowers. A close relative to the fragrant sweet pea, it is much more vigorous and can become a thug if not kept in check. There is a pure white variety called 'White Pearl'.

Lathyrus odoratus (sweet pea). There are many cultivars of *L. odoratus*, the beautiful and fragrant sweet pea. The flowers grow in clusters; some are one colour, while others are bicoloured or variably marked. These are some of the earliest seeds we can plant out in the garden. They make excellent cut flowers and because they are annuals, the more flowers you pick the more the plant will produce. Deadhead all spent flowers. (See "Annual seeds to be sown directly into the garden" in the May chapter.)

Lonicera spp. (honeysuckle). The flowers of many of the honeysuckles are small and not particularly showy, but they are abundant, and most of them are very fragrant. *L. japonica* 'Halliana' (Japanese honeysuckle) is the most vigorous and widely grown. It climbs to about 20 feet (6 m) with sweetly fragrant white flowers fading to yellow. It thrives in full sun or light shade.

There are three abundantly blooming, sweetly scented *L. periclymenum* varieties that deserve mention. 'Belgica' (early

Dutch honeysuckle), cultivated since the 17th century, has yellow blooms flushed with purple and red; 'Graham Thomas' has white flowers maturing to yellow; and 'Serotina' has rich red-purple flowers. Plant in sun or light shade, and mulch annually with well-rotted compost. To keep trained plants in shape, prune shoots back by one-third after flowering.

The flowers of *Lonicera* x *tellmanniana*, although unscented, are a lovely, coppery-orange colour and bloom from late spring well into summer. The attractive, elliptical, deep green leaves are a whitish-blue on the underside. This climber will tolerate full sun but produces better flowers if planted in partial shade.

Parthenocissus spp. Deciduous vines that climb by aerial roots. They are noted for their brilliant fall colouring and thrive in sun or shade, growing to heights of over 50 feet (15 m). Think carefully before growing them on house walls, as their adhesive tendrils are hard to remove at repainting time, and they have a tendency to creep under wood or shingle siding. Plant them in humus-rich, well-drained, but moist soil, and provide initial support for young stems until they become self-clinging. *P. quinquefolia* (Virginia creeper) is a great cover for ugly walls. *P. tricuspidata* (Boston ivy) grows more densely than Virginia creeper.

Passiflora caerulea (common passion flower). This is a fast-growing climber valued for its exotic, large, blue and purple flowers and shiny, dark, evergreen leaves. In a sunny sheltered site protected from winter cold and wet, it will grow to a height of 30 feet (9 m). 'Constance Elliott' bears pure white flowers and has the same growth habit as the species.

Plumbago auriculata (Cape leadwort).
A scrambling, semi-evergreen shrub in frost-free climates, it doubles as a climber when trained. It bears clusters of sky-blue flowers from midsummer to late autumn. Plants do well in containers and can be overwintered indoors in a cool room. Grow in well-drained fertile soil in full sun. It can grow up to 20 feet (6 m).

Polygonum aubertii (silver lace vine). A very rapid deciduous climber that is capable of covering a large area in a single season. Masses of fleecy cream flowers cover the vine from early summer to fall. *P. bald-schuanicum* is similar to silver lace vine in appearance, growth and vigour. The flowers are somewhat larger and have a faint pink tinge. It can be hard to find. Both these climbers can be used as a fast-growing screen, but to keep them under control, prune them down to the ground each year. They thrive in sun or shade.

Rhodochiton atrosanguineum. Grown as an annual in our climate, this unusual-looking climber grows to a height of 10 feet (3 m). The hanging flowers have black to dark purple tubes inside red-purple, bell-shaped skirts. Grow in moist but well-drained fertile soil in full sun. The roots should be shaded. Pinch out the shoot tips to encourage a bushy habit.

Solanum spp. *Solanum crispum* 'Grasnevin' is a semi-evergreen woody climber that may survive our winters only if protected. It will scramble to a height of 30 feet (9 m) and bears fragrant, deep blue-purple flowers in clusters and small whitish-yellow berries in autumn. Grow in moist, fertile soil in full sun or partial shade. Weak stems can be pruned in spring. *S. jasminoides* 'Album' is similar to 'Grasnevin', but bears fragrant, star-shaped, white flowers with yellow anthers, followed by dark black fruit in autumn.

Tropaeolum spp. *Tropaeolum majus* (annual nasturtium climber) is easy to grow from seed and many varieties are available. These fast-growing climbers are very useful to cover a trellis or fence quickly in the summer months. 'Climbing Mixed' and 'Jewel of Africa' climb to 9 feet (3 m) and are covered with striking, brightly coloured flowers all summer long. Grow in full sun. *T. speciosum* (vermilion nasturtium) is a herbaceous climber that will grow to 15 feet (3.5 m). It produces long-spurred, vermilion-coloured flowers all summer long, followed by small, bright blue berries. It looks very effective scrambling through shrubs and dark green hedges. Grow in moist, humus-rich, acidic soil in full sun or semishade. *T. tuberosum* 'Ken Aslet' is a herbaceous climber to 8 feet (2.4 m). The tubular flowers are yellow streaked with red outside and orange on the inside, with red sepals. The leaves are bluish-green. It blooms profusely from midsummer into autumn. It is a good idea to dig up the tubers and store in a frost-free area in winter.

Tweedia caerulea. A tender woody climber native to Chile, it grows to 4 feet (1.2 m). Its flower clusters are pale azure blue when they first open and then the star-shaped blossoms fade to lilac. Grow as an annual or protect it from winter cold.

Vitis spp. (grape vines). For a permanent climber with wonderful fall foliage and fruit, add a grape vine to an arbour or trellis. Vines should be planted in deep, moist, well-drained soil in a sunny position if they are to produce ripe fruit and good fall colour. *V. coignetiae* is a very vigorous climber to 85 feet (26 m) with large, wrinkled, veiny leaves that turn purplish and red in autumn. The fruit is small, black and barely edible. *V. vinifera* (common grape) will grow up to 120 feet (37 m) in the wild but in the garden it is generally pruned to no more than 10 feet (3 m). It has large lobed leaves and small, pale green flowers that bloom in spring, followed by purple and red grapes in autumn. There are many varieties to choose from. Make your selection according to your taste in grapes and the fall colour of the leaves.

Wisteria **spp.** Perhaps the most beautiful of all the climbers, capable of reaching a height of 70 feet (21 m). Unless kept in check it is not a plant for a small space. Wisterias grow best in humus-rich soil in full sun. Cut back shoots in February to within two or three buds of the previous year's growth. *W. floribunda* (Japanese wisteria) has fragrant, violet, violet-blue or white blooms which appear with the leaves in April and May. The best form is 'Macrobotrys', with violet-purple spires up to 3 feet (90 cm) long. *W. sinensis* (Chinese wisteria) blooms before the leaves open in April or May. The flower clusters are shorter than those of Japanese wisteria, but they open all together. The flowers are mauve or deep lilac, and there is a beautiful 'Alba' form, which is more strongly and sweetly scented. 'Black Dragon' has deep purple, double blooms and 'Plena' has mauve double blooms.

Down the Primrose Path

There are over 500 species of primula and many are worth growing for their sweetly scented, colourful flowers and their compact garden form. They are often referred to as the heralds of spring and most are native to the Alps, Dolomites and Himalayas. Generally speaking, those from the Himalayas, Japan and China require a moist, humus-rich soil and shady conditions. This group includes all of the popular candelabra primulas and the drumstick primulas (*Primula denticulata*). They grow well in boglike conditions near streams and in moist shade under shrubs and trees. European species (*P. auricula*, *P. veris* and *P. vulgaris*), on the other hand, will do well with a more loamy soil, sunshine and drier conditions. The Pacific Northwest, with its cool, moist climate, is ideal for growing many species and varieties of primulas, including polyanthas (*P.* x *polyantha*). Polyanthas are the brightly coloured hybrids readily available in grocery stores and garden centres. They are grown as annuals during late winter and early spring, in containers and as border plants.

At UBC Botanical Garden there is an extensive collection of primulas and for several months of the year there is a continuous display of various species in flower, starting in late February.

The majority of primulas available in nurseries and garden centres are easily grown in our cool, moist climate. They blend well with other shade-loving plants in a natural woodland setting or in sunny, well-drained soils.

The plants need to be divided every two years and replanted in fresh topsoil to which manure or compost has been added. The best time for division is in May when there are a million other more pressing things that need to be done in the garden; however, if you leave it until later in the summer you probably will notice that they will not flower as they should the following year.

Some primulas, such as *P. auricula,* are best grown in pots. Use a good potting mixture of 1/3 fresh potting soil, 1/3 sand or grit and 1/3 leaf compost. Many primulas are not difficult to grow from seed, and plant catalogues and UBC Botanical Garden have an excellent selection of seeds to choose from.

Watch out for slugs and snails in your primula patch. They love to feast among the leaves.

The following is a list of primulas worth growing and available locally.

P. auricula. A very handsome species with strong stems and evergreen rosettes of thick fleshy leaves. The bell-shaped flowers are carried in clusters. The flowers of the species are yellow, but many hybrids have been developed in a wide range of colours, predominantly red, yellow and purple, with a paler contrasting eye. They grow 6 to 9 inches (15 to 23 cm) tall, need moist, fast-draining soil, and are good in rock gardens. Good cultivars are 'Argus', handsome, very fragrant flowers with pink edging and a creamy white centre; 'Chorister', canary yellow with a frosty white centre; 'Dales Red', single pink, cream centre; 'Marie Crousse', double-flowered, purple; 'Mrs. J. H. Wilson', deep lilac-mauve, yellow centre; 'Queen Alexandra', pale yellow, cream centre; 'Rowena', powdery lilac-pink edging, purple middle and sulphur-yellow centre.

P. denticulata (drumstick primrose). A lovely little primula from the Himalayas, it grows best in moist, humus-rich soil—almost bog conditions—but will grow in ordinary soil if not too dry. In April, globe-shaped clusters of white, lilac or purple flowers are produced on foot-high (30-cm) stems. The wavy-margined grey-green leaves don't fully develop until after flowering. Plant in the front of a border, and propagate by division immediately after flowering. Several good cultivars are available, such as 'Alba', white; and 'Ruby', rose-purple.

P. elatior (oxlip primrose). Native to Europe, this traditional primrose is found in many cottage gardens throughout Europe. The bright yellow flowers are held in a tight clump on top of a 1-foot (30-cm) stalk. It thrives in chalky soil.

P. florindae (giant cowslip). Strong 2- to 3-foot (60- to 90-cm) stems bear hanging clusters of fragrant, yellow, bell-shaped flowers. It blooms in July, one of the last of the primulas to bloom. It thrives in damp soil, and will grow in shallow running water by the side of a stream. While the species is yellow, there are hybrids in shades of light orange or red. This species is native to western China and was introduced into cultivation early in the 20th century.

P. juliae. Growing to a height of 3 inches (7 to 8 cm), it bears purple flowers with a small yellow eye from February to April. This species from the Caucasus is the parent of many lovely hybrids we have today. Referred to collectively as Juliana Hybrids, they may also be named *Primula* x *pruhoniciana.* Good hybrids include 'Schneekissen', with a pure white flower; 'Dorothy', a delicate, petite plant with pale yellow flowers; 'Lady Greer', a herbaceous perennial that grows to 5 inches (12 cm) with clusters of primrose-yellow flowers;

and 'Wanda', the most widely grown of the Juliana Hybrids, bright purple with a yellow centre.

P. x *polyantha* (**polyanthus**). This primrose needs no introduction, as every garden centre and supermarket has tantalizing displays of them as early as January. They are naturally occurring hybrids and were first recorded in botanical chronicles in 1663. Since then they have gone through several transformations, and the modern hybrids have surpassed any previous polyanthus in floral size, colour range, form and stem strength. They are ideal for window boxes, pots or baskets by the front door, and are tolerant of all sorts of soil and locations.

P. rosea. A native of the Himalayas, this perennial grows to 8 inches (20 cm) and produces vivid, rosy-pink flowers on a short stalk in early spring. Plant in moist, acidic soil in a semishady area or in full sun.

P. sieboldii (**Sakurasoh**). These hardy perennials grow to a height of 6 to 9 inches (15 to 23 cm). They are a tufted hairy species with pale green, bluntly toothed leaves. The flowers are large and showy in shades of pink, purple and white. The petals are usually notched or frilled. The plants go dormant in summer. Good cultivars include 'Dancing Ladies', pale lilac and pink with white centres; 'Geisha Girl', pink with fringed petals; and 'Winter Dream', pure white.

P. veris (**cowslip**). The stout stems of 4 to 8 inches (10 to 20 cm) carry dense clusters of sweetly scented, nodding, bright yellow flowers in early spring. It is semi-evergreen and grows best in moist, well-drained, fertile soil in semishade or full sun.

P. vialii. This is the most unusual primula. The lavender-blue flowers are produced on dense conical spikes. A short-lived herbaceous perennial, it will grow in full sun with moist soil or in semishady conditions.

P. vulgaris (**English primrose**). This much-loved native of the British Isles has dainty, sweetly scented, pale yellow flowers with deeper yellow centres. It can flower as early as February and is a lovely reminder that spring is around the corner. Although yellow is the colour we most associate with primroses, they come in shades of red, purple, pink and white, in single or double forms. From the species, many hybrids have been bred, including 'Francesca', 6 inches (15 cm) high, found originally in the Surrey, B.C., garden of Francesca Dart. It blooms over a long period of time and produces lime-green flowers with a yellow eye. 'Mahogany Sunrise' is also a local primrose bred by Dr. John Kerridge. It grows to a height of 4 inches (10 cm) with deep mahogany-red flowers edged in gold with a gold centre. 'Sue Jervis' has shell-pink double flowers; *P. vulgaris* ssp. *sibthorpii* has a single mauve-pink flower and buttery eye; and 'Quakers Bonnet' is an early-flowering pale violet with double flowers.

Candelabra types. This group includes primulas where the flowers are arranged in whorls up the stem. These natives of Japan, China and, in particular, the Himalayan region are grown most successfully in a richly humus, moist soil in light shade underneath a canopy of trees or shrubs, in open meadows and in bog-like conditions. They are among the easiest of primulas to grow. In order to keep the species pure, it is important to plant the different types as far from each other as possible, or stick to one species.

P. beesiana. This is a strong-growing species with lilac-purple flowers carried in tiers along 2-foot (60-cm) stems in June and July. It requires rich, moist—even wet—soil, preferably in a waterside location in sun or part shade.

P. bulleyana. A perennial that grows to 2 1/2 feet (75 cm) tall, producing golden yellow flowers from a reddish bud in summer.

P. japonica (**Japanese primrose**). One of the hardiest and easiest to grow of the candelabra primulas. It is a tall variety, growing to 2 feet (60 cm), and thrives in rich, moist soil. Colours range from white and pale pink to crimson and purplish-red. It is a somewhat short-lived plant but seeds itself freely, gradually making large colonies, with the resulting plants flowering in the full range of colours. Three good cultivars are 'Miller's Crimson', 'Postford White' and 'Rosea'.

P. prolifera. The leaves are smooth, large and evergreen in mild climates, unlike other candelabras. The flowers are golden yellow and the stalks can reach 4 feet (120 cm) in height.

P. pulverulenta. The leaves are 1 foot (30 cm) in length, deep green and wrinkled; the flowers are red to purple on 3-foot (90-cm) stems thickly dusted with a white meal. The Bartley Hybrids have flowers in a pink and salmon colour range.

Recipe for primula seed potting mix

To grow plants from seed is rewarding, challenging and exciting. The difference between success and failure is often one small factor. Here is a recipe for a potting mix that will get your primulas off to a good start.

In a container, mix equal parts of peat, pumice and granite grit. Water thoroughly. Cover the mix with a thin layer of wet sphagnum moss, water again, sprinkle the seeds on the damp mix and cover them with perlite.

Water carefully from the bottom and wait for the seedlings to germinate.

Violets

Make room for a clump of violets in your garden. They grow happily in the shade under shrubs and at the base of fences and hedges. They are also a lovely addition to vegetable and herb gardens. Next to a door they look charming planted in shallow containers where they form a nice mound.

Violets, pansies and violas are all part of the large Violaceae family. There are over 400 species and many are native to North America, Europe, South America and Australia. Which do we choose to grow in our gardens? There are many species and hybrids but garden centres and nurseries have a very limited selection, so if you are looking for interesting violets, often it is necessary to grow them from seed.

What a thrill to start a plant from seed and watch it go through its life cycle, especially the violet, with its often unpredictable habits. Here today, gone tomorrow is how we can describe many of the violets we have grown in our gardens. Some disappear because they are naturally short-lived perennials. Others travel with their seeds, dispersing at a great distance from their parent plant; these little plants turn up unexpectedly in the most unusual places in the garden, including cracks in the sidewalks, where they are always a welcome sight. Violets produced from seed in the garden are rarely true to form. Selected seeds bought through plant catalogues are the most reliable.

Our experience suggests that growing violets from seed is an exercise in patience. Germination of seed can take weeks to months. One thing to remember is that most violet seeds (those native to the northern hemisphere) need a cooling period before they will germinate. Mix seeds with a damp light compost or peat alternative in a see-through plastic bag. Allow air into the bag, seal with a twist tie and leave at room temperature for two days to allow the seeds to absorb the moisture. Then transfer the bag to the coolest part of the fridge (not freezer) and leave for 4 to 6 weeks, checking periodically to make sure germination has not begun. When germination has started, remove the bag from the fridge and sow the seed mixture in a light compost in seed trays or small pots; do not cover the seeds and do not allow the soil to dry out. Place them in a north-facing window where there is lots of indirect light.

When the plants are 1 inch (2.5 cm) tall, prick them out, making sure you do not injure the root, which is often long and straight. Transfer the seedlings into small pots or trays in a multi-purpose compost mix and keep in a semishaded position until they can be planted outdoors. Watch for slugs, red spider mites and aphids.

The following, almost foolproof list of violets is one that will ensure you have a member of this family blooming for many months of the year, including winter.

Viola canadensis (Canada violet). Native from Alaska to Oregon, including much of the coastal mountain area of B.C. and the Rocky mountain area, it forms neat clumps 2 feet (60 cm) wide and grows to a height of 1 foot (30 cm). The blossoms are near white, flushed violet and with a yellow throat. This violet blooms from May through July and needs a light, moist, cool position to grow well. The plant can be divided in autumn.

V. cornuta (horned violet). Native to the Pyrenees, this is a vigorous, clump-forming, evergreen perennial groundcover. The flowers range from a rich deep violet to a lilac-blue colour and bloom in early summer. The plants grow to a height of 9 inches (23 cm.) If the clumps are cut down after flowering they may produce blooms again late in the season, often up to December. It grows best in moist but well-drained soil in sun and partial shade. This viola is an important parent to many good perennial violas. 'Lilacina' and 'Boughton Blue' are two lovely blue-flowering varieties. They look especially good when planted near *Alchemilla mollis*. 'Alba' is pure white and 'Chantreyland' produces apricot-coloured blossoms. Divide in autumn.

V. corsica (syn. V. bertolonii). This is often called the largest-flowering of all the viola species. The flowers are a deep violet-blue with a veined centre. It is long-lived where winters are mild. It can easily be propagated from cuttings.

V. glabella (stream violet). This native plant blooms from March to July with canary-yellow flowers neatly veined with a purple centre. This common species is often seen growing near streams and in moist woodland. It grows to a height of 12 inches (30 cm). It should definitely have a place in any native garden and is a valuable asset to every garden.

V. jooi. Native to Transylvania, this little violet grows best in a sunny, well-drained alpine setting or rockery. The flowers are a soft pinky-lilac colour and fragrant. It has a habit of seeding itself all over the garden.

V. *nigra* 'Bowles Black'. One of our favourites. It is grown as an annual but seeds itself in the most unexpected places far from the mother plant. The flowers are numerous and quite small. This is also an excellent plant for containers.

V. *odorata* (sweet violet). This is one of the earliest flowers to bloom in our area, often appearing in February. The purple flowers are sweetly scented. There are many named cultivars with *V. odorata* as a parent; the following are available through local plant catalogues. 'Princess of Wales' has been in cultivation since 1899 and has highly fragrant, soft blue-lavender flowers with a white centre. 'Royal Robe' is sweetly scented, associated with the making of perfume and soaps and is referred to in romantic English literature. 'Sulphurea' is an apricot-yellow form with a very faint fragrance, unfortunately common with yellow sweet violets. 'Alba' has pure white flowers and is often mistaken for a clump of snow in a shady area of the garden. 'Queen Charlotte' has dark blue flowers on long stems and makes a good cutting flower.

V. *sororaria* 'Freckles'. An eastern North American plant, this variety has pale blue flowers specked with purple and blooms in spring. It is short-lived but is fun to see growing in moist shade.

V. *tricolor* (johnny-jump-up). This is one of the most charming wildflowers. It flowers from spring into late summer with three colour combinations, yellow, blue and violet. Growing well in sun and shade, its casual look makes it a wonderful addition to the vegetable and herb garden.

Keep an eye out for the following cultivars. They are best propagated from cuttings taken in late summer. Young cuttings should be taken from the centre of the plant. Dig a little trench next to the parent plant, line it with sand and plant the new cuttings.

'Ardross Gem'. Produces a succession of purple and yellow flowers on 6-inch (15-cm) tall stems.

'Irish Molly'. A reliable perennial with an unusual and wonderful colour combination of bronze, green and brown.

'Jackanapes'. Named after Gertrude Jekyll's monkey. The upper two petals of the flower are a lovely reddish brown and the lower three petals are a cheerful yellow.

'Maggie Mott'. Silver-mauve with a pale centre.

'Molly Sanderson'. Grey-black with a yellow centre.

Recommended Reading

Organic and common-sense gardening

A Gardener's Guide to Pest Prevention and Control in the Home Garden. Ministry of Agriculture and Food, Province of British Columbia, 1999.

Ball, Jeff. *Rodale's Garden Problem Solver: Vegetables, Fruits, and Herbs.* Rodale Press, Emmaus, Penn., 1988.

Buczacki, Stefan and Keith Harris. *Pests: Diseases and Disorders of Garden Plants.* Harper Collins, London, 2nd ed. 1998.

Damrosch, Barbara. *The Garden Primer.* Workman Publishing, New York, 1988.

Gershuny, Grace. *Start with the Soil.* Rodale Press, Emmaus, Penn., 1993.

Gilkenson, Linda, Pam Pierce and Miranda Smith. *Rodale's Pest & Disease Problem Solver: A Chemical-Free Guide to Keeping Your Garden Healthy.* Rodale Press, Emmaus, Penn., 1996.

Hessayon, D.G. *The Biofriendly Gardening Guide.* pbi Publications, London, 1990.

The Organic Gardener's Handbook of Natural Insect and Disease Control: A complete problem-solving guide to keeping your garden and yard healthy without chemicals. Ed. by Barbara Ellis and Fern M. Bradley. Rodale Press, Emmaus, Penn., 1996.

Pest or Guest: A Guide to Alternative Pest Control in the Home. Society Promoting Environmental Conservation (SPEC), Vancouver, 1985.

Rodale's Organic Gardening. Rodale Press, Emmaus, Penn., 1989.

Rubin, Carole. *How to Get Your Lawn and Garden off Drugs.* Whitecap Books, Vancouver, 1990.

Clematis

Evison, Raymond J. *Making the Most of Clematis.* Eloraprint, Wisebach, England, 1987.

Fisk, Jim. *Clematis: A Wisley Handbook.* Royal Horticultural Series, London, 1986.

Fisk, Jim. *Clematis: The Queen of the Climbers.* Cassell Publishers, London, 1989.

Lloyd, Christopher. *Clematis.* Collins, London, 1977.

Climbers

Perkins, Harold O. *Espaliers and Vines for the Home Gardener.* Iowa State University Press, Iowa, 1979.

Phillips, Roger and Martyn Rix. *Climbers for Walls and Arbours.* Pan Publishers, London, 1998.

Phillips, Roger and Martyn Rix. *Perfect Plants.* Random House, 1996.

RHS Good Plant Guide: 2000 award-winning plants. Dorling Kindersley Books, 1998.

Tebbler, Stephen. *Climbers, Plants and Wall Shrubs.* The Crowood Press, Swindon, England, 1990.

Also see Further Reading.

Primroses

Shaw, Barbara. *The Book of Primroses.* David and Charles, London, 1990.

April

O ne of the loveliest sights of the whole year has to be ornamental cherry trees in full bloom. In Vancouver and Victoria the streets are lined with clouds of pink as the wind picks up the dark and light blossoms and tumbles them into a carpet under our feet. Started by far-sighted city Parks Board people as far back as the 1930s, the tradition of planting flowering trees on our city streets has given us some of the most beautiful, welcoming cityscapes anywhere.

The cherries mark the full flowering of spring. Under their spreading branches, late spring daffodils and tulips open to rain and sun, and spring-flowering shrubs, such as the star magnolia (*Magnolia stellata*), viburnums and daphnes, bring freshness and colour at every turn. To help you choose spring-flowering shrubs for your garden, we feature them this month. We also show you how and when to propagate from cuttings.

Rhododendrons and azaleas begin their main flowering season now, reaching their peak in May. They are such a feature of west coast gardens that we discuss them at some length in this chapter. Watch also for early-flowering clematis, especially evergreen *Clematis armandii* (see the March chapter), whose lovely scented white flowers trail over back fences, arches and doorways.

Before you get busy in the garden, spare some time to visit local bulb shows, especially at Bradner in the Fraser Valley, and in the Skagit Valley in Washington State. This is the time to order unusual daffodils and tulips direct from the growers, for delivery next fall. If you're thinking of buying a spring-flowering tree, visit local parks and gardens to identify your favourites. Many crabapple trees, for example, are excellent small flowering trees for a city-size lot.

Perennials are pushing up vigorous green growth, and many of the woodland plants, such as barrenwort (*Epimedium*), navelwort (*Omphalodes*), Solomon's seal (*Polygonatum*), and lungwort (*Pulmonaria*) are in bloom. Look for delicate pasqueflowers (*Anemone pulsatilla*), whose pale mauve, white or rosy pink heads surrounded by a silvery, silklike softness are in startling contrast to the strong colours and forms of spring bulbs. Pasque-flower's fluffy seed heads are excellent for flower arranging.

Now that spring is truly here, there is a lot to be done in the garden: beds to be dug, trees and shrubs to be planted, seeds to be sown and lawns to be cut. Weeds grow overnight and, before you know it, dandelion seeds are blowing gaily across the lawn. Listen to the cheerful birds as they make their nests, and revel in the joy of spring.

Garden Highlights

*indicates fragrance

Bulbs

Anemone blanda (windflower), *Erythronium* spp. (dog-tooth violet or fawn lily), *Fritillaria imperialis* (crown imperial lily), *Ipheion* *uniflorum* (star flower), *Muscari* spp. (grape hyacinth), *Narcissus* spp. (daffodil),* *Puschkinia scilloides*,* *Scilla* spp. (squill), *Trillium* spp., *Tulipa* spp. (tulips).

Perennials

Alyssum montanum (perennial alyssum) and *Aurinia saxatilis* (formerly *Alyssum saxatilis*); *Anemone pulsatilla* (pasqueflower); *Aubrietia deltoidea* (aubretia); *Bellis perennis* (English daisy); *Bergenia* spp.; *Dicentra* spp. (bleeding heart); *Epimedium* (barrenwort); *Helleborus orientalis* (Lenten rose); *Myosotis* spp. (forget-me-not); *Omphaloides* (navelwort); *Polygonatum* x *hybridum* (Solomon's seal); *Pulmonaria* (lungwort); *Sanguinaria canadensis* (bloodroot).

Climbers

Clematis alpina, Clematis armandii (evergreen clematis).*

Shrubs

Berberis darwinii (Darwin's barberry), *Camellia japonica, Chaemomeles* spp. (Japanese flowering quince), *Cytisus praecox* (broom),* *Daphne cneorum* (garland daphne),* *Exochorda* spp. (pearlbush), *Kerria japonica, Magnolia stellata* (star magnolia), *Osmanthus* x *burkwoodii*,* *O. delavayi*, *Rhododendron* spp. and hybrids (rhododendrons and azaleas), *Spiraea* x *arguta* (bridal wreath), *S. prunifolia* (bridal wreath), *Viburnum* spp.

Trees

Magnolia denudata,* *M. soulangeana, Malus* spp. (flowering crabapple), *Prunus* spp. (flowering cherry).

April Checklist

Annuals, perennials and bulbs

- Deadhead daffodils but leave seed pods on squills and grape hyacinths to seed themselves. Don't remove foliage until it has started to yellow. Feed with fish fertilizer.
- Divide up primroses and polyanthus after flowering.
- Edge flower beds, weed well and check carefully for invading pests and diseases.
- Stake perennials that need it, and mulch perennials if not already done.
- Continue to sow seeds of hardy annuals in ground.

Trees, shrubs and climbers

- Rose pruning should be completed by the beginning of the month (see the June chapter). Mulch with aged manure or well-rotted compost. Check for aphids and rub off, or use an insecticidal soap.
- Shear winter-flowering heathers after flowering.
- Continue planting trees and shrubs.
- Prune early-blooming shrubs such as *Spiraea thunbergii* and *Forsythia* spp. after flowering.
- Evergreen and conifer hedges can be clipped now.
- Check vines growing on the house to make sure they are not invading window frames or working their way under gutters and shingles.

Fruits, vegetables and herbs

- April 1 to 15, plant early potatoes, green onion, bulb onion, kohlrabi, cabbage and leeks.
- April 16 to 30, sow beets, carrots, Swiss chard, broccoli, cauliflower, parsnip, kale and lettuce. Set out earlier-sown vegetables from the cold frame (see the July chapter for cold frame information).
- Sow zucchini, cucumbers and tomatoes indoors in a sunny window or a cold frame (see the July chapter for information on cold frames).
- Keep the vegetable garden well weeded, and keep a lookout for signs of pests and diseases.
- Plant out new strawberry plants.

Other garden activities

- Continue preparing new lawns and repairing worn patches on existing ones. The first three lawn mowings should be done with the blades set higher than usual.
- Aerate lawn if not already done.
- Start planting water plants in pool.
- Turn compost and keep it moist.

Rhododendrons and Azaleas

People come from all over the world to see the rhododendrons and azaleas in the Pacific Northwest. At their finest in late spring, a bewildering variety of these plants, many bred locally, can be seen in gardens and nurseries in British Columbia. Outstanding collections are on public view in Butchart Gardens and Beacon Hill Park on Vancouver Island, and VanDusen Gardens, Stanley Park, and University of British Columbia David Lam Asian Gardens in Vancouver.

Pioneer growers started a strong tradition

Some of the plants in these gardens are over a hundred years old. For example, rhododendrons planted in 1889 at Fountain Lake in Beacon Hill Park still flourish today. They were installed under the direction of Canada's first rhododendron specialist grower, George Fraser, who set up his nursery in remote Ucluelet on the west coast of Vancouver Island. Other early growers also settled on the island, ensuring a strong tradition of rhododendron culture on B.C.'s west coast.

Of special interest to Vancouver park lovers are two other pioneer growers, Ted and Mary Greig, who gave nearly 1,000 plants in the early 1950s to the University of British Columbia to start UBC's rhododendron collection. In 1965, the Greigs sold the balance of their rhododendron stock for a fraction of its value to the Vancouver Park Board, and these plants can now be seen at VanDusen Gardens (the species plants), Stanley Park (hybrids, especially the summer-flowering ones), and Queen Elizabeth Park.

Native species flourish here

There are three species of rhododendron native to British Columbia: *Rhododendron albiflorum*, *R. lapponicum* and *R. macrophyllum*. *R. albiflorum* is deciduous, and can only be found at elevations above 2,500 feet (762 m) near the coast and above 4,000 feet (1219 m) in the interior. *R. lapponicum* is also an alpine, growing to a maximum height of 12 inches (30 cm). It has bright purple flowers. *R. macrophyllum*, the pink or California rhododendron, has pink or deep rose flowers and can easily be seen blooming in spring adjacent to the Hope-Princeton highway about 21 miles (34 kilometres) from Hope, and just south of Parksville on Vancouver Island, 9 miles (14 kilometres) in from the highway on Macmillan Bloedel property, near Northwest Bay Depot.

Our acid soil, mild climate and high annual rainfall provide an ideal environment for growing a wide variety of these lovely flowering shrubs.

What is a rhododendron?

Rhododendrons are part of the heath family or *Ericaceae*. Other members of the family include the heaths, heathers, blueberries, mountain laurel and lily-of-the-valley shrub, and all like the same growing conditions as rhododendrons.

Many people imagine a rhododendron to be a medium-sized bush with shiny, evergreen, dark green leaves and huge, purple, pink or red flowers in April or May. In fact, the genus *Rhododendron* is extremely large, with more than 800 species and many thousands of hybrids, ranging in height from dwarf, creeping alpines only a few inches (10–12 cm) high to huge trees growing up to 40 feet (12 m). The leaves vary from 1/4 inch (.6 cm) to almost 2 feet (60 cm) in length, and the flowers can be many different shades of purple, blue, red, pink, orange, yellow or white.

Some rhododendrons are deciduous, losing their leaves in winter, but the majority are evergreen. Evergreen rhododendrons are prized as much for their leaves as for their flowers, and several species have a distinctive, soft, feltlike covering on their leaves, generally on the underside, known as indumentum. The leaves provide restful greenery in the garden year-round, even though the blooms are short-lived. Azaleas are also members of the genus *Rhododendron*, and can be either evergreen or deciduous.

Rhododendron species and hybrids for the small garden

Since most city gardens are small, with no room for many of the larger rhododendrons, rhododendron breeders continue to develop compact hybrids from the smaller rhododendron species. Two of the most popular of the small species plants are *R. williamsianum* and *R. yakushimanum*.

R. williamsianum is a charming dwarf species. It is easily recognized by its foliage, with small, oval, smooth leaves, bronze when they first unfurl. It has bell-shaped pink flowers on loose trusses, and is best grown in an open site, protected from frost, since new growth is early. Good hybrids include 'Bow Bells', clear pink; 'Linda', rose pink; 'Maureen', orchid pink; and 'Willbrit', deep pink with lighter edges.

The semidwarf species *R. yakushimanum* is also extremely attractive and, with its hybrids, is currently in great demand. Introduced from Japan in 1934, it is hardy, cold and heat tolerant, and compact. It has striking foliage, with leaves that start as silver spears covered with brown felt, becoming rounded and dark green above, with thick, fuzzy, brown indumentum below. The flowers are dark pink fading to white as they open fully, and the plants bloom profusely. *R. yakushimanum* is parent to hundreds of desirable hybrids, including 'Coral Velvet', coral pink opening to pale salmon; 'Ken Janeck', deepest pink opening to white, with a larger leaf and plant size than most of this group of hybrids; 'Koichiro Wada', deep pink opening to white; and 'Yaku Princess', apple-blossom pink.

Deciduous azaleas

There are many beautiful deciduous azalea species, some delightfully fragrant and many with excellent fall colour, such as *R. luteum*, with yellow flowers, and *R. occidentale*, white flushed with yellow and/or pink. Hybrids of *R. occidentale*, like the species plant, are all useful for their late flowering.

There are four main deciduous azalea hybrid groups: Ghent, Mollis, Knaphill/Exbury and Occidentale. Many are strongly scented, and they add welcome colour in late

May and early June. The many hybrids include 'Coccinia Speciosa', brilliant orange scarlet; 'Daviesii', creamy white with orange-yellow blotches; 'Gibraltar', rich red; 'Irene Koster', pale pink with yellow throat; and 'Silver Slipper', white flushed pink with a yellow blotch.

Perhaps the most outstanding of all the azaleas is *R. schlippenbachii*, the 'Royal Azalea', with translucent, pale pink flowers in April, followed by large leaves with rounded ends, turning warm red in the fall. New growth is early, so the plant does need to be protected from the wind.

Evergreen azaleas

The evergreen azaleas are a large, miscellaneous group of small evergreen and semi-evergreen shrubs that are often referred to as Japanese azaleas, and they incude the familiar indoor pot plants. There are many wonderful hybrids to choose from, producing a profusion of colourful flowers in late spring.

If you buy an evergreen azalea hybrid, it is a good idea to make your selection when the plant is in bloom, since some of the colours can be quite dramatic. For example, 'Hino Crimson', with brilliant crimson-red flowers, and 'Purple Splendour', with bright purple blooms, need careful placing if they are not to overwhelm the other plants around them. They would have quite a colour battle with some of the deciduous azalea hybrids in the orange, flame and yellow colour range.

Basic care for rhododendrons

Rhododendrons and azaleas need acid soil to grow well, with a pH range of about 4.5 to 6.0. The roots need well-drained, well-watered soil and should be kept cool and moist year-round. In our climate this means they will need to be watered frequently, especially in the first year after planting, and during dry spells in the summer and early fall.

Ideally, rhododendrons and azaleas should be planted from October to March. However, since they have a compact, shallow root system they are easy to move at any time, except when the ground is frozen, provided they are given adequate moisture.

How to plant

If the rootball is dry, it should be soaked thoroughly before planting. Do not plant too deeply, since this may cause the roots to rot. Instead, make sure that the top of the rootball is at the surface or slightly above the ground. Cover the roots of the plant with a light layer of organic mulch, such as ground bark or well-rotted compost, to help the roots stay cool and moist.

What to feed

The best feed for rhododendrons is a mixture of well-rotted compost and leaf mould, applied as a mulch around the extremity of the plant's rooting system in winter or early spring. This will help to ensure good blooming for the season. Do not apply mulch directly over the rootball, since this will eventually bury the plant too deeply and it may not flower.

Chemical fertilizers can be used, but organic ones, such as canola meal, are preferable. Fertilizer should be applied once before flowering and again after flowering, but no later than July.

Once the plants have finished blooming, remove the spent blossoms as soon as you can. Deadheading enables the energy of the plant to go into fresh growth for next year's blooms. Be careful not to disturb the growing buds immediately beneath.

Where to plant

Sunlight and temperature requirements vary considerably among different rhododendrons and azaleas. Some require almost full sun, while others need full or partial shade. As a general rule, the larger the leaf size, the more shade the plant needs. Some will tolerate temperatures as low as -25°F (-32°C), while others do not tolerate any frost at all.

It is very important, therefore, to select the correct plant for the environmental conditions in your garden. If the conditions do not suit a given type—if it is too wet, too dry, too cold, and/or too sunny—the plant will become stressed. Stressed plants are much more susceptible to damage from insects and diseases.

Rhododendrons and azaleas look best in a city garden if they are planted in semiwoodland conditions. This may mean layering them under medium-sized trees that provide dappled sun and offer wind protection, and underplanting with smaller shrubs, bulbs, and other plants (see the February chapter, "Creating a Native Garden"). These other plants should have the same acid soil requirements as rhododendrons.

Knowing what to buy is important

Which rhododendrons and azaleas to buy? The choice today is enormous, so resist the temptation to pick up the first you see. As well as the points just mentioned, be guided by your garden space and design requirements and also by personal preferences in shape and colour. For example, if your garden can accommodate a 3- to 4-foot (.9- to 1.2-m) plant, and you have a pink, blue and white colour scheme, you might be attracted to a small white rhododendron. However, it might be a plant that grows to 20 feet (6 m) within ten years, one that will dwarf everything around it. It's much better to look for a white-flowering hybrid of *R. yakushimanum*.

When buying rhododendrons or any other shrub for your garden, it's important to make sure it will be hardy in our climate. In exceptionally cold winters it is worth protecting any that might be vulnerable to extreme cold. Buy your plants from reputable sources if you are interested in purchasing authentically named varieties; so many different hybrids are produced today that sometimes they are wrongly labelled.

Colour selection is extremely important; mixed groupings of colours that clash can be really hard on the eye in a small space. Rhododendrons generally look best where their colours can be shown individually, to full advantage, or where they can blend and harmonize with each other. Thus it is important to plan a colour sequence for the plants, so that different areas of the garden provide colour and focus at different times, rather than shrubs competing or clashing with each other. Odd-numbered groupings of identical plants (3, 5, 7 or 9) can be used for a strong visual effect, unifying and harmonizing the garden.

Be sure to choose some of the fragrant azalea hybrids such as the Ghent and Occidentale groups, mentioned above. Their heady perfume is a bonus in any garden.

Rhododendron problems

If your rhododendron is having problems there are several possible causes to investigate. The first thing is to assess the plant's habitat, noting such things as exposure to sun, soil moisture over long periods, pesticide usage, fertilizers applied, or any other environmental conditions you may observe. Contact your nearest plant help line and describe the problems, including a summary of environmental conditions. If the problem cannot be diagnosed over the phone, take a sample to your nearest garden centre or Master Gardener clinic, and they will likely be able to help you.

By far the most common insect problem for rhododendrons and azaleas is the root weevil. These small, hard-backed little pests leave telltale irregular notches on leaf edges, resulting in very unsightly plants. The weevils live around the base of the plant during the day in debris and old rhododendron leaves, and eat the plant at night. They move slowly so can be caught easily at night (with the aid of a flashlight) and destroyed.

The commercial product Tanglefoot can also be used. Wrap sticky masking tape around the trunk of the plant, and cover the tape with Tanglefoot. Make sure that none of the branches of the plant are close to the ground, so that the weevils can only climb up via the trunk and will be caught in the sticky Tanglefoot.

The tape should be firmly wrapped, but not too tightly, or it may cut off circulation from the roots to the rest of the plant. Removal of all debris from the base of the plant also helps to discourage the weevils. Many rhododendron and azalea hybrids or species are bred for their resistance to weevils. Selecting resistant varieties minimizes maintenance and damage.

Another problem is root rot, or stem dieback. Symptoms include wilting of one limb, or of the whole plant. It can happen almost overnight, especially in hot weather, and is caused by a number of fungi belonging to the genus *Phytophthora*. These organisms are most active in poorly drained soil, so prevention is one of the most important ways of controlling the disease. To minimize the risk, always plant rhododendrons and azaleas in well-drained soil, and keep the roots cool and moist with a light mulch.

Rhododendron and azalea chart

	Ht.	Red	Ht.	Pink	Ht.	White	Ht.	Blue	Ht.	Yellow
January, February and early March			L	*R. dauricum*						
			M	*R. mucronulatum*						
			M	'Olive'						
			L	'Christmas Cheer'						
Late March and early April	M	*R. barbatum*	SD	'Cilpinense'	T	'Beauty of Littleworth'	L	'Praecox'	L	'Bo-peep'
	M	'Etta Burrows'	SD	'Pink Snowflakes'			T	'P.J.M.'	M	'Ann Carey'
			L	'Rosamundi'	SD	'Snow Lady'				
			SD	*R. williamsianum*						
			L	'Seta'						
			D	'Rose Elf'						
Late April	M	'Anthony Waterer'	M	'G.W. Leak'	L	'Unique'	D	'Ramapo'	D	'Shamrock'
	T	'Taurus'	D	'Pink Drift'	SD	'Dora Amateis'	SD	'Blue Bird'	D	'Chikor'
	SD	'Creeping Jenny'	D	'Wigeon'	SD	'Olympic Lady'	SD	'Blue Tit'	L	'Moonstone'
	L	'Grace Seabrook'	SD	'Molly Ann'	M	'Sir Charles Lemon'	T	*R. augustinii*	SD	'Cream Crest'
	D	'Carmen'	SD	'Lori Eichelser'	SD/L	*R. yakushimanum*	D	*R. impeditum*	D	'Curlew'
	SD	'Elizabeth Hobbie'	L	'Bow Bells'					M	*R. lutescens*
	SD	'Cary Ann'	M	'Pink Cameo'					SD	'Princess Anne'
	L	'Elizabeth'	M	*R. schlippenbachii*						
			M	*R. vaseyi*						
			SD	'Ginny Gee'						
			L	'Winsome'						
Early May	M	'Mother's Day'	M	Temple Belle'	T	'Alice'			L	'Second Honeymoon'
	SD	'Baden Baden'	M	'Cotton Candy'	M	'Loder's White'			L	'Medusa'
	M	'Jean Marie de Montague'	M	'Hurricane'	M	'Boule de Neige'			T	'Hotei'
			T	'Loderi Venus'	M	'Helene Schniffner'			L	'Jalisco Goshawk'
	L	'Thor'	M	'Trude Webster'					L	'Mrs. Betty Robertson'
	T	'Red Walloper'	T	'Walloper'	T	'Loder King George'			M	'Virginia Richards'
			M	'Lem's Cameo'					M	*R. luteum*
			M	'Buchanan Simpson'	T	'Sappho'			T	'Crest'
			T	'Anna'					SD	'Fabia'
			T	'Marinus Koster'						
Late May	M	'Mayday'	T	'Pink Pearl'	M	'Cunningham's White'	M	'Purple Splendor'	L	'Whitney's Orange'
	T	'G.A. Sims'	M	'Dawn's Delight'			M	'Blue Pacific'		
	M	'Vulcan'	M	'Countess of Derby'	M	'Lodestar'	M	'Dorothy Amateis'	M	*R. luteum*
	T	'Princess Elizabeth'	T	'Anna Rose Whitney'						
June and July			M	*R. auriculatum*	M	'Mrs. T. H. Lowinsky'				
			T	*R. fortunei* ssp. *discolor*	T	'Polar Bear'				

Height at 10 years:

D	= dwarf	(less than 1 1/2 feet/45 cm)
SD	= semidwarf	(less than 3 feet/90 cm)
L	= low	(less than 4 1/2 feet/1.4 m)
M	= medium	(less than 6 feet/1.8 m)
T	= tall	(over 6 feet/1.8 m)

Colour:
red — includes crimson and orange-red
pink — includes deep rose and salmon
blue — includes lavender
yellow — includes orange and apricot

Spring-flowering Shrubs

There are many other interesting spring-flowering shrubs besides rhododendrons. Listed below are favourites that would be a handsome addition to any garden.

***Berberis darwinii* (Darwin's barberry).** Spectacular clusters of deep red-orange buds opening to deep yellow flowers in April make this shrub desirable. Darwin's barberry is evergreen, growing to 9 feet (2.7 m), with glossy, deep green, prickly leaves, and blue-mauve berries in summer. It is good for hedging, may be pruned to shape and thrives in full sun or light shade. 'Nana' is a small compact shrub with rich yellow flowers. 'Prostrata' is a low-growing shrub with orange buds opening to a golden yellow.

***Camellia japonica* (camellia).** Camellias are amongst the most popular and valuable of evergreen shrubs, and flourish here in our acid soil. They may be planted in semi-shade or full sun, but a hot, dry situation is unsuitable. Most camellias want partial shade, cool roots and a sheltered position. They are valued for their exquisite blossoms and glossy evergreen foliage. The flowers are single, semidouble or double, in pink, red or white. They flower in late winter or spring. There are hundreds of varieties to choose from; the following are some suggestions. 'Adolphe Audusson' is a semidouble red-flowered shrub to 20 feet (6 m). 'Bob Hope' has very dark red, large, semidouble flowers on a compact shrub reaching 10 feet (3 m). 'Debutante' has light pink, double flowers on a 20-foot (6-m) shrub. 'Lady Clare' has deep clear peach-pink, semidouble flowers; grows to 7 feet (2.1 m) tall with a lax and pendulous growth habit. 'Otome' has pale pink petals surrounding yellow stamens on a shrub reaching 15 feet (4.5 m). 'Rubescens Major' has double crimson flowers with darker veins and grows to 12 feet (3.6 m). For more camellias, see, "Trees and shrubs for winter and early spring interest" in the November chapter.

***Ceanothus* spp. (California lilac).** Native to California, this group comprises evergreen and deciduous shrubs. The evergreens particularly are not known for their hardiness and do require the protection of sunny walls. However, in spite of this, they are worth a try and are a glorious addition to the garden for their attractive foliage and stunning blue flowers. *C. impressus* is an evergreen species with a height and spread of 10 feet (3 m) or more. The small, dark green leaves are glossy and cover rigid stems that bear small, deep blue flowers in May. 'Puget Blue' is probably the finest form. 'Concha' is a dense shrub growing to 7 feet (2.1 m) high and wide. It has small, dark green leaves and clusters of deep blue flowers. 'Ray Hartman' is a shrub or shrubby tree, from 12 to 20 feet (3.6 to 6 m) high. It has large, dark green leaves and medium blue 3- to 5-inch (7.5- to 10-cm) clusters of flowers *C. arboreus* 'Trewithen Blue', a large evergreen shrub, grows to 24 feet (7 m) with a short trunk. The flowers are a deep blue and lightly scented. This shrub can be trained in a fan style against a sunny wall.

Tip of the Month: Bananas for Roses

Place banana skins just below the soil surface around rose bushes. The skins are a rich source of magnesium, sulphur, calcium, phosphates, silica and sodium. These trace elements added to the soil will help ensure a magnificent display of blossoms.

'Delight' is a hardy hybrid that grows to 24 feet (7 m) with rich blue flowers in long panicles.

***Chaenomeles* spp. (flowering quince).** A deciduous shrub, suitable for espaliering, especially against a sunny south wall. It should be pruned hard after blooming, since it flowers on old wood. In fall some of them bear edible fruit suitable for preserves. There are many beautiful named cultivars, in shades of pink, red and white.

***Choisya ternata* (Mexican orange).** An evergreen that will grow in well-drained soil in sun or partial shade to a height of 6 feet (1.8 m) or more. It is related to the citrus family and its glossy green leaves shine throughout the year. Its white, sweetly scented blossoms appear in late spring, growing from the leaf axils at the end of the shoots. No regular pruning is necessary, but cut out frosted shoots at the base in spring. Trim to shape after flowering.

***Corylopsis pauciflora* (buttercup winter hazel).** Closely related to the witch hazels (*Hamamelis*), this medium-sized deciduous shrub can grow to 6 feet (1.8 m). Its flowers are primrose yellow, bell-shaped and fragrant. Much loved by flower arrangers and easily grown in woodland soil, but it should be protected from cold winds. It grows best in semishade, and prefers soils low in lime.

***Daphne* spp.** *D. cneorum* (garland flower) is a low, evergreen shrub, 1 foot (30 cm) in height, with a spread of 2 to 3 feet (60 to 90 cm). The stems have dusky green, narrowly oblong leaves and carry terminal clusters of fragrant, rose-pink flowers. Suitable for the rock garden or pathway and a lovely addition to any garden. *D. x burkwoodii* 'Somerset' is semi-evergreen with a height and spread of 3 to 4 feet (.9

to 1.2 m). Its attraction is its fragrant soft pink flowers in May, but it needs some careful companion planting to enhance it for the rest of the year. A little easier than other species of daphne, and a very nice addition to the border.

***Exochorda* x *macrantha* 'The Bride' (pearlbush).** This lovely garden hybrid is a deciduous hardy shrub grown for its usually freely borne clusters of dainty, pristine flowers. It can be used in mixed or shrub borders, or as a specimen. It associates well with rhododendrons and azaleas and does well in sun or light shade in any good garden soil. After flowers fade, prune out old, weak wood to reduce crowding and maintain vigorous growth. It grows to a height of 10 feet (3 m).

***Forsythia* x *intermedia* (forsythia).** Deciduous, easily grown and perhaps the most popular and best known of all the spring-flowering shrubs, forsythia is a quick-growing shrub up to 9 feet (2.7 m). It thrives in ordinary garden soils and grows well in city gardens, sun or partial shade. The flowers are deep yellow, clustering along the branches during March, and are borne on wood from the previous year's growth. Prune after flowering, removing old and damaged wood, and shorten young shoots by one-third to keep shrubs tidy. When in bloom, forsythia looks good underplanted with blue grape hyacinths, although it is unfortunately somewhat insignificant after flowering. Good forms are 'Beatrix Farrand', 'Lynwood Gold', and 'Spectabilis'.

***Fothergilla* spp.** These hardy, deciduous shrubs are noted for their brilliant fall colours. The flowers have no petals but consist of numerous, long, creamy white stamens in bottlebrush spires. Two good species are *F. major* and *F. monticola*, both of them growing to 6 to 8 feet (1.8 to 2.4 m), with a similar spread.

Kerria japonica. During late spring this deciduous shrub bears shaggy yellow flowers on elegant, arching stems. The leaves are small, bright green and heavily veined. If you like yellow, it is a good selection for foundation planting and borders. It grows in sun or shade and tolerates poor soil. Prune out older wood occasionally to maintain vigour. The species has five-petalled flowers that resemble those of potentilla, and it grows to a height and spread of 4 to 6 feet (1.2 to 1.8 m). Its slender green stems are hidden by blooms throughout late spring. Good in shade, with attractive green bark in winter. 'Pleniflora' bears abundant, rounded, double flowers in brilliant yellow, which cause branches to bend gracefully beneath their weight. It may reach 10 feet (3 m). 'Variegata' has white-edged foliage and single yellow flowers. It is much smaller, only growing to 2 1/2 feet (75 cm).

Magnolia stellata (star magnolia). Lovely deciduous shrub or small spreading tree. It takes years to mature, but flowers when still young. Plant in full sun or partial shade in lime-free, well-drained soil. It is interesting in structure at all times of the year, and the fragrant, double, star-shaped white blossoms emerge from furry grey winter buds before the leaves appear. This is a very useful shrub in a small garden. It makes a fine lawn specimen or focal point, and is lovely underplanted with squill (*Scilla sibirica*) for simultaneous blooming.

Osmanthus spp. Useful shrubs that make dense, bushy shapes of small, dark, shining leaves. The white flowers have a wonderful scent, making it ideal for planting beside a window. It does well in full sun or partial shade in any good garden soil. *O. x delavayi* may grow to 8 feet (2.4 m). It has dark, glossy, ovate leaves, sharply toothed, and clusters of very fragrant, small, white starry flowers in April. It is not always hardy, depending upon location and severity of winter. *O. x burkwoodii* forms a tidy, domed shrub 6 to 10 feet (1.8 to 3 m) high and wide, suitable for hedging, with lustrous, dark green leaves and fragrant, tubular white flowers in April and May. It is hardier than *O. x delavayi*.

Pieris spp. (lily-of-the-valley shrub). A genus of evergreen, compact, flowering shrubs. They are acid-loving, and are best planted in damp, peaty soil in semishade. They are unsuitable for very dry or cold positions, but perfect for a woodland setting. In spring they bear clusters of waxy, lily-of-the-valley–like flowers, hence their common name. There are several lovely species and hybrids. The following would be suitable for a smaller garden. 'Forest Flame' is grown primarily for its brilliant red young foliage, which appears in spring and gradually turns pink then green. The white flowers are in large terminal clusters. *P. japonica* 'Valley Rose' is a low-growing, compact shrub with lovely drooping sprays of waxy pink flowers at the branch tips, and bronzy-red new foliage. 'Variegata' is a slower-growing cultivar with narrower, pale green, white-edged leaves. The flowers, which are borne in March, are white. This is an ideal shrub for a container, and is charming underplanted with miniature spring bulbs.

Rosmarinus officinalis (rosemary). One of the classic Mediterranean herbs, with narrow, highly aromatic, glossy leaves, green above, white-felted below, and light blue flowers in late spring. Although loving full sun and well-drained, gritty soil, it will usually survive the winter if it is covered during very cold weather and located in a protected position. There are cultivars with flowers in other shades of blue and even pink that are less hardy than the species. A wonderful culinary plant, especially with roast lamb.

Spiraea spp. A group of undemanding shrubs that thrive in any well-drained soil in an open, sunny position. *S.* x *arguta* (bridal wreath) is one of the best known. It bursts into bloom in late spring, its arching branches weighed down with tiny white flowers. When the flowers fade, small green leaves follow. Prune flowering shoots hard as the blossoms die, but do not cut away any of the new leafy shoots, for these will bear the blossoms next year. *S. thunbergii* has larger white flowers that appear before the leaves in March and April.

Viburnum spp. A wonderful group of shrubs, with one type or another blooming nearly all year. The two listed here are exceptional ones that bloom in spring. *V. carlesii* 'Aurora' (Korean spice viburnum) is an old favourite and an excellent shrub for a small garden, growing slowly to a compact bush of 4 to 5 feet (1.2 to 1.5 m). It is deciduous and happy in any soil. It has downy, oval leaves, and large, rounded, intensely fragrant clusters of tiny white flowers that open in late spring from porcelainlike buds of deep rosy-pink. It makes an excellent standard, and gives good fall colour too.

V. x *burkwoodii* is taller than its parent *V. carlesii*, reaching a height of 8 feet (2.4 m). It is more open in structure, semi-evergreen, with bright green, glossy leaves that turn scarlet in the fall. It's a good choice for town gardens as it will tolerate a city atmosphere, and is very desirable in any garden. It is a vigorous grower, with white, waxy, sweetly scented flowers opening from pinkish buds. It is happy in acid and alkaline soils.

Weigela spp. One of the most beautiful is *Weigela florida* 'Variegata'. It holds interest for six months of the year, beginning in May when its arching branches bear funnel-shaped, sweetly scented, fresh pink blossoms that attract hummingbirds. Following this it develops striking, variegated foliage of cream and pale green. It is reliable and easy to grow in any soil. A deciduous shrub reaching a height of 6 feet (1.8 m), it is suitable for an open border or light woodland setting.

Propagating Plants from Cuttings

Propagating plants from cuttings is an easy, rewarding and inexpensive thing to do. A cutting is more or less what its name suggests: a small part cut from a mature plant and prepared and treated in such a way that it can grow into a new plant.

There are different types of cuttings and we will guide you through the adventure of taking softwood, semihardwood and hardwood cuttings throughout the year. Some general rules are: take cuttings only from healthy plants, choose healthy shoots to propagate, clean your cutting tools and containers, and be patient.

Use the general guide on the following pages to take cuttings throughout the year. There is a great deal of flexibility, so don't feel restricted by the dates—you can vary it by a month or even two, particularly with softwood and semihardwood cuttings.

Softwood cuttings

These are cuttings taken from the current year's growth, usually during the late spring and early summer months. The shoots you remove should break off easily using your fingers. Trim the cuttings with a clean knife to a length of 3 to 4 inches (8 to 10 cm) just below a node. Remove all the lower leaves.

Insert the cutting up to half of its length into a potting mixture of one-half damp compost or peat and one-half sand. The container should then be labelled and covered with a clear plastic bag. Place the cuttings in their containers in a sheltered shady area and do not let the plants dry out. When a strong root system has developed, you have a new addition for your garden. It is a good idea to keep a journal to record your methods, your successes and your failures.

Semihardwood cuttings

Semihardwood cuttings are taken from the current year's growth later in the summer when the shoots are ripe and woody at the base but still soft at the tip. Select healthy stems, trim off the soft tip and remove the lower leaves. Cut to a length of 4 to 6 inches (10 to 15 cm). At the base of the cutting, wound the side of the bark with the knife and insert the cutting into rooting hormone.

Plant the cutting into a mixture of one-half peat or compost and one-half sand. Remember to keep the soil mixture damp at all times. Label and water regularly. If the cuttings are to be kept outdoors in a cold frame or a cold greenhouse over winter, protect them from frost by covering with a blanket or burlap, and protect them from direct sunlight. This method of keeping them outdoors may slow the development of roots, but by the following autumn many plants should have a strong enough root system to be planted out into the garden.

Some plants are very easily propagated from semihardwood cuttings and the cuttings can be directly planted into the garden. Lavender, some hebe, skimmia, euonymous, senecio and boxwood can go straight into the ground; others need to be a little more pampered. Your experience will be your best guide.

Figure 1

Figure 2

Hardwood cuttings

Hardwood cuttings are taken from the previous year's growth when the wood is dormant in late fall or early winter. Cuttings can include a heel or stem. Often heel cuttings are more successful with difficult plants. Lateral twigs are pulled away from the old wood, leaving a heel-shaped base on the cutting

(Fig. 1). With scissors, trim away the ragged area around the heel (Fig. 2). At this point the hardwood cuttings can be bundled and left in a cold frame until a later date.

When you're ready to plant, prepare the containers with a one-half compost, one-half sand mix, and water it down. Insert the cuttings into a rooting hormone and then into the soil mixture. Place in a cold frame sheltered from the sun. Eventually your hard-wood cuttings should root. If you bring the cuttings indoors, the rooting process will be speeded up.

Remember to label and date all your cuttings. It is important to keep in mind that some plants take weeks to produce roots, others months, and still others will disappoint you by not rooting at all. The main thing is to enjoy and keep learning from the process of propagating through cuttings.

Propagation method and month

Plant name	Softwood	Semihardwood	Hardwood
Abelia	July		Nov.-Dec.
Akebia	July		
Amelanchier		Sept.-Dec.	
Arbutus unedo			Dec.
Arctostaphyllos		Sept.-Dec.	Feb.
Azalea		Sept.-Dec.	
Buddleia	July		Oct.-Dec.
Buxus	April		
Calluna	May		Dec.-Feb.
Camellia	June (*C. japonica*)	Sept.-Dec.	Dec. (*C. sasanqua*)
Campsis	July		
Caryopteris			Mar.-Apr.
Cassiope			Mar.-Apr.
Ceanothus		Sept.-Dec.	
Choisya	Aug.		
Cistus	Aug.	Sept.-Dec.	
Clematis	July		
Cornus	June		
Cotoneaster	June		
Daphne	July		
Deutzia	June		Nov.-Jan.
Enkianthus	May		
Erica		April	Feb.
Escallonia		Sept.-Dec.	
Euonymus	July	Sept.-Dec.	
Forsythia	May	Sept.-Dec.	
Fothergilla	June		
Fuchsia	May		

Propagation method and month (cont.)

Plant name	Softwood	Semihardwood	Hardwood
Garrya elliptica	July		Feb.
Gaultheria	June		
Genista	Aug.		
Hamamelis	July		
Hebe		Sept.-Dec.	
Hydrangea macrophylla			Feb.
Hydrangea petiolaris	May		
Hypericum	June		
Ilex	July		Dec.
Kerria	June		Oct.-Dec.
Laburnum			Dec.
Lavandula	July	Sept.-Dec.	
Lavatera	Aug.		
Lonicera			Dec.-Jan., Apr.
Magnolia	July		
Mahonia	July		
Nandina	July		Nov.-Dec.
Osmanthus	June-Aug.		Nov.-Jan.
Passiflora	July		
Pernyetta			Nov.-Jan.
Photinia			Oct.-Dec.
Pieris	June		Jan.
Potentilla fruticosa	June		
Rhododendron (medium and large-leafed)			Sept.-Dec.
Ribes	June		Oct.-Dec.
Rosa			Oct.-Dec.
Salix	June		Feb.
Sarcococca	May		Nov.-Dec.
Senecio	July		
Skimmia	Aug.	Sept.-Nov.	Nov.-Dec.
Spiraea	June		Dec.
Styrax	June		
Syringa		August	
Tamarix			Dec.
Taxus		Sept.-Dec.	Dec.-Jan.
Vaccinium ovatum		Sept.-Dec.	April
Veronica	July	Sept.-Dec.	
Viburnum	June, Aug.		
Vitis	July	Sept.-Dec.	
Weigela	June		
Wisteria	July		

Recommended Reading

Rhododendrons and azaleas

All About Azaleas, Camellias and Rhododendrons. Ortho Books, San Francisco, 1985.

Cox, Kenneth. *A Plantsman's Guide to Rhododendrons.* Ward Lock, London, 1989.

Greer, Harold E. *Greer's Guidebook to Available Rhododendrons, Species and Hybrids.* Offshoot Publications, Eugene, Oregon, 1988.

Leath, David. *Rhododendrons of the World.* Charles Scribner's Sons, New York, 1961.

Phillips, Roger and Martyn Rix. *Shrubs.* Random House, New York, 1989.

Rhododendrons and Azaleas. A Sunset Book, Lane Books, Menlo Park, California, 1973.

Rhododendrons on a Western Shore. Victoria Rhododendron Society, Victoria, 1989.

Spring-flowering shrubs

Bartels, Andrea. *Gardening with Dwarf Trees and Shrubs.* Timber Press, Portland, Oregon, 1987.

Grant, John A. and Carol L. Grant. *Trees and Shrubs for Coastal B.C. Gardens.* Whitecap Books, Vancouver, 1990.

Hessayon, D.G. *The Tree and Shrub Expert.* pbi Publications, London, England, 1983.

Phillips, Roger and Martyn Rix. *Shrubs: Over 1900 Shrubs in Full Color Photographs.* Random House, New York, 1989.

Cuttings

Browse, Phillip M. *Plant Propagation.* Simon and Schuster, New York, 1984.

Propagation for the Home Gardener. Brooklyn Botanic Garden, Brooklyn, 1984.

May

*I*t's easy to see why Shakespeare called it the "merrie month of May." This late spring month can bring fine warm weather, colour is everywhere, and even the garden's slow starters are beginning to unfurl their leaves. Late-flowering street trees, such as crabapples and horse chestnuts, open their buds, and the pastel blooms of wisteria hang heavily from arches and pillars. Many perennials are in bloom, and the last of the spring-flowering bulbs are up.

Although some varieties of rhododendron flower as early as January, May is really their prime time. If you are interested in adding any new varieties to your garden, this is the month to find out which ones. The Rhododendron Walk at VanDusen Gardens and the David Lam Asian Garden at UBC are exceptionally good places to visit, since the plants are carefully labelled. (See the April chapter for information on azaleas and rhododendrons.)

Another shrub that flowers now is the lilac, with its intense, haunting fragrance. This old favourite has been improved greatly in recent years: new hybrids include some developed in Canada that are hardy, vigorous, fragrant and disease free. Small varieties of lilac, growing to a maximum height of 5 feet (1.5 m), are perfect for a mixed border in a small garden.

A lovely tree that flowers at this time but is not recommended for residential gardens is the laburnum. Its yellow, sweet pea–shaped flowers hang from the tree in dense clusters. The sight is especially striking when several laburnums are planted either side of a walk and underplanted with bluebells, as in VanDusen Gardens. However, all parts of the laburnum are poisonous, especially the seed pods, making the tree particularly dangerous for young children.

Garden centres have had huge, colourful displays of bedding plants for weeks now, but don't be tempted to buy them until the third week of the month. The ground is simply too cold for these tender plants and there is always the danger of a late frost. It's much better to wait until the weather is reliably warm and annuals can flourish without setbacks; you'll be much happier with the final result. There are many other things to do in the garden at this time: staking and supporting taller plants, pinching back leggy growth, transplanting, weeding, sowing seeds and taking care of lawns.

This chapter features both annuals and perennials, providing fairly extensive plant lists to choose from. Some of them are not as readily available as others, but it is usually worth the extra effort to seek out the unusual ones.

 # Garden Highlights

*indicates fragrance

Bulbs

Allium spp. (ornamental onions), *Anemone blanda* (windflower), *Convallaria majalis* (lily-of-the-valley),* *Endymion hispanicus* (Spanish bluebell), *Leucojum aestivum* (summer snowflake), *Muscari* spp. (grape hyacinth),* *Narcissus* spp. (daffodils and narcissus),* *Ornithogalum umbellatum* (star of Bethlehem).

Perennials

Aquilegia spp. (columbine), *Armeria maritima* (thrift), *Astrantia* spp. (masterwort), *Brunnera macrophylla*, *Centaurea montana* (mountain bluet), *Centranthus ruber* (valerian), *Delphinium* hybrids, *Dianthus* spp. (pinks),* *Euphorbia* spp. (spurge), *Gentian acaulis* (gentian), *Geranium* spp. (hardy geranium), *Geum* spp., *Helianthemum* spp. (sun rose, rock rose), *Heuchera* spp. (coral bells), *Hosta*, *Iberis sempervirens* (candytuft), *Lupinus* spp. (lupine), *Meconopsis* spp. (blue poppy), *Paeonia* spp. (peony),* *Papaver* spp. (poppy), *Saxifraga* x *urbium* (London pride), *Stachys byzantina* (woolly lamb's ears), *Trillium*.

Climbers

Clematis alpina, *C. macropetela*, *C. montana*,* *Wisteria*.*

Shrubs

Ceanothus (California lilac), *Choisya ternata* (Mexican orange),* *Cistus* spp. (rockrose), *Deutzia* spp., *Kalmia latifolia* (mountain laurel), *Kolkwitzia amabilis* (beauty bush), *Rhododendron* spp. and hybrids (rhododendrons and azaleas), *Rosa* spp. (rose),* *Spiraea thunbergii* (spirea), *S.* x *vanhouttei*, *Syringa* spp. (lilac),* *Viburnum plicatum*, *V. opulus*, *Weigela* spp.

Trees

Aesculus hippocastanum (horse chestnut), *Cornus nuttallii* (western white dogwood), *C. florida*, *Crataegus* spp. (hawthorn),* *Gleditsia triacanthos* (honey locust), *Laburnum* (golden chain tree), *Magnolia sieboldii*,* *Malus* spp. (crabapple).

May Checklist

Annuals, perennials and bulbs

- Buy bedding plants and plant out after the middle of the month. Plant up tubs, hanging baskets and window boxes.
- Thin out annuals that were sown earlier, retaining the best and strongest plants.
- Pull up spring bedding plants, such as wallflowers and forget-me-nots, and add to compost pile. Sow seeds of these biennials now for next year.
- Pinch out growing tips of chrysanthemums and asters to promote bushy growth.
- Stake tall perennials, such as delphiniums.
- Lightly shear back early spring–flowering perennials, such as aubrietia, arabis and perennial alyssum.
- As flowers fade, tie back clumps of daffodil leaves neatly, or dig them up and heel them into a spare patch of ground to die back. Feed them with fish fertilizer so they will flower well next year.
- Plant out dahlia tubers, making sure to drive in the stakes first, to avoid damage to tubers.

Trees, shrubs and climbers

- Check for aphids on roses, and either rub them off or apply an insecticidal soap. Mulch around the roses if not already done.
- Train or tie in young shoots of climbers to cover the desired space evenly. After flowering, reduce some of the tangled growth of *Clematis montana* if space is restricted (see the March chapter).
- Prune deciduous shrubs after flowering (see the April chapter).

- Remove seed heads from rhododendrons and azaleas. Mulch them lightly at the extremity of the rootball (not on top of the rootball) with well-rotted compost. This will help to retain moisture and protect roots from drying out. Do this also for other shallow-rooted evergreens, such as camellias.

Fruits, vegetables and herbs

- Continue successive sowings of lettuce, carrots, spinach, radishes, bush beans, pole beans, peppers and potatoes.
- Start winter crops of cauliflower, broccoli, Brussels sprouts, cabbages and pumpkins. Start main crop of potatoes. Plant asparagus.
- Feed tomato plants, remove side shoots and plant out after the middle of the month. Also plant out peppers, eggplants and squash, including zucchini.
- Sow corn, cucumber and squash at the end of the month. Plant corn in blocks for better pollination.
- Keep vegetable garden well weeded and keep a lookout for signs of pests and diseases. Slugs are a particular problem with tender young seedlings.
- Cut off strawberry runners.
- Take cuttings of rosemary, sage and thyme.

Other garden activities

- Keep newly turfed or sown lawns well watered.
- Continue preparing new lawns and repairing worn patches on existing ones.

Annuals with a Difference

Annuals, easily raised from seeds for cuttings, give quick results and are in fashion once again! Gardeners are weaving sophisticated compositions from a mixture of annuals and perennials. We can choose from a palette of soft pastels or hot fiery shades. We are nostalgic for old plants that are gradually being reintroduced and experimenting with semi-tropicals for dramatic summer accent. And we are using edible annuals for their wonderful foliage shapes and colour. Local garden centres offer new selections each spring, but mail order catalogues from around the globe offer an even richer choice.

What is an annual?

A true annual grows from seed, flowers, sets seed and dies within one season. Some of these temporary visitors to the garden are hardy, such as sweet peas, cornflowers, godetia, poppies and love-in-a-mist, and can be sown directly into the ground in fall or early spring. Others are half-hardy, and need to be started indoors and planted outside when all danger of frost is past. This includes nicotiana, French marigolds and petunias.

We grow many plants as annuals even though they are actually perennials, such as marguerites, impatiens, begonias, fuchsias and geraniums. Although they are unable to survive our winters outside, they can be overwintered successfully if brought inside into a cool room, basement or garage.

Bedding plants can be irresistible

It is the half-hardy annuals and tender perennials we go into the garden centres to buy as bedding plants. These plants have been started in greenhouses by commercial growers and are often in full bloom when they arrive at the garden centre, making them irresistible to all but the most hardened gardener.

Gardeners are dazzled by the riot of colour and masses of blooms the garden centre can offer. Buying mature bedding plants, taking them home and planting them is the easiest form of flower gardening. The plants give spectacular results with relatively little labour. Edges, borders, walkways, containers and window boxes come instantly to life. Presto, a garden is made. This form of gardening appeals to many who enjoy the beauty of flowers but whose hearts are on the golf course, by the seaside, on the tennis court or, heaven forbid, at the office.

However, if you have the time and the space, it is much less expensive, and very satisfying, to start summer bedding plants from seed yourself, especially if you have a greenhouse or sunny, south-facing window. In this way you can grow interesting and unusual plants not usually offered for sale by garden centres.

When to buy bedding plants

If you are buying bedding plants, do not plant earlier than the third week in May. It is usually too cold before then. Buy healthy plants with sturdy stems and healthy foliage. Plan your garden border and containers ahead of time, including the varieties and numbers of plants you will need. Otherwise you may find yourself with twice as many bedding plants as you need.

Seeds: the annual miracle

One of the special pleasures of annuals comes from sowing seeds and watching them go through their life cycle all within a year. In a short period of time, annuals give all their energy to flowering, so that the seeds can form and the annual can perpetuate its species. If the flowers are cut, the plant will try again and again. The more annuals are cut, the more they bloom, and most annuals make excellent cutting flowers.

Be daring and experiment! Seek out unusual and different varieties and try them in your garden, mix them into perennial beds as fillers when the perennials fade, and sow every few weeks for continuous blooming. Your efforts will be rewarded when neighbours stop on their evening walks to admire your stunning bed of poppies, or your garden full of cosmos daisies. Following are some of our favourites you may want to try.

Annual seeds to be sown directly into the garden

Asperula orientalis (**annual woodruff**). This little annual bears clusters of tiny, blue, very fragrant flowers. The flower stems trail along the ground. Annual woodruff is at home in a moist, shady spot. It makes a fine edging plant and is a good, short-stemmed cut flower. Scatter seeds outdoors in masses as soon as the ground can be cultivated in the spring. Plants bloom 10 to 12 weeks after sowing.

Brassica (**cabbage and kale**). Brassicas are among the best of all decorative foliage annuals; they also make fine stir-fry and salad greens and are one of the most cold-hardy crops for winter. Sow seeds mid-June to mid-July in moderately good garden soil for a fall and winter crop, or May–June for summer use. 'Lacinato', the black Tuscan kale, has impressive, deep bluish-grey, deeply blistered leaves on a strong stem that can reach 3 feet (90 cm) or more. The curly red kale 'Redbor' makes foaming 18- to 24-inch (45- to 60-cm) mounds of deep mahogany-red and is also great in flower arrangements; 'Red Peacock' has wonderful, deep purple ribs. Swiss chard 'Bright Lights' glows brilliant red or chartreuse when backlit by the sun. All can enhance the colour of adjacent flowers. See catalogues and our vegetable list in the July chapter for more interesting foliage ideas to spice up your borders.

Calendula officinalis (**pot marigold**). This cheerful plant has cream, lemon, bright orange, and yellow blossoms 2 to 4 inches (5 to 10 cm) across. It thrives in full sun, cool growing conditions and fertile soil. Plant seeds outdoors as soon as the ground can be cultivated in the spring. A second sowing in early summer will ensure a fall crop.

Centaurea cyanus (**cornflower, bachelor's button**). The name "cornflower" comes from the fact that these flowers grow wild in the grain fields of Europe. The ragged blue flower is always a delight, and it's easy for children to grow. Newer cultivars are pink, white, lavender and red. Look for interesting taller forms like the 'Frosted Queen' mixture and the Boy Series that comes in separate colours: black (more a deep purple), white, red and blue. Sow cornflower seeds outdoors any time in the fall so that the plant will begin to grow before the frosts arrive. This will ensure early blooms in the spring.

Cerinthe (**honeywort**). *Cerinthe major* var. *purpurascens* has grabbed the fancy of plant lovers with its beautiful blue-purple colouring. This plant self-sows easily about your garden and looks great next to golden oregano or thyme.

Chrysanthemum carinatum (**annual chrysanthemum**). Annual chrysanthemums are very different in appearance from their perennial cousins. Their leaves are generally smaller, and their flowers resemble daisies. Flower heads are single or semidouble, and colours include yellow, purple, orange, salmon and white, with a ring of contrasting colour near the centre of each flower. Most grow to about 2 feet (60 cm) in height. Annual chrysanthemums are easy to grow, and make excellent cutting flowers. In early spring, scatter seeds thinly over prepared soil, and rake them lightly. Thin seedlings to 18 inches (45 cm) apart. They transplant very easily.

***Clarkia amoena* (godetias, farewell to spring).** Native to the western United States. Cuplike blossoms are clustered along stems varying in height from 10 inches (25 cm) to 2 1/2 feet (75 cm). Flowers are white, pink, red or lilac, and the foliage is grey-green. Godetias make wonderful cut flowers. Sow seeds in early fall or spring in their permanent position, 6 to 12 inches (15 to 30 cm) apart.

Clarkia unguiculata. These beautiful flowers originated in the western United States and were named for Captain William Clark of the Lewis and Clark expedition. *C. unguiculata* is single-flowered, with 1-inch (2.5-cm) blossoms borne all along the 2- to 3-foot (60- to 90-cm) stems. It comes in shades of salmon, pink, mauve, purple, red and white. Sow weeds outdoors in spring as soon as the ground can be worked, or in the previous fall for earlier flowering.

***Coleus* x hybridus.** This house plant or tropical perennial is fast becoming popular as an annual that adds dazzle to summer borders and containers with its vibrant foliage. There are numerous choices. 'Pallisandra' has broad, deep velvety black leaves with lightly serrated edges. 'El Brighto' is orange with lime-green edges;

'Coral Glow' is a deep coral variegated. Give them afternoon shade and enough water; pick off the flower stems and pinch out the top to encourage branching.

***Consolida ambigua* (annual delphinium, larkspur).** Native to southern Europe, this annual is loved for its tall spires of flowers in shades of blue, salmon, rose, lilac, purple or white. The plants grow 3 to 5 feet (.9 to 1.5 m) tall, perfect as a background planting along a fence or wall. They are also an excellent cut flower. They can be grown from seed outdoors in the fall, and also in the early spring. Sow seeds where they are to remain in the garden, and space plants about 10 inches (25 cm) apart. Taller plants may need staking. Needs fertile, well-drained soil.

***Cosmos bipinnatus* (cosmos) and *C. sulphureus* (yellow cosmos).** Native to Mexico, cosmos will grow 4 to 6 feet (1.2 to 1.8 m) tall (yellow cosmos is a bit shorter). They are valuable as a filler in perennial borders, as background planting and as cut flowers. The blossoms are daisylike, and about 3 to 4 inches (7.5 to 10 cm) across. The wide pink, white or red petals of cosmos encircle yellow centres; yellow cosmos blossoms are all yellow. The foliage is feathery and delicate-looking. These flowers love the sun. Sow seed indoors in March, or outdoors after all danger of frost is past. Cosmos often self-seed, giving enjoyment year after year.

***Eschsholzia californica* (California poppy).** The state flower of California, this poppy grows easily in our climate. It was found on the Pacific coast by a Russian explorer in 1815 and named after a member of the Russian expedition, Dr. Johann Friedrick Eschscholz. The silky blossoms of the California poppy come in tones of gold, bronze, scarlet, terra cotta, apricot and white. Plants do best in full sun and well-drained, sandy soil. Sow seeds in the autumn or spring in their permanent position. They do not transplant easily.

***Helianthus annuus* (sunflower).** The common sunflower is an effective, temporary hedge and screen. This annual is a must for bird lovers, who will enjoy the many bird visitors in the fall when the seeds have ripened. It thrives in poor soil, with little moisture, and will tolerate light shade. Plant seeds outdoors 1/2 inch (1 cm) deep and 2 feet (60 cm) apart when the danger of frost is past in the spring.

***Lathyrus odoratus* (sweet pea).** Sweet peas can be used as climbers, border and bedding plants, container plants, and in hanging baskets. They come in all colours, and the blossoms resemble little sunbonnets. They have a delightful fragrance, and summer gardens seem incomplete without them. The best sweet pea seeds available here are the English "Boltons" seeds, found only in some specialty stores, but worth searching for. Non-climbing varieties grow to about 8 inches (20 cm), and make excellent cut flowers and container plants.

There is a secret to growing sweet peas successfully. Dig a deep trench and fill it with organically rich soil. Soak the seeds in warm water for about an hour before planting. Plant the seeds in early fall or early spring, about 1 inch (2.5 cm) deep, in the rich, well-worked soil. When the seedling is about 4 inches (10 cm) high, pinch it back so that it will develop strong side branches, and build up the soil around it to make the stem stronger.

***Lavatera trimestris* (mallow).** Native to the Mediterranean region, mallow is related to hibiscus. Plants grow up to 4 feet (1.2 m) in height, and make fine screens. The pink or white flowers resemble those of hibiscus. Sow seeds where you want them to bloom as soon as the soil can be worked in the spring. Space 2 feet (60 cm) apart.

***Linaria maroccana* (Morocco toadflax).** This relative of the snapdragon loves our cool summers, but needs to be planted in a sunny spot. Plants grow 9 to 12 inches (23 to 30 cm) in height, and the dainty, 1/2-inch (1-cm) blossoms come in shades of yellow, blue, lavender, red and white. They are excellent for a rock garden, or as an edging plant in a border. Linaria make good, long-lasting cut flowers. Sow outdoors in early spring, spaced 6 inches (15 cm) apart.

***Linum grandiflorum* and *L. usitatissimum* (flower flax and common flax).** A native of North America, flowering flax has 18-inch (45-cm) stems topped with colourful flowers about 2 inches (5 cm) in diameter. Colours are predominantly red. Common flax, from which linen and linseed oil are made, is sky blue, and makes an excellent garden flower, particularly when planted in masses throughout a flower bed. It likes our cool summers. Sow seeds where you want them to grow in the fall or early spring, when the ground can be worked. Sow seeds at three- to four-week intervals, as the plant blossoms for only three to four weeks.

***Nigella damascena* (love-in-a-mist).** Native to the Mediterranean region, this delicate annual loves full sun and ordinary soil. Love-in-a-mist faintly resembles the cornflower in shape, but its blooms are more delicate. Colours are blue, white, pink, rose, mauve and purple. The blooms are replaced by striking pale green seed pods with brown markings, which look interesting in dried flower arrangements. Sow the seeds in fall or early spring in a permanent position in the garden, spaced 8 inches (20 cm) apart. Two sowings a month will ensure an extended flowering season.

Papaver **spp. (poppies).** Poppy flowers are delightful to have in any garden. The flowers look like crinkled silk, and some are fragrant. *P. alpinum* (alpine poppy) has wiry stems 6 to 10 inches (15 to 25 cm) high, with blossoms in orange, apricot, yellow, white, pink and scarlet. *P. nudicaule* (Iceland poppy) is found in the arctic and mountain regions, and forms clumps 10 to 12 inches (25 to 30 cm) wide with slender stems topped with fragrant blooms in many colours. The lovely Shirley poppy is a cultivar of the famous scarlet wildflower, the corn poppy (*P. rhoeas*) of the fields of Flanders. The Shirley poppy was bred by the Reverend W. Wilks of Shirley, England. Shirley poppies have yellow or white stamens, and the blooms are white, pink, orange and shades of red.

Poppies look best when massed in borders by themselves. Sow seeds in the fall to bloom the following spring. The seeds are very tiny. When sowing, mix with sand and scatter seeds directly onto the ground. Thin the plants as they emerge. Space alpines 6 inches (15 cm) apart, the others 8 to 12 inches (20 to 30 cm) apart. Spring-sown poppies are not as robust as fall-sown plants. Poppies make excellent cut flowers, but require extra care. Cut them just as the nodding buds become erect, but before the flowers open. To conserve their moisture, sear the stem ends immediately by dipping the ends in boiling water or searing them with a match.

Rudbeckia hirta 'Gloriosa Daisy' **(gloriosa daisy).** These hybrid versions of black-eyed susans were first developed in the United States. Brown centres are surrounded by yellow gold or mahogany petals. The plants are 2 to 3 feet (60 to 90 cm) tall and make excellent border plants and cutting flowers. The dwarf cultivars look superb in containers by themselves. Sow seeds outdoors in autumn or early spring, spaced 12 to 15 inches (30 to 38 cm) apart. They are easy to transplant.

Tropaeolum majus **(common nasturtium),** *T. peregrinum* **(canary bird flower) and** *T. speciosum* **(flame flower).** Nasturtiums grow wild in Mexico and come in double- and single-flowering varieties of both climbing vines and bushy plants. Dwarf varieties grow 1 foot (30 cm) high. Climbers grow 6 to 10 feet (1.8 to 3 m). Dwarf varieties make excellent edging for flower beds and vegetable gardens. Vines cover fences, trellises, old stumps and rocks. Young nasturtium leaves may be used in salads. Sow outdoors when all danger of frost has passed in the spring. Space dwarf varieties 6 inches (15 cm) apart, vines 12 inches (30 cm) apart. Watch for aphids and, when they appear, dislodge them with a hard spray from a garden hose. Don't use insecticidal soap since it will damage the leaves.

Half-hardy plants grown as annuals

You can start these plants from seed indoors, or look for bedding plants at the garden centre.

Amaranthus **spp. (amaranthus).** Big, bold and lush, these foliage plants add a subtropical look to the garden when combined with other foliage plants like castor beans, dark-leafed coleus 'Black Knight' and banana plants. Startling, colourful, 3-foot (90-cm) 'Poinsettia Mixed' and 'Joseph's Coat' (scarlet, yellow and green) are varieties of *A. tricolor*. Shorter varieties, such as 'Green Thumb', grow to about 2 feet (60 cm), with divided green plumes that look great with variegated or yellow-leaved shrubs. 'Pygmy Torch' is just about 12 inches (30 cm) tall and has dusky maroon foliage and dense heads in a similar colour. Given a sunny, sheltered location and rich soil, they can also be planted in containers. Amaranthus is a grain crop, as well as an ornamental.

***Browallia speciosa* and *B. vicosa* (browallia, amethyst flower).** Browallias have attractive, pointed, bright green leaves and striking blue or white flowers. They are easy to grow, and are excellent for window boxes, hanging baskets and rockeries. 'Sapphire' is deep blue, 'Marine Bells' is indigo and 'Silver Bells' is white.

***Cleome hasslerana* (cleome, spider flower).** Cleome's dramatic height of 3 to 5 feet (.9 to 1.5 m) and large airy flowers are an asset to any border, particularly a fading perennial one. Cleome is a native of tropical climates and needs warm weather to get going, but it is a striking plant. It comes in shades of pink, lavender and white, and blooms from July to September.

***Cobaea scandens* (cup-and-saucer vine).** This vigorous climber is a native of Mexico and requires full sun and a rich soil. Its blossoms are about 2 inches (5 cm) long and 1 1/2 inches (4 cm) wide and appear to be sitting in large green saucers of foliage. The colours of the cups range from white through greenish-purple to violet. If you see this annual in the garden store, grab it. It will cover a wall, trellis or fence in a hurry, and it's an interesting addition

to any garden. Lovely as cut flowers, and blooms from July to September.

***Coleus* x *hybridus*.** These natives of the South Pacific make spectacular additions to beds, borders and window boxes, and are grown for their exotic foliage. They thrive in shady spots.

***Dorotheanthus bellidiformis* (mesembryanthemum, Livingstone daisy).** This succulent plant, a native of South Africa, makes a wonderful summer garden addition. Flower colours range from brilliant reds, pinks, lavenders and whites to very soft pastel tones. They grow about 6 inches (15 cm) high, and love the sun and dry soil. They look beautiful as a single planting in window boxes.

***Felicia amelloides* (blue marguerite) and *F. bergerana* (kingfisher daisy).** These South American natives have low, dark green mounds of foliage from which grow an abundance of blue daisies. Both species love dry pockets of rock gardens. They are also excellent as edging plants for walkways and flower beds, and in containers. They make good cut flowers.

***Gaillardia pulchella* (blanket flower, Indian blanket).** Descendants of wild plants in the American West, these make interesting additions to the garden. Annuals grow to about 18 inches (45 cm), some with single and semidouble daisylike blossoms. Other cultivars have ball-shaped flower heads about 3 inches (7.5 cm) in diameter. Colours range from creamy white to yellow, orange and red, and many are bicoloured. They love the heat and tolerate dry soil. Excellent for containers.

***Gazania* x *hybrida* (African daisy).** Natives of South Africa, these plants grow 6 to 12 inches (15 to 30 cm) tall. They have daisylike blossoms that can be yellow, gold, cream, pink and bronze-red. Gazanias grow well in windy places and are excellent container plants. They love the sun and the blossoms close in cloudy weather.

Matthiola longipetala ssp. bicornis (night scented stock) and M. incana (common stock). Evening scented stocks grow to 12 inches (30 cm), with spires of small, lilac-coloured flowers that close during the day and open at night. Cultivars of common stocks vary in height from 1 to 3 feet (30 to 90 cm) and bear flowers in all colours. At night and on cool or rainy days, evening stock is loved for its fragrance. Common stocks are excellent bedding plants and cut flowers. Stocks do best in rich soil and sun.

Moluccella laevis (bells of Ireland). This native of the Mediterranean area makes an excellent cut flower. The 2- to 3-foot-high (60- to 90-cm) stems have green bells along their entire length. The bells are actually not flowers but enlarged calyxes. However, they look like flowers and are excellent in dried flower arrangements. They need sun to grow well.

Nicotiana alata (flowering tobacco plant). These natives of South America are especially appreciated for their fragrance. The blossoms are white, pink, wine, chartreuse or chocolate, depending on the cultivar. The stems are 1 to 3 feet (30 to 90 cm) tall and flowers are 2 inches (5 cm) in diameter. Excellent for flower borders. *N. alata* Nickie Series cultivars are short-lived, semidwarf and very fragrant. 'Nicki Red' has red flowers. *N. langsdorffii* bears nodding panicles of tubular, apple-green flowers and grows to 5 feet (1.5 m). *N. sylvestris* produces short, densely packed panicles of nodding, sweet-scented, trumpet-shaped white flowers on stems 5 feet

(1.5 m) tall. *N.* x *sanderae* 'Sensation Mix' cultivars stay open all day into evening and bear fragrant flowers in shades of pink, red and white that are 2 1/2 feet (75 cm) tall.

Papaver spp. (poppy). *P. somniferum* (opium poppy) has glaucous blue-green leaves and bears stems with large, solitary pink, mauve-purple, red or white bowl-shaped flowers to 4 inches (10 cm) across. These are followed by large, blue-green seed pods that are great for dried arrangements. 'Peony Flowered' has frilly double flowers in red, purple, pink, salmon-pink, maroon-red or white. 'White Cloud' has white double flowers; 'Seriously Scarlet' has striking scarlet flowers with a dark purple-blue centre; 'Black Peony' is a dark-flowered double; 'Cedric Morris' is a mix of soft pastels.

Portulaca grandiflora (moss rose). Moss rose is a native of Brazil, grows about 6 inches (15 cm) high, and produces many flowers in beautiful shades of rose, salmon, pink, orange, yellow and white. It loves hot, dry locations. Containers, rock gardens and dry banks are all excellent homes for this pretty little annual.

Ricinus communis (castor oil plant). An old favourite for bedding out, this large, dramatic, foliage plant creates a bold subtropical effect and needs a sheltered spot. *R. zanzibarensis* will reach 6 feet (1.8 m) and comes in purple or bronze shades, or a mix of dark greens. 'Carmencita', with red flowers, and 'Carmencita Pink' are shorter and flower dependably.

Salpiglossis sinuata (painted-tongue). A relative of the petunia, these flowers are useful as bedding plants and fillers in perennial borders. The plants are 2 to 3 feet (60 to 90 cm) tall, topped by trumpet-shaped flowers in muted shades of gold, scarlet, rose, mahogany and blue. All are decorated with a delicate veining. They require sun and protection from the wind. They make excellent cut flowers.

Salvia spp. (sage). There has been a bit of a revolution in salvias. Many new colours, plus taller and bushier types are coming to market. Some are perennials and some are best grown from cuttings, but many seed-grown varieties are now also available. _S. horminum_ has large, colourful bracts in pink, purple or white atop the 18-inch (45-cm) plant spike. Look for deep blue _S. patens_, in lavender, salmon, white or red; _S. coccinea_, a 2 1/2-foot (75-cm) plant; as well as the traditional deep purple (_S. farinacea_ 'Blue Victory') shades. Sow seeds mid-February with good light and moisture.

Schizanthus hybrids (butterfly flower, poor man's orchid). A native of Chile, butterfly flower is particularly useful in hanging baskets and window boxes where it can cascade over edges. Some cultivars are up to 2 feet (60 cm) in height; others only reach 1 foot (30 cm). The blossoms resemble a variety of orchid and are usually bicoloured with combinations of pink, violet, purple and white. All are heavily veined with gold.

Verbascum spp. (mullein). Although they may be perennial, the spiky, vertical, front-of-the-border verbascum are best grown as biennials by sowing fresh seed every two years. _V. bombyciferum_ has elegantly cut silvery leaves in a rosette the first year and yellow flowers to 6 feet (1.8 m) the second. _V. chaixii_ 'Album' has a white flower with contrasting purple stamens on dark stems above a base of large, prominently veined midgreen leaves. Popular named cultivars include 'Helen Johnson', 'Raspberry Ripple', and 'Purple Parasols'. They like full sun with well-drained soil.

Verbena spp. (verbena). _V. bonariensis_ has magenta flowers floating atop 6-foot (1.8-m) wiry stalks. It likes sun, tolerates drought and looks great at the very front of the border intermingled with other see-through plants like _Nicotiana sylvestris_ or cosmos. It self-sows and germinates freely. Other varieties are difficult to grow from seed and succumb to mildew. Start seeds with bottom heat in shade, and grow them on the dry side, being not too generous with food; or look for plants raised from cuttings. 'Silver Anne', a hybrid with large, shell-pink flowers flushed with rose; 'Peaches and Cream', a soft pastel; and 'Homestead Purple', a bright purple, bloom all summer long and are also good in hanging baskets.

Viola (pansy). The romantic garden pansy hybrids are best treated as annuals, biennials or very short-lived perennials. These favourites prefer shade to semishade in average soil. Their faintly scented round flowers are compact. Some bloom profusely all summer; others are winter- or spring-flowering and are ideal with bulbs. They may seed themselves about, filling in gaps. Pansies are available in an amazing range of colours ("black" to lavender to peach to pale yellow), and are now being bred with picotee (ruffled) edges! The species violets tend to be smaller and more fragrant; they are perennial and make a great woodland groundcover. For more information, see "Violets" in the March chapter.

Perennials Come in from the Wild

Every year in late spring, the wild lupines bloom. The banks of the Trans-Canada Highway in West Vancouver are covered with their blue, purple and white flowers, intermingled with bright yellow broom. A little later, in more remote areas of the province, wild blue and yellow columbines, blue delphiniums and hundreds and hundreds of other native perennials come into bloom.

These lovely flowers remind us that the ancestors of all the perennials we plant in our gardens originally came from the wild. However, most of them have come a long way since the early plant gatherers harvested their ancestors. Delphiniums, for instance, have now been produced in shades of red, and lupines and columbines are available in many pastel colour combinations. Perennials have been bred for colour, shape, size, hardiness and disease resistance, until their ancestry is barely recognizable.

Perennial borders are back in style

Perennial borders became popular in the late 19th century as a result of the work of people such as Gertrude Jekyll and William Robinson. Today perennials are popular again, and nurseries and specialty growers are responding to the demand by increasing the availability of interesting and unusual cultivars.

In residential gardens, perennials are not often grown on their own, since they die back to the ground during winter months, leaving a bare and uninteresting border. Instead, perennials are usually planted in a mixed border with bulbs, trees, shrubs, roses and annuals, and each plant receives the fertilizer or soil amendments it needs to thrive. Unfolding leaves of perennials will hide the dying foliage of bulbs; trees and shrubs will bloom in their season; roses come out when many of the early perennials are finished and annuals have not begun; and annuals and later-flowering perennials provide colour for the summer and early fall months. When winter arrives and perennials and annuals are over for the year, it is the structure, texture and form of trees and shrubs that helps to sustain interest in the garden.

Some perennials are especially precious because they bloom when little else is flowering. Perhaps the most important of these are the hellebores, which include the winter and lenten roses. They are detailed in the December chapter.

Perennials are easy care

Most perennials are grown for the beauty of their flowers, but some are grown for their foliage alone. By and large they are easy to grow, last many years and produce blooms year after year with a minimum of care. They range in height from tall, majestic hybrid delphiniums to prostrate carpeting plants like the soft, grey-green, woolly lamb's ears.

Since they come in so many different shapes and sizes, perennials are great fun to arrange in a border. Most of them can be moved easily, and benefit from regular division and replanting. There are exceptions to this. Peonies, for example, should be left undisturbed except for regular feeding and watering. Given the right conditions, they will flourish and continue to produce more flowers year after year. Like all perennials, peonies benefit from an annual top dressing of rich organic material, either good compost or well-rotted manure.

Colour choices reveal personality

If you plan carefully, it is possible to change colour schemes in the same area of the garden from season to season, and to have something in flower from January to November. The flower border is another place where the personality of the gardener comes out, because there are few restrictions on your choice of plants and colours.

Famous gardeners have written at length about the virtues of one colour scheme or another. For example, Vita Sackville-West's all-white garden at Sissinghurst, England, was created in the 1930s and still attracts thousands of visitors each year. Gertrude Jekyll wrote extensively about using colour themes in the garden, and contemporary garden expert Penelope Hobhouse has devoted a whole book to the subject.

Experimenting is the key to success

Ultimately the choice is yours alone. The only advice we offer is to experiment, as long as you choose your plants carefully. Some plants, such as the lovely Japanese anemone (*Anemone* x *hybrida*), grow and spread very quickly. This may be an advantage when you're starting out, but the plants can quickly take over and smother less robust neighbours unless they are carefully positioned.

Make sure you buy healthy plants and find out what they need to thrive, including the amount of sun or shade they need, whether they prefer acid or alkaline soil, and whether they like to be divided regularly or left undisturbed. Give them the right conditions, the right amount of food and water, and sit back and enjoy the results.

Make your own Friendship Garden

One of the nice things about growing perennials is sharing them with your friends.

Siberian iris, for instance, will at least double its clump size in a year. Hardy geraniums, such as *Geranium endressi*, and plants such as lady's mantle (*Alchemilla mollis*) self-seed very easily. Before you know it, you'll have lots of seedlings to give away and trade with friends. As you look around your garden, you'll remember the people who gave them to you, and plants from your Friendship Garden will be shared with a widening circle of friends.

Perennial favourites

Everyone has their own perennial favourites. The following list contains most of ours. It will help to get you going, and introduce you to some of the many lovely perennials available today. You may have to search for some of the less usual cultivars in local specialty nurseries (see the listings in Resources).

Achillea spp. (yarrow). These attractive, hardy plants demand little and give a lot. They have lovely fernlike foliage and durable clusters of flowers with flat flower heads that are excellent for cutting and drying. They rarely need staking. Plant in well-drained soil in a sunny position and divide every two to three years. *A. filipendulina* (fernleaf yarrow) cultivars are all yellow. Good ones to look for are 'Coronation Gold' and 'Gold Plate'. *A. millefolium* cultivars are shorter than the fernleaf yarrows, in shades of white through to pinks and reds. Good ones are 'Cerise Queen', bright pink; 'Fire King', deep red; and 'Rosea', soft pink. Look for the new hybrids from Germany in softer colours of salmon, pink and yellow. One excellent hybrid to look for is *A.* 'Moonshine', which has beautiful silvery leaves and lemon-yellow flowers. However, avoid the species *A. ptarmica* (sneezeweed) as it is very invasive.

***Aconitum* spp. (monkshood).** All parts of this plant are poisonous, especially the roots, so do not plant it near a children's play area or vegetable garden, where it may be eaten by mistake. Monkshood are attractive plants with tall blue spires of hooded or helmet-shaped flowers. They are easy to grow, providing they have rich moist soil and a partially shaded location. A good garden species is *A. carmichaelii*, with violet-blue flowers in August and September. Hybrids of *A. henryii*, *A. napellus* and *A. pyrimindale* bloom in July and August, and rarely need staking. Good cultivars include 'Bressingham Spire', violet-blue; 'Newry Blue', deep blue; and 'Spark's Variety', deep violet-blue. *A. lycotonum* 'Ivorine' is a lovely cultivar but hard to find. It is a compact plant with hooded ivory white flowers that bloom in late spring and early summer.

***Alchemilla mollis* (lady's mantle).** A beautiful plant that forms a 1-foot (30-cm) mound of pleated, downy, grey-green leaves with sprays of yellowish-green flowers from early June to late August. It seeds freely, but rarely becomes invasive. The flowers are excellent for cutting and drying. It grows anywhere, in sun or shade. Raindrops are held like jewels on the leaves after a rainfall.

***Allium* spp. (ornamental onions).** Until recently, onion and garlic have been neglected in our decorative gardens. Although they have added spice to diets since ancient Egypt, been used in witchcraft to repel vampires, and were traded by First Nations people a hundred years ago on Vancouver Island, only now do we finally also appreciate their beauty. These spring- and summer-blooming perennial bulbs are good additions to borders, containers or rock gardens and when dried their airy starburst heads continue to provide interest over winter. *A. cernuum*, 8 to 12 inches (20 to 30 cm), is our native, pink-flowered nodding onion found in woodland and meadow. Try it with fescues and campanulas. *A. aflatunense*, 2 to 4 feet (60 cm to 1.2 m), with rose-violet heads, is one of the easiest drumstick alliums to grow. It flourishes in open borders. 'Purple Sensation' features 4-inch (10-cm) heads of rich reddish-violet on 3-foot (90-cm) stems. They are hardy in well-drained sunny spots. *A. christophii* is a well-known and popular bulb with short stems, 6 to 16 inches (15 to 40 cm), that support large, pale violet-blue, globular flowering heads up to 8 inches (20 cm) in diameter. The seed head dries beautifully and is much used in floral arrangements. *A. giganteum* has a large spherical umbel, packed with star-shaped flowers, usually purple-violet, occasionally white, on 32- to 80-inch (80- to 200-cm) stems.

***Anthriscus sylvestris* 'Ravenswing' (Queen Anne's lace).** This is the dark leaf form of Queen Anne's lace. Its finely dissected, deep purple, almost black foliage topped with white flower umbels is irresistible. It blooms in spring to early summer before going dormant in the summer heat. It may stay green through mild winters and is easy to grow.

***Aquilegia* spp. (columbine).** Columbines are old favourites, with their ferny leaves and pretty, nodding flowers. They grow best in partial shade, but will tolerate full sun. They grow easily from seed, are relatively short-lived, and are best replaced every four or five years. The most striking garden varieties are selected hybrid strains with large, showy flowers with long spurs.

The McKana Giant hybrids are noted for vigorous growth and large bicoloured flowers. Other good cultivars include 'Crimson Star', large, long-spurred crimson and white flowers; 'Rose Queen', long-spurred white and soft rose flowers; and 'Nora Barlow', double ruffled pink tipped with white.

Artemisia **spp. A** very useful group of plants, grown for their striking, aromatic, silvery foliage, the perfect foil for other, stronger-coloured plants. They need a sunny location and well-drained soil. *A. absinthium* (common wormwood) is a subshrubby deciduous species with beautiful silver-grey foliage, reaching a height of 3 feet (90 cm). 'Lambrook Silver' and 'Powis Castle' are both lovely. Unfortunately, the latter is not hardy in our climate. *A. schmidtiana* forms a cloud of silvery, silky-haired foliage. 'Nana' is a dwarf cultivar only a few inches (several cm) high, and 'Silver Mound' is the most commonly grown, reaching a height of 1 foot (30 cm). A very useful plant for the front of a border. *A. lactiflora* 'Guizho' (white mugwort) is not a silver-grey foliage plant for dry open sites, but a moisture-loving selection with dark stems and purple-green leaves. Its finely dissected foliage forms a clump with tall flower stalks waving huge, white, astilbe-like flower panicles. It is a midsummer bloomer that likes semishade and good soil.

Aster **(Michaelmas daisy).** This large family of plants is important for fall colour. All are easy to grow. The earliest bloom in late July, and others continue to the first frost. Most asters flower best in full sun and should be divided every two to three years. *A. amellus* cultivars bloom in August and grow to 2 feet (60 cm). They have very large flowers with prominent yellow centres. *A.* x *frikartii* is a hybrid of *A. amellus* and *A. thompsonii*, with large, clear blue flowers and contrasting yellow centres. It needs winter protection. A well-known cultivar is 'Wonder of Staffa', a lavender-blue, which grows to 2 feet (60 cm). *A. novae-angliae* (New England aster) blooms from September to October. It is tall, growing to 5 feet (1.5 m), with rough hairy stems and leaves. It likes full sun and rich soil. Good cultivars are 'Barr's Pink', rose-pink; 'Harrington's Pink', clear rose; and 'September Ruby', deep rose. *A. novi-belgii* (New York aster, Michaelmas daisy) has smooth leaves and branching stems with masses of flowers. Cultivars vary in height from a few inches (cm) to 6 feet (1.8 m). There are dozens of cultivars to choose from. Many benefit from pinching back the growing tips early in the season to encourage busy growth. Good tall cultivars are 'Ada Ballard', mauve-blue; 'Ernest Ballard', deep rose-red. Dwarf ones are 'Audrey', pale blue; 'Jenny', double violet-purple; and 'Snowsprite', white.

Astilbe x *arendsii.* These plants are excellent for a shady border, although they will tolerate sun if they have moist, humus-rich soil. The plant has attractively divided leaves and bears upright plumes of red, pink or white flowers from late June to August. Astilbes should be divided and replanted every three to four years in the spring. The hybrids are a big improvement over the species from which they were developed. Some good cultivars are 'Bressingham Beauty', 3 feet (90 cm), late blooming, rich pink; 'Deutschland', 2 feet (60 cm), early, pure white; 'Fanal', 2 feet (60 cm), early, dark red; and 'Federsee', 3 feet (90 cm), early, rose-red.

***Astilboides tabularis* (formerly *Rodgersia tabularis*).** This is a strongly architectural foliage plant, suitable in a cool, moist woodland garden or growing beside a pond in partial shade. Beware of its roots becoming either waterlogged or dried out. Its huge, 2 1/2-foot (75-m) olive-green leaves are supported by long bristly stems. The ivory plume of flowers reaches 5 feet (1.5 m) and droops at the tip.

***Astrantia* (masterwort).** These are lovely plants, but will self-seed extravagantly unless the flowers are removed before they go to seed. *A. major* is a pretty, old-fashioned–looking perennial with clump-forming leaves that throw up many branched stems of pincushion-shaped flower heads in several pleasing colours. It tolerates sun and part shade, will bloom all summer until frost, lasts a long time and dries well, so it's perfect as a cut flower. *A. major* 'Rubra' has wonderful starlike flowers with dark maroon-red bracts and delicate pink stamens. 'Hadspen Blood' is a wonderful, deep plum-red. *A. maxima* is pink and has more rounded petals, which gives the flowers more substance.

Campanula* spp. *(bellflower). This useful and reliable group of perennials ranges from the small, mound-forming clumps of *C. carpatica* (Carpathian harebell) to the stately spires of *C. lactiflora*. *C. carpatica* is useful for the front of a border or a rock garden. It is very hardy and adaptable, and forms neat clumps of foliage 4 to 6 inches (10 to 15 cm) tall, with white, purple or blue bell-shaped flowers from early summer to fall. 'White Clips' is white; 'Blue Clips', violet-blue. *C. glomerata* (clustered bellflower) grows 1 to 2 feet (30 to 60 cm) and bears dense clusters of bell-shaped flowers from late spring to midsummer. It thrives in moist soil in full sun or shade. Try 'Alba', white; 'Joan Elliot', deep violet; and 'Superba', bright purple. *C. persicifolia* (peach-leaf bellflower) is the best bellflower for borders. It grows to 2 feet (60 cm), its slender flower spikes covered with upward-facing blue or white bells. It grows well in most locations, sun or partial shade. Good cultivars are 'Blue Belle', rich blue; 'Snowdrift', white; and 'Telham Beauty', rich blue. *C. lactiflora* (milky bellflower) is the tallest of the campanulas and thrives in part shade. It bears an

---

Tip of the Month: Beware of Gifts

Warning bells should go off when you hear the words, "Would you like some such and such? I've got masses of it and am happy to dig you some!" Think of an excuse quickly, such as, "No thanks, I'm only growing orange flowers with blue stripes this year." Say anything, but beware: if you accept the offer, you too will soon have masses of it.

Here is a starting list of seeders and spreaders. These plants are too lovely to banish from the garden, but must be watched carefully. One way to curtail the spreaders is to plant them in large black plastic pots set in the ground.

The seeders are *Centranthus ruber, Foeniculum vulgare, Galega officinalis, Alchemilla mollis, Euphorbia* 'Chameleon', *Verbena bonariensis, Sisyrinchium striatum, Fuchsia magellanica*. The spreaders are *Euphorbia amygdaloides* var. *robbiae, Artemisia* spp., *Lysimachia clethroides, Persicaria bistorta* 'Superbum', *Petasites* spp., *Salvia uliginosa, Anemone* x *hybrida, Cerastium tomentosum, Convallaria majalis, Epilobium angustifolium, Vinca* spp., *Campanula cochleariifolia* 'Elizabeth'.

abundance of white, pale blue or pink flowers on tall stiff stems. Good cultivars are 'Loddon Anna', soft pink, and 'Pritchard's Variety', violet-blue. *C. latifolia* (broad-leaf bellflower, great bellflower) is very hardy, flourishing in semishaded positions and bearing spires of lilac-purple flowers. Good cultivars are 'Alba', white; and 'Macrantha', blue-purple.

Canna **spp. (canna lily).** These exotics are excellent plants for a tropical effect and wonderful summer colour. They are hardy if the roots do not dry out, but protect them in winter with a generous dry mulch or bring them into the basement, garage or cool greenhouse. Huge, paddle-shaped, translucent, variegated leaves in greens through terra cottas support brightly coloured flowers. Hundreds of hybrids have resulted from complex crosses and many are becoming available locally as we push the limits of our climatic zone in the garden. Several are giants, growing to 5 to 7 feet (1.5 to 2.1 m). 'Phaison' has stunning, variegated, burnt orange leaves with dark veining; 'Bengal Tiger' has midgreen leaves with yellow striations. Plant all where you'll see the sun shining through the leaves.

Chrysanthemum **spp.** This is a large and diverse group of more than 200 species, most of which are easy to grow, providing they are given sunny positions and well-drained soil. The plants we commonly call chrysanthemums come under the group name of *C. x morifolium*, a vast and extremely complex group that has been divided into 13 classes with hundreds of species and cultivars in each class. Root cuttings or small plants are available from garden centres in late spring, but the best sources of show plants and interesting types are the chrysanthemum societies and clubs. Pinching back the growing tips once or twice before midsummer will help the plants to bush out, and they should be divided every second year in early spring, replanting single shoots from the outside of the clump and discarding the centre. *C. x superbum* (shasta daisy) is one of the most common of the chrysanthemums to be used for perennial borders. It has coarse leaves with white, yellow-centred, daisy-like, single or double flowers on strong stems. Shastas need rich, moist, but well-drained soil and frequent division. Keep them bushy by pinching or shearing them back early in the season, and they will bloom continuously from June to August. Several good cultivars include 'Esther Read', double; 'Wirral Pride', semidouble; and 'Wirral Supreme', double white.

Cimicifuga **(bugbane).** These are aristocratic foliage plants for moist soil. *C. racemosa* flowers midsummer with tall white bottle-brush spikes over dark green leaves on black wiry stems that reach 5 feet (1.5 m). *C. simplex* is smaller and flowers later, in the autumn. *C. simplex* 'Atropurpurea' is recommended for its almost black foliage that blends with cool or hot colours. It is striking when planted with gold-leafed plants like *Hosta* 'August Moon' or where it can echo the red veining of Japanese painted fern (*Athyrium niponicum* 'Pictum'). *C. simplex* 'Brunette' also has sweetly fragrant white blossoms on 6-foot (1.8-m) stalks in late summer, and it maintains its dark purple-black foliage colour even in the shade.

Coreopsis verticillata **'Moonbeam'.** This is a mounding plant that produces masses of lemon-yellow daisylike flowers on 2-foot (60-cm) stems. Blooms until frost if you deadhead.

Crocosmia **(montbretia).** These easy-to-grow attention grabbers are now available in interesting apricot through red colours. In late summer their flower sprays arch above spear-shaped leaves and make a good addition to hot borders in full sun. They look good partnered with nasturtium, dahlia and kniphofia, along with the muted tones of heucheras, fennel or cotinus. 'Lucifer' stands 5 feet (1.5 m) tall with vermilion-red flowers. 'Golden Fleece' has soft yellow flowers and amber buds. 'George Davidson' has light burnt-orange flowers and reaches just 1 1/2 feet (45 cm), so it's good for containers.

***Cynara cardunculus* (cardoon).** These statuesque plants have thistlelike flower heads that are edible, attractive to insects and useful for flower arrangements. Spiny, silvery-grey leaves grow on grey, woolly, 5-foot (1.5-m) stalks. Plant in rich soil in full sun, sheltered from strong winds and protected in winter with dry mulch. Great focus for the back or front of the herbaceous border.

Dahlia. These midsummer-flowering tuberous perennials are enjoying a resurgence. They are available in countless varieties, from soft pastels to brilliant colours, and several cultivars have desirable dark foliage. See the August chapter for suggestions.

***Delphinium* spp.** The most widely grown delphiniums in this area are the Giant Pacific Hybrids. Plant breeders are still seeking new delphiniums, emphasizing shorter growth times and the introduction of new colours in brilliant pinks and reds. Delphiniums like a position in full sun, and with their towering spires of bloom, they are ideal for the back of a border. They require careful staking, as the heavy flower spikes will break off under the pressure of heavy rain. After they have finished flowering in June, their spikes should be cut off at the base, so that the plants can bloom again in late summer. Plants can

easily be started from seed, or you can buy young plants in May. The young shoots are particularly susceptible to slug damage. Some Giant Pacific Hybrids to watch for are 'Summer Skies', light blue; 'Blue Bird', medium blue; 'Blue Jay', dark blue; and 'Galahad', white. *D.* x *belladonna* cultivars are not as eye-catching as the large-flowered hybrids, but neither are they as susceptible to rain and wind damage. These are strong, sturdy plants that grow to 2 feet (60 cm), with deeply cut leaves and airy flower clusters. Good cultivars are 'Belladonna', light blue; 'Cliveden Beauty', turquoise-blue; 'Pink Sensation', pink; and 'Casa Blanca', white. *D. grandiflora* (*D. chinense*) comes from China, and is a short-lived, bushy plant, reaching a height of 1 foot (30 cm). It blooms in June and July. Good cultivars are 'Blue Mirror', gentian-blue; 'Tom Thumb', deep blue; and 'White Butterfly', white.

***Dianthus* spp. (carnations, pinks).** Pinks are valued for their neat mounds of silver or green foliage and their deliciously fragrant flowers, which are excellent for cutting. All varieties require a sunny position in full sun and well-drained, sandy soil. They can be propagated very easily by heeled cuttings. *D.* x *allwoodii* (carnation-pink, border carnation) were made by crossing an old-fashioned pink with a perpetual-flowering carnation. They produce more blooms than the old-fashioned pinks, and are usually double. They bloom in June and July and sometimes again during the fall. Good cultivars are 'Daphne', single pink with crimson eye; 'Doris', semidouble salmon-pink, very fragrant; 'Lilian', white, fragrant; and 'Robin', double red. Most sold here are grown from seed.

D. plumarius hybrids (cottage-pink, grass-pink) make attractive border plants, with grey foliage and fragrant single or double flowers. Good cultivars are 'Pike's pink', clear pink; 'Inchmery', pale pink; and 'Mrs. Sinkins', a lovely double white, intensely fragrant.

***Dicentra* spp. (bleeding heart).** These are graceful plants with arching sprays of pendulous flowers, suitable for shady borders or a woodland setting. All except the Japanese *D. spectabilis* are native to North America and all do best in humus-rich soil. *D. cucullaria* (Dutchman's breeches) is a native of eastern and central Canada. It is a lovely plant for a shady area, with white or pinkish-white pantaloon-shaped flowers tipped with yellow. They bloom in May. *D. eximia* (fringed bleeding heart) has narrow, heart-shaped flowers carried in loose clusters above fernlike grey-green leaves. It does best in shade, but the hybrids are more tolerant of sun. 'Alba' is a white cultivar. *D. formosa* is our native bleeding heart and is very similar to *D. eximia.* Flowers are pink to deep rose. 'Sweetheart' is a dainty white form. *D. spectabilis* (Japanese, or common, bleeding heart) is taller and larger-leafed, with large, rosy-pink flowers on graceful arching branches. There is a white cultivar, 'Alba'. Like the other three species, it dies back in the summer, so should be planted with hostas, astilbes or ferns to fill in the gap.

***Echinacea purpurea* (coneflower).** A North American native valued for its medicinal uses, it blooms with rich colours in late summer. It is essential for a meadow garden or with grasses; it's good for cutting; and it produces beautiful seed heads and attracts butterflies. It likes full sun in moist but well-drained soil and grows to 3 feet (90 cm). 'Bright Star' has purple-red flower heads with a maroon centre disk; 'White Swan' has creamy white flower heads with an orange-brown disk.

***Echinops* spp. (globe thistle).** These are easy, undemanding plants to grow, with thistle-like leaves and glove-shaped, metallic-blue flowers. They last all summer and are excellent as cut flowers and for drying. For best results, cut the flowers before they are fully open. They grow best in a sunny location and rarely need division. Globe thistles grow to 3 to 4 feet (.9 to 1.2 m). Good cultivars are 'Taplow Blue', vigorous with blue flowers; and 'Veitch's Blue', with grey-green leaves and bright blue flowers.

***Eryngium* spp. (sea holly).** These striking plants vary in height from 2 to 4 feet (.6 to 1.2 m). The flowers have a central cone surrounded by a ruff of prickly, metallic bracts. In contrast, the leaves are mostly smooth and rounded. Sea holly thrives in a sunny location in well-drained soil. They are good for cutting and dry well. *E. alpinum* 'Donard' is a good cultivar, with metallic-blue flowers.

***Euphorbia* spp. (spurge).** Remarkably long-blooming greenish "flowers" (actually bracts) and excellent foliage made these plants a garden staple. You will find them in every corner of the globe, but several are native to temperate climates and are well suited to our gardens. *E. characias* and its subspecies *wulfenii* is the best known and best loved. Gertrude Jekyll wrote: ". . . though its immense yellow-green heads of bloom are at their best in May, they are still of pictoral value in June and July, while the deep-toned, grey-blue foliage is in full beauty throughout the better part of the year. It is valuable in boldly arranged flower borders, and holds its own among shrubs. . . ." It grows to 3 feet (90 cm). *E. dulcis* 'Chameleon' has rich burgundy leaves and purple-tinted, yellow-green flushed bracts. It prefers semishade with soil on the dry side. This plant can become a real pest by seeding itself everywhere, and is hard to control. *E. griffithii* 'Fireglow' grows to 3 feet (90 cm) and is enjoyed for its fiery red bracts with a golden glow to the centre. It blooms in spring and its foliage provides a striking backdrop through the summer before turning brilliant vermilion in the fall. 'Great Dixter' is slightly more compact than 'Fireglow', has darker foliage and deeper orange bracts. *E. myrsinites* has a sprawling growth habit, with blue-grey leaves and lime-green blooms that mix well with sedums in a dry summer spot. It grows to 8 inches (20 cm). *E. polychroma* grows to 1 1/2 feet (45 cm) and is a reliable, slow-spreading, spring-blooming plant for semishade to full sun. It too has showy yellow-green bracts and foliage that turns bright red in autumn.

Geranium spp. (cranesbill, hardy geranium). These are the true geraniums. The bedding plants we commonly call geraniums are, in fact, pelargoniums. Geraniums are more modest in flower and very versatile. Phoebe Noble, who gardens just north of Victoria and who wrote *My Experience Growing Hardy Geraniums,* suggests "they will thrive in sun or shade, are drought resistant, disease free and tolerant of neglect."

Here are a few locally available favourites. 'Ann Folkard' is a hybrid cross that has purple-magenta flowers from June to October. *G.* x *cantabrigiense* 'Cambridge' is a versatile cultivar that will easily carpet a small border or rock garden with pink flowers. *G. cinereum* is low-growing and suitable for rock gardens or a raised bed. It grows to about 6 inches (15 cm) and blooms from June to August. Good cultivars include 'Ballerina', purplish-pink; and 'Lawrence Flatman' and 'Giuseppe', which are similar but with darker blotches at their centres.

'Cotton Candy' is a hybrid with unusual brown-coloured foliage and light pink flowers. A 5-inch (12.5-cm) plant, it looks good in the front of a border. *G. dalmaticum* has glossy evergreen foliage and bright pink flowers. It prefers a sunny rock garden and needs frequent division to flower well. *G. endressii* sports pink blossoms all summer and fall, and is hardy and very easy to grow. When crossed with *G. versicolor*, it has produced some popular hybrids, such as *G.* x *oxonianum* 'Anmore', a lovely pastel silky pink with beautiful olive-green foliage that thrives in dry semishade; 'Phoebe Noble', a clear and vibrant lipstick-pink; 'A.T. Johnson', a floriferous silvery-pink; and 'Wargrave Pink', a pale pink. *G. himalayense* forms a dense cover of dark green that turns bright autumn colours and has long-blooming flowers of soft violet-blue from June through August. A good cultivar is 'Plenum', double violet-blue.

'Johnson's Blue' is a dainty plant that flowers in June. If you shear it to the ground before it gets too untidy, it will form fresh new leaves and flowers. 'Brookside' has less flop and a longer season of blue. *G. macrorrhizum* is a valuable species that thrives in sun or shade. The flowers are magenta, and the leaves are fragrant with attractive fall tints. It makes an easy groundcover, with above-ground rhizomes that will spread to fill in bare spots, but it's easy to pull out if it's out of place. A good cultivar is 'Ingwersen's Variety', soft pink. Phoebe Noble says: "If in doubt, plant *G. macrorrhizum*." *G. phaeum* (mourning widow) is a tall variety, named for its dark colour. It loves shade and even thrives in dry conditions. 'Lily Lovell' has larger flowers and 'Album' has pure white flowers to brighten a dark corner.

'Samobor' has interesting dark blotched leaves and soft pink flowers. *G. pratense* (meadow cranesbill) grows 18 inches to 3 feet (45 to 90 cm) and blooms from June to August. The large flowers are mid-blue and grow on long stalks above handsomely cut, dark green foliage. It should be sheared to the ground as soon as the flowers fade. This will promote a new growth of leaves and prevent unwanted seedlings. 'Spinners' is a fine hybrid for small borders. Look for 'Victor Reiter Jr.' and 'Midnight Reiter', more compact and with dark flowers. *G. renardii* is a little treasure for an alpine or rockery garden. Its appeal is the solid clump of round, felted, grey-green leaves, with nondescript small white flowers.

G. sanguineum (bloody cranesbill) grows to 18 inches (45 cm) and flowers from May to August in purplish-magenta that combines well with soft pinks, greys and silvers. Good cultivars are *G. sanguineum* var. *striatum*, pale pink; 'Album', pristine white; and 'Shepherd's Warning', bright pink. *G. sylvaticum* is a desirable woodland plant that also enjoys sunny spots. It is available in mauvish-blue; a good blue called 'Mayflower'; and a white named 'Album'. *G. wallichianum* 'Buxton's Variety' bears sky-blue flowers with large white eyes from June through October. Support its trailing stems with attractive neighbours, such as lady's mantle.

Geum spp. This is a family of easy-to-grow perennials that has been improved over the past decade or so. The bright yellow, red, or orange flowers need careful placing so as not to clash with their neighbours. Geums require good drainage and good, fertile soil. They thrive equally well in full sun or partial shade and should be lifted and divided every two to three years. Some begin to bloom in May and others are still in bloom in August. Two of the most popular cultivars are 'Lady Stratheden', with clear yellow semidouble flowers, and 'Mrs. Bradshaw', with scarlet semidouble flowers.

Gypsophila paniculata (baby's breath). A great plant for the border, growing to 3 feet (90 cm). From June to August it produces an airy cloud of white or pink flowers, borne in clusters on thin wiry stems. A lovely contrast to heavier border plants. The flowers are excellent for cutting and drying. It combines well with other plants and is useful for hiding fading leaves of early bloomers. It is easily grown, but may need staking since the large sprays of flowers cause the plant to get top-heavy. It thrives in a sunny location, and added lime improves growth. Good cultivars include 'Bristol Fairy', double white and 'Rosy Veil', double soft pink.

Helleborus spp. (winter rose). See the December chapter for details of these charming winter bloomers.

Hemerocallis spp. (daylily). Daylilies are easy to grow and come in every colour but true blue. They are valued for their long display, are often fragrant, tolerate a wide range of soils, and, except for slugs, are relatively pest and disease free. They establish themselves as clumps of grassy blue to green foliage with a profusion of blossoms that seem to float in air from late spring to late summer. There are daylilies that are only 10 inches (25 cm) and giants over 60 inches (150 cm). Flower sizes range from 1 to 11 inches (2.5 to 28 cm) in diameter. Yellow, cream, white and pink pastel varieties are almost always fragrant and do best in full sun to bring out their colour. Many red and purple cultivars benefit from partial shade in the hot part of the day. Although each flower lasts only one day, new blooms arrive continuously over a long period. The old common orange daylilies carry 12 to 15 buds per stem and bloom for one month; but the new, more vigorous hybrids can carry up to 50 buds per stem and some rebloom continuously for up to five months. Daylilies prefer moist, well-drained soil, and to maximize flowering should be divided every two to five years. With over 39,000 registered varieties available, favourites other than 'Joan Senior', white; 'Stella de Oro', yellow; and 'Siloam Double Classic', double peach-pink are simply too numerous to mention. Visit display gardens at Erikson's Daylily in Langley or Beachwood Daylily in Aldergrove, as well as local nurseries.

Heuchera spp. (coral bells). Their showy evergreen leaves and lovely flower sprays make heucheras a good addition to any well-drained garden or container. The plant forms mounds of rounded, lobed, often deeply veined foliage; the flowers are good for cutting and attract bees and hummingbirds. They like sun or semi-shade and complement other foliage plants such as grasses and hostas. There are too many new varieties to list, but here are a few favourites. 'Chocolate Ruffles' has glossy mahogany-brown leaves with a ruffled edge and flowers of creamy white. 'Huntsman' has deep green foliage and blood-red repeat-blooming flowers. *H. americana* 'Palace Purple' has variegated glossy mahogany leaves, with flowers of ivory white. *H. americana* 'Pewter Veil' has silver leaves with purple undertones and charcoal-grey veins and tiny bluish-white flowers, tinged purple and green.

Iris spp. There are over 300 different species of iris. Some grow from rhizomes, some from bulbs. The bulbs are discussed in the September chapter. Of the rhizomatous iris, water lovers such as *I. laevigatae* (see "The Water Garden" in the August chapter) like boggy ground, whereas the majestic bearded iris needs to have its large tubers resting on well-drained soil, absorbing sunshine. Others, such as the Siberian iris, have such short rhizomes they almost look like bulbs, and they need moist, but not soggy, soil. By carefully choosing plants, you can have irises in flower from April to July.

The German bearded irises form a large group with many different cultivars, and it's hard to choose among them, except on a basis of colour preference. It's well worth a visit to a grower or public garden when they are in bloom. Dwarf bearded irises need similar conditions to those required for the tall bearded varieties. Since they are shorter, they are very useful at the front of a border. Good cultivars are 'Little Sapphire', silvery-blue; 'White Gem', white; and 'Joyful', yellow. *I. sibirica* (Siberian iris) is the easiest of all the irises to grow. It is not as showy as the tall bearded irises, but is becoming more widely grown as gardeners come to appreciate its usefulness and resistance to disease. It does best in full sun, but will tolerate some shade. The flowers are small and dainty, and their clumps of rushlike foliage provide continuing interest through the summer. The clumps tend to double in size each year, so they should be divided every second year in early spring, by slicing the clump into sections with a sharp spade. Good cultivars are 'White Swirl', white; 'Persimmon', clear blue; and 'Royal Ensign', purple.

Lupinus (lupine). *L. polyphyllus*, one of our native lupines, is probably one of the parents of the Russell Hybrids that are grown so widely in gardens around the world. These are large spreading plants, growing up to 5 feet (1.5 m) in height, with densely packed spires of bloom. The colourful flowers, many of which are bicoloured, bloom in May from a base of soft green, finely cut leaves. They can be grown from seed or bought as plants. Unfortunately they are short-lived, and should be replaced after three or four years when they begin to lose their vigour. They do best in full sun and a lime-free soil. Most are grown here from seed.

Osteospermum spp. Osteospermum are neat, compact plants with dense evergreen foliage and prolific, starry, daisy blooms. Some recently bred varieties are hardy perennials in our climate, others are less vigorous and best treated as container or bedding-out plants. They are sun-lovers for well-drained, fertile soil. Regular deadheading will continue their flower display from early summer to autumn. Wonderful colours and a long season make them superb for small gardens. 'Buttermilk', with brown-backed yellow flowers; 'Silver Sparkler', with blue-backed white flowers with a blue eye; 'Langtrees', pink; and 'White Pim', a pure white, are all tough plants that look striking with grey-leaved artemisias, blue-grey grasses or helichrysum.

Paeonia spp. (peony). These are among the loveliest of all the hardy perennials, and some of the most rewarding to grow. Hardy, dependable and resistant to most pests, peonies grow in practically any soil in full sun or light shade. They are extremely long-lived and should not be disturbed if they are growing and flowering well. They are heavy feeders, and flowering is improved by a fall application of well-rotted manure or compost and a spring application of bone meal. The secret to successful blooming is to not plant them too deeply. The dormant buds at the top of the fat tubers should be just about 1 inch (2.5 cm) below the soil surface. Stake them early in the season before growth appears to protect them from being beaten to the ground during summer rains. *P. delavayi* has deep purplish-red flowers. Many lovely hybrid forms are available: 'Banksii', purple-red double flowers with white tips; 'Godaishu' (syn. 'Five Continents'), white semidouble flowers; 'Hana-Kisoi' (syn. 'Floral Rivalry'), shell-pink semidouble flowers. The list of mouth-watering choices is very long.

P. lactiflora (Chinese peony) is one of the parents of most of today's peonies. Hundreds of named cultivars are on the market and new ones are produced every year, so it is difficult to single out a few that are best. Impressive though the new hybrids are, the older hybrids are still worth growing. 'Festiva Maxima', white with crimson flecks, for instance, is glorious, and was developed over a hundred years ago. Some other good double cultivars are 'Angel Cheeks', fragrant, pale pink flowers with red-striped central petals; 'Ballerina', paler pink; 'Duchess de Nemours', white with good scent; 'Sarah Bernhardt', apple-blossom pink, fragrant; and 'Karl Rosenfeld', wine-red. Good semidoubles are 'Cytherea', bright pink; and 'Nathalie', clear pink. Good singles are 'Avant Garde', pink; 'Le Printemps', cream; 'Bowl of Beauty', pink with lots of yellow stamens; and 'Rose Diamond', salmon-rose. Good Japanese hybrids are 'Isani Gidui', white; 'Ama-no-sode', pink; and 'Gay Paree', red outer petals, creamy pink centre.

P. lutea var. *lutea* is a lower-growing plant to 3 feet (90 cm); it flowers yellow and red. *P. officinalis* (common peony, apothecary's peony) is a medicinal peony that has been grown for hundreds of years. It is an old favourite in the garden, and one of the earliest peonies to bloom. It has single, scarlet-red flowers and deeply cut foliage. Good cultivars are 'Alba Plena', double white; 'Rosea Plena', double rose; and 'Rubra Plena', double dark red. *P. mlokosewitschii* (molly the witch) is early blooming, with grey leaves and yellow flowers. *P. suffruticosa* (tree peonies) are woody, upright, deciduous shrubs to 7 feet (2.2 m). They produce bowl-shaped, occasionally scented, pink, white, gold, apricot, red or purple, single to semidouble flowers in late spring and early summer.

Papaver orientale (Oriental poppy). Cheerful, bright red poppies have been popular for a long time in the June border. New cultivars have increased the choice of colours to salmon, white, and deep pink, in double or single forms. Poppies prefer a position in full sun, but will tolerate partial shade. Their one drawback is that they are slightly untidy after flowering, so grow something like baby's breath, asters or daylilies near them to hide decaying foliage and fill gaps after flowering. Good varieties include 'Cedric Morris', large, pale buff-pink flowers with black blotches; 'Mrs. Perry', salmon pink; 'Black and White', white petals with black blotches; 'Patty's Plum', deep plum petals with black centre blotches; and 'Coral Reef', vivid coral pink with a dark centre.

Penstemon spp. (penstemon). There is a resurgence of interest in penstemon, a semi-evergreen clumping perennial that is grown for its foxglovelike, tubular flowers from early summer through fall. Regular deadheading will help guarantee a constant display of flowers. Wonderful colours in the pink, carmine, purple and maroon range, an old-fashioned elegance and a preference for dry sun make it a good choice for containers as well as borders and rock gardens. Some favourites include 'Huskers Red', 1996 Perennial Plant of the Year, 3 feet (90 cm) tall, a vigorous evergreen with deep maroon foliage and pale pink tubular flowers that naturalizes well with ornamental grasses; 'Midnight', 3 feet (90 cm), with dark indigo-blue blooms; 'Blackbird', 2 feet (60 cm), a large-flowered deep maroon-purple hybrid that mixes nicely in a border with pale-coloured achillea or *Geranium endressii*; 'Apple Blossom', with pale pink flowers with white throats; 'Garnet', with small, deep wine-red flowers; and 'Purple Haze', 6 to 12 inches (15 to 30 cm), a University of British Columbia introduction with a compact shrubby form and lavender-blue summer flowers.

Phlox spp. For fragrance, spectacular long-lasting flowers, and ease of culture, phlox is deservedly popular. It is particularly useful as it blooms midseason. Phlox needs a rich, well-cultivated soil. The plants should be spaced far enough apart to allow good air circulation, thus helping to prevent powdery mildew. To maintain a succession of bloom, remove flower trusses as they fade. *P. maculata* (meadow phlox) is a native of eastern North America. It is an easy plant to grow, thriving in sun or partial shade, and is a compact plant growing to 3 feet (90 cm). Good cultivars are 'Alpha', lavender pink; 'Delta', blush pink; and 'Omega', white. The popular phloxes are hybrids of *P. paniculata* (border phlox, summer phlox), in colours of white, pink, salmon, scarlet and purple. Heights vary from 18 inches (45 cm) to 4 feet (1.2 m), so there are hybrids suitable for any position in the border. Self-colours, those with the eye the same colour as the petals, are the most popular, but many varieties have flowers with an eye of a contrasting colour. Good cultivars are 'Mother of Pearl', blush white; 'Norah Leigh', variegated foliage, mauve flowers; 'Prince of Orange', salmon-orange; and 'Sandringham', rose-pink.

Polemonium caeruleum (Jacob's ladder). The leaves of this plant are arranged in pairs resembling the rungs of a ladder, on upright or arching stems. Clusters of pale blue or white, bell-shaped flowers bloom from June to July. They are not very long-lived plants, but they seed themselves freely. They are best in partial shade, in cool moist conditions, but will tolerate sun if the roots are kept moist. Good cultivars are 'Blue Pearl', dark blue with a yellow eye; and 'Lacteum', white flowers.

Rodgersia spp. This bold plant is rewarding for its striking foliage. *R. aesculifolia* is an attractive tropical-looking plant, ideal at water's edge; it prefers damp soils in sunny sites or fertile rich soils in partial shade. Creamy white flower panicles appear in midsummer. Its large leathery leaves resemble horse chestnut leaves. *R. pinnata* has young bronze leaves that become emerald green as they mature, then turn to copper. In July it sprouts sprays of pink and white flowers. 'Alba' is the white form; 'Superba' has leaves that remain bronze. The leaves of *R. podophylla* are similar to *R. aesculifolia*, and its creamy white flowers are the nicest of all the rodgersias.

Rudbeckia spp. (black-eyed susan). These tall daisylike flowers with bronze/green centre cones contribute long-lasting displays of glowing yellow, orange and russet from late summer through autumn. They make a good addition to borders or naturalized in meadow or woodland gardens. *R. nitida* 'Herbstonne' grows to 5 to 6 feet (1.5 to 1.8 m) and makes a stately clump of large golden flowers; *R. fulgida* 'Goldsturm' was Perennial Plant of the Year for 1999.

Salvia spp. (sage). The salvia-obsessed can find many outstanding, easy-to-grow perennial salvias to add mounds of colour from summer through fall. They rebloom when deadheaded and last forever as cut flowers—but leave some end-of-season seed heads. *S. nemorosa* 'Blue Hill' is a compact 18 to 24 inches (45 to 60 cm) with sky-blue flowers. 'East Friesland' has deep blue flowers. *S. x superba* 'May Night', the 1997 Perennial Plant of the Year, has deep indigo-blue flower spikes to 28 inches (70 cm) in May and June. 'Rose Queen', 30 inches (75 cm), has rose-pink flowers and grey tinted leaves. *S. uliginosa* (bog sage), 2 to 4 feet (.6 to 1.2 m), sends up tall stems with sky-blue racemes in fall, and likes moist soil and full sun. *S. officinalis* (common sage) is a culinary herb with woolly aromatic leaves; 'Purpurascens' has red-purple young leaves.

Sedum (stonecrop). There are many good varieties of this late summer bloomer for the sunny or semishaded dry parts of the garden or containers. 'Matrona', the European Plant of the Year 2000, has large, purple-red foliage clumps and large rose-pink flowers. 'Autumn Joy' opens with bright, salmon-pink flowers that darken to mahogany for the winter. 'Bertram Anderson' is a more prostrate form with very dark mahogany foliage and deep rose flowers. It grows to 6 inches (15 cm) and combines well with heucheras and fine-textured festuca grasses.

Sempervivum **spp. (houseleek or hens and chicks).** These spiky, compact little plants tucked into pots, on walls or along pathways are perfect for small gardens. Their plump, sculpted leaves in subtle colours are the main attraction, but starry spring flowers (mainly red or yellow) are a bonus. They like sunny, well-drained sites, tolerate neglect and are easy to grow. For containers, add plenty of grit to your soil mix, so they don't get waterlogged. Protect them from excessive winter rains with a shelter of glass or plastic, or overwinter in a cold frame or unheated greenhouse. They reproduce with offset "babies" around the base of the plant; these can be left to root and form a cushion of rosettes, or they can be detached and grown separately. Hundreds of varieties are available, but they are generally either of the spidery type that develop dense webbing between leaf tips, or the fleshy varieties with smooth, succulent leaves that form striking rosettes.

Stachys byzantina, **syn.** *S. lanata* **(woolly lamb's ears).** This is one of the most appealing and useful plants for the front of the border. It has thickly felted, woolly grey leaves that make a dense, weed-smothering mat. It looks very attractive with dianthus and old roses, and plants with pink or blue flowers. It thrives in well-drained soil in sun or partial shade. The woolly, grey-white flower spikes with small purple flowers are excellent for dried flower arrangements.

Thalictrum **spp. (meadow rue).** This tall, fairylike plant has elegant glaucous foliage on stiff stems and large airy plumes of flowers from June through September. It prefers part sun and moist but well-drained soil. It can grow up to 7 feet (2.1 m) and is a wonderful filler plant that can be placed near the front of the border to appreciate its daintiness. *T. aquilegifolium* is a popular form with powder pink or ivory flowers. *T. delavayi* 'Album' has pure white flowers. *T. flavum* spp. *glaucum* has lime-coloured flowers. *T. finetii* has 1-inch (2.5-cm) lavender flowers with yellow stamens.

 # Guided by Colour

Colour is often the determining factor that creates a sense of space, of coolness or of warmth in our gardens. Whether we choose harmonizing or contrasting schemes is a matter of personal choice, but successful combinations can be visualized before planting. Consider your favourite colours and think about focal points as well as background to create a satisfying whole picture.

Silver-grey foliage softens and blends the background. Dark, almost black foliage can add drama, and yellow-greens provide sunny accents. Here are some colour ideas. The lists include plants for their stem colour, flowers and fruit, as well as foliage.

Silver-grey foliage

Use silver-grey to set off and unify other colours. It enhances white, brightens pastels, softens brilliant, buffers warring and unifies diverse. Remember, these plants generally prefer full sun and well-drained soil.

Trees. *Cedrus atlantica* var. *glauca* (Atlas cedar), *Eucalyptus* spp., *Chamaecyparis lawsoniana* 'Pembury', *Cytisus battandieri* (pineapple broom), *Elaeagnus angustifolia* (Russian olive), *Pinus sylvestris* (Scots pine), *Pinus koraiensis* (Korean pine), *Pyrus salicifolia* 'Pendula' (willowleaf pear).

Shrubs. *Artemisia* 'Lambrook Silver', *A.* 'Powis Castle', *Hebe* spp., *Lavandula* (lavender), *Rosa glauca, Santolina* spp.

Perennials. *Cynara cardunculus* (cardoon), *Dianthus* spp. (pinks), *Festuca glauca* (blue fescue), *Helichrysum petiolare, Hosta* spp., *Onopordum* (Scotch thistle), *Perovskia atriplicifolia* (Russian sage), *Salvia argentea, Stachys byzantina* (syn. *S. lanata*) (lamb's ears), *Verbascum* (mullein).

Black beauties

Flowers and foliage in shades of maroon or purple appear as black as garden beetles and create bold drama. They are a strong counterpoint to vivid red, orange or yellow petals, a formal complement to whites and a dramatic enhancement to contemporary architecture or even painted surfaces. Keep in mind that too much black may be gloomy, so don't overdo it.

Trees and shrubs. *Acer palmatum* 'Dissectum Nigrum' (maple), *Berberis thunbergii atropurpurea* (Japanese barberry), *Cercis canadensis* 'Forest Pansy' (eastern redbud), *Corylus maxima* 'Purpurea' (filbert), *Cotinus coggygria* 'Royal Purple' (smoke bush), *Phyllostachys nigra* (black bamboo), *Prunus* 'Nigra' (purple-leaved plum), *Salix gracilistyla* 'Melanostachys' (willow).

Annuals and perennials. *Alcea rosea* 'Nigra' (hollyhock), *Angelica sylvestris* 'Purpurea', *Anthriscus sylvestris* 'Ravenswing', *Antirrhinum* 'Black Dragon' (snapdragon), *Beta vulgaris* 'Bull's Blood' (black-leaved beet), *Carex nigra, Dahlia* 'Arabian Night', *Dianthus barbatus* Nigrescens Group (sweet william), *Euphorbia dulcis* 'Chameleon', *Geranium pratense* 'Victor Reiter', *Heuchera* 'Pewter Veil', *Helleborus orientalis* 'Black Strain', *Hemerocallis* (daylily), *Iris chrysographes* 'Before the Storm', *I.* 'Black Dragon', *I.* 'Hello Darkness', *I.* 'Michael Paul',

I. 'Paint it Black', *Knautia macedonica, Lysimachia* 'Purpurea' (loosestrife), *Ocimum basilicum purpurascens* (purple-leaved basil), *Ophiopogon planascapus* 'Nigrescens' (black mondo grass), *Phormium tenax, Rodgersia podophylla, Sedum* 'Vera Jameson', *Solenostemon* 'Midnight' (coleus), *Trifolium repens* 'Purpurascens Quadrifolium' (clover), *Tulipa* 'Black Parrot', 'Queen of the Night', 'Ebony Queen', *Viola* 'Black Magic'.

Yellow-green plants

Chartreuse, lime-green, lemon or butter-yellow all provide strong accents when paired with dark green backgrounds and contrasting flowers, especially in full sun.

Trees and shrubs. *Acer japonicum* 'Aureum', *Catalpa bignonioides* 'Aurea', *Ginkgo biloba, Gleditsia triacanthos* 'Sunburst', *Lonicera nitida* 'Baggesen's Gold' (boxleaf honeysuckle), *Philadelphus coronarius* 'Aureus' (mock orange), *Physocarpus opulifolium* 'Dart's Gold', *Robinia pseudoacacia* 'Frisia', *Rhododendron lutescens, Rosa* 'Fruhlingsgold', *Sorbus aria* 'Aurea', *Spiraea japonica* 'Goldflame'.

Perennials. *Alchemilla mollis* (lady's mantle), *Anthemis* 'E.C. Buxton', *Carex elata* 'Aurea', *Coreopsis* 'Moonbeam', *Euphorbia amygdaloides robbiae, E. polychroma, E. characias wulfenii, Hedera helix* 'Gold Heart', *H. helix* 'Buttercup', *Helichrysum petiolare* 'Limelight', *Helleborus argutifolius, Hemerocallis* (daylily)—various cultivars, *Hosta* 'Gold Standard' and many other cultivars, *Humulus lupulus* 'Aureus' (golden hops), *Iris* 'Green Spot', *I. pallida* 'Variegata', *Kniphofia* 'Green Jade', *Limnanthes douglasii* (poached egg plant), *Milium effusum* 'Aureum' (Bowles golden grass), *Origanum vulgare* 'Aureum' (golden marjoram), *Verbascum* 'Gainsborough'.

Creating a White Garden

The cool, classical purity of an all-white garden can give the illusion of tranquillity in a crowded city. It makes even the tiniest yard feel more spacious and serene, and it helps to harmonize the surroundings. White flowers become more prominent towards dusk, as other colours fade into their surroundings, and many are strongly scented. Plants with grey foliage are very useful, providing a transition between dark green leaves and stark white flowers. Flowers that are just off-white add contrast and interest.

Below is a planting plan to help you create a white garden. All these plants are described in the book and the appropriate, white cultivars are listed here, although you may have to search a bit for some of them. All the plants given are perennials except for *Rosa* 'Iceberg', and *Hebe pinguifolia* and *Philadelphus coronarius*, both shrubs.

back

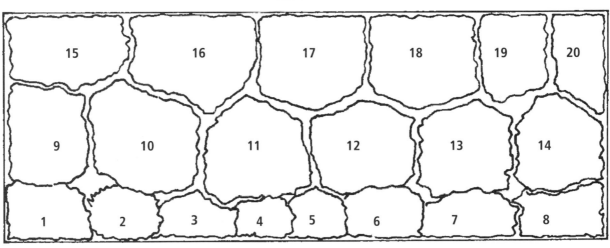

1. *Dianthus* 'Mrs. Sinkins' (cottage pink)
2. *Hebe pinguifolia* (hebe)
3. *Stachys byzantina*, also called *S. lanata* (woolly lamb's ears)
4. *Dianthus* x *alwoodii* 'Lilian' (border carnation)
5. *Campanula carpatica* 'White Clips' (Carpathian harebell)
6. *Artemisia schmidtiana* 'Silver Mound' (artemisia)
7. *Aster novi-belgii* 'Snowsprite' (aster)
8. *Iris* 'White Gem' (dwarf iris)
9. *Geranium sanguineum* 'Album' (hardy geranium)
10. *Iris sibirica* 'White Swirl' (Siberian iris)
11. *Paeonia* 'Isanu Gidui' (peony)
12. *Eryngium alpinum* (sea holly)
13. *Campanula persicifolia* 'Snowdrift' (peach-leaf bellflower)
14. *Gypsophila paniculata* 'Bristol Fairy' (baby's breath)
15. *Phlox maculata* 'Mother of Pearl' (meadow phlox)
16. *Philadelphus coronarius* (mock orange)
17. *Delphinium* Pacific Hybrid 'Galahad' (delphinium)
18. *Rosa* 'Iceberg' (rose)
19. *Hemerocallis* 'Joan Senior' (daylily)
20. *Chrysanthemum* x *superbum* 'Wirral Pride' (shasta daisy)

Recommended Reading

Annuals

Hessayon, D.G. *The New Flower Expert.* pbi Publications, London, 1996.

Phillips, Roger and Martyn Rix. *Perfect Plants.* Random House, New York, 1996.

Rice, Graham. *Discovering Annuals.* Timber Press, Portland, 1999.

Taylor, Norman. *Taylor's Guide to Annuals.* Houghton Mifflin, Boston, 1986.

Perennials

Hendy, Jenny and David Tarrant. *New Perennials: The Latest and Best Perennials.* Whitecap Books, Vancouver, 1999.

Jones, Carolyn. *The Complete Guide to Perennials for Amateurs and Experts.* Whitecap Books, Vancouver, 1990.

Lovejoy, Ann. *The Border in Bloom: A Northwest Garden Through the Seasons.* Sasquatch Books, Seattle, 1990.

Phillips, Roger and Martyn Rix. *The Random House Book of Perennials, Vol. 1 Early Perennials, Vol. 2 Late Perennials.* Random House, New York, 1991.

Colour and design

Hobbs, Thomas. *Shocking Beauty.* Raincoast Books, Vancouver, 1999.

Lawson, Andrew. *The Gardener's Book of Colour.* Frances Lincoln, London, 1996.

Pope, Nori and Sandra. *Color by Design.* Soma, San Francisco, 1998.

June

June is a very rewarding time for gardeners. All the hard work and preparation of earlier months has paid off, the weeds are under control, annuals are planted and perennials are in bloom. Long June evenings are ideal for puttering in the garden, relaxing after a busy day and listening to friends admire your hard work. Compliments are always welcome, and you might pick up some gardening tips as well.

This is, of course, the month for roses. For centuries these lovely flowers have been prized and cultivated by rose lovers around the world, from ancient Persian rulers and Chinese emperors to early B.C. settlers. Today private and public gardens display an amazing range and variety of roses, and it's hard to imagine planning a garden without at least one favourite bush. In our cities you find them tumbling over backyard fences, struggling bravely beside derelict buildings, and enjoying the luxury of special beds and tender care.

June is also the time for strawberries. Although we can now obtain these tender fruits year-round, the imported ones bear no resemblance to our own sweet, juicy berries fresh from the garden. Several varieties are specially suited to our climate, and two of the best of these are 'Totem' and 'Tristar'. The biggest problem in growing strawberries is virus diseases, so try to make sure the plants you buy are certified virus-free. If you have no strawberries in your garden, take your buckets, friends and children out to the nearest "U-pick" field.

Many perennials are in bloom this month, especially the showy delphiniums, peonies, irises, poppies and bellflowers. Look for dainty Siberian iris as well as its more dramatic relative, the German bearded iris. There are some lovely shrubs in bloom now, including weigela and beauty bush (*Kolkwitzia amabilis*), both of which are especially attractive to hummingbirds. This month we feature the shrubs that bloom during the months of May to September.

Although there is plenty to do in the garden this month, especially if you have a vegetable garden, the most important thing is to take time to relax and enjoy it.

Garden Highlights

indicates fragrance

Bulbs

Allium spp. (ornamental onions), *Camassia* (camas), *Eremurus robustus* (foxtail lily), *Lilium candidum* (Madonna lily),* *L. regale* (lily).*

Perennials

Achillea (yarrow), *Aconitum* spp. (monkshood), *Alchemilla mollis* (lady's mantle), *Aruncus dioicus* (goatsbeard), *Astilbe*, *Campanula* spp. (bellflowers), *Delphinium* hybrids, *Dictamnus albus* (gas plant),* *Digitalis* spp. (foxglove), *Filipendula* spp. (meadowsweet), *Hemerocallis* spp. (daylily),* *Iris sibirica* (iris), *I. versicolor* (iris), *Lychnis* spp., *Papaver* spp. (poppy), *Paeonia* spp. (peony), *Phlomis* spp. (Jerusalem sage), *Polemonium caeruleum* (Jacob's ladder), *Thalictrum* spp. (meadow rue), *Tradescantia* spp. (spiderwort), *Trollius* spp. (globeflower), *Verbascum* spp. (mullein), *Zantedeschia aethiopica* (calla lily).

Climbers

Hydrangea anomala ssp. *petiolaris* (climbing hydrangea), *Lonicera* spp. (honeysuckle),* *Rosa* spp. (climbing and rambling roses),* *Solanum crispum* (potato vine).

Shrubs

Buddleia alternifolia (butterfly bush), *Kolkwitzia amabilis* (beauty bush), *Philadelphus* spp. (mock orange),* *Potentilla* spp. (cinquefoil), *Rosa* spp. (roses),* *Weigela*.

Trees

Cornus kousa (Japanese dogwood), *Robinia pseudoacacia* (black locust), *Styrax japonica* (Japanese snowbell tree).*

June Checklist

Annuals, perennials and bulbs

- Keep planting out bedding plants. Feed regularly with organic fertilizer and water well. Keep an eye on containers and hanging baskets, as they dry out very quickly.
- Keep watering bulbs until the leaves have turned yellow, and can be pulled off gently.
- Continue staking tall perennials, and keep perennial beds neat by picking fresh flowers for indoor display and faded flowers for the compost.
- Divide up German bearded irises after flowering.
- Sow perennials, such as phlox, yarrow, columbine, lupine and delphinium, in a seed bed for next summer.
- Mulch lilies with compost or well-rotted manure.

Trees, shrubs and climbers

- Prune back deciduous shrubs, such as mock orange, after flowering.
- Start taking shrub cuttings (see the April chapter).
- Cut back suckers on lilacs, and prune off faded flower heads.
- Deadhead rhododendrons and azaleas, and mulch if not already done.
- Keep newly planted hedges, trees and shrubs well watered.
- Check for aphids, mildew and black spot on roses, and pick off and destroy diseased leaves.

Fruits, vegetables and herbs

- Remove about one-third of the immature apples to get bigger fruit and prevent branches breaking from too much weight later on.
- Plant out tomatoes, zucchini and cucumbers (see the July chapter).
- Thin out earlier sowings and continue to sow lettuce, carrots, spinach and radishes (see the July chapter).
- Keep vegetable garden well weeded and watch for signs of pests and diseases.
- Continue to nip out side shoots of single-stemmed varieties of tomatoes, and support with stakes.
- Continue sowing winter vegetables (see the July chapter). Start rutabagas and late cole crops.
- Cut off flowers of chives to encourage new foliage.

Other garden activities

- Finish all pool planting (see the August chapter).
- Mow lawn regularly, keeping it at least 2 inches (5 cm) high, and keep it well watered.

- Turn compost.
- Maintain a regular check for disease and insect problems.
- Feed house plants and move outside into a shady spot for their annual summer holiday.

 # Roses

Of all flowers, none is as universally loved, written about and romanticized as the rose. The rose was the flower of Aphrodite, the Greek goddess of love and beauty, and of Venus, the Roman goddess of love. Even Cleopatra succumbed to its charm, and first greeted Mark Antony in a room knee-deep with rose petals. Today the role of the rose as a romantic symbol continues undiminished, and it may be no coincidence that June, the month of roses, has always been the month of brides.

One of the most ardent rose growers of all time was the Empress Josephine, wife of Napoleon I. In the magnificent gardens of her Château Malmaison she attempted to grow every known variety of rose, and by the time she died in 1814 she had collected 250 different hybrids. She even commissioned Pierre-Joseph Redouté to do a series of engravings of her roses so that they would be preserved for future generations to know and enjoy.

Roses come in an incredible variety of forms, colours and fragrances, with a rose for every occasion. They are extremely versatile and can be used as shrubs, climbers, hedges and groundcover. They may be trained to cover arbours, trellises and walls, and can even be grown in containers. They make superb cut flowers and are attractive grown in a mixed border with perennials, shrubs and annuals.

Choosing roses

Some roses are a bit fussy and need a lot of care, but remember that roses originally grew happily in the wild long before they were cultivated. Select healthy specimens of disease-resistant varieties that are appropriate for our climate and suited to your specific garden site, and you can grow many roses that thrive on simple basic care and maintenance. Before choosing your roses, it's a good idea to visit some of the wonderful rose gardens in our area for inspiration. Stanley Park, VanDusen Gardens, the Rose Garden on the University of British Columbia campus and Butchart Gardens will all encourage you. Take time to think about the colours, shapes and fragrances you like, consult local rose society recommendation lists, local rose nursery catalogues and the lists included here, and then go rose shopping with your preferences in mind.

Buying roses

Roses are sold either bare-root or in containers. Container-grown roses are the most popular, and are easy to get from garden centres. They are the only ones sold during the growing season. They have the advantage that you can see what you are buying.

Bare-root roses are lifted from the ground at the nursery during the dormant season, from October to March, and are usually purchased by mail order from specialist suppliers. Buying bare-root roses enables you to get exactly what you want, not what the local stores have to offer.

Some roses are sold prepackaged in polythene or waxed cardboard, with moist peat around the roots. These roses tend to be cheaper, but you'll need to choose and inspect them carefully before purchasing, and they should only be bought during the dormant season.

Where to plant

Roses do best in full sun. Most like at least six hours of sun a day, but there are some roses that tolerate partial shade. They love rich, moisture-retentive, well-drained soil, and need to be sheltered from strong winds. They should be planted away from trees and shrubs that will deprive them of nourishment.

If possible, it is best to prepare the planting site a month or two before receiving the plants. Dig the bed thoroughly, remove any weeds and mix in lots of well-rotted manure or compost. The deeper the soil is prepared the better, even to a depth of 18 to 24 inches (45 to 60 cm).

When to plant

Bare-root roses can be planted at any time during the dormant season, usually between late October and late March, and the ideal month is November. They should not be planted when the ground is frozen. Container-grown roses can be planted at any time during the year, although spring or fall is preferable.

Planting distances

Rose growers recommend the following planting distances for roses.

Average-sized hybrid teas and floribundas	2 feet	(60 cm)
Tall hybrid tea and floribundas	3 feet	(90 cm)
Low-growing shrub roses	3 feet	(90 cm)
Standard roses	4 feet	(1.2 m)
Average-sized shrub roses	5 feet	(1.5 m)
Climbers	7 feet	(2.1 m)
Ramblers	10 feet	(3 m)

How to plant

Prepare a planting mixture, about a bucketful per rose, of soil to which you add a handful each of well-rotted compost and bone meal.

When you have unpacked your new, bare-root roses, check them carefully. Remove any damaged shoots by cutting back to the first healthy bud below the damage. Cut out any decayed or thin shoots and remove leaves or hips. At the same time, cut back any damaged or long roots to 12 inches (30 cm). Put the roses in a bucket of water and give them a good drink.

Dig the planting hole, making sure it is deep enough for the budding union—the point where the plant is budded onto the root stock—to be 1 inch (2.5 cm) below soil level, and wide enough for the roots to fan out as evenly as possible all round.

Hold the rose in position and cover the roots carefully with the planting mixture, firming down the earth by gentle treading. Add more planting mixture until the hole is full. Tread down again gently, water well and firm the soil once more.

The planting hole for climbing roses should be at least 15 inches (38 cm) away from the wall or fence. This will help to provide adequate air circulation and prevent dryness at the roots.

Planting container-grown roses

Prior to planting, give the rose a good soak. Move it carefully from its pot, so as not to disturb the soil packed around its roots, and place it carefully into a container prepared with the rose potting mix mentioned above.

If the rose has been grown in a fibre pot and you buy it during the growing season, plant it in its pot, rather than risk damaging the roots. Soak the plant, pot and all, for 24 hours to soften it, make a few slits in the side of the pot, peel back the rim to below soil level, and plant. Fill in the space between the pot or the rootball and surrounding soil with more soil mix, making sure the budding union is just below soil level. Firm down and water frequently until the plant is established.

How to care for roses

If they are planted properly and fed and watered regularly, roses will grow and flower with very little attention. However, they do need plenty of water during the growing season. During prolonged dry spells they should be soaked thoroughly once or twice a week, depending on the moisture capacity of the soil. In most cases it is best to water early in the morning, applying the water directly to the soil, not the foliage. Water on rose leaves encourages development of diseases such as powdery mildew.

All roses benefit from a good mulch of well-rotted animal manure or compost in the spring, which can be worked into the top inch (2.5 cm) of soil in the fall. They need regular feeding with organic fertilizers such as fish and seaweed products, applied to the leaves in dilute solution. They will benefit from slow-acting bone meal dug into the soil at planting time or scratched into the topsoil. A top-dressing of sulphate of potash in the spring, or an application of wood ash, which also contains potash, helps to ripen the stems and improve the flowers. Regular removal of dead blooms encourages a succession of strong flowering shoots throughout the growing season.

Pruning

In order that your roses perform at their best, they need regular pruning to achieve a balance of flower production and shrub form.

You cannot kill a rose by pruning, and you can always do better next year, so fear not, just get out your secateurs and loppers, study your rose to decide whether it is to be short and bushy or long and rambling, and go to it.

Most roses produce their flowers on growth of the current year and can be pruned in early spring. Roses that flower on last season's wood, such as the true ramblers, many of the species roses, old garden roses and some of the modern shrub roses, should be pruned as soon as flowering is over in summer or autumn. Some ramblers and old garden roses develop graceful arching branches without much pruning at all.

All pruning cuts should be finished cleanly and made immediately above an outward-facing bud. Dead or diseased wood should be removed, and weak, damaged or crossing shoots should be removed entirely. Always prune to an outward-pointing bud to allow light and air to reach the centre of the plant.

Pests and diseases

The best protection against pests such as aphids and spider mites and disease such as black spot and powdery mildew is prevention. The first step is to select healthy, disease-resistant varieties that enjoy our climate. After planting well, feeding and watering regularly, you need to remember good hygiene. Always clean up pruning debris and litter because insects and disease spores overwinter in dead matter left under the plants. Be tolerant of some imperfection, handpick the blemishes and ruthlessly "shovel prune" the hopeless failures to thrive.

For more specifics, check the section on Common Pests and Diseases, and the detailed care of roses given in each month's checklist.

A selection of roses

There are nearly 5,000 different roses. Listed below are some interesting, unusual and lovely species and hybrids that are available here and suited to our climate. Although more nurseries are carrying a wider variety, you may have to search for them from the specialty growers (see "Specialty Nurseries, General Nurseries and Garden Centres" in the Resources section). As much as possible, roses are listed here according to their age: old roses first, modern hybrids last.

The originals: species roses and their hybrids

The originals are the wild roses, some of the 200 ancestors of all our present-day roses. Nearly all of them bloom only once with lovely, usually single blooms that can last for several weeks. Species roses are easy to grow, thrive on healthy neglect and require little pruning. They are ideal for the beginning rose grower. Many of them have been crossed to create handsome hybrids with the hardiness and form of the species. Some lovely species, all suitable for woodland planting, are *Rosa dupontii*, with pure white flowers and golden brown stamens; *R. glauca* (*R. rubrifolia*), with plum-coloured new shoots and mauve-pink flowers; and *R. moyesii*, with bright red flowers and spectacular hips in the fall. If you would like to add native rose species to your garden, look for *Rosa nutkana* (Nootka rose) or *Rosa woodsii* (Wood's rose). These shrubs, to about 5 feet (1.5 cm), have clear lilac-pink flowers, gold autumn leaves and fat red hips in winter. The UBC Plant Introduction Scheme has brought out a seedling of the Wood's rose called 'Kimberley'. It is a superior, compact shrub with pale pink flowers and good rose hips, suitable for mass plantings.

Old garden roses

Fragrant, hardy and tolerant of imperfect growing conditions, the old garden roses have replaced hybrid tea roses. Although many have a short flowering season, they make up for it with their wonderful variations of colour, form and fragrance, and most produce good hips in the fall, often with good fall leaf colour. Gardeners are in love with them, and the growers have responded to demands, so that the old garden roses are readily available. Under this heading come the gallica, cabbage, moss, damask, Portland, alba, China, Bourbon, noisette and hybrid perpetual roses. Quite a list! Here is our selection.

Gallica roses (*Rosa gallica*). These were the first garden roses cultivated and are very important in the evolution of modern roses. They are easy to grow, tolerate poor soil and bloom once. Their flowers can be either single or double and they have a delicate fragrance. Two of the most venerable are the deep, soft pink French rose, *R. rubra*, and the Red Rose of Lancaster or Apothecary Rose, *R. gallica officinalis*, which was used in the Middle Ages for herbal remedies. *R. gallica* 'Versicolor' ('Rosa Mundi') is a lovely striped rose of light crimson and white; 'Belle Isis' is a delicate soft pink, highly perfumed double; and 'Complicata', the hybrid, is a wonderful rose with large, pink, single flowers with golden stamens, blooming profusely in midsummer. 'Tuscany Superb' is a larger version of 'Tuscany', the "Old Velvet Rose," and has deep rich red, almost-double flowers with golden stamens; it is well scented and grows to 4 feet (1.2 cm).

Cabbage roses (*Rosa* x *centifolia*). Cabbage roses are aptly named. Their large, full, double, intensely fragrant flowers make them the epitome of old garden roses. They produce long arching stems which require some form of support, especially since the blooms are so heavy. Two lovely hybrids are 'Fantin Latour' and 'Rose de Meaux'. 'Fantin Latour', the most famous of the centifolias, has delicate pink, fragrant flowers; 'Rose de Meaux' is much smaller and double pink.

Moss roses (*Rosa* x *centifolia mucosa*). These roses are distinctive because of their somewhat hairy sepals and stalks, reminiscent of moss. They are hardy, sweet-smelling roses that bloom once a year. The pink 'Common Moss' is best known and intensely perfumed, and 'Capitaine John Ingram' is grown for its strong scent and dark crimson to purple colouring. Another special hybrid is 'Alfred de Dalmas', a lovely little rose bearing clusters of medium-sized, creamy pink, semidouble flowers from June to October.

Damask roses (*Rosa damascena*). These lovely, very fragrant roses were used as early as the first century B.C. to prepare attar of roses. They are quite resistant to disease. Damasks produce tremendous clusters of flowers in groups of three to five. They are thorny shrubs, superbly fragrant, with tall arching canes that need some support. Lovely hybrids are 'Belle Amour', pink with rich yellow stamens; 'Celsiana' and 'Ispahan', both pink semidoubles; and the blush pink to white double 'Leda'. Other special favourites are 'Gloire de Guilan', with beautiful, clear pink double flowers; 'Mme. Hardy' with clusters of pure white, double blossoms set off by bright green foliage; and 'Quatre Saisons' with its double pink blooms, excellent for making potpourri.

Portland roses. The Portlands are an interesting group of small roses, ideal to grow where space is limited. Two nice cultivars are 'Comte de Chambord', with lovely pink, highly perfumed, double blossoms, and 'Jacques

Cartier', with fragrant, soft pink blooms, suitable for containers and shade-tolerant.

Alba roses (*Rosa* x *alba*). This vigorous group is both disease- and pest-resistant. The blooms are beautifully scented, borne mainly in a single flush in midsummer. Lovely ones include the White Rose of York (*Rosa* x *alba*), and the pink hybrids 'Celestial', 'Félicité Parmentier and 'Köningin von Dänemark'.

China roses *(Rosa chinensis)*. It is, of course, the repeat-flowering habit of these roses, which bloom all summer, that contributed so much to the development of modern roses. The hybrids available today are medium- to small-sized shrubs with a branching habit. Nice hybrids include 'Cécile Brunner', the sweetheart rose, with dainty, pink, delicately fragrant flowers; and 'Irène Watts', with free-flowering, double white, pink-tinted blooms. 'Mutabilis' has small, single, slightly fragrant flowers that begin as vermilion buds, open to pale yellow, change to pink and to crimson before the petals fall. This continuous bloomer is recommended by the University of British Columbia Plant Introduction Scheme.

Bourbon roses (*Rosa* x *borboniana*). These roses are probably a cross between the autumn damask and the China rose. Much loved by the Victorians, they bear fragrant, large, many-petalled flowers. Some bloom continuously, while others are recurrent or produce a single flush. They make very good garden shrubs and climbers. Excellent hybrids include 'Adam Messerich', 'Boule de Neige', 'Bourbon Queen' and 'La Reine Victoria'. Special favourites include bright rose-pink 'Louise Odier'; deep pink, shaggy 'Mme. Isaac Pereire'; pink, semidouble 'Kathleen Harrop'; and the lovely cerise-pink 'Zéphirine Drouhin'.

Noisette roses. The noisette roses are robust shrubs or climbers but may be badly damaged in a severe winter. They are capable of reaching 20 feet (6 m). They are a hybrid of the China and musk rose, and usually bear medium-sized flowers in heavy clusters in summer and fall. The noisettes brought the colour yellow to climbers and ramblers. The many lovely hybrids include white 'Aimée Vibert', yellow to creamy white 'Alister Stella Gray', pink 'Blush Noisette', primrose-yellow 'Céline Forestier' and mixed yellow 'Desprez à Fleurs Jaunes'. However, the best known is probably 'Mme. Alfred Carrière', with lovely, large, highly scented white blossoms tinged with pink. It is vigorous, blooms almost continuously, and can be grown in semishade, on a north wall.

Hybrid perpetuals. These emerged in the 1830s as a result of hybridization between several other groups of old garden roses, and many remain with us today. Four lovely hybrids are the rose-pink 'Baroness Rothschild', creamy white 'Gloire Lyonnaise', pink 'Mrs. John Laing', and violet-coloured 'Reine des Violettes'.

Hybrid tea roses (large-flowered roses)

These roses date back to the 19th century, when the European hybrid perpetual rose was crossed with the China tea rose, producing the first hybrid tea rose, 'La France', in 1865. This marked the beginning of a new era in rose cultivation. Hybrid teas are the most widely grown of roses; available in both bush and standard form, they are generally upright plants of fairly even growth.

These roses are prized for their flowers of classic beauty, produced from summer to fall, borne singly or with several side buds. Many are fragrant, and their colour range is tremendous. They make excellent cut flowers for indoors, and are suitable for massed planting, or individual planting in a mixed border.

Here are 10 hybrid tea roses recommended for the west coast.

'Blessings'. Very free-flowering, shapely rose of soft salmon. Ideal for mass planting and blooms over a long season. Growth vigorous and upright. Good disease resistance.

'Chicago Peace'. A "sport" of the world favourite 'Peace', it is a healthier, more vigorous bush, with golden-yellow buds, some with a flash of shocking pink, opening to sunset colours. Give it adequate space and just a light pruning.

'Dainty Bess'. Lovely, large, silver-pink single flowers with stunning golden-brown stamens. Continuous bloomer; average disease resistance. Availability limited to specialist suppliers.

'Folklore'. Recommended for the coast. Orange flowers with good scent. Good disease resistance.

'Loving Memory' (**Burgund 81**). Large, vibrant red blooms borne on strong stems. Bushy and upright with glossy foliage. A continuous bloomer, it is moderately fragrant and good for bedding or group planting. Good disease resistance.

'Peaudouce' (**'Elina'**). Lovely pale primrose flowers turning to ivory when mature. Bushy upright growth with ample foliage. A good choice for cutting. A continuous bloomer with a slight fragrance, it is good for bedding or mass planting. Good disease resistance. Availability may be limited.

'Polar Star'. Free-flowering, creamy white flowers borne on sturdy stems. Does need adequate space. Continuous bloomer and good for bedding or group planting. Excellent for cutting.

'Pristine'. Lovely fragrant white flowers with pink blush. The upright bushes are good for bedding or in groups. Good disease resistance.

'Rosemary Harkness'. Voted Rose of the Year 1999 by the Vancouver Rose Society, this vigorous grower has delicate peach and apricot flowers and a fruity perfume. It is disease resistant and an early bloomer.

'Silver Jubilee'. Very free-flowering rose with silvery-pink and apricot flowers produced in clusters. Foliage dense and glossy. Moderately fragrant. Suitable for hedging, bedding and growing in containers. An excellent rose with good disease resistance.

Floribunda roses (cluster-flowered roses)

Floribunda roses were cultivated in Denmark in the early part of this century, the result of the crossing of polyantha and hybrid tea roses. This union resulted in a shrubby, larger rosebush, with flowers somewhat smaller than those of the hybrid tea. Although they are not usually fragrant, they produce abundant, colourful clusters of blooms throughout the summer and fall.

Floribundas are easier than other roses to grow, and they are now available in a wide range of colours. They may be used in beds or borders, as hedging plants or among other shrubs; some are suitable for containers, but may need protecting in winter. They also make very good cut flowers.

The following floribundas are recommended for the West Coast.

'Betty Prior'. Reminiscent of a wild rose, with single pink blooms over a long season. Good disease resistance.

'Escapade'. A lovely rose, with scented semi-double blooms of white-centred lilac surrounding yellow stamens. Has a long flowering season and is excellent for cutting. Good for bedding and hedging. Average disease resistance.

'Eyepaint'. Vigorous bushy plant with single blooms of scarlet with a white eye, borne all summer. Good as a hedging plant or a border. Average disease resistance.

'Fragrant Delight'. Soft orange and salmon semidouble blooms, combined with a strong fragrance, make this rose desirable. Continuous bloomer and suitable for hedging.

'Iceberg'. One of the best floribundas, with shapely buds opening to flat, pure white blooms. Will flower continually if given space; lovely as a specimen, hedge or standard. Average disease resistance.

'Pink Parfait'. Prolific semidouble blooms in several shades of pink. Growth upright and bushy; foliage semiglossy. A lovely rose, good for bed, border or as a specimen. Has a slight fragrance. Good disease resistance.

'Queen Elizabeth'. An outstanding rose that is commonly known as a grandiflora but is classified as a floribunda. It has large clear pink blooms. Vigorous, upright and tall; not suitable for a small bed. Excellent as a cut flower, and good disease resistance. Continuous bloomer and suitable for hedging.

'Sexy Rexy'. Bush growth with double flowers of pink and soft salmon. Good disease resistance and suitable for hedging and growing in containers. Slight fragrance.

'Trumpeter'. A compact 2-foot (60-cm) bush; continuous bloomer with glowing vermilion-red flowers, suitable for small gardens.

Modern shrub roses

These are a very diverse group of roses, introduced as a result of the 20th-century landscaping demand for easily maintained plants with a long flowering season. These shrubs make good garden plants and some can be adapted to make small climbers.

Hybrid musks. These were introduced at the beginning of the century and are valuable for their clusters of fragrant flowers borne throughout the growing season. They are a very useful shrub, suitable for the average-sized garden. Some lovely hybrids include 'Ballerina', pink with a white centre; 'Buff Beauty', yellow; 'Felicia', silver-pink; 'Pax', pure white; and 'Penelope', creamy pink.

Rugosa hybrids (*R. rugosa*). Originally from Japan and China, the rugosa roses are valuable garden shrubs. They are easy to grow, and most are strongly scented, with good hips

Tip of the Month: Compost Tea

A soil drench or foliar spray of compost tea can actually help eliminate many pests and diseases by increasing the soil's diversity of bacteria and fungi, protozoa and beneficial nematodes.

To make the tea, simply place well-rotted manure or compost and fresh green comfrey leaves in a burlap "tea bag." You may add molasses to the compost to help feed the tiny biota, some kelp meal to add trace elements and further feed, and a bit of rock dust to give the beneficial fungi an attachment point. Tie the burlap with twine, suspend it on a broom handle or stick and submerge it in a container of chlorine-free water, such as rainwater. Steep it until it is the colour of weak tea, agitating it occasionally. Overnight may be sufficient time for a small watering can, or several days may be needed to brew a larger container, such as a bucket or small barrel.

Put the compost tea in a spray bottle and mist both upper and lower plant leaf surfaces, or drench the soil around the plant root zones. Use this high-nitrogen tea within 12 hours to prevent it from becoming anaerobic (without oxygen), a state that promotes pathogens rather than beneficial bacteria. Repeat periodically through the growing season to keep your soil and plants well fed and happy. Your roses will love it!

and colour in the fall. They are generally healthy, and flower throughout most of the summer. Five attractive examples are 'Blanc Double de Coubert', lovely pure white double flowers; 'Frau Dagmar Hastrup', silver-pink flowers; 'Hansa', double cerise-violet flowers with a spicy scent; 'Roseraie de l'Hay', large crimson-purple blooms; and 'Thérèse Bugnet', very hardy, with reddish-pink blooms.

David Austin roses. Of the many introductions in the modern shrub rose group, one of the most recent and most interesting has been the "New English rose" from David Austin, a British nurseryman. Austin has crossed the old roses, such as gallicas and damasks, with modern hybrid teas and floribundas to produce hybrids that have the look and fragrance of old garden roses, with the hardiness and blooming reliability of hybrid teas. As a whole they are compact shrubs, well suited to the smaller garden. To produce the best effect, David Austin recommends planting several plants of one variety closely in a group. Spaced more closely than normal, at a distance of 18 inches (45 cm), a group of three or five will quickly grow together. There are now over 80 different varieties; following are some lovely examples.

'**Abraham Darby**'. Large, coppery apricot flowers with a strong scent.

'**Chianti**'. Large Gallica-like flowers of rich crimson that become purplish-maroon, with a powerful fragrance.

'**Constance Spry**'. The original English rose, with large, soft pink blooms and a strong myrrh fragrance.

'**Evelyn**'. A more compact shrub to 3 1/2 feet (105 cm) with pleasing, deliciously scented flowers of apricot and yellow with a hint of pink.

'**Gertrude Jekyll**'. A strong-growing shrub with warm pink flowers and a powerful fragrance.

'**Glamis Castle**'. Dainty white flowers with a strong myrrh scent on a 3-foot (90-cm) shrub.

'**Graham Thomas**'. A rich yellow, good as a shrub or climber.

'**Heritage**'. Soft, shell-like, medium pink flowers with a honey scent.

'**Leander**'. Small, exquisite, deep apricot flowers on a vigorous, upright, 3-foot (90-cm) shrub that is also great as a climber.

'**Mary Rose**'. A good all-round disease-resistant shrub with continuous blooms of rose-pink.

'**Pat Austin**'. Named after his wife, the blooms are an unusual copper and amber colour.

'**The Prince**'. Opens a deep rich crimson and turns royal purple; grows to 2 feet (60 cm) with a spreading habit useful for the border edge.

Climbers and ramblers

Consider using beautiful thorny ramblers as security devices. These descendents of the vigorous wild roses have long canes and are easily trained along a fence to form a 20-foot (6-m) impenetrable barrier. These roses bear scented, often recurrent flower clusters in a cloak of green foliage that turns yellow or red in the fall, has fat red hips all winter, and is clothed in miserable sharp prickles to deter intruders! Every household needs one.

Climbing roses may be trained to climb through shrubs and trees, up arches and balconies as well as along fences and hedges.

Some lovely hybrids are 'Aloha', salmon-pink; 'Albertine', coppery-pink; 'Altissimo', scarlet; 'America', apricot; 'Dublin Bay', blood red; 'Meg', buff-yellow to apricot; *R. mulliganii*, huge sprays of single white flowers; 'New Dawn', soft pink, the Vancouver Rose Society's Rose of the Year 2000; 'Seagull', waves of fragrant white; and 'Westerland', dazzling gold-apricot.

Miniature roses

These charming little roses grow from 6 to 12 inches (15 to 30 cm) high, and are replicas of the larger roses. They are now widely available in Canada and are excellent choices for groundcover, edging borders and window boxes. They require the same basic conditions and care as other roses. Some pretty hybrids are 'Baby Darling', orange-pink double blooms; 'Beauty Secret', cardinal-red blooms; 'Cinderella', white with pink edging, thornless; 'Cupcake', pale pink with lemon centre; 'Green Ice', white with hints of chartreuse and pink, glossy leaves; 'Reiki', scented clear pink; 'Sandalwood', tender but an unusual smoky terra cotta colour; 'Snow Carpet', tiny white flowers; 'Sweet Chariot', scented flowers, grape and blackberry coloured with a hint of cream at the centre on long arching stems.

Roses suitable for groundcover

There are some lovely little roses that have been bred for use in mass planting, and are excellent for groundcover. They are also effective in containers and tumbling over retaining walls. Some nice hybrids include 'Alba Meidiland', white; 'Bonica 82', salmon-pink; 'Dunwich rose', creamy yellow; 'Fiona', dark red; 'Pearl Drift', whitish-pink; 'Pink Meidiland', deep pink; 'Swany', pure white; and 'The Fairy', pale pink.

Roses with hips!

Rose hips—luscious, brilliant, seed-containing berries—keep roses beautiful well past Christmas and also attract birds to our gardens. As long as you leave the flowers to fade on the shrub, the rose hips will grow into a spectacular autumn display. Wild and species roses, including ramblers and their hybrids, seem to have great hips as well as fiery-golden fall foliage.

Our native *Rosa nutkana* produces showy red hips; the rugosa roses and their hybrids, like 'Hansa', 'Fru Dagmar Hastrup', and 'Therese Bugnet', produce hips like red crabapples. Species roses like *R. moyesii*, with single red flowers, have generous orange-red hips and *R. mulliganii* produces tiny orange beads. 'Hebe's Lip' bears crimson marbles and 'Bonica' has round orange fruit.

The single-blooming climber 'Madame Gregoire Staechelin' produces lovely green to soft terracotta berries and 'Mutabilis' provides a continuous summer bloom of soft, single-petal flowers, followed by a generous crop of red berries. 'Dortmund' develops a good crop of large erect hips after red flowers and 'Fred Loads' bears attractive winter berries after its bright orange flowers of summer. Ramblers like 'Kiftsgate' and 'Rambling Rector' are prolific in flower and produce shiny hips that hang in clusters through February.

Many roses will give you mellow autumn richness as specimen shrubs or as superb hedges and can be brought indoors to brighten festive table centrepieces. A bonus is that rose hips have a high vitamin C content and can be used to make jellies and wine.

Summer-flowering Shrubs

The following list of shrubs can help you plan for colour in your garden from the end of May until the end of September. For ease of planning, the shrubs are organized into three groupings: early summer (late May to June), midsummer (June and July), and late summer (July to September).

Early summer (late May to June)

Deutzia spp. A group of easily cultivated deciduous shrubs that thrive in all soils in sun or part shade. The flowers are usually white and unscented and appear in clusters on the previous year's wood. Prune out some of the old wood after flowering to encourage new flowering shoots. They are trouble free and very resistant to pests and diseases. *D. gracilis* (slender deutzia) is a dense, compact shrub growing to about 3 feet (90 cm), with slender branches carrying clusters of snowy white star-shaped flowers. The slightly toothed leaves are a fresh, bright green. *D. x rosea* 'Carminea' is a compact shrub with a height and spread of 3 feet (90 cm). Arching branches carry open, bell-shaped flowers, white inside and rosy pink on the outside. *D. scabra* is a hardy species growing to 6 feet (1.8 m), with rough, oval green leaves. The flowers bloom in upright clusters, 3 to 6 inches (8 to 15 cm) long. A good cultivar is 'Pride of Rochester', with double white flowers tinged with purple on the outside.

Fuchsia magellanica (hardy fuchsia). Look for these hardy varieties that won't need to overwinter indoors with their more tender fuchsia relatives that we use for summer bedding. These deciduous upright shrubs have distinctively attractive, pendulous, tubular flowers from early summer to autumn frost. They are great in open borders or hedges and tolerate sun or shade in average soil. 'Alba', to 4 feet (1.2 m), has delicate, almost white flowers; 'Folia Variegata' is low-growing to 2 feet (60 cm) and has unusual white and green variegated foliage against pale pink flowers. 'Hawkshead' is a delicate white variety. 'Genii' is bushy to 3 feet (90 cm) with red-purple flowers against lime-green leaves and red shoots when grown in full sun.

Hebe pinguifolia 'Pagei.' A very attractive evergreen shrub that is, unfortunately, unlikely to survive a severe winter here unless well protected. It is low-growing to 12 inches (30 cm), with rounded blue-grey leaves and abundant clusters of little white flowers near the ends of the branches. It does not require regular pruning.

Kalmia latifolia (mountain laurel, calico bush). A lovely shrub with glossy, oval, evergreen leaves and beautiful clusters of saucer-shaped flowers. It is slow-growing to about 5 feet (1.5 m) and requires moist acid soil in light shade. It is closely related to the rhododendron and is native to the eastern United States. Some good cultivars are 'Ostbo Red', with deep red buds opening to pink; 'Nipmuck', 'Pink Charm' and 'Pink Star', all pretty pinks; 'Elf' and 'Alpine Pink', dwarf pinks; 'Shooting Star' and 'Silver Dollar', white; and 'Fresca', white with deep purple edging.

Kolkwitzia amabilis (beauty bush). This lovely deciduous shrub can reach 12 feet (3.7 m) and is one of the most valuable of the summer-flowering shrubs. It is most reliable, and although it needs full sun it will grow in any soil. It was first introduced early this century from West China by E.H. Wilson, the botanist, collector and explorer who is said to be responsible for introducing more than 1200 species of trees and shrubs to the west. The stems of beauty bush are clustered with small, pink, yellow-throated bells that arch them over from the weight of the blossoms. In the fall the leaves turn to rich red. It should be pruned after flowering or in the winter. For an informal look, plant with naturalized perennials, such as hellebores, foxgloves, Japanese anemones and hardy geraniums.

Lonicera nitida (**boxleaf honeysuckle**). A bushy evergreen that grows to 5 feet (1.5 m) unless pruned to shape; it has glossy leaves and creamy white flowers. 'Baggesen's Gold' has long arching shoots; the folige is chartreuse when grown in partial shade or bright yellow in full sun. It is easy to propagate from stem cuttings and is useful for hedging.

Philadelphus **spp.** (**mock orange**). These are lovely deciduous shrubs up to 10 feet (3 m) tall with white, often intensely fragrant, single or semidouble flowers much coveted by flower arrangers. They will thrive in any well-drained garden soil in sun to part shade and love a good feed before blossoming. Prune out after flowering, since blooms are produced on the previous year's wood. *P. coronarius* is a strong grower, up to 10 feet (3 m) tall. 'Aureus' has clusters of very fragrant flowers in June, with bright golden leaves that last all summer. *P. lewisii* is an elegant, loosely branched deciduous shrub to 10 feet (3 m) that is native to British Columbia. It bears clusters of beautiful, fragrant white flowers with golden stamens at the ends of its branches. It is hardy, showy and very adaptable to a wide variety of garden sites. *P. x virginalis* is a hybrid that has produced several garden cultivars, usually with double flowers. 'Minnesota Snowflake' and 'Natchez' are both 6 to 8 feet (1.8 to 2.4 m) in height, and 'Dwarf Minnesota Snowflake' grows to 3 to 4 feet (.9 to 1.2 m).

Potentilla fruticosa (**shrubby cinquefoil**). A most useful little shrub, up to 4 feet (1.2 m) in height. It flowers continuously all summer, with flowers like small wild roses. It prefers full sun but can take part shade, and it will thrive in any soil. There are many good cultivars, including 'Katherine Dykes', primrose-yellow; 'Red Ace', bright vermilion; 'Mount Everest', pure white with yellow-centred flowers; and 'Tangerine', which has yellow flowers when planted in sun and orange flowers when planted in shade. 'Yellow Gem' is a University of British Columbia plant introduction that forms a tidy low mound of hairy, grey, lobed leaves and bright yellow flowers with ruffled petals from May through to a hard frost. It can be mass-planted for cover on a sloping bank or used as a grouping or accent in the front of a border.

Sambucus nigra (**elder**). A deciduous shrub to 12 feet (3.7 m), it can be hard-pruned to contain its size. It likes dappled sun and is grown for its coloured foliage and musk-scented, dense, flat-topped ivory flowers that are followed by glossy black fruits. 'Aurea' has gold-yellow leaves; 'Aureomarginata' has yellow-margined, dark green leaves; 'Guincho Purple' has dark green leaves that turn blackish-purple, then red in autumn, and pink-tinged flowers with purple stalks.

Spiraea **spp.** (**spirea**). Twiggy, hardy, deciduous shrubs that bear small starlike blooms arranged in clusters. The harder the plants are pruned, the larger the flower heads they carry. They are best grown in a sunny, open position, in almost any soil. *S. x bumalda* 'Anthony Waterer' is a popular garden cultivar, 3 to 4 feet (.9 to 1.2 m) high, with clusters of bright carmine flowers and leaves variegated with pink and cream. 'Limemound' is useful for its lovely, lime-green foliage. It is a dwarf shrub with pink flowers and leaves turning to orange-red in the fall. 'Goldflame' is valuable for its bronze leaves that turn yellow as they grow, then turn green. *S. japonica* 'Little Princess' is under 20 inches (50 cm) tall with long summer bloom in rose-pink.

Symphoricarpos albus (snowberry). A native, deciduous, suckering upright shrub that grows to 6 1/2 feet (2 m). Pink flowers in May to July are followed by spongy white berries. It likes moist soil and sun or part shade.

Syringa spp. (lilac). Lovely deciduous shrubs or small trees. The flowering season is short, but the heady fragrance of the large flower heads makes these shrubs hard to resist. Lilacs are easily grown, though they are greedy feeders. They respond to a good chill in the winter, and all love limey soils. The small tubular flowers, which appear in clusters, are often intensely fragrant and are in various shades of white, cream, pink, lilac, deep violet and mauve. It is important that the old flower heads are removed as soon as they fade, but do not prune heavily, since this results in the loss of much of next year's growth. *S. vulgaris* (common lilac) reaches a height of 8 to 12 feet (2.4 to 3.7 m), with a spread of 5 to 10 feet (1.5 to 3 m). It is available in many good garden cultivars, such as 'Mme Lemoine', double white; 'Charles Joly', double magenta; 'Belle de Nancy', double pink; and 'President Lincoln', single, light bluish-violet. *S. microphylla* is a hardy, small lilac that grows to only 4 to 5 feet (2.1 to 1.5 m), just the thing for a small garden. Its fragrant, lilac-coloured blooms appear in erect clusters during June. Not always easy to get.

Viburnum spp. *V. plicatum* 'Mariesii' is a lovely shrub, best planted as a specimen. It is deciduous, grows to 9 feet (2.7 m), and its horizontal tiered branches are laden with clusters of white lacecap flowers in early summer. It has good fall colour, is easy to grow and does best in rich, slightly moist soil, sun to part shade. Another UBC plant introduction, *V. plicatum* 'Summer Snowflake' is a deciduous shrub to 6 1/2 feet (2 m). Clusters of white flowers are produced in two rows along the tops of its branches, beginning with a major flush in May and continuing until frost. It likes full sun to light shade, can be pruned to a smaller size and is disease and pest resistant. It makes a great specimen plant and works well in mixed borders. *V. opulus* (guelder rose) is a deciduous upright hardy shrub, growing to 12 feet (3.7 m) in any moist soil. Its leaves are shaped like maple leaves, and it is desirable for its white blooms, loved by flower arrangers, and its showy red berries in the fall. The cultivar 'Compactum' is a smaller form.

Midsummer (June to July)

Buddleia davidii (butterfly bush). A deciduous shrub, reaching a height of 10 feet (3 m), with long, tapering, dark green leaves that are white and felted underneath. Small fragrant flowers appear in dense, arching, plume-shaped clusters from mid-July onwards. Butterflies are attracted to the flowers, so it is worth growing for that reason alone. It thrives in full sun, and is tolerant of lime. Prune hard in the spring, taking out the old flowering wood, and remove faded flower clusters after flowering. Some good cultivars are 'Black Knight', a deep purple; 'Charming', deep pink; 'Dubonnet', reddish-purple; and 'White Bouquet', white.

Cotinus coggygria (smokebush). A deciduous shrub grown for its large, oval, purple or green summer foliage that colours well in the fall, and for its delicate pink flower plumes in summer, from which it gets its common name. 'Royal Purple' has dark red-purple leaves that turn scarlet in the fall. 'Grace' bears masses of deep pink flowers. Its intense, wine-red new foliage darkens to plum-red at maturity before it turns bright orange-red in the fall. Grow it in full sun for the best dark red colour and prune it quite hard to control its size and produce bigger leaves. This relatively drought-tolerant shrub is also great for containers.

Escallonia hybrids. These are useful evergreen shrubs and a good addition to seaside gardens, since they are tolerant of coastal winds and dry conditions. They carry short tubular flowers in terminal clusters on last year's growth in June, and bloom continues into fall on the current season's growth. They flower best in full sun and benefit from annual mulching with compost. Prune to shape after flowering. A number of excellent hybrids have been developed. Among the best are 'Apple Blossom', compact to 5 feet (1.5 m) with pale pink flowers; 'C.F. Ball', one of the hardiest, up to 8 feet (2.4 m), with tubular red flowers; and 'Pink Princess', up to 5 feet (1.5 m), with rose-pink flowers.

Hydrangea spp. A group of hardy, dependable shrubs with big bold leaves and large clusters of flowers that remain for a long period of time. All require rich, well-drained soil with ample moisture and a position in light shade. Prune out old gnarled wood in early March, and mulch with well-rotted compost or manure. *H. macrophylla* are deciduous shrubs up to 6 feet (1.8 m) tall, with coarsely toothed, light green leaves. This species is divided into two groups: the lacecap group, with flattened clusters of tiny fertile florets, surrounded by a ring of larger sterile flowers; and the Hortensia group, with round "mopheads" of flowers, less elegant than the lacecaps, but making a more striking display with their large round heads of sterile flowers. On acid soil the pink varieties may turn blue or purple, and on alkaline soil the blue varieties turn pink or purple. Good lacecaps are 'Blue Wave', a vigorous grower in pink or blue; and 'Mariesii', a rich pink or blue. Good Hortensias are 'Bluebird', pink or blue; 'Bouquet Rose', pink or blue; and 'Revelation', red or blue. *H. arborescens* 'Annabelle' is a lovely hydrangea growing to about 4 feet (1.2 m) tall and producing enormous clusters of greeny-white flowers from June to September.

Lavatera spp. (tree mallow). This fast-growing shrub with single, hollyhocklike flowers blooms continuously until frost, likes sun and is quite drought tolerant. Prune in spring to keep its open growth habit compact. 'Barnsley' grows to 8 feet (2.4 m) and has pale pink flowers with a red eye. 'Rosea' is a more compact 4 feet (1.2 m) with clear pink flowers.

Santolina chamaecyparissus (lavender cotton). A low-growing shrub with attractive, silvery-grey, finely divided leaves. Usually grown for its foliage at the expense of the bright yellow buttonlike flowers, which are clipped off before they bloom. An excellent shrub for the front of a border, and easy to grow from cuttings if the parent plant gets old and woody. Grows to about 2 feet (60 cm), but is usually kept much lower by shearing. It likes a position in full sun.

Late summer (July to September)

Abelia x *grandiflora.* A useful semi-evergreen shrub up to 8 feet (2.4 m) high. A hybrid of spreading and arching habit, with small bronze-green leaves, it is usually hardy in our area. From July to October it bears slightly fragrant, tubular, pink and white flowers. It likes well-drained humus-rich soil and will grow in sun or part shade. Can be used for hedging. A nice dwarf cultivar is 'Edward Goucher'.

Caryopteris x *clandonensis* (**bluebeard**). The lovely combination of cool blue flowers and grey-green foliages makes this one of the most valuable of the late-flowering shrubs. It is sometimes damaged in a hard winter and needs protection in cold weather. It wants full sun and should be pruned hard each spring. Two good cultivars are 'Heavenly Blue', with lovely deep blue flowers, useful in a confined space; and 'Blue Mist', with profuse blossoms, also good for small gardens.

Ceratostigma willmottianum (**hardy plumbago**). A deciduous, twiggy shrub up to 3 feet (90 cm), valuable for its small clusters of pure mid-blue flowers in July and tinted red foliage in the fall. Plant in full sun in light loamy soil. No regular pruning is required, but old or damaged shoots should be cut back to ground level in the fall.

Clethra alnifolia (**sweet pepper bush, summer sweet**). Deciduous medium-sized shrub, valuable for its late flowering and the colour of its foliage in the fall. Plant in sun to part shade, in damp, lime-free soil. The fragrant, small, white or pink blossoms grow in terminal spikes, and on opening emit a pungent scent. A good cultivar is 'Rosea', pale pink flowers.

Hibiscus syriacus (**rose-of-sharon**). This deciduous species is another valuable late-flowering shrub. It grows to a height of 10 feet (3 m) and is bushy and broad, with erect growth. Plant in a sunny position in any well-drained garden soil. It is unusual for its late leafing, and needs no regular pruning. It's a good choice for the city garden. Among the best cultivars are 'Blue Bird', violet-blue hollyhock-like blooms with a crimson blotch at the base; 'Red Heart', white with a scarlet-red basal blotch; 'Diana', large white blooms; and 'Woodbridge', large, deep rosy-pink blooms with a maroon blotch at the base.

Hydrangea spp. *H. paniculata* (peegee hydrangea) is an erect shrub that grows 12 to 15 feet (3.7 to 4.6 m) in our area. It is lovely as a specimen plant, and flowers freely during August and September. A good cultivar is 'Grandiflora'. The oak-shaped leaves of *H. quercifolia* (oak-leaf hydrangea) distinguish it from other hydrangea species. It is deciduous and makes a bush 4 to 5 feet (1.2 to 1.5 m) high. It thrives in moist woodland conditions. It bears round-topped clusters of white flowers in late summer, and in the fall its large leaves take on a wonderful autumn hue. Hydrangeas need generous feeding, and should be given a good dressing of compost in early spring.

Lavandula angustifolia (**English lavender**). A native of the Mediterranean, this small evergreen shrub is evocative of cottage gardens and rose beds. It can grow to a height of 3 to 4 feet (.9 to 1.2 m), but is better if kept shorter by pruning in March or April. Both the flowers and foliage are aromatic, the flowers being very fragrant and true lavender in colour. Lavender thrives best in full sun in a well-drained, not-too-rich soil. To prune, trim after flowering and cut it back almost to the base in early spring, which will promote bushy new growth. With its silvery-grey foliage and blue flowers it makes an attractive small hedge. Smaller cultivars include 'Hidcote' and 'Munstead', which grow to a height of about 18 inches (45 cm).

Recommended Reading

Roses

Allen, Christine. *Roses for the Pacific Northwest.* Steller Press, Vancouver, 1999.

Austin, David. *English Roses.* Conran Octopus, London, 1993.

Beales, Peter. *Classic Roses.* Harper and Row, New York, 1985.

Beales, Peter. *Twentieth-Century Roses.* Harper and Row, New York, 1988.

Hessayon, D.G. *The New Rose Expert.* pbi Publications, London, 1996.

Phillips, Roger and Martyn Rix, *The Quest for the Rose.* BBC Books, London, 1993.

Phillips, Roger and Martyn Rix, *Roses.* Random House, New York, 1988.

The Rose Bed. Vancouver Rose Society, monthly bulletin for members.

Summer-flowering shrubs

See Recommended Reading in the April chapter.

January: garden design at
UBC's Nitobe Memorial Garden
(page 5)

January: garden design
(pages 5–11)
DORIS FANCOURT-SMITH

February: crocus 'Pickwick'
(page 13)

February: hostas in the garden
of E. Carey (pages 16–17)

March: *Primula* 'Ceperley Hybrids' in VanDusen Botanical Garden (pages 53–56)

March: *Viburnum opulence* with *Clematis macropetala* (page 43)

April: spring-flowering shrubs such as forsythia and ribes (pages 68–71)

April: deciduous azalea such as *Rhododendron schlippenbachii* in the garden of Glen Patterson (page 64)

May: annuals and
perennials (pages 79–101)
DORIS FANCOURT-SMITH

May: wisteria (page 78)

May: yellow garden featuring golden feverfew,
Crambe cordifolia, Helianthemum (pages 101–102)

May: annuals such as *Agapanthus* 'Bressingham Blue', *Campanula persicifolia, Verbena canadensis* 'Home-stead Purple', phlox (pages 88–101)

July

Sometime around the middle of July summer really starts, bringing at least four to six weeks of sunny, balmy weather before the first rains fall again. The rhythmic hiss of water coming from sprinklers and garden hoses is punctuated by the harsher sounds of mechanical lawn mowers. We can relax and smell the flowers, sit out in the evening's warmth and enjoy the night sky, as the fragrance of lilies, night-scented stocks, flowering tobacco, lavender and herbs fill the air.

Nature's summer garden is also at its peak. This is the time to hike to alpine meadows in our nearby mountains and enjoy the beauty of hundreds of species of wildflowers, including wild lupines, Indian paintbrush, alpine harebells, columbines, gentians, saxifrages, mariposa lilies and many more. It is also a good time to visit the Gulf Islands and coast forest areas. The Gulf Islands have some of the most varied flora in the province, including large numbers of Canada's only native broadleaf evergreen tree, the arbutus. Even cacti grow and thrive in some hot, dry areas.

Back home, gardens are full of colour, fragrance and vitality. Sweetly scented old roses and clematis cover walls, trellises and arbours, and sweet peas begin to bloom. Many annuals and summer-flowering perennials are at their peak, and tubs, window boxes and pots that were planted in May are in full bloom. An unusual and lovely summer bulb for containers is lily-of-the-Nile (*Agapanthus*), whose spectacular round flower heads of blue or white bloom from July to September. White lily-of-the-Nile, edged with variegated ivy, can make even the most humble container look exotic.

Increased awareness of the need to conserve water has stimulated a general interest in drought-tolerant plants, and most garden centres now carry a good selection. This chapter includes a section on water-wise gardening and looks at the interesting variety of drought-tolerant plants we can grow in the city and by the ocean, with special emphasis on some of the attractive and unusual grasses and bamboo available today. The seaside and island garden section looks at some of the challenges and rewards for those who garden in and around B.C.'s coastal waters.

Many herbs and vegetables from the garden are ready for picking, and if you follow the tips in this chapter, you will easily be able to create an unusual and colourful salad from your own garden. It's also the time to begin harvesting herbs and flowers for drying and to pick fresh raspberries. Some of the world's foremost raspberry breeders are here in B.C., and there are many excellent cultivars to choose from. 'Tulameen' is a new introduction from B.C. and a great find for home gardeners. It produces exceptionally large, light red, aromatic fruit with a fine flavour. 'Tulameen' has a 50-day fruiting season, producing raspberries right through July and August. Herbs

and berry fruits are ideal for making flavoured vinegars, and this chapter includes instructions on how to make them.

Garden Highlights
*indicates fragrance

Bulbs

Allium spp. (ornamental onions), *Begonia*, *Camassia* (camas), *Cardiocrinum giganteum* (giant Himalayan lily),* *Gladiolus* spp.,* *Lilium* spp. (lilies),* *Tigridia* spp. (tiger flower).

Perennials

Acanthus spp. (bear's breeches), *Agapanthus africanus* (lily-of-the-Nile), *Alstroemeria* (Peruvian lily), *Campanula lactiflora* (bell-flower), *Chrysanthemum* x *superbum* (shasta daisy), *Echinacea purpurea* (purple cone-flower), *Echinops* spp. (globe thistle), *Erynigium* spp. (sea holly), *Gaillardia* x *grandiflora* (blanket flower), *Helenium autumnale* (sneezeweed), *Kniphofia* spp. (red hot poker), *Liatris* spp. (gay feather), *Lysimachia punctata* (yellow loosestrife), *Monarda didyma* (bergamot),* *Nepeta mussinii* (catmint),* *Penstemon* spp. (beard-tongue), *Phlox* spp.,* *Rodgersia*, *Rudbeckia* spp. (coneflower or black-eyed Susan), various ornamental grasses.

Climbers

Clematis hybrids, *Jasminum officinale* (poet's jasmine),* *Lathyrus latifolius* (perennial sweet pea), *Passiflora* spp. (passion flower),* *Rosa* hybrids (climbing roses).*

Shrubs

Escallonia spp., *Fuchsia magellanica* (hardy fuchsia), *Hebe* spp., *Lavandula angustifolia* (lavender),* *Rosa* hybrids (roses),* *Senecio* 'Sunshine', *Spiraea* 'Anthony Waterer' (spirea), *Tamarix* spp. (tamarisk), *Yucca* spp.

Trees

Liriodendron tulipifera (tulip tree), *Magnolia grandiflora* (southern magnolia).*

July Checklist

Annuals, perennials and bulbs

- Water flowers in containers and hanging baskets daily.
- Regularly deadhead annuals and perennials to encourage flowering.
- When delphiniums fade, cut to ground level to stimulate second bloom.
- Make sure tall plants have support.
- Lift bearded irises after flowering, divide and replant.
- Pinch back chrysanthemums and asters to promote bushiness.
- Dry flowers for winter decoration.
- Plant autumn bulbs such as colchicum and autumn crocus.
- Take geranium (*Pelargonium* spp.) cuttings.

Trees, shrubs and climbers

- Prune deciduous shrubs, such as weigela, mock orange and deutzia, after flowering.
- Prune hedges lightly to keep them tidy.
- Deadhead roses and water well. Feed with rose food.
- Take cuttings of plants such as hebe, senecio and lavender (see the April chapter for a more extensive list).

Fruits, vegetables and herbs

- Harvest vegetables and continue sowing of lettuce, peas, kale, leeks, Swiss chard, broad beans, bush beans, beets, carrots, green onions and winter vegetables, such as winter cauliflower and purple sprouting broccoli.
- Continue feeding vegetables and water them regularly.
- Stop cutting rhubarb now, so that the plant can store energy. Keep it well watered.
- Harvest raspberries and strawberries. Remove unwanted strawberry runners and throw out plants that have cropped for three summers.
- Harvest bush fruits and cut out fruited canes.
- Cut herbs for freezing and drying.

General garden activities

- Mow lawn regularly and keep edges trimmed.
- Add waste from vegetable garden to compost. Keep it moist and turn regularly.
- Keep garden well watered.

Water-wise Gardening

In most areas water is, or is becoming, an increasingly scarce commodity, and this has accentuated the importance of water-wise garden practices, including selecting plants that can withstand low water levels for prolonged periods of time. Throughout the Lower Mainland and Vancouver Island, municipalities and organizations, such as City Farmer in Vancouver and the Compost Education Centre in Victoria, are working to educate the general public about natural land cultivation and water conservation. General principles for water-wise gardening are simple.

Care for the soil. Add humus, compost or decomposed organic matter, digging them into the ground and applying them as mulch. This helps increase the capacity of the soil to retain moisture and provides nutrients needed for plant growth without the addition of chemical fertilizers. Mulching also cools the soil and helps slow weed growth.

Save water. Trap and contain winter rain for the summer garden. Water will collect in low-lying areas and provide a habitat for moisture-loving plants. Divert rain into rain barrels and use it during dry summer spells.

Choose drought-tolerant plants. This includes many plants native to our region and others that are adapted to grow with little or no supplemental water. Be sure to leave wild plants in place in their natural habitat and buy only plants that have been grown in the nursery from collected seeds or cuttings. (See list below.)

Location, location, location. Choose the right plant for the right place. A sunny, south-facing slope that dries out fast will suit sun-loving plants with low water requirements, while thirsty plants can be grouped together for easier watering. Plants can be layered to provide shade and reduce evaporation and watering needs.

Water wisely. Only water when your plants are thirsty. An occasional deep soaking develops strong, deep roots. Check the soil an inch (2.5 cm) below the surface. If the soil is still moist, wait to water. Apply water directly to the roots. Soaker hoses are ideal for this, putting water where it is needed, reducing evaporation and helping to prevent disease. Water in early morning or evening so that the water soaks into the soil rather than evaporating.

Drought-tolerant plants

The plants listed here can survive our summers with little or no supplemental water once they are established, as long as they are planted in the right spot.

The plants can be used in both city and island gardens, with the exception of *Arbutus menziesii*, a distinctive native tree with thin bark that peels off, exposing the tree's warm, cinnamon-coloured trunk and branches. Arbutus trees are rarely found far from the shoreline and do not transplant well. They are a distinctive sight in coastline areas, extending in range from the northern Gulf Islands down to northern Baja California. If you are fortunate enough to have one on your property, protect and enjoy.

Native B.C. plants are marked with an asterisk(*).

Trees

Acer circinatum* (vine maple), *Arbutus unedo* (strawberry tree), *Arbutus menziesii** (arbutus), *Cornus nuttallii** (Pacific dogwood), *Pinus contorta** (two-needled pine), *Sorbus* spp., *S. sitchensis** (mountain ash).

Shrubs

Arctostaphylos uva-ursi* (kinnikinnik, bearberry), *Artemisia* spp. (southernwood, wormwood, absinthe), *Buddleia davidii** (butterfly bush), *Calluna vulgaris* (heather), *Ceanothus velutinus** (snowbrush), *Choisya ternata** (Mexican orange), *Cistus* spp. (rock rose), *Cotinus* spp. (smokebush), *Cotoneaster* spp., *Gaultheria shallon** (salal), *Lavandula* spp. (lavender), *Mahonia nervosa** (low Oregon grape), *Paxistima myrsinites** (falsebox), *Philadelphus* spp.* (mock orange), *Potentilla fruticosa** (cinquefoil), *Ribes sanguineum** (flowering currant), *Rosa nutkana* (Nootka rose), *Rosmarinus officinalis* (rosemary), *Sambucus caerula,** *S. racemosa** (elderberry), *Santolina chamaecyparissus** (cotton lavender), *Symphoricarpos alba** (snowberry), *Vaccinium parviflorum,** *V. ovatum** (huckleberry).

Perennials

Acanthus spp. (bear's breeches), *Achillea* spp.* (yarrow), *Agapanthus africanus* (lily-of-the-Nile), *Allium cernuum** (nodding onion), *Alstroemeria* spp., *Anaphalis margaritacea** (pearly everlasting), *Antennaria microphylla** (woolly pussytoes), *Armeria maritima** (thrift), *Baptisia tinctoria* (wild indigo), *Bergenia* spp. (bergenia, elephant ears, saxifrage), *Camassia* spp.* (quamash lily), *Catananche caerulea* (cupid's dart), *Centaurea* spp. (bachelor's button), *Coreopsis* spp. (tickseed), *Dianthus* spp. (pinks), *Dodecatheon* spp.* (shooting star), *Echinacea purpurea* (purple coneflower), *Echinops* spp.* (globe thistle), *Erigeron* spp. (fleabane), *Eryngium maritimum* (sea holly), *Erythronium* spp., *Fritillaria* spp.* (rice root, chocolate lily), *Gaillardia* x *grandiflora* (blanket flower) *Geranium* spp. (hardy or true geranium, cranesbill), *Iris germanica, I. florentina* (bearded iris), *Lilium columbianum** (tiger lily), *Monarda didyma* (bergamot), *Nerine bowdenii, Penstemon* spp.* (beard-tongue), *Polygonum bistorta, Scabiosa caucasica* (pincushion flower), *Sedum* spp.* (stonecrop), *Stachys byzantina* (woolly lamb's ears), *Verbena* spp. (vervain), *Veronica* spp. (speedwell).

Grasses

How can you tell a grass from a sedge or a rush? This tip from Eva Antonijevic of Westridge Farms may help.

> Sedges have edges,
> Rushes are round,
> Grasses are hollow
> with nodes to the ground.

Many, but not all, ornamental grasses are custom-built for drought tolerance. The selection available in garden centres today is excellent, with an astonishing range of heights, sizes, colours and flowering times. They range in size from delicate grasses only a hand-span in height to majestic, towering, plume-crested sheaths that grow to more than 10 feet (3 m). Some are attractively striped or banded. Others have showy flower plumes, spikes or seed heads, and several provide dramatic and lasting interest throughout the winter months.

The following grasses are widely available and highly recommended for various locations. The sun-lovers are the most drought tolerant.

***Calamagrostis* x *acutiflora* 'Karl Foerster' (Foerster's feather reed grass).** One of the best grasses for a strong vertical effect, with stiffly upright clumps of green foliage and narrow white flower spikes that fade to a pinkish-brown and last well into winter. It blooms from June to September and grows to a height of 4 to 5 feet (1.2 to 1.5 m) and a width of 18 inches to 2 feet (45 to 60 cm). It needs sun.

***Carex morrowii* 'Aureo-variegata' (variegated Japanese sedge).** Although the sedges are not true grasses, they are similar in appearance. They form compact tufts of foliage with usually insignificant flowers. 'Aureo-variegata' is an extremely useful, short-growing, evergreen plant that really likes shade but will tolerate sunshine. Its green leaves have a central stripe of creamy yellow, and it bears pale green flowering spikes in spring. It's excellent for brightening up shady areas and combines well with hostas. It grows to a height and spread of 12 inches (30 cm).

***Chasmanthium latifolium* (northern sea oats).** This is one of the best grasses for shady sites. It is native to North America and hardy to Zone 3. It forms upright clumps of dark green foliage that resemble dwarf bamboo, and its dangling, decorative flower spikes look like flattened oats. It grows happily in the shade, reaching a height of 2 1/2 to 3 feet (75 to 90 cm) and width of 12 inches (30 cm).

***Festuca cinerea* (blue fescue).** The fescues are low, tufted, clump grasses with fine-textured foliage that ranges in colour from silver-blue to green. They are excellent grasses for windy, dry, hot conditions and are at their best in spring and early summer. A good example is *F. cinerea* 'Elijah Blue', a low-growing grass with bright, silvery-blue, very stiff foliage that maintains its colour right through the season. It forms a compact 8- to 10-inch (20- to 25-cm) mound and grows in sun or part shade.

***Hakonechloa macra* (hakone grass).** This attractive, cascading plant has delicate, bamboolike, bright green foliage that turns pinkish-red in the fall. It is an elegant ornamental grass, especially good for a shady spot, and looks beautiful on its own in a medium-sized pot. It grows to 18 inches (45 cm) and combines well with more upright grasses, such as *Imperata cylindrica* 'Red Baron' (Japanese blood grass). It dies back in winter.

***Helictotrichon sempervirens* (blue oat grass).** This evergreen forms perfectly rounded clumps of intensely blue leaves and is the best blue grass for general-purpose use. It does not spread, but always stays in a clump. Tan-coloured flower spikes rise 3 feet (90 cm) above the foliage on graceful arching stems from May to July. It grows to a height and spread of 12 to 18 inches (30 to 45 cm). This grass grows best in the sun and it blends well with grey and silver foliage plants and pink and purple flowers.

***Imperata cylindrica* 'Red Baron' (Japanese blood grass).** The bright green vertical leaves of this strikingly attractive grass emerge in the spring with wine-red tips, and the foliage becomes more and more red in summer, turning blood-red in the fall. It grows up to 18 inches (45 cm) and prefers moist soil in full sun, although it tolerates light shade.

***Miscanthus sinensis* (Japanese silver grass).** At least 40 different cultivars have been selected from this superb species grass, and they make excellent specimen plants. All bloom in late summer or fall and hold their shape well into winter, fading to shades of tan or cream. Cultivars vary in leaf colour, height and form. A particularly attractive and readily available cultivar is 'Silberfeder', an architecturally striking, refined and erect plant that has long leaves arching down from stout stems. Its silvery-white flower heads appear in August and last well into winter. It grows to a height of 5 to 6 feet (1.5 to 1.8 m) and spread of 18 to 24 inches (45 to 60 cm). It likes sun.

***Pennisetum setaceum* 'Rubrum' (purple-leafed fountain grass).** This is a medium-sized clump grass with excellent fall and winter colour and outstanding burgundy-red foliage throughout the season. The foliage grows to a height and spread of 3 to 4 feet (.9 to 1.2 m) and showy, rosy-red, bottlebrush plumes arch from the clump in late summer and fall. Its close relative, *P. alopecuroides*, forms clumps of cascading, bright green leaves in spring that change to gold, red-tipped, as the seasons progress, and finally to white before they die back for the winter. It grows to a height and spread of 2 to 3 feet (60 to 90 cm) and bears buff-coloured feathery spikes from August to October. Both prefer sun.

Bamboo

Bamboos have become, quite understandably, popular plants to grow. They can be used for dramatic effect in a pot and as a screening hedge, and they make a lovely rustling sound in the wind. Many are subject to damage by the bamboo mite, *Schizotetranychus celarius*, which scars the leaves, but otherwise these broad-leaved evergreens are easy to grow. They do have a few drawbacks, however. For instance, leptomorphic, running-type bamboos send out long rhizomes that are strong enough to crack an asphalt driveway. Running-type bamboos can be kept in bounds with a barrier, whereas pachymorphic, or clumping bamboos do not even need a barrier. Bamboos have cyclical flowering, although some species will wait up to 150 years to do this. Flowering occurs synchronously throughout the world, such as happened with *Phyllostachys flexuosa* in the mid-1990s. How this occurs is not understood. Although flowering is often fatal for the bamboo, new plants can emerge from the scattered viable seed. The bamboo varieties listed here are recommended by bamboo expert Graeme Bain from Southlands Nursery and Merle and Doug Box from The Bamboo Ranch.

Fargesia utilis. Any one of the handsome, clumping *Fargesia* species are worth growing. *F. utilis*, one of the tallest at around 15 feet (4.6 m), grows in a tight clump with small, delicate-looking leaves, and is hardy to 0°F (−18°C). The lovely evergreen *F. nitida* is even hardier and looks best in partial shade.

Indocalamus tessellatus. This is a dramatic, tropical-looking bamboo with leaves up to 2 feet (60 cm) long and 4 inches (10 cm) wide, the largest bamboo in cultivation. The leaves can be used to wrap food for cooking instead of banana leaves or corn husks. This bamboo grows well in pots and as a house plant. It is hardy to −5°F (−20°C) and is best grown in a protected area; its leaves will shred if exposed to strong wind.

Phyllostachys aurea. Also called golden bamboo, this species is one of the most commonly grown and, once established, it is extremely drought resistant. It has an upright habit and is graceful as a specimen, in pots or as a hedge. It grows to 21 to 27 feet (6.1 to 8.1 m) and is hardy to 0°F (−18°C). *P. nigra* (black bamboo) grows to 24 to 30 feet (7 to 9 m), is hardy to −5°F (−20°C), and is prized for its jet black culms (stems). New culms emerge green and turn black in two to three years. Black bamboo is dramatic as a container plant but prefers room to grow well. *P. nuda* is the tallest of the three at 34 feet (10.2 m), and the hardiest, to −15°F (−26°C). It likes full sun and bears supple foliage on dark green culms. Its new shoots are good to eat.

Pleioblastus chino murakamianus. Highly variegated leaves with vivid white stripes and some leaves that are pure white make this bamboo a striking accent in the garden. It grows to 6 to 10 feet (1.8 to 3 m), is hardy to 0°F (−18°C) and likes some shade.

Pseudosasa japonica. Japanese arrow bamboo is probably the most commonly grown of all the bamboos. It makes an excellent screen or tub plant and is quite happy indoors in pots. Its culms grow up to 18 feet (5.3 m) with persistent sheaths and large handsome leaves, 5 to 13 inches (12.5 to 32.5 cm) long and almost 2 inches (5 cm) wide. It is hardy to 0°F (−18°C) and likes some shade.

Semiarundinaria fastuosa. Narihira bamboo is a stately plant with stiffly erect, purplish-brown mature culms. This running bamboo makes a great hedge that grows up to 30 feet (9 m) in height and is hardy to –6°F (–21°C). *S. yashadake* 'Kimmei' has bright yellow culms with green grooves and green leaves striped with yellow. It makes a dramatic accent plant, good in pots. It grows to 25 feet (8.3 m), hardy to 0°F (–18°C). Both bamboos prefer full sun.

Shibatea kumasaca. Has a unique appearance in that the slender culms are obscured by dense, swirling, short but broad leaves. It also has very prominent nodes and is an interesting bamboo to use in containers. It grows up to 7 feet (2.1 m), is hardy to –6°F (–21°C), and prefers moist, acidic soil and partial shade.

Seaside and Island Gardening

It's hard to imagine anything more appealing than living beside the sea in our lovely inland coastal areas. The scenery is spectacular, bald eagles, cormorants and seals are a common sight, and if your home is located near their cruising grounds, there are even pods of killer whales. The view is constantly changing, the climate is mild, and the sunsets can take your breath away.

However, gardening by the sea can be quite a challenge. Strong winds, salt air, and blowing sand can be very damaging to plants, unless the plants are well protected or specifically suited to shoreline conditions. Erosion and problems with deer can be additional hazards, and most areas of the Gulf Islands suffer from a lack of water in the summer.

Make use of the view

The first thing to consider when planning a seaside garden is its location and design. Since your greatest asset is the view, try to create a setting that keeps the ocean as the focal point and frames it. Make use of natural features such as boulders and cliffs, and vegetation such as native arbutus and evergreen trees so that the garden enhances its environment.

Wind, salt, sand and erosion

In some areas, especially on southern Vancouver Island, the late fall and winter winds can be strong, changeable and quite destructive. Salt and sand carried by the wind and rain can also be damaging to garden plants. If your garden does not have a natural weather screen, it is a good idea to plant trees and shrubs that are capable of withstanding these elements and will protect your garden.

In some areas the shoreline is eroding quite seriously, partly due to construction and development. When plants are removed that would normally stabilize the earth and retain moisture, the soil becomes vulnerable, and prolonged and heavy winter rains may wash it away. If this is happening in your garden, you will want to include plants that will stabilize the soil. The long, spreading roots of trees are extremely good for this purpose, making it even more important that existing trees are preserved.

Islands suffer from summer drought

Most seaside gardens in our area are quite rocky, with little topsoil. This is particularly a problem in the islands since they receive very little rain from May to September, although there is usually plenty of rain in winter.

If you want to grow a variety of plants, and you live on one of the islands, you will need to have access to a good water source, probably from your own well. Better still, look for plants that are already adapted to these conditions, and feature B.C. native plants (see listing of drought-tolerant plants above). A totally natural seaside garden containing well-placed indigenous trees, rushes and sea grasses is hard to beat, easy to maintain and best suited to our extremes of wet and dry.

Deer: love them or hate them?

Visitors to the Gulf Islands are always enchanted by their first sight of these delicate little creatures as they wander down to the ocean and graze in the meadows at dusk. However, seasoned island residents are not quite so enchanted. The island deer are just as fond of garden plants as they are of meadow grass, and they will eat nearly everything in their path. This is frustrating to gardeners, who have developed ways to protect their plants, as you will want to do.

The first thing to do is to erect a stout chicken-wire fence around the vegetable garden. It may be necessary to spread the wire over the top of the garden too, because deer have been known to jump a 6-foot-high (1.8-m) fence. You can, of course, use this technique to protect any part of the garden, but in most cases it is impractical to do so. Sometimes deer will be deterred by a rope hung across vulnerable access points, but usually not for very long.

Most islanders try to grow mainly plants the deer don't like, and then provide special protection for the ones that they do. Unfortunately, deer will eat almost anything if they are hungry enough. The only thing we could find that they never touch are daffodils and marguerites, although they do seem to be put off by yellow-flowered plants.

Some people claim to have good success with the following shrubs: rhododendrons (as long as their blooms are at least 5 feet/1.5 m above the ground), barberry (*Berberis* spp.), Mexican orange (*Choisya*), lavender (*Lavandula* spp.), lily-of-the-valley shrub (*Pieris japonica*), Oregon grape (*Mahonia aquifolium*), cinquefoil (*Potentilla* spp.), heath and heather, camellia (*Camellia* spp.), forsythia (*Forsythia* spp.), laurustinus (*Viburnum tinus*), abelia (*Abelia* x *grandiflora*), escallonia (*Escallonia* hybrids), aucuba (*Aucuba japonica*), California lilac (*Ceanothus* spp.), flowering quince (*Chaenomeles* spp.) and junipers (*Juniperus* spp.).

Among the groundcovers and perennials with deer-proof claims are artemisias (*Artemisia* spp.), *Rubus calycinoides*, cotoneaster (*Cotoneaster* spp.), tickseed (*Coreopsis* spp.), globe thistle (*Echinops*), the hellebores or "winter roses" (*Helleborus* spp.), flowering tobacco plant (*Nicotiana* spp.), peonies (*Paeonia* spp.), white and yellow irises (*Iris* spp.) and ferns. Among the summer bedding plants, French marigolds (*Tagetes* spp.), pot marigolds (*Calendula officinalis*) and zinnias (*Zinnia* spp.) are worth a try.

After years spent trying to outwit the deer, most islanders have become quite philosophical about the subject. Life, they say, is too short to worry about the loss of a few petunias or roses.

Seaside plants

The following plants, all mentioned elsewhere in the book, grow well beside the sea. We encourage you to ask other seaside gardeners what they do, and continue to experiment yourself.

Trees and shrubs suitable for dry conditions. *Arbutus menziesii* (native arbutus), *Arbutus unedo* (strawberry tree), *Artemisia* spp. (southernwood, wormwood, absinthe), *Ceanothus* (California lilac), *Choisya ternata* (Mexican orange), *Cistus* spp. (rock rose), *Lavandula* spp. (lavender), *Pinus contorta* (two-needled pine), *Potentilla fruticosa* (cinquefoil), *Rosmarinus officinalis* (rosemary), *Santolina chamaecyparissus* (cotton lavender).

Trees and shrubs suitable for seaside conditions. *Acer pseudoplatanus* (sycamore maple), *Buddleia davidii* (butterfly bush), *Calluna vulgaris* (heather), *Cotoneaster* spp., *Cytisus* spp. (broom), *Eleagnus angustifolia* (Russian olive), *Escallonia* hybrids (escallonia), *Erica arborea* var. *alpina* (tree heath), *Fuchsia magellanica* (hardy fuchsia), *Hebe* spp., *Hippophae rhamnoides* (sea buckthorn), *Ilex opaca* (American holly), *Juniperus* spp., *Mahonia aquifolium* (Oregon grape), *Photinia fraseri*, *Pyracantha* spp. (firethorn), *Rosa rugosa*, *Skimmia* spp., *Symphoricarpos* spp. (snowberry), *Tamarix* spp. (tamarisk), *Vaccinium ovatum* (evergreen huckleberry), *Viburnum opulus* (guelder rose), *Viburnum tinus* (laurustinus).

Perennials suitable for seaside conditions. *Achillea* spp. (yarrow, milfoil, sneezeweed), *Agapanthus africanus* (lily-of-the-Nile), *Alstroemeria* spp., *Armeria* spp. (thrift), *Bergenia* spp. (bergenia, elephant ears, saxifrage), *Catananche caerulea* (cupid's dart), *Centaurea* spp. (bachelor's buttons), *Dianthus* spp. (pinks), *Echinops* spp. (globe thistle), *Erigeron* spp. (fleabane), *Eryngium maritimum* (sea holly), *Geranium* spp. (hardy or true geraniums, cranesbill), *Iris* spp. (irises and flags), *Nerine bowdenii*, *Penstemon* spp. (beard-tongue), *Polygonum bistorta*, *Scabiosa caucasica* (pincushion flower), *Sedum* spp. (stonecrop), *Stachys byzantina* (woolly lamb's ears), *Veronica* spp. (speedwell).

 # Growing Herbs

It's hard to imagine a garden without herbs. Fragrant, flavourful and colourful, they are among the most delightful and useful plants in the garden. In our area, we can grow an amazingly wide range of them, from sun-loving rosemary, thyme and lavender to shade plants like sweet woodruff, cowslip, sweet violet and Solomon's seal. Wherever you live, whether your garden is a large city loft or an apartment window box, shady or sunny, dry or wet, you can grow some of your favourite herbs.

Many herbs are disease resistant and pest free. Some, such as garlic, French marigolds and nasturtiums, act as powerful insect repellents. Culinary herbs, such as thyme, rosemary, sage, parsley and oregano, have been indispensable ingredients in the kitchen for centuries.

Herbs can turn an ordinary green salad into an exotic creation with the addition of different colours—azure-blue borage flowers, red rose petals, sweet violet flowers, orange nasturtium blooms—and flavours—tangy mints, lemony French sorrel, celery-flavoured lovage leaves, peppery arugula, pungent sage. Your salad selection is limited only by the number of edible plants you can grow.

If you are looking for ideas for your own garden, it's a good idea to visit a demonstration garden. If possible, try to see the UBC Botanical Garden's Physick and Food gardens, located next to each other on the north side of Southwest Marine Drive. The Physick Garden carries an extensive collection of medicinal herbs, and the Food Garden has many unusual varieties of fruit trees, berry bushes, soft fruits, culinary herbs and vegetables. Guides are on hand to answer your questions, and you will be able to gain some idea of the range of edible plants you can grow and the conditions they like.

Our climate enables us to grow nearly all but the most tender, heat-dependent herbs and vegetables. If your space is limited, the most important thing is to grow the herbs and vegetables you like to eat. If, for example, you are the only one in the house who likes zucchini, then six plants will be far too many, unless you have lots of non-gardening friends who will welcome your garden's bounty.

Herbs for the kitchen

If you are just starting to grow herbs, it is a good idea to begin with some of the most useful culinary ones, and we give a list of these in this chapter, as well as a planting plan for a herb garden. Most kitchen herbs prefer well-drained soil and plenty of sun, and many do well in pots. It's best to plant them in a protected, south-facing location which is, ideally, near to the house so that you can pick them easily when you need them. If left to their own devices, some herbs, such as mint, become untidy or spread wildly, so they will need pruning and containing. Make sure to find out the habits of each herb before you plant it, and treat it accordingly. Then plan your herb garden carefully on paper, and it will help you to avoid making costly mistakes.

Perennial and annual herbs can be interspersed to preserve a pleasing design in the garden all year round. Some perennials, such as thyme and golden oregano, make good borders. Others, such as rosemary, sage and curry plant, make attractive evergreen hedges, although your herb garden will need to be in a well-protected spot, since rosemary and curry plants may be damaged or killed in severe winters. Herb gardens make wonderful feeding grounds for bees and butterflies, especially if there are early and late bloomers,

helping to provide continuous nectar throughout the season.

Planning a herb garden

Putting aside an area of the garden for herbs is an idea that goes back many centuries. Traditional herb gardens are either square or rectangular and are divided into four sections. Many have a bird bath or sun dial in the centre, which acts as a focal point and draws attention to the shape of the garden. In the 16th century these focal points had the charming name of herbal "conceits."

Since the design is so important to the overall effect of the herb garden, the edging plants should be chosen carefully, to emphasize the shape of the beds. The best plants to use for edging are low-growing, compact ones that keep their form and look attractive throughout the year. Good choices are dwarf varieties of lavender, boxwood and santolina, common and lemon thyme, curry plant, germander and golden oregano.

The prevailing colours in a herb garden are generally subdued, with soft green or grey foliage and lavender, mauve, blue or white flowers. However, bright splashes of vivid colours, such as pot marigolds and nasturtiums, will blend well with the softer colours. Foliage can also be used to add colour, with such herbs as variegated thyme or mint, silvery-curry plant, santolina and lavender.

The plan on the following page is one traditional arrangement for a herb garden. The plants are described in the list of culinary and medicinal herbs below, with the following exceptions: boxwood (see shrub listings in "Shade Gardens, Native Plants and Wildflowers" in the February chapter), lady's mantle (see "Perennial Favourites" in the May chapter), and lavender (see "Summer-flowering shrubs" in the June chapter).

A traditional herb garden

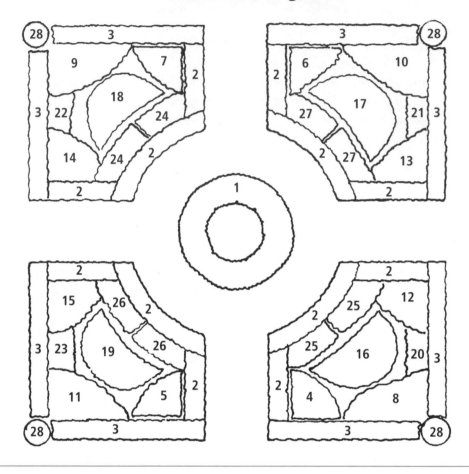

1. Lady's mantle (*Alchemilla mollis*)
2. Lavender (*Lavandula angustifolia* 'Hidcote' or 'Munstead')
3. Boxwood (*Buxus sempervirens* and *B. microphylla*)
4. Chives (*Allium schoenoprasum*)
5. Parsley (*Petroselinum* spp.)
6. Thyme (*Thymus* spp.)
7. Greek oregano (*Origanum vulgare hirtum*)
8. Fennel (*Foeniculum vulgare*)
9. Lovage (*Levisticum officinale*)
10. Angelica (*Angelica archangelica*)
11. Marshmallow (*Althea officinalis*)
12. Sorrel (*Rumex acetosa* and *R. scutatus*)
13. Sage (*Salvia officinalis*)
14. French tarragon (*Artemisia dracunculus*)
15. Lemon balm (*Melissa officinalis*)
16. Basil (*Ocimum basilicum*)
17. English marigold (*Calendula officinalis*)
18. Bergamot, bee balm (*Monarda didyma*)
19. Garlic (*Allium sativum*)
20. Dill (*Anethum graveolens*)
21. Purple coneflower (*Echinacea purpurea*)
22. Coriander (*Coriandrum sativum*)
23. Borage (*Borago officinalis*)
24. Alpine strawberries (*Fragaria vesca*)
25. Stevia (*Stevia rebaudiana*)
26. Summer and winter savoury (*Satureja* spp.)
27. Rosemary (*Rosmarinus officinalis*)
28. Mint (*Mentha* spp.), planted in pots, to contain it

Culinary and medicinal herbs

The culinary herbs are listed with their common names first, botanical names in brackets, because it is by their common names that all these plants are best known.

Alpine strawberries *(Fragaria vesca).* A perennial plant, it propagates easily by seed and by runners. The fruit is small, sweet and succulent, either white or red, similar to a cultivated strawberry. The young leaves can also be used to make a refreshing tea.

Angelica *(Angelica archangelica).* Angelica is one of the stately beauties of the herb garden. It is an aromatic biennial and grows to about 6 feet (2 m) in its second year, with large, bright green, aromatic leaves. The leaves are used to add flavour and sweetness to desserts, and the stems can be candied for decoration.

Basil *(Ocimum basilicum).* The most popular culinary basil, this annual grows to 8 inches (20 cm), with white flowers and large, succulent, finely flavoured leaves. It prefers well-drained soil and full sun. It is very tender and often only survives outside here from mid-June to mid-August, depending upon the season. Basil is a warming, aromatic herb that helps to improve digestion and is a key ingredient in pesto sauce and many tomato-based dishes. It is great in salads and makes an excellent garnish.

Bergamot *(Monarda didyma).* This perennial grows to 3 feet (90 cm), with highly fragrant, broad, pointed leaves and heads of unusual, decorative red, pink or mauve flowers in mid- to late summer. It divides easily in spring and spreads rapidly. Leaves can be floated on drinks and the flowers make an unusual addition to salads.

Borage *(Borago officinalis).* An annual, growing to 3 feet (90 cm) with bristly leaves and star-shaped blue flowers. It self-seeds easily, and will tolerate poor soil and shade. The young leaves are pleasant in salads and the flowers look decorative in salads and drinks.

Chervil *(Anthriscus cerefolium).* This annual grows to 2 feet (60 cm) high with delicate, anise-scented leaves. It is best grown in light shade and moist, rich soil, and it self-seeds easily. It is a good flavouring for light, savoury dishes and has been used for centuries as a cleansing spring tonic.

Chives *(Allium schoenoprasum).* A bulb that multiplies rapidly, chives grow to 1 foot (30 cm), with round, pink flower heads. The leaves have a delicate onion flavour and are excellent for many uses, including soups and salads.

Coriander *(Coriandrum sativum).* A delicately leafed annual, the whole plant is strongly aromatic and the dried seeds are scented like orange peel. Coriander likes good soil and a sunny location. It is an excellent herb for helping to improve digestion and is especially used in East Indian cooking.

Dill *(Anethum graveolens).* An annual that grows to 5 feet (1.5 m), dill has fine, delicate leaves, decorative yellow flower heads and aromatic seeds. Dill likes a sunny, sheltered position in good, light soil. It is used in preparations to ease colic in babies and is known for its ability to settle gas in the stomach. A common ingredient in northern European cooking, it is good with fish, sour cream dressings or sauces.

Fennel *(Foeniculum vulgare).* A perennial that grows up to 6 feet (1.8 m), fennel has finely cut leaves and a yellow umbel of flowers. It self-seeds very readily, so beware. Fennel likes well-drained soil and a sunny location. It is a very useful aromatic herb; the leaves are eaten raw and the stems cooked and used to flavour fish dishes. The seeds are an excellent after-dinner digestive. The annual Florence fennel is harder to grow here but the bulb is readily available in stores and makes a delicious vegetable.

Garlic *(Allium sativum).* One of the most important of all herbs, garlic has a powerful antiseptic and disinfectant action. It has a rich, pungent flavour and is used widely, both raw and cooked. Garlic is a bulb and flowers in its second year. It can be planted in late fall or very early spring, for an early fall harvest.

Lemon balm *(Melissa officinalis).* This perennial grows to 3 feet (90 cm) and has strongly lemon-scented leaves. It is easy to cultivate in sun or semishade and self-seeds. The leaves make a refreshing, calming, soothing tea, and they are an excellent flavouring for fruit salads and stuffings. The fresh leaves can be used to soothe insect bites.

Lovage *(Levisticum officinale).* This perennial grows to 6 feet (1.8 m), is strongly aromatic and tastes like strong celery.

Lovage grows easily from seed and prefers good soil and a sunny position. Its leaves are excellent for soups and stews.

Marigold, pot or English *(Calendula officinalis).* This is an annual with large yellow and orange flowers that bloom from late spring onwards. It likes to grow in the sun, in any soil, and starts easily from seed. Pot marigold is a useful medicinal herb, prized for its soothing qualities. It is an excellent flavouring for soups and salads and was used in Shakespeare's day to flavour and colour breads.

Marshmallow *(Althea officinalis).* A stately perennial, closely related to hollyhock, marshmallow is greatly valued for its soothing, healing properties. It is not affected by the rust virus that makes hollyhock leaves unsightly and is an attractive addition to the herb garden. It can grow to a height of 8 feet (2.4 m) and bears white flowers with lavender centres along the stem from midsummer into fall.

Mint *(Mentha* **spp.***)* A well-known family of perennials with square stems, pointed leaves, and whorls of flowers in summer. The mints spread rapidly from creeping stems and must be contained as they are very invasive. They are easily propagated

---

Tip of the Month: Custom Salads

Many gourmet stores carry ready-prepared salad mixes of unusual greens, herbs and flowers. These are expensive, however, and it is easy and fun to grow your own ingredients.

The ideal location for the bed is near the house, in a spot that receives good morning sun and is easy to water.

One tablespoon (15 mL) of mixed salad seeds should cover a square yard (square metre) of soil. Try a variety of lettuces, spinach, arugula, cresses, mache or corn salad, mustard and Oriental greens. Culinary herbs, such as basil, coriander, dill, fennel, parsley, sage, rosemary, salad burnet, thyme, lovage and mint, can also be planted in the bed. Time successive sowings from the last frost in spring through to August plantings for fall and winter salads.

Harvest regularly, cutting young, new leaves close to the ground so that the plant will sprout a second and third time. Amend the soil with fish fertilizer or canola seed meal between cuttings, and water well. Early morning harvests yield the most succulent leaves.

and grow best in rich, moist soil and light shade. Mints are strongly scented, with a delicious flavour, and are very soothing to the digestive system after a meal, hence the use of after-dinner mints and peppermint tea. The most important mints are peppermint (*M. x piperita*) and spearmint (*M. spicata*).

Oregano (*Origanum spp.*). There are several species, both annual and perennial. The species with the most flavour are those from hot climates, such as Greek oregano, *Origanum vulgare hirtum*. Good Greek oregano has a zippy bite to it and is commonly used with onions and tomatoes in Mediterranean cooking.

Parsley (*Petroselinum crispum*). A biennial that self-seeds easily, parsley grows in sun or light shade. It is an important culinary herb, rich in vitamins A, B, C and minerals.

Purple coneflower (*Echinacea purpurea*). Purple coneflower is an upright perennial with lance-shaped, dark green leaves. Its large, daisylike, deep crimson-pink flower heads with conical brown centres are borne singly on strong stems in summer and bring a splash of colour to the herb garden. They grow from 2 to 2 1/2 feet (60 to 75 cm) in height. The herb is a North American native plant, greatly valued for its medicinal properties, especially for its ability to stimulate the immune system.

Rosemary (*Rosmarinus officinalis*). A perennial that will usually survive our winters if grown in well-drained soil in a very sheltered, sunny, southern exposure. It will grow to 3 feet (90 cm), but needs protection from frost in winter. It has blue flowers in late spring or early summer and grows easily from cuttings. Rosemary is a powerfully flavoured herb with highly fragrant leaves and is widely used in cooking, especially lamb dishes. Rosemary is an important medicinal herb, too, gently stimulating circulation and digestion and helping to lift the spirits. A cup of rosemary tea is a nice pick-me-up on a bleak day.

Sage, common (*Salvia officinalis*). This shrubby, woody, strongly aromatic perennial with grey leaves and purple-blue flowers grows to 2 feet (60 cm). Sage is a pungent flavouring herb and grows well from seed and cuttings. It is used widely in stuffings for poultry and pork. Sage is antiseptic and relaxing, and makes an excellent and effective tea for a sore throat.

Salad burnet (*Sanguisorba minor*). A perennial with long leaves divided into leaflets, salad burnet grows easily from seed in a sunny, well-drained position. It is excellent for salads, with a faintly bitter and nutty flavour. It can be harvested all year except during severe winter months.

Savoury (*Satureja spp.*). Summer savoury (*S. hortensis*) is an annual; winter savoury (*S. montana*) is a perennial. The annual has a more delicate, pungent flavour, but both are used for flavouring in soups and stews. Both grow best in well-drained soil and a sunny position.

Sorrel (*Rumex spp.*). Sorrel is a perennial, and is a sharp-tasting, lemony salad herb that can be harvested from very early spring to late fall. It is excellent in soups and sauces. Garden sorrel (*R. acetosa*) is the most common; French sorrel (*R. scutatus*) is more delicate in flavour.

Stevia (*Stevia rebaudiana*). Stevia is a tender perennial herb with very sweet-tasting leaves. The plant comes from South America, where it has been used for centuries as a sweetener for food and drinks. Stevia grows easily from cuttings and likes a sunny spot and well-drained soil.

Tarragon, French *(Artemisia dracunculus).* A perennial that grows up to 1 1/2 to 2 feet (45 to 60 cm), tarragon dies back in winter. The leaves have a distinctive, hot, but subtle flavour. Tarragon grows from cuttings or divided roots, and prefers a well-drained, sunny location. It is an essential ingredient in Béarnaise sauce, and is very popular for veal and chicken dishes.

Thyme *(Thymus* spp.*).* There are many types and flavours of this perennial, which has small, strongly scented leaves. All grow well from seeds, cuttings and layerings into low, compact, bushy plants. Thymes prefer good drainage and a sunny position. One of the most important culinary herbs, thyme also has a strong antiseptic and antifungal action, making it an important herb for helping to preserve food.

The year-round vegetable garden

It is not necessary to have a large garden with a separate vegetable-growing area in order to eat your own fresh produce. Many vegetables and fruits are ornamental and decorative and can be mixed right into the flower border, or grown in pots on the patio. Tomatoes, for example, will produce prolifically when they are located in a sunny spot in pots, and fed and watered regularly.

Garden stores become very busy around the beginning of May, when most people rush in to buy vegetable seeds and seedlings for summer harvesting. However, if you plan your vegetable growing carefully, you can har-

vest in our area 12 months of the year, except on very cold, snowy winter days. For example, certain hybrids of Brussels sprouts, broccoli, cabbage and cauliflower are planted in early June, and can be harvested from mid-September through to the end of March. Hybrids of beets, carrots, fennel, kale, mustard, parsnips, rutabaga, scallions, and Swiss chard are planted in early July for harvest from mid-September to the end of March. Other hybrids of broccoli, cauliflower, endive, mustard, onions and spinach are planted in mid-July for harvest from mid-February to mid-May.

Locally developed strains work best

When planning your vegetable garden, choose from those that are recommended or grown specifically for this area. For information on local seeds see "Mail-Order Gardening" in the Resources section of the book.

One thing to watch for are interesting and different salad ingredients, most of which are very easy to grow. Lettuce, for example, includes exotic varieties like 'Red Sails', deeply fringed, green tinged with deep red; 'Continuity', a large butterhead, pretty enough for the flower garden; and 'Winter Density', extra-dark romaine/butter crunch cross, frost tolerant. Other interesting salad greens include mildly nutty corn salad, juicy and tart garden purslane, pungent and peppery arugula, and piquant edible chrysanthemum leaves that look like those of the ornamental plant.

Salad ingredients don't have to take up much space, and if you plant a few seeds every two weeks, you'll have a continuous supply of salad from early spring to late fall.

Preparing the vegetable beds

First select a site that provides as much sun as possible, preferably a southern, sunny, open exposure protected from wind. Mark out beds, leaving 3 to 5 feet (.9 to 1.5 m) between them to prevent people from walking on the beds and compacting the soil. Prepare the soil by digging it over to at least a foot (30 cm) deep, and enriching it with organic matter, such as well-rotted manure, seaweed or compost. Do not enrich if the bed is to be used to grow light feeders such as carrots.

It is best to raise the beds into mounds with flat or slightly rounded tops and sides sloping down to the path. You can also make raised beds by containing the sides with concrete blocks, bricks, rocks, or wood, but the sides of the beds tend to become hiding places for slugs. Raising beds helps to increase their yield, and the beds are easier to keep weed free, watered and fertilized. In addition, excess moisture will drain faster after heavy rains, and the beds will warm up faster in spring.

Plan the garden so that the most heat-dependent plants, such as tomatoes and corn, are in the sunniest, most protected spots, with at least six hours of sun a day. Begin planting, according to your plan, as soon as the soil can be worked in the spring. Many vegetables are heavy feeders and will need to be fed regularly with an organic food such as liquid fish fertilizer.

Crop rotation

Vegetable crops should be rotated (grown in different parts of the vegetable garden each year). Crop rotation is an important way to minimize the buildup of soil-borne insects and diseases and to prevent the depletion of soil nutrients. Most insects and diseases prey on specific groups of plants and overwinter in nearby soil. If their preferred hosts, and any related plants, are relocated the next year, it discourages the spread of insects and diseases.

Crop rotation also helps to maintain the nutritive balance of the soil. Crops can be divided into three groups depending upon whether they take nutrients out of the soil or put them back in. They are classified as heavy feeders, light feeders and soil builders. For example, members of the cabbage family, tomatoes, potatoes, the squash family, rhubarb and lettuce are all heavy feeders, while carrots, parsnips, the onion family, peppers and Swiss chard are light feeders. The soil builders include clover, green manure (planting a crop of fall rye, for instance), peas and beans. Members of each of the three groups should be rotated so they're grown once every three years in a particular spot. Members of the cabbage family grow best in sweet soil; add lime to the soil where they are grown if necessary.

Getting an early start in spring

Starting vegetable seeds indoors is an excellent way to give yourself a head start in spring. However, you will also be able to plant and harvest outdoors much earlier than usual if you use a cold frame to protect plants against cold and frost in early spring. It is easy to make a cold frame by constructing a base of wooden boards and covering the top with a piece of glass in a frame—an old window works very well. The top should be attached to the base and hinged so that the frame opens to the south for maximum sun and shelter, and then it is ready to use.

During the day, prop up the glass so that air can circulate around the plants inside the frame and close it up again at night. The plants will be well protected from cold weather and will mature early.

Successive planting

Many fast and easy-to-grow summer vegetables, such as lettuce, radish and arugula, mature quickly and should be planted once every couple of weeks from spring onwards in order to ensure a continuous harvest.

Companion planting

For centuries, gardeners have grown particular plants together, believing that some plants help others to grow, and some protect others from insects and diseases. The chemicals given off from one plant can even prevent another plant from flourishing. The concept of companion planting has come to prominence again in recent years as more and more gardeners work towards gardening organically. There is controversy about whether it works or not, but we feel that anything that reduces the use of pesticides is worth a try. Experiment with some of the ideas below and see how they work for you.

- Garlic and chives planted around roses or between susceptible vegetables, such as peas and lettuce, may reduce the number of aphids.
- French marigolds, asters, chrysanthemums, pyrethrum daisy, anise, coriander and basil are believed to repel a broad spectrum of insects. When planted in clumps in the flower bed, or among vegetables, they may help to discourage some harmful insects in your garden.
- If you have a problem with the neighbourhood cats using your garden as kitty litter, it might help to plant rue (*Ruta graveolens*) in various parts of the garden. Rue has a strong smell that cats dislike intensely.
- Nasturtiums planted between rows of broccoli may help to control aphids, since the aphids will first attack the nasturtiums.
- Mixtures of rosemary, thyme, sage, catmint and hyssop may help to keep cabbage butterflies away from the cabbages, cauliflowers, broccoli and Brussels sprouts.
- Tansy is said to be a very useful herb for keeping harmful insects away. Planted between cabbages, it may help to control cabbage worms and cutworms, and planted near doors it may keep ants out of the house.

Some recommended vegetable varieties for our area

The B.C. Ministry of Agriculture and Fisheries no longer provides lists of recommended vegetable varieties for our area. The best sources for seed are local seed companies that test and develop their own seed. Local seed catalogues are available in the fall. The following list shows some of the varieties they recommend.

Vegetable	Recommended variety
Asparagus	Larac, Jersey Knight, UC157.
Beans (broad)	Aquadulce, Broad Windsor
Beans (bush)	Venture, Jade, Blue Lagoon, Dragon Tongue, Dwarf Bees, Gina, Golden Rocky, Labrador, Nugget, Royal Burgundy, Early Hukucho Soybean
Beans (filet)	Maxibel, Nickel
Beans (dry)	Black Coco, Cannellini, Montcalm, Speckled Bays
Beans (pole)	Blue Lake, Cascade Giant, Fortex Pole Filet, Goldmarie, Kentucky Blue, Musica Romano, Purple Peacock
Beans (runner)	Painted Lady, Scarlet Emperor

Vegetable	Recommended variety
Beets	Albina Vereduna, Chioggia, Detroit Supreme, Early Wonder Tall, Forono, Golden, Red Ace, Pacemaker III, Kestrel, Winterkeeper, Beet Blend
Broccoli	Everest, Green Valiant, Packman, Shogun, Southern Comet, Minaret, Green Goliath, Spring Raab, Purple Sprouting, White Sprouting Late
Brussels sprouts	Royal Marvel, Red Rubine, Vancouver
Cabbage (summer)	Charmant, Derby Day, Early Jersey Wakefield, Early Savoy Express, Parel
Cabbage (late)	Melissa, Super Red 80, Bently, Danish Ballhead, Embassy, January King, First Early Market
Carrot	Autumn King, Bolero, Cleopatra, Danvers, Flyaway, Healthmaster, Merida, Minicor, Mokum, Novo Kuroda, Scarlet Nantes, Thumbelina, Royal Chantenay
Cauliflower (early)	Fremont, Idoi, Rosalind, Snow Crown
Cauliflower (fall)	White Rock, Armado Spring Plus, Purple Cape
Celery	Ventura, Golden Self Blanching, Mentor RS
Corn	Golden Jubilee, Seneca Horizon, Sugar Dots, Bodacious, Chief Ouray, Miracle, Sugar Buns, Jubilee Super Sweet, Seneca Appaloosa, Golden Bantam
Corn (ornamental)	Chinook
Cucumber (slicing)	Slicemaster Select, Amira, Armenian, Lemon Cucumber, Marketmore, Seneca Longbow, Orient Express, Salad Bush, Sweet Slice, Tasty Green
Cucumber (pickling)	Homemade Pickles, Cool Breeze, County Fair
Eggplant	Dusky, Ichiban, Short Tom
Kale	Lacinato, Redbor, Improved Siberian, Squire, Red Russian, Winterbor
Kohlrabi	Kongo, Rapid, Superschmeltz
Leek	King Richard, Durabel
Lettuce (butter)	Arctic King, Buttercrunch, Continuity, Esmeralda, Optima
Lettuce (French)	Cardinale, Loma, Nevada, Sierra
Lettuce (iceberg)	Salinas, Summertime
Lettuce (looseleaf)	New Red Fire, Red Sails, Redcurl, Revolution, Simpson Elite, Grand Rapids TBR
Lettuce (oakleaf)	Brunia, Mascara, Salad Bowl, Sunshine, Tango
Lettuce (romaine)	Little Leprechaun, Baby Green, Majestic Red, Rouge d'Hiver, Valmaine, Winter Density
Onion (sweet Spanish)	Ailsa Craig, Blanco Duro, Walla Walla
Onion (storage)	Buffalo, First Edition, Copra, Redwing
Onion (overwintering)	Buffalo, Walla Walla

Vegetable	Recommended variety
Oriental vegetables	Chinese cabbage—China Express; choi sum—Yu Tsai Sum; gai lan—Veg Gin; dai gai choi—Bau Sin; komatsuna—Komatsuna and Tendergreen; mibuna—Green Spray; mizuna—Kyona; leafy mustard—Southern Giant Curled and Giant Red; pac choi—Ching Chiang, Joi Choi and Pac Choi; shiso—Perilla; shungiku—Edible Chrysanthemum; Tah Tsai
Parsley	Dark Green Italian Plain, Forest Green, Hamburg
Parsnip	Andover, Gladiator
Peas (shelling)	Alderman, Maestro, Olympia, Oregon Pioneer, Oregon Trail Pea, Tacoma, Waverex
Peas (snap)	Mega, Sugar Daddy, Sugar Snap, Oregon Giant, Oregon Sugar Pod II
Peppers (mildly hot)	Anaheim College, Ancho, Fajita Bell, Mulato Isleno
Peppers (hot)	Early Jalapeno, Habanero, Long Thin Cayenne, Scotch Bonnet Red,
Surefire,	Thai Dragon
Peppers (sweet)	Chocolate Beauty, Golden Bell, Gourmet, Purple Beauty, Jupiter, Northstar, Pimento Elite, Staddon's Select
Peppers (small sweet)	Banana Supreme, Gypsy, Jingle Bells, Pepperoncini, Red Bull's Horn
Potato (early)	Warba, Rode Eesteling
Potato (midseason)	Yukon Gold, Ruby Gold, Red Pontiac, White Rose
Potato (late)	Netted Gem, Banana, All Blue
Pumpkin	Big Moon, Rouge Vif d'Etampes, Frosty, Howden, Jack Be Little, Lumina, Prizewinner, Small Sugar, Snack Jack
Radicchio	Bianca Di Milano, Palla Rossa Special
Radish	Altaglobe, Black Spanish Round, Early Scarlet Globe, Easter Egg II, French Breakfast, Icicle Short Top, Plum Purple, Long Scarlet
Rutabaga	Marian
Salad greens	Arugula, Italian Dandelion, Belgian Endive Flash, Corn Salad—Valgros and Vit, Curly Cress, Upland Broadleaf Cress, Watercress, Golden Purslane, French Sorrel
Spinach	Bloomsdale Savoy, Mazurka, Olympia, Skookum, Space, Tyee, New Zealand
Squash (summer)	Black Beauty Zucchini, Butterstick, Gold Rush, Spacemiser Zucchini, Benning's Green Tint, Scallopini, Sunburst, Ronde de Nice, Tromboncio, Yellow Crookneck
Squash (winter)	Gem, Hi-Beta Gold, Spaghetti Squash, Table King Acorn, Delicata, Sugar Loaf, Sweet Dumpling, Ambercup, Autumn Cup, Buttercup, Gold Nugget, Hubbard Blue, Sweet Meat, Nicklow's Delight, Zenith
Swiss Chard	Fordhook Giant, Bright Lights, Rhubarb Chard, Perpetual Spinach

Vegetable	Recommended variety
Tomato (extra early)	Siletz, Oregon Spring, Santiam
Tomato (ultra early)	Alicante, Kootenai, Oregon Eleven, Prairie Fire, Stupice, Sweet Cluster
Tomato (early)	Early Cascade, Early Girl, Big Beef, First Lady, Nicklow's Doubletake, Super Fantastic
Tomato (late)	Celebrity, Moneymaker, Longkeeper, Monix, Principe Borghese, Oregon Star, Viva Italia
Tomato (heritage)	Black Krim, Persimmon, Brandywine, Yellow Brandywine
Tomato (cherry)	Red Currant, Gold Nugget, Gardener's Delight, Red Cherry, Sungold, Sweet Million, Sweetie, Tumbler, Yellow Pear
Tomatillo	Rio Grande, Toma Verde
Turnip	Purple Top White Globe, Shogoin

Outdoor planting dates for vegetables in our area

These guidelines are those recommended by B. C. Ministry of Agriculture and Fisheries. The dates apply to years with average weather. Dates can be advanced by two weeks if cold frames are used.

March 1 to 15	Broad bean, radish, garlic
March 16 to 31	Peas, spinach, leaf lettuce, Chinese vegetables, turnip, onion sets, shallot
April 1 to 15	Early potato, green onion, bulb onion, kohlrabi, cabbage, leek
April 16 to 30	Beet, carrot, Swiss chard, broccoli, cauliflower, celery transplants, onion and leek transplants, parsnip, kale, head lettuce
May 1 to 15	Cauliflower, broccoli and cabbage transplants, main crop potatoes, parsley, asparagus
May 16 to 31	Tomato, pepper and eggplant transplants, squash, pumpkin, cucumber, Brussels sprout, bean, corn
June 1 to 15	Rutabaga, late cole crops other than Brussels sprouts
Up to July 15	Carrot, beet, green onion, broad bean, transplants of cole crops, pea, bush bean, Swiss chard, head lettuce, kale, leeks
Mid-July	Winter cauliflower, purple-sprouting broccoli
Up to August 15	Leaf lettuce, Chinese vegetables, winter radish, turnip, radish, spinach
September	Fall rye for green manure
Mid-October to early November	Garlic, shallot, overwintering onions

Frost-free dates

The Canadian Department of Agriculture divides the climate of the country into 10 zones, based on minimum winter temperatures, frost-free periods, quantity of precipitation and wind velocity. Our area, which is the most temperate part of Canada, falls mainly into Zone 8, although there is one balmy bit of southern Vancouver Island that is considered Zone 9.

Depending upon your particular location, your frost-free dates may vary a bit from the ones given below. These are the averages for Vancouver.

Last day of frost	April 1
Safe to sow seeds of tender annuals outdoors	April 15
Safe to transplant tender cultivars of common bedding plants outdoors	May 1
Date for digging up and storing corms and gladiolus	October 15
First day of frost	November 5

Making Flavoured Vinegars

Bottles of herbal and fruit vinegar are great additions to the kitchen, and they allow you to enjoy the taste and benefits of fresh herbs year round. The best vinegar to use is apple cider vinegar, organic if possible. It helps to regulate the acid/alkaline balance in the body, and is an excellent digestive tonic. It also tastes good.

To make herbal vinegar, pick the herbs in the morning, after the dew has dried but before the heat of the day has driven off the plant's essential oils. Use only perfect leaves, flowers and fruits, discarding any that have turned brown or show signs they have been eaten by garden pests.

Chop the fresh herbs finely and pack loosely into a sterilized glass, ceramic or stone jar. Warm the vinegar to just below boiling point, and pour it over the herbs so that they are completely covered. Cover with a glass, ceramic or stone lid and place the jar in a warm place. Leave for 4 to 6 weeks, mixing occasionally. Strain and rebottle. Store the vinegar in a cool, dark place away from light and heat.

Raspberry vinegar is another favourite. It makes one of the very best dressings for salad and when sweetened it is a great tonic drink for small children—and adults too. It is simple to make. Simply fill a stone crock with fresh raspberries and cover with apple cider vinegar, heated as described above. Leave to sit, covered, for 2 or 3 weeks, strain, rebottle and use for salad dressings.

To turn it into a drink for summer sipping, add 1 pound (454 g) of sugar to each pint (475 mL) of raspberry vinegar and warm gently to the simmering point. Skim off any scum that forms on the top, bottle when cold and store in a cool, dark place. To make a refreshing drink, pour a little of the sweetened vinegar into a glass and top with still or sparkling water.

Recommended Reading

Water-wise and drought-resistant gardening

Chatto, Beth. *The Dry Garden*. Dent, London, 1978.

Christopher, Thomas. *Water-Wise Gardening*. Simon and Schuster, New York, 1994.

Ellefson, Connie; Tom Stephens; and Doug Welsh. *Xeriscape Gardening*. Macmillan, London, 1992.

Ferguson, Nicola. *Right Plant, Right Place*. Macmillan, London, 1996.

Rice, Braham. *Plants for Problem Places*. Timber Press, Portland, Oregon, 1988.

Taylor, Jane. *Drought-Tolerant Plants*. Prentice Hall, London, 1993.

Walters, James and Balbir Backhaus. *Shade and Color with Water-Conserving Plants*. Timber Press, Portland, Oregon, 1992.

Grasses, bamboo, and seaside/ wild places

Darke, Rick. *The Colour Encyclopedia of Ornamental Grasses*. Timber Press, Portland, Oregon, 1999.

Greenlee, John. *The Encyclopedia of Ornamental Grasses*. Rodale Press, Emmaus, Penn., 1992.

Grounds, Roger. *The Plantfinder's Guide to Ornamental Grasses*. Timber Press, Portland, Oregon, 1998.

Harrington, H.D. *How to Identify Grasses and Grasslike Plants*. Swallow Press, London, 1977.

King, M. and Piet M. Oudolf. *Gardening with Grasses*. Timber Press, Portland, Oregon, 1996.

Pojar, Jim and Andy MacKinnon. *Plants of Coastal British Columbia*. Lone Pine, Vancouver, 1994.

Robinson, William. *The Wild Garden*. Timber Press, Portland, Oregon, 1994.

Wang and Shen. *Bamboos of China*. Timber Press, Portland, Oregon, 1987.

Herbs

Bown, Deni. *Encyclopedia of Herbs and Their Uses*. Dorling Kindersley, New York, 1995.

Chevallier, Andrew. *The Encyclopedia of Medicinal Plants*. Dorling Kindersley, London, 1996.

Foster, Steven. *Herbal Renaissance*. Peregrine Smith Books, Layton, Utah, 1993.

Hoffman, David. *The Complete Illustrated Holistic Herbal*. Element Books, Shaftesbury, Dorset, U.K., 1996.

McIntyre, Anne. *Folk Remedies for Common Ailments*. Key Porter Books, Toronto, 1994.

Tolley, Emelie and Christopher Mead. *Herbs: Gardens, Decorations and Recipes*. Clarkson and Potter, New York, 1985.

Trewby, Mary. *A Gourmet's Guide to Herbs and Spices*. Salamander Books, Los Angeles, 1989.

Wood, Matthew. *The Book of Herbal Wisdom*. North Atlantic Books, Berkeley, California, 1997.

Vegetables and flowers

Chan, Peter. *Better Vegetable Gardens the Chinese Way*. Garden Way Publishing, Pownal, Vermont, 1985.

Newton, Judy. Vegetables. *The Complete Guide for Amateurs and Experts*. Whitecap Books, Vancouver, 1991.

Solomon, Steve. *Growing Organic Vegetables West of the Cascades*. Sasquatch Books, Seattle, 1989.

Vilmorin-Andrieux. *The Vegetable Garden*. Ten Speed Press, Berkeley, California. Over 100 years old, reprinted. An invaluable gem.

Wilkinson Barash, Cathy. *Edible Flowers from Garden to Palate*. Fulcrum Publishing, 1993.

August

There's a certain bittersweet quality to August. It begins with the hottest weather of the summer: tantalizing fragrances hang in the soft warmth of late evening air, annuals are at their best, and the vegetable garden is producing abundantly. But by the end of the month there's dew on the grass in the mornings, the temperature has dropped considerably, and fall is just around the corner.

In August the garden seems to get carried away with itself. Fragrant honeysuckles and sweet peas ramble everywhere. Runners of rampant squash plants escape from the vegetable garden and start advancing on the house. The first tomatoes ripen, zucchinis need harvesting daily, and pole beans are ready for eating. Gardeners find themselves cutting back excessive vegetation, harvesting produce and pulling the odd weed, but otherwise leaving the garden to take care of itself.

Water-wise gardening becomes very important, and the need to water some plants, especially vegetables, continues until the rain begins in earnest. Some years the dry weather continues right into the middle of October, and many plants will suffer damage unless they are well sited and watered appropriately. If you are away a lot during the summer you may want to install an irrigation system.

Flowering herbs, such as oregano, hyssop and pineapple sage, bloom now, and their sweet nectar attracts honey bees, bumblebees and butterflies. The bees won't hurt you as long as you don't disturb them, and it's quite a sight to see dozy bumblebees sleeping on the hyssop flowers after gorging themselves on the nectar.

Some of the star bloomers of the month are hydrangeas, dahlias and marguerites, and they usually flower prolifically right up to the end of September. August, however, is the best time to visit dahlia growers. Their fields are in full bloom and you can choose your tubers for delivery and planting next spring. The information given here should help you make your selection.

This is also an excellent time to pick flowers for drying, make potpourris, and enjoy fragrance in the garden—all topics highlighted in this chapter. We also discuss water gardens, which are at their most appealing in the middle of summer. A water garden may sound like a luxury—and a lot of work—but it is an invaluable addition to a garden. Even the smallest patch of water helps to create a feeling of peace and tranquillity.

Garden Highlights
*indicates fragrance

Bulbs

Acidanthera murieliae,* *Agapanthus africanus* (lily-of-the-Nile), *Crocosmia* spp. (*montbretia*), *Dahlia* spp. and hybrids (*dahlias*), *Galtonia* spp. (summer hyacinth),* *Lilium* spp. (lilies).*

Perennials

Althaea spp. (hollyhock), *Artemisia* spp. (wormwood), *Chrysanthemum* spp. (florists' chrysanthemum), *C. frutescens* (marguerite daisy), *Gypsophila paniculata* (baby's breath), *Heliopsis* spp. (oxeye daisy), *Hypericum calycinum* (St. John's wort), *Inula* spp. (elecampane), *Salvia superba* (salvia).

Climbers

Clematis spp. and hybrids, *Jasminum officinale* (jasmine),* *Lonicera* spp. (honeysuckle), *Rosa* hybrids (climbing and rambling roses),* *Tropaeolum speciosum* (flame creeper).

Shrubs

Abelia x *grandiflora* (abelia), *Calluna vulgaris* (heather), *Caryopteris* x *clandonensis* (bluebeard),* *Clethra alnifolia* (summersweet),* *Hydrangea* spp. (hydrangea), *Rosa* spp. (roses).

Trees

Clerodendrum trichotomum (glorybower),* *Magnolia grandiflora* (southern magnolia)*

August Checklist
Annuals, perennials and bulbs

- Water plants where necessary and keep deadheading annuals and perennials.
- Dry flowers for winter decoration.
- Feed plants in tubs, window boxes and hanging baskets with fish fertilizer.
- Plant out perennial seedlings, such as delphiniums, and biennials, such as wallflowers, that were started earlier.
- Take cuttings of alpines, such as pinks (*Dianthus* spp.).
- Continue taking cuttings of garden geraniums (*Pelargonium* spp.).
- Collect the seeds of plants you wish to propagate.
- Plant fall-flowering bulbs.
- Order peonies from catalogues to plant in the next few months.

- Select and order dahlias for planting next spring.

Trees, shrubs and climbers

- Keep evergreens well mulched.
- Continue taking cuttings from shrubs such as camellia, escallonia, weigela and butterfly bush (*Buddleia davidii*) (see the April chapter.)
- Prune back wisteria and other vigorous climbers to control vegetative growth.
- Keep deadheading roses and keep them well watered. Order roses for planting in late fall and winter. Finish pruning rambler roses. (See the June chapter for information on roses.)
- Clip lavender as flowers fade.
- Trim hedges.

Fruits, vegetables and herbs

- Harvest vegetables frequently and keep vegetable plants well watered.
- Keep sowing winter vegetables, lettuce, spinach, radishes, turnips and Chinese vegetables up to August 15 (see the July chapter).
- Cut raspberry canes that have finished fruiting to ground level, and tie new canes to supports.
- Continue to collect herbs for freezing and drying, and take cuttings of rosemary, lavender, oregano, rue and bay laurel.
- Summer-prune espaliered fruit trees (see the January chapter).
- Remove the tops of single-stemmed tomato plants (not bush types) at the fourth truss and fertilize.

General garden activities

- Mow lawn regularly and prepare ground for sowing new lawns next month.
- Turn compost and keep moist.

Dahlias— They're Back!

Dahlia facts

- The dahlia is the national flower of Mexico. In nature, dahlia species are found almost exclusively in Mexico and Central America.
- Dahlia tubers and flowers are edible. Hollyhock Farm on Cortes Island and Sooke Harbour House on Vancouver Island both grow the flowers for use in the kitchen and for decoration. At Sooke Harbour House they also grow the tubers for eating.
- Dahlias are named for Dr. Anders Dahl, a Swedish botanist of the late 18th century.
- There are 17 classifications of form recognized by the American Dahlia Society: Formal Decorative, Informal Decorative, Semicactus, Straight Cactus, Incurved Cactus, Lacinated (or Fimbriated), Ball, Miniature Ball, Pompom, Water Lily, Peony-flowering, Anemone-flowered, Collarette, Single, Mignon Single, Orchid-flowering and Novelty.

Dahlias have been in and out of fashion for the last 200 years, ever since their discovery in Central America.

They were banished from many gardens in the last decade as gardeners fell in love again with the pastel colours and subtly shaded groupings of the Gertrude Jekyll–style border. Today dahlias are trendy again and growers are producing an even wider selection of forms and hues, a wonderful addition to any garden, whatever the taste of the gardener.

Dahlias begin blooming in midsummer and continue to the first frost. Their flowers range in size from 2 to 12 inches (5 to 30 cm) across, and in colour from white through pinks and lavenders, yellows and oranges to red and deep magenta, with many that are striped, streaked, spotted or edged. As well as adding a whole new dimension to the late summer border, some varieties make excellent cut flowers. Flowers are best cut when fully opened, in the cool of the early morning.

How to grow

Dahlias can be started from tubers, grown from seed or rooted from cuttings. Most of the dahlias we grow are hybrids, and plants grown from seed do not come true to type. To ensure you have the plant you want, source tuberous roots of named cultivars and save the tubers from year to year.

What is a tuber?

A tuber is a short, thickened, subterranean branch, used for food storage by the plant. It has growing points, called "eyes," at the join of the root and the previous year's plant stalk.

Tuber storage

Dahlias are hardy to Zone 8, and in Zones 8, 9 or 10 they can be left in the ground to over-winter. (See "Frost-free dates" in the July chapter.) However, their survival depends on soil drainage and the severity of the winter. It is usually best, therefore, to lift tubers in the fall and store them for replanting the following spring.

In preparation for storage, cut the foliage back to about 4 inches (10 cm) above the ground after the first hard frost. Lift each clump with a garden fork, being very careful not to spear the tubers. Gently brush the soil off the roots, spread the clumps apart in a well-ventilated but shaded area and turn the tubers upside down to ensure that all the water drains from the stems. Label them well and leave for a few days to harden off.

When the tubers are dry and free of soil, place them, still labelled, on top of a few inches of peat moss, sawdust or vermiculite in wooden flats or cardboard boxes. Cover them with the same material, leaving the stems exposed, and store for the winter in a very cool, frost-free place.

How to divide

Tubers should be divided in the early spring. The "eyes" should be evident as little nubs on the tubers, but not yet sprouted. If the eyes have sprouted it means they were stored in too warm a place or they have been left too long in the spring before planting.

Handle the tubers carefully so as not to damage the emerging nubs; cut the tubers with a sharp knife, making sure that each has at least one nub to produce a new plant.

When, where and how to plant

Plant when all danger of frost has passed. That generally means around the middle of April for gardeners in Victoria and the Lower Mainland and a bit later or earlier elsewhere, depending upon your specific climatic conditions. Dahlias love the sun, and deep, fertile, well-drained soil, sheltered from strong winds. They need a minimum of six hours of sun a day to do well.

When planting, dig a hole about 8 inches (20 cm) deep and 12 inches (30 cm) wide. Loosen the soil in the bottom of the hole, incorporate some compost and refill to about 6 inches (15 cm).

This is the time to put in a stake, which should be at least three feet (1 m) high, and tall enough to support the eventual height of the plant. If you try to stake plants after planting you run the risk of damaging the tuber.

Set the stake at the side of the hole and then set the tuber on its side, with the growing shoot or eye facing upward and close to the stake. Cover with 2 to 3 inches (5 to 7.5 cm) of soil and continue to fill in around the plant with soil as the dahlia grows and develops until the soil surface is even.

Dahlias that grow up to about 3 feet (1 m) tall can be planted about 2 feet (60 cm) apart, the taller ones about 3 feet (1 m) apart.

Plant care

Keep the plant well supported by tying it to the stake when it reaches a height of about 1 foot (30 cm). Apply a mulch to the soil to help conserve moisture, and water when necessary, depending upon the weather. Like most plants, dahlias prefer a thorough watering rather than frequent sprinkling.

Slugs and cutworms are the worst enemy of dahlia plants in the early stages, so check regularly for these pests (see the section on "Common Pests and Diseases").

Pinch out (remove) the growing tip when the plant is about 1 foot (30 cm) high, and this will result in a more compact, floriferous plant. If you want to increase the bloom size you can remove some lateral buds, a technique called disbudding. Flower buds come in groups of three, with the central bud producing the largest bloom. To disbud, either pinch off the two side buds or cut to the base of the leaf axil.

Growing from cuttings or seed

Cuttings may be taken from new growth and should be 3 to 4 inches (7.5 to 10 cm) long. (See "Propagating Plants from Cuttings" in the April chapter.) Rooted plants from cuttings must be hardened off gradually before you can plant them in the ground. In general, the best time to transplant them is when the roots start emerging from the bottom of a 4-inch (10-cm) pot. Try to plant late in the day or when the forecast calls for cool cloudy weather for a few days. Otherwise shield them from direct sun for a few days.

Growing from seed is most often used for bedding dahlias. They will not come true to cultivar because of cross-pollination. Harvest

---

Tip of the Month: Overwintering Pelargoniums

Taking pelargonium cuttings and overwintering them is satisfying and easy, and the best time to do this is from July to September.

For cuttings. Choose a healthy shoot without flowers or flower buds. Using a sharp knife, cut the shoot off just below a node, so that the cutting is 3 to 4 inches long (7.5 to 10 cm). Remove the lower leaves but leave at least three leaves per cutting.

Fill a 3-inch (7.5-cm) pot three-quarters full with potting mixture, and make a hole for the cutting with a pencil or a piece of dowel. Drop the cutting into the hole, press firmly in place, and add more mixture. Water it well and then keep it on the dry side, giving it a little water when necessary so that it does not wilt. Water sparingly during the winter months and keep in a cool, light room.

Harden off in April or May by setting plants out during the day and bringing them in at night or by placing them in a cold frame. Plant in the garden at the end of May.

To overwinter pelargonium plants. Dig them up in late September and shake off the soil, being careful not to damage the roots. Plant in fresh potting mixture in pots large enough to contain each plant's roots. Cut the stems down to half their height, removing all yellow leaves and dead flower heads.

Place the pots on a south-facing window ledge in an unheated room or in an unheated greenhouse. Water sparingly and do not fertilize during the winter months.

In spring, move the plants to a well-lit area and increase the amount of water. Harden them off in April, as above.

seeds in September and October and store in sealed containers. Seed can be sown indoors in February and March.

Dahlia shows and sales

Local dahlia societies have annual shows where you can see wonderful displays of dahlias. These shows are usually judged events and it's a great opportunity to talk to the experts (see the section on "Monthly Special Events").

Dahlias Galore and Ferncliff Gardens are two excellent nurseries in our area where you can buy plants and see the plants in bloom. Their show gardens are open to the public every day from early August to early October and both have catalogues. Ferncliff also has a video. (See "Specialty Nurseries, General Nurseries and Garden Centres" in the Resources section for times and locations.)

The Dahlia Trial Garden in Victoria

This is the only dahlia trial garden in Canada and a great place to view new varieties. It was established in 1994 at the Horticultural Centre of the Pacific (see "Public Parks and Gardens" in the Resources section for further details). New varieties of dahlias are sent here by growers who wish to introduce them the following year. The dahlias are planted, looked after and evaluated by members of the Victoria Dahlia Society as well as visiting judges from other dahlia societies. Each variety on trial is assessed against standards set by the American Dahlia Society and must score at least 85 out of 100 to be recognized for introduction.

Dahlia Species

Dahlia coccinea. Growing to a height of about 2 feet (60 cm) with red stems and yellow, orange or red flowers, this dahlia is probably one of the parents of the modern hybrids.

D. merckii. A delightful species, growing to 2 feet (60 cm), with small, mauve-pink, nodding flowers on slender reddish stems and very finely dissected green leaves. 'Hadspen Star', a white version of the species with very dainty, starlike flowers, is a selection from Nori and Sandra Pope at Hadspen House.

D. imperialis (tree dahlia). This may be hard to find, but if you have the space it will be worth hunting for. A dahlia with treelike proportions, this one grows to 12 feet (3.7 m) and bears small pink or white flowers in very late summer and early fall. It is not likely to get much in the way of bloom, but what a great talking point!

D. tenuicaulis. Another tree dahlia, this one grows to 8 feet (2.4 m) and has mauve flowers and light purple foliage. It blooms earlier in the season than *D. imperialis*.

Award-winners

With over 40,000-plus named dahlias in 12 categories of form, there is no end of choice. Here are a few award-winning dahlias from 'The Fabulous Fifty' list put out by the American Dahlia Society in its 1999 Bulletin.

'Alloway Candy' (novelty). An easy-to-grow dahlia with perfect form and pink blooms; to 4 feet (1.3 m).

'Brookside Snowball' (ball). A perfect white ball with strong stems.

'Creve Coeur' (giant). They just don't get any bigger or better than this, with spectacular 13-inch (32-cm) dinner-plate–sized red blooms on ramrod-stiff, vigorous, 5-foot (1.5-m) stems.

'Edna' (formal decorative). Yellow. An outstanding, recurved form and show winner; to 4 feet (1.2 m).

'Ferncliff Daybreak' (informal decorative). Light tangerine-cream with yellow tones. Outstanding and abundant early bloomer with long stems; to 5 feet (1.5 m).

'Hamari Accord' (semicactus). A very striking and easy-to-grow dahlia with good stems and 8-inch (20-cm) yellow flowers; to 5 feet (1.5 m).

'Hy Clown' (formal decorative). Six-inch (15-cm) rich yellow flowers with petals tipped and outlined in red. Very showy, to 4 feet (1.2 m).

'Inland Dynasty' (semicactus). Outstanding form and colour with huge, 10-inch (25-cm) yellow blooms; to 4 feet (1.2 m).

'Islander' (semicactus). Dark pink, salmon tones and an inner yellow glow. Twisted, waved petals, good depth; to 3 1/2 feet (1.1 m).

'Jessica' (cactus). Another show-stopper, this one with yellow flowers and red tips; to 5 feet (1.5 m).

'Just Peachy' (semicactus). Peachy blend of pink and yellow. Excellent garden variety with healthy green leaves; to 4 feet (1.2 m).

'Kenora Lisa' (formal decorative). Distinctive 6-inch (15-cm) salmon-pink blooms; to 4 feet (1.2 m).

'Lauren Michelle' (water lily). Glowing lavender with deep purple reverse; to 4 feet (1.2 m).

'Magic Moment' (semicactus). Beautiful 6- to 8-inch (15- to 20-cm) white blooms with a tinge of light purple at the tips as it matures; to 6 feet (1.8 m).

'Red Velvet' (water lily). Red with rose tones and lighter centre. Very pleasing; to 4 feet (1.2 m).

'Rose Toscano' (formal decorative). This dahlia has perfect form and long stems with glowing, pale orange flowers; to 4 feet (1.2 m).

'Show 'n' Tell' (semicactus). Another knock-out, this one with 8-inch (20-cm), orange-red flowers tipped with gold, and lacinated petals; to 5 feet (1.5 m).

'Spartacus' (informal decorative). Has 9-inch (23-cm), dark, velvety-red flowers. Excellent colour and form; to 4 feet (1.2 m).

'Stellyvonne' (laciniated). Creamy yellow with a slight tinge of pink at the edges; to 4 feet (1.2 m).

'Verda' (semicactus). Wonderful white flowers that glisten in the sun; to 4 feet (1.2 m).

'Wildwood Marie' (water lily). Dark pink blooms with strong stems; to 6 feet (1.8 m).

'Yvonne' (water lily). Salmon-pink and good for cutting; to 4 1/2 feet (1.4 m).

'Zorro' (informal decorative). Rated one of the best with dark red blooms; to 5 feet (1.5 m).

Dahlias with dark purple foliage

These dahlias are stunning and worth growing for their foliage alone. They are compact, bedding-type dahlias that need no staking.

'Bednall Beauty'. A smaller version of 'Bishop of Llandaff' with decorative burgundy foliage and single scarlet flowers.

'Bishop of Llandaff'. Low-growing to about 3 feet (1 m), this is a wonderful plant with dark, rich, bronze-purple leaves and small, single to semidouble scarlet flowers.

'Ellen Huston'. Striking orange flowers and almost black foliage. It is very free flowering.

'Fire Mountain'. This is another with a bright red flower and very dark foliage.

'Moonfire'. A splendid orange with vermilion at the base of the petals. A lovely contrast to its black foliage.

The Water Garden

Few things look as cool and inviting on a hot summer's day as a water garden. Fish swim lazily under the surface, dodging between the lily pads, looking for stray aphids and other tasty insect morsels. Iridescent dragonflies skim the water's surface, hovering for a few seconds before they dart off again. Pristine water lilies open their delicate flowers, watched by a large, concrete frog that sits benignly in the middle of the pond, water gently spurting from its open mouth.

A water garden is a great addition to any backyard and will give you countless hours of enjoyment. However, there are some important things you need to consider before you go out with the shovel and start digging.

Children, dogs and other impediments

Any body of water that is not completely fenced off presents a danger for small children and animals. Since there is little point in installing a water garden if you have to surround it with a high fence, you'll probably want to wait until your children are old enough and your animals well trained enough to be completely safe around water. Similarly, if you do install a water garden, make sure your garden is securely fenced, so that children and animals cannot enter unattended.

Where should the water garden be sited?

Even a small garden probably has room for a pond, but if your lot is very small, there may not be room for anything else. So make sure you really do have room for one before you go to the expense of creating a water garden. If you don't really have room, but like the idea,

you can always consider making a mini-garden in a pot, keeping it outdoors in summer and indoors in winter.

As a general rule, ponds should be located at the low point in a garden. This is their natural siting in nature, and anything else can be jarring to the eye. Exposure, however, is equally important, since water plants need at least six hours of direct sunlight a day. The pond should be in an open, sunny location, free of large overhanging deciduous trees that would drop leaves into the water in the fall. The leaves decay, using up precious oxygen just as the oxygenating plants are becoming less active, and this will foul the pond.

What should it look like?

Ponds can be formal or informal, depending upon the atmosphere of the surrounding garden. If your garden has a casual "woodsy" feel, then a formal pond would look out of place, but if your garden is designed along more structured lines, then the pond should be formal too.

The shape and design of the pond will have a bearing on where you put different kinds of water plants. Marginal plants, such as water iris and marsh marigolds, like to be in shallow water, with their heads dry and feet wet. This can be achieved by providing a ledge at the edge, covered with about 6 inches (15 cm) of water, and then dropping the contour sharply, so that the rest of the pond is about 2 feet (60 cm) deep, ideal for water lilies, oxygenating plants, and fish.

There is a drawback to this kind of pond in our area—raccoons love it. Standing on the shallow ledge, they can destroy water plants and clean out the fish population in no time. One solution is to make the entire pond 2 feet (60 cm) deep with vertical sides, so that the raccoons cannot feel the bottom. You can always make a special platform in the middle of the pond for marginal plants.

What are the best materials to use?

Ponds are made from concrete, prefabricated fibreglass forms, or heavy butyl rubber sheeting. There are pros and cons to each material, but concrete is generally regarded as the best method for the long term. The easiest to install is the prefabricated fibreglass form, and you can do this yourself, but they are quite expensive to buy.

It is also relatively easy to make a pond yourself with butyl rubber sheeting. First you need to dig a hole to the required contour and depth, and line it with the sheeting, preferably in black or dark grey. It is important to leave enough liner at the top, camouflaged with rocks and plants, so that the water stays in the pond rather than leaking around the edge. The pond is then ready to use. Butyl sheeting works well for shallow ponds with shelved sides. It can be a problem, however, if you want your pond to have vertical sides, since the sides might be unstable and cave in. Although the liner is made from tough material, there is also the risk that you might puncture it. It will last for five to ten years.

A pond lined with concrete is a much more permanent structure. You'll need to pour a concrete floor, build a wooden form for the sides, and pour concrete into them. Properly made, a concrete pond is excellent, but improperly made, it can be subject to cracks and leaks. The concrete layer should be 6 inches (15 cm) deep and reinforced. Unless you are confident you can do this properly yourself, it's well worth hiring a professional to install it for you.

The concrete used for fish ponds must be specially treated so that lime does not leach out into the water, killing plants and fish. This should be done as the pond is built, and it is important to consult with experts if you plan to do it yourself, and follow instructions carefully. You must then flush the pond with water several times before it is ready to use. Properly built, the pond will last for many, many years.

Planting around the water garden

Take a critical look at the location of your water garden, and its surrounding vegetation. Does it look like it belongs? A pond in the middle of the lawn needs a border edging of some kind. This might be grasses, bog plants, primroses, hostas, irises, small shrubs, or many other plants, depending upon the formality or informality of your garden, and the other planting. The water garden should be linked to its surroundings with plants, so that it seems to fit in, rather than being isolated.

Planting the water garden

Once your pond is finished and filled with water, and you are satisfied that all traces of chlorine from the water and lime from the concrete (if used) are gone, then the fun of stocking it begins. Before you introduce fish, you'll need to stock the pond with water plants and leave them for a minimum of six weeks to become established and acclimatized to their surroundings. A pond that has the right balance of different kinds of plants and animals will be completely self-sufficient, and require a minimum of attention.

The essential plants are the submerged oxygenating plants, which manufacture oxygen for the pond, helping to keep everything else alive. In the shallow areas you'll want marginal plants, with their roots in water and heads in the air, and in the deeper areas you'll put true pond plants, such as water lilies, whose roots are planted at the bottom of the pond and whose leaves sit on the surface.

Floaters, such as fairy moss, will drift on the surface.

In a medium-sized pool, approximately 9 feet by 6 feet (2.7 by 1.8 m) and 2 feet (60 cm) deep, you'll need about 20 to 25 bunches of oxygenating plants (one bunch for every 2 feet/60 cm of surface area), 8 marginal plants, 7 floating plants, and 3 others, of which at least one should be a water lily. Water plants are much more readily available than they used to be, and several local garden stores carry a selection, although it is often hard to locate oxygenators (see "Specialty Nurseries, General Nurseries and Garden Centres" in the Resources section of the book).

Of all the plants, water lilies deserve a special mention, since they are such a valuable addition to a pond. There are many different cultivars, varying not only in colour but also in habits, including flowering time, length of flowering season, the depth of water they like and how vigorously they grow. The ones you choose will depend upon your preferences and the size and depth of your pool. Many are fragrant, and there are over a hundred cultivars that are hardy enough to be left in the pond all year. When you buy the one or two water lilies you need for your pond, it's best either to consult an expert, or to visit nurseries that carry water plants early in the season.

Pond animal life

Fish and water snails are a very important addition to a pond. Goldfish will eat up unwanted pests, such as aphids and mosquito larvae, and snails will clean up debris and generally help to keep the water clear and fresh. For a medium-sized pond you'll want about 8 to 10 small goldfish and half a dozen water snails. You may be able to get these from your local pet shop.

Predators, pests and diseases

There are few garden sights as memorable as the great blue heron in the first light of day, gazing intently into the depths of your pond. Once startled, he'll leave with a great swish of wings, at least 5 feet (1.5 m) from tip to tip. But he'll be back for the fish he missed, until your pond is cleaned out. One way to protect your fish is to string fishing line around the edge at a height of 6 inches (15 cm). Herons won't step over this, and after failing to make a catch several times in a row, will eventually go and look for easier prey.

The other main predator is, of course, the raccoon, which has already been mentioned. Some people install movement-activated electric lights that come on when the raccoons step in the path of the beam: it startles the animals and may cause them to move on. Covering the pond with wire mesh or installing a low electrified wire around the pond can be effective, but unsightly. The best deterrent is to have a pond with vertical sides and make sure plants and ornaments are in the middle of the pond, out of reach.

Controlling pests such as aphids and other small insects is not hard when you have fish in the pond. Simply knock the insects into the pond with a high-pressure jet of water and the fish will take care of the rest. When introducing plants and fish into your pond for the first time, it is most important to make sure they are disease free. Dip plants in a weak solution of permanganate of potash before planting: this will help to prevent transmitting pests and diseases from one pool to another. It is also a good idea to put fish into water containing a proprietary fungus-control solution before putting them into the pool.

All this may sound like a lot of work. It is, in the beginning. However, once your water garden is established and you can sit back and enjoy it, you will be thankful you made the effort. The information given here is enough to get you thinking; we recommend you consult the reading list at the end of the chapter for further information.

Water plants to grow

Oxygenating plants

These are the plants that live submerged in the water and release oxygen. They are essential for the life of fish and the other plants and will be your first priority. However, be warned. Many of these seemingly innocent plants are actually extremely vigorous growers and will increase a lot in bulk over the growing season. As a rule of thumb, plant material should not be allowed to occupy more than one-third of the overall volume of the pond.

Ceratophyllum demersum (**hornwort**). A hardy, floating plant with long, spreading growth that breaks off easily and starts to root and grow. The foliage is dark green and prefers good light conditions and relatively deep water.

Eleocharis acicularis (**hair grass, needle spike rush**). The fine, grasslike leaves of this hardy evergreen plant are mid-green and produce dense underwater cover in shallow pools, up to 12 inches (30 cm) deep.

Elodea canadensis (**Canadian pondweed**). A semi-evergreen plant that forms a dense sward of foliage underwater and has dark green leaves. Fish feed on the plant and use its cover for spawning. It grows rapidly and is not really suitable for small ponds.

Lagarosiphon major (**curly water thyme**). This is hardy, evergreen, and one of the best oxygenators. It grows in a similar way to *Elodea*. The stems are covered in narrow, dark green leaves. It is often sold under the name *Elodea crispa*.

Potamogeton crispus (**pondweed**). The wavy, seaweedlike foliage of this hardy aquatic has a bronze tone that colours more vividly in strong light conditions.

Ranunculus aquatilis (**water crowfoot**). A hardy plant and one of the most attractive oxygenators, it has dissected foliage below the water line and three-lobed, floating leaves. Tiny white flowers form in spring.

Vallisneria spp. (**eel grass**). An evergreen, submerged water plant, frost tender, it requires sun or semishade and needs thinning out from time to time. It can be propagated by division in spring or summer.

Submerged and floating plants

Floating plants cover the surface of the water, keeping it cooler and helping to reduce algae by lessening the amount of light that penetrates into the water. Shallow water plants are known as marginals, and their containers can be quite shallow. A 6-inch (15-cm) depth of water is fine, as long as the water is always kept topped up so that the plants do not dry out.

Acorus calamus '**Variegatus**' (**variegated sweet flag**). This semi-evergreen perennial has swordlike, tangerine-scented leaves with cream stripes, flushed rose-pink in spring. It prefers sun and grows to a height of 30 inches (75 cm). A much smaller relative is *A. gramineus* 'Variegatus', which has grasslike leaves and no scent. It grows to a height of 10 inches (25 cm).

Aponogeton distachyos (**water hawthorn, cape pondweed**). Long, straplike floating leaves decorate the water surface, accompanied by strongly scented white flowers, produced throughout the growing season. Plant at a depth of 6 inches (15 cm) and move to 12 to 18 inches (30 to 45 cm) deep when established. Prefers sun.

Azolla caroliniana (**mosquito fern, water fern**). This tiny, deciduous water fern is red to purple in full sun and pale green to blue-green in shade.

Butomus umbellatus (**flowering rush**). A deciduous, rushlike perennial with narrow, twisted leaves and umbels of pink to rose-red flowers in summer. It grows to a height of 3 feet (90 cm) and likes sun.

Caltha palustris (**marsh marigold**). A deciduous perennial with attractive, rounded, dark green leaves and clusters of bright, golden-yellow, buttercup-shaped flowers in spring. It grows to a height of 24 inches (60 cm) and prefers sun. The cultivar 'Flore Plena' has double flowers.

Eichhornia crassipes (**water hyacinth**). A deep-water plant that has glossy evergreen leaves floating on air-filled leaf stalks, it prefers sun and bears spikes of blue-lilac flowers in summer.

Hottonia palustris (**water violet**). Dense whorls of divided green leaves form a spreading mass of foliage on this deciduous plant. Lilac or whitish flowers appear above the water surface in summer. Very useful for shallow pools.

Hydrocharis morsus-ranae (**frogbit**). A deciduous plant with rosettes of kidney-shaped, olive-green leaves and small white flowers during summer. The plant drops overwintering buds to the bottom of the pool in winter and they rise to the surface in late spring when new growth begins.

Iris laevigata (**beardless Japanese iris**). This rhizomatous iris grows to 2 to 3 feet (60 to 90 cm) in height and bears blue, blue-purple or white flowers in early summer to midsummer. It grows well in sun or semi-shade in moist conditions or in shallow water.

Menyanthes trifoliata (**bog bean**). A deciduous marginal plant that has tripartate leaves and fringed white flowers in spring. Prefers sun.

Nymphaea spp. (**water lilies**). These are the roses of the water garden, and they are available in almost any colour, in double or single blooms. Their growth habits, preferred planting depths, flowering times and rates of growth vary tremendously. Your local supplier or garden centre should be able to help you make a choice suitable for your situation. Lily pads provide shelter for fish and help to reduce the spread of algae. Most water lilies need at least six hours of sunshine a day in order to bloom. Here are some hardy, recommended varieties.

N. alba is the most common European species grown and one of the most beautiful with its pure white, cup-shaped flowers and green leaves. It is a vigorous plant, best in a large pond. Each plant may spread to 8 feet (2.4 m) and needs at least a 3-foot (90-cm) depth of water. *N. odorata* is white-flowered and fragrant, prefers a water depth of 1 to 2 feet (30 to 60 cm) and room to spread to approximately 6 feet (1.8 m). 'Alba' is a smaller form and grows well in a container. It has pure white flowers and a strong scent. *N. tetragona* is a small white variety. It will spread to 1 1/2 feet (45 cm) and needs a water depth of 1 1/2 to 3 feet (45 to 90 cm). 'Alba' syn. *N. pygmaea* is white, and is one of the smallest of all the water lilies, excellent for containers. *N.* 'Pink Opal' is a small plant with star-shaped pink flowers and a strong scent. It has a spread of 3 feet (90 cm) and needs a water depth of 1 1/2 feet (45 cm). *N.* 'Laydekeri Rosea' is very small and has strongly scented, deep rose-coloured flowers. It has a spread of 3 feet (90 cm) and needs a water depth of 1 1/2 to 2 feet (45 to 60 cm). *N.* 'James Brydon' is a rich red with orange stamens. It is an excellent small water lily and tolerates some shade. It has a spread of 4 feet (1.2 m) and needs a water depth 1 1/2 feet (45 cm). *N.* x *helvola* has marbled leaves and soft, sulphur-yellow flowers. It is very small and grows well in containers. It spreads to 16 inches (40 cm) and needs a water depth of 10 inches (25 cm).

Pistia stratiotes (shell flower, water lettuce). This lovely, evergreen floating plant must be brought in during the winter, except in tropical climates. It has hairy, soft green foliage that is arranged in lettucelike whorls and produces insignificant greenish flowers.

Pontederia cordata (pickerel weed). A deciduous marginal plant with lance-shaped, glossy, dark green leaves, it bears dense spikes of blue flowers in late summer and prefers sun.

Saururus cernuus (lizard's tail, swamp lily, water dragon). A deciduous perennial with clumps of heart-shaped leaves and racemes of creamy flowers in spring. It prefers sun and grows to a height of 10 inches (25 cm).

Sparganium erectum, syn. S. ramosum. A vigorous deciduous or semi-evergreen perennial with narrow leaves, this marginal water plant is one of the few that does best in full shade. It bears small, greenish-brown burrs on flower spikes in the summer and grows to a height of 3 feet (90 cm).

Typha minima (dwarf cattail). A deciduous perennial with grasslike leaves and spikes of rust-brown flowers in late summer, followed by decorative, cylindrical seed heads. It grows to a height of 18 to 24 inches (45 to 60 cm) and likes sun.

Recommended Reading

Dahlias

Ferncliff Gardens Catalogue (see "Specialty Nurseries, General Nurseries and Garden Centres" in Resources).

Hammett, Keith. *The World of Dahlias.* Reed, London, 1980.

Water gardens

Chatto, Beth. *The Damp Garden.* Dent, London, 1982.

Dutta, Reginald. *Water Gardening Indoors and Out.* Crown Publishing, New York, 1977.

Heritage, Bill. *Ponds and Water Gardens.* Blandford Press, London, 1981.

Robinson, Peter. *The American Horticultural Society Complete Guide to Water Gardening.* Dorling Kindersley, London, 1997.

Skinner, Archie and David Arscott. *The Stream Garden.* Ward Lock, London, 1994.

Slocum, Perry D. and Peter Robinson. *Water Gardening, Waterlilies and Lotuses.* Timber Press, Portland, Oregon, 1996.

Swindells, Philip. *Waterlilies.* Croom Helm, London, 1983.

Swindells, Philip and David Mason. *The Complete Book of the Water Garden.* Ward Lock, London, 1989.

Wilson, Andrew. *The Creative Water Gardener.* Ward Lock, London, 1995.

June: roses such as
Rosa 'Dortmund' in a
garden by Phoenix
Perennials
(pages 107–116)

June: roses such as
Rosa 'Graham Thomas"
(pages 107–116)

June: summer flowering
shrubs (pages 116–122)
DAGMAR HUNGERFORD

June: roses (pages 107–116)
ANN BUFFAM

Opposite
June: summer flowering
shrubs such as mountain
laurel (page 117)

July: vegetables in the garden of Sue Evanetz (pages 138–143)

July: grasses (pages 127–128)

DAGMAR HUNGERFORD

July: grasses such as blue fescue (page 128)

August: water gardens such as this one in the garden of Ann Buffam (pages 153–158)

August: sweet pea 'Mattucana' (page 146)

September: lilies such as *Lilium* 'Casa Blanca' (pages 168–173)

October: Japanese maple in the fall at VanDusen Botanical Garden (pages 175, 180)

November: evergreens such as *Pinus contorta* in the garden of Glen Patterson (page 192)

December: plants such as mountain ash to feed birds (pages 207–208)

September

September is often the loveliest month of the year. It's usually warm in the daytime, the air feels fresh and skies are generally clear. At night the temperature starts to drop, and the smell of dampness signals the end of summer. Annuals put on their last, glorious bursts of activity before the weather gets too cold, apples and pears are ready to be picked, and it's harvest time in the vegetable patch. Fall-blooming perennials, such as Japanese anemones, Michaelmas daisies, dahlias and chrysanthemums, are in full bloom, and give much-needed warmth to the fading flower beds.

It seems appropriate that many of the fall-flowering plants come in bright oranges, reds, purples and hot pinks, in defiant contrast to the cool yellows, blues and whites of early spring. Deciduous trees are part of this colourful show, their green leaves turning various shades from soft yellow to deep red, until they tumble to the ground and are raked into piles, ready for the compost heap.

As the perennial plants, trees and shrubs prepare for winter, sending their energy back into their roots, gardeners get busy with the fall clean-up. This process can last right through to the end of November, since it seems a shame to cut back anything that is still energetically flowering. It's a good time to trim hedges, plant new lawns and take the last cuttings of the season from bedding plants, such as geraniums, begonias and marguerites.

It's also time to look ahead to next spring and think about bulbs. Garden stores begin to get their bulbs in now, and you'll want to buy your spring-flowering bulbs while the selection is at its best. The hardy, summer-flowering bulbs are in too, especially lilies, and they are well worth a corner of the garden. Although there are some, such as *Acidanthera murieliae*, that must be bought and planted in spring because they are too tender to survive the winter, many bulbs are just right for fall planting.

This is also a good time to plant a large container for pleasure and interest through the winter and early spring months.

Garden Highlights

* indicates fragrance

Bulbs

Colchicum autumnale and *Crocus* spp. (autumn crocus)*; *Crocosmia* spp. (montbretia); *Cyclamen hederifolium*, also called *C. neopolitanum* (hardy cyclamen); *Dahlia* spp.; *Freesia* x *hybrida* (freesia)*; *Leucojum autumnale* (autumn snowflake); *Nerine bowdenii* (nerine).

Perennials

Anaphalis spp. (pearly everlasting), *Anemone* x *hybrida* (Japanese anemone), *Aster* spp. (Michaelmas daisy), *Chrysanthemum* spp., *Liriope muscari* (lily turf), *Physalis alkekengi* (Chinese lantern), *Schizostylis coccinea* (Kaffir lily), *Sedum spectabile* (stonecrop), *Solidago* hybrids (goldenrod), *Stokesia laevis* (Stokes' aster).

Climbers

Clematis orientalis, *C. paniculata*,* *C. tangutica*, *Polygonum aubertii* (fleece vine, silver lace vine).

Shrubs

Callicarpa bodinieri (beautyberry), *Calluna vulgaris* (heather), *Cotinus coggygria* (smoke bush), *Erica cineria* (scotch heath, bell heather), *Hydrangea paniculata* 'Grandiflora' (Peegee hydrangea), *Spartium junceum* (Spanish broom).*

Trees

Magnolia grandiflora (southern magnolia).*

September Checklist

Annuals, perennials and bulbs

- Keep deadheading annuals and perennials and save seed pods of flowers you wish to propagate.
- Divide perennials and plant new ones.
- Plant peonies this month and next.
- When leaves of gladiolas turn brown, the corms can be lifted and sun-dried for 10 days. Store in a cool, well-ventilated, frost-free place.
- Plant sweet peas, poppies and cornflowers now for early-summer flowering.
- Plant out wallflowers and add lime to soil.
- Begin planting spring-flowering bulbs. Shop early for best selection. Pot up some for flowering indoors.
- Dry flowers, including hydrangeas, for winter arrangements.
- Continue taking geranium (*Pelargonium* spp.) cuttings, and take fuchsia, heliotrope and marguerite cuttings.

Trees, shrubs and climbers

- Order new roses and prepare new rose beds for planting in November.
- Prune summer-flowering heathers. Give hedges a final light trim.
- Continue taking shrub cuttings (see the April chapter).

- Prepare soil for planting trees and shrubs in winter.

Fruits, vegetables and herbs

- Keep harvesting fruits and vegetables. Pull up tomato plants by the end of the month. Unripened fruit will ripen indoors.
- Continue sowing winter vegetables, lettuce, spinach, Swiss chard and kale, and thin out earlier sowings (see the July chapter).
- Start taking cuttings of bush fruits.
- Order new fruit trees and bushes to plant in winter. Prepare sites by digging in compost and manure.

 # Spring-flowering Bulbs

Bulbs are some of the easiest and most rewarding plants to grow in the garden. With the minimum of care, many will blossom and multiply over the years, adding interest and colour to the smallest space. In September the garden shops start carrying an impressive selection of over 350 different cultivars. The majority are imported from Holland, but we also have very good local bulb growers.

Most bulbs are sold with excellent information sheets, including instructions on how and where to plant, blooming times, and a colour photo of the flowers. This makes it much easier to make your choices. By choosing bulbs carefully, you can have blossoms in your garden as early as mid-January.

Spring is the time to look at bulbs

If you didn't already do so this year, make a note to visit public gardens for inspiration next spring. Queen Elizabeth Gardens, UBC Botanical Gardens, VanDusen Gardens and Butchart Gardens have excellent bulb displays.

When it comes to daffodils and narcissi,

some of the best are grown locally, and these local bulbs are usually less expensive than imports. There are many different varieties available. Every April, growers exhibit their blooms at the Bradner Flower Show in the Fraser Valley, and take orders for delivery in the fall. Fields around Bradner are covered in cheerful yellow and white blooms, and many growers welcome visitors to their fields.

If you are willing to venture farther afield, the towns of La Conner and Mount Vernon in the Skagit Valley, Washington State, about one hour's drive from the border, are well worth the visit. Daffodils and tulips are grown in fields all around the towns. This is a great way to spend a sunny day, especially if you take a picnic, your camera and any friends and family you can round up. (See the section on "Monthly Special Events" for details about the Bradner Flower Show and the Skagit Valley Tulip Festival.)

What is a bulb?

A bulb is a tiny, fully formed plant surrounded by white, fleshy, overlapping scales. Inside the bulb is everything that the plant needs to grow and flower at the appropriate time. At the base of the bulb is an area called the basal plate, which contains the roots of the plants. A thin papery outer covering called a tunic surrounds the bulb, which remains in its dormant state until moisture and the right temperature conditions spur it into action.

Corms, tubers and rhizomes

Some spring "bulbs" are not bulbs at all, but the term has come to mean any plant with an underground storage system. Crocuses and cyclamen, for example, are produced from corms. Bulbs and corms look very similar, the only visible difference being that corms tend to be somewhat flatter in shape. In corms however, food is stored in an enlarged basal plate rather than the scales, and it is a more solid structure.

Tubers, on the other hand, look quite different from bulbs and corms, and come in a variety of shapes and sizes, either singly or in clusters. A tuber is an enlarged or thickened subterranean stem.

Rhizomes are similar to tubers in having a thickened modified stem, but rhizomes tend to grow horizontally on, or just below, the surface. The iris springs to mind when we think of a plant with this type of food storage container.

When to plant?

In our climate, spring bulbs can be planted any time from mid-September through to late November. In low-lying areas, such as Richmond, where drainage is poor, some gardeners plant them even later.

What to buy

Make sure the bulbs you buy are plump, firm and healthy. Choose four or five of your favourites, and buy them in quantities of 10 or more. You can always buy more of the ones you like the following year, and add other varieties. Put your bulbs into separate paper bags, each carefully labelled and complete with information sheet, and you're ready to plant.

What to plant where?

Spring-flowering bulbs generally do best in well-drained soil and a sunny location. Part shade, however, is fine, and some, such as squills, do very well in full shade. Before planting, walk around your garden. Become familiar with each shrub and tree, and imagine every bare corner as a potential spot for spring bulbs.

Plant snowdrops in clumps of 25 or more

under a deciduous tree or in front of low-growing evergreen shrubs or conifers. Most important, however, is to plant them near a path where you can see them easily, even on the dullest, rainiest days.

Another very early, lovely little bulb is *Iris reticulata*, a miniature iris that only grows to about 5 inches (13 cm) high. These bulbs look most natural when planted in a rock garden among low-growing heathers or conifers, in front of dwarf azaleas, or under a Japanese maple. They should be in a sunny spot, in groups of at least 10.

Consider what else will be in bloom at the same time, and use your bulbs to accent or complement other plants. For example, the delicate, starlike blue flowers of glory-of-the-snow (*Chionodoxa luciliae*) are an excellent contrast to a yellow-flowering forsythia or other early-flowering deciduous shrubs. They also associate well with yellow and white crocuses or miniature daffodils.

How to plant bulbs

It is very important to plant bulbs at the right depth and with the right nutrients in order for them to give their best blooms. First, dig out the soil to the proper depth, loosen it and add bone meal and any necessary soil amendments. If the soil is sandy, add peat moss or leaf compost. If it is heavy and clay-based, add sand or peat moss.

Plant the bulbs firmly in the soil, pointed end up, in the desired numbers and arrangement. Cover the bulbs with soil and water well.

Growing spring bulbs in outdoor containers

Many spring bulbs, especially dwarf cultivars, can be used effectively in containers (see "How to Plant a Large Container for Winter Pleasure" later in this chapter). You can create a spring scene by underplanting a potted conifer with hyacinths and narcissi, or by planting bulbs with evergreen plants, such as ivy, so that the bulbs come up through the ivy. Once they have been used in a container, the bulbs should be planted into the garden, since they will not do well in a container for two years running.

Some common bulb problems

Plants that stop flowering and degenerate into masses of small, grasslike leaves, or die, may have been attacked by the narcissus bulb fly. The adult fly resembles a small bumblebee. It is the maggot of the fly that attacks snowdrops, daffodils, hyacinths, tulips and other bulbous plants. Bulbs are tunnelled and usually rot. Look for a tiny brown hole where the maggot has entered the bulb. The best way to control the problem is to dig up the bulbs after the foliage has died down and destroy the wormy bulbs.

Slugs are another common problem. They love tender young shoots. The best way to prevent slug destruction is to clean up the garden really well in fall and again in early spring, eliminating any slug hiding places, and maintain a vigilant watch for any sign of these pests.

If all signs of your bulbs have disappeared, you may be the victim of squirrels or mice, who love to nibble at bulbs. Planting the bulbs slightly deeper in the fall may help to eliminate this problem.

It is worth keeping a record of the bulbs you have bought, where you have planted them, and ones that you want to buy. Note the quantity, description and price of the bulbs and where they are planted. This is also a good place to jot down bulbs you might want to plant next year.

Daffodils

These are among the most popular and dependable of all the spring-flowering bulbs and look best planted in huge drifts or naturalized in grassy meadows or orchards. For those of us with small city gardens, they can be naturalized under deciduous trees and shrubs instead. No matter where we plant them, they do look best massed in as large a group as possible. Bulbs should be planted 6 inches (15 cm) deep in fertile well-drained soil, in a sunny or partly shaded location. Planted in grass or elsewhere in the garden, they should be left undisturbed until the leaves have begun to yellow, which is usually about six weeks after they have flowered. Given the right conditions, they will flower year after year, increasing in quantity.

It used to be that the choice was between yellow and white, but now there are many pink, scarlet and orange-cupped cultivars to make the already difficult task of choosing daffodils more difficult still. When choosing, make a note of height as well as blooming times, but whatever you choose, daffodils look best when planted in groups of the same variety rather than mixed. Here are some to look for, varying in size from the large-flowered cultivars to the dainty miniatures.

'Acropolis'. Huge 4-inch (10-cm) flower with multilayered white petals splashed crimson at the centre. Blooms in midspring and grows to 18 inches (45 cm).

'Broadway Star'. A large 3-inch (7.5-cm) white flower with the central petals splashed with orange stripes down the middle. Grows to 16 inches (40 cm).

'Daydream'. Sunny yellow petals with a creamy white, flared trumpet edged in yellow. Strong stems to 16 inches (40 cm).

'February Gold'. A very early narcissus, with yellow, slightly reflexed petals and a darker yellow trumpet. Grows to 12 inches (30 cm).

'Hawera'. A small multistemmed cultivar flowering in April with lemon-yellow flowers to a height of 7 inches (18 cm). Good for containers.

'Ice Wings'. Clusters of pure white flowers to a height of 8 inches (20 cm).

'Jack Snipe'. White petals with a lemon-yellow cup blooming midspring. A height of 8 inches (20 cm) makes it a good candidate for containers.

'Peeping Tom'. Another early-flowering cultivar, this one has bright yellow, reflexed petals and a narrow, flanged trumpet. Grows to a height of 18 inches (45 cm).

'Tahiti'. A fully double flower that is 4 1/2 inches across (11 cm), yellow with a bright orange-red centre. Grows to 18 inches (45 cm).

'Tête-à-Tête'. A lovely little narcissus growing to a height of 6 inches (15 cm). Golden-yellow, slightly reflexed petals with a yellow-orange cup.

'Thalia'. A dainty white cultivar, usually with two flower heads per stem. Flowers have funnel-shaped cups and slightly twisted petals. Grows to a height of 14 inches (35 cm).

'Yellow Cheerfulness'. Sweetly scented, double, golden-yellow flowers in clusters of three or four. It grows to 18 inches (45 cm) and blooms in midspring.

Tulips

At this time of year garden centres have a large selection of tulips in a wide variety of colours, shapes and flowering times, making the choice a daunting one. The important thing to remember is that the tulip cultivars can be treated like annuals. Experiment, for they are not permanent additions to the garden. Mass plant, mingle them among border shrubs and other bulbs or plant them in containers.

Grow tulips in a sunny spot, sheltered from strong winds, in well-drained fertile soil. You can dig the bulbs up after the foliage has died down, store them in a dry cool place (garage or basement) over the summer and replant them in the fall. But do not be surprised if they do not bloom as successfully as the first year.

The following list is meant to give you a variety of colour, shape of flower and blooming time.

'Ancilla'. A Kaufmanniana tulip, it blooms early with a soft pink colour on the outside of the petals and white on the inside. It grows low to the ground on a short stem 6 inches (15 cm) high.

'Apeldoorn'. A Darwin hybrid tulip, orange to cherry red, it grows to 24 inches (60 cm).

'China Pink'. This lily-flowered, clear pink tulip blooms in late spring and grows to 20 inches (50 cm).

'Dreamland'. A cup-shaped tulip that grows to a height of 24 inches (60 cm) and flowers in late spring. It is described as "spinel-red flamed cream" (ruby red and cream) in one bulb catalogue.

'Hamilton'. A fringed tulip with buttercup-yellow blossoms produced in midspring; grows to 20 inches (50 cm).

'Marilyn'. Another late lily-flowered tulip, white with a fuchsia to purple feathered flame marking the white petals. Grows to 24 inches (60 cm).

'Oriental Splendor'. Has the characteristic mottled leaves of *T. greigii*; the flowers are carmine-red edged with lemon and grow to a height of 12 inches (30 cm).

'Peach Blossom'. An old cultivar that produces double, peachy-pink flowers early in spring and grows to a height of 11 inches (28 cm).

'Princess Irene'. This single early tulip is a unique combination of orange and purple and grows to a height of 14 inches (35 cm).

'Red Riding Hood'. A red, early-flowering tulip growing to a height of 8 inches (20 cm) with attractive blue-green leaves marked purple.

'Spring Green'. A late-flowering ivory-white tulip feathered with green, growing to a height of 16 inches (40 cm).

'West Point'. A primrose-yellow, lily-shaped tulip with exceptionally strong stems growing to a height of 24 inches (60 cm).

'White Triumphator'. A late bloomer with lily-shaped, white flowers, it combines well with early greys and greens in a border, and grows to a height of 28 inches (70 cm).

Tip of the Month: Dividing Irises

September is the one time when the garden looks after itself, so it's a great time for dedicated gardeners to take a vacation. Lock up the toolshed, arrange for someone to water occasionally and head for your favourite vacation spot. However, if you decide to stay home, you could be dividing irises.

Irises need to be lifted and divided every three years or so. They can be divided in early summer immediately after flowering, but they can suffer if they're not given adequate water when replanted. Late August and early September is an excellent time to divide them and get them well rooted before winter.

Lift the clumps and carefully split the new rhizomes away from the old unproductive rhizome in the centre. Discard the old section and cut the leaves of the new sections into a fan shape about 6 inches (15 cm) long. Plant firmly with the top of the rhizome just showing above the soil.

Flaming tulips

An interesting fact is that the "breaking" of plain-coloured tulips into "flames" and stripes of different colours is not the result of clever tulip breeding, but an infection caused by the "tulip breaking virus," which is spread by aphids. In Holland during the height of the tulip craze, people spent fortunes to get hold of these unusual plants, not realizing what caused this mutation.

Tiny treasures

Most of the spring bulbs mentioned so far are cultivars, but here is a look at some of the species bulbs that are becoming more available. There has been a reluctance to buy them, as it was feared that they were being dug up from the wild. That certainly was the case at one time, but that trade has all but ceased and the species bulbs that are available now are grown from seed in nurseries. Of course, the time and work involved in raising them from seed is often reflected in the price.

Many of the species have a simplicity and grace that the large-flowered hybrids don't possess. Apart from the beauty of their flowers, the great advantage of the species bulbs is that they will naturalize if conditions suit them. There isn't the space in this book to talk about them all, but a look at a few fritillarias, tulips and daffodils show what treasures are there to discover.

Fritillaria species

Fritillarias are grown for their exquisite bell-shaped flowers, subtle colours and characteristic chequered or mottled markings. Easy to grow, their chief requirement, like most bulbous plants, is well-drained soil in sun, though some, as you will see, thrive in shady woodland areas.

A checklist of spring-flowering bulbs

The following chart will help in planning your selection of bulbs. The chart includes planting depth, spacing between bulbs and height of mature plants. Bulbs with an asterisk are especially recommended as a beginner's selection.

Flowering time	Planting depths		Spacing		Flower height
Early spring					
Galanthus spp. (snowdrops)*	5 inches	(13 cm)	3 inches	(7.5 cm)	VL
Eranthis hyemalis (winter aconite)	5 inches	(13 cm)	3 inches	(7.5 cm)	VL
*Iris reticulata**	5 inches	(13 cm)	3 inches	(7.5 cm)	VL
Crocus spp.*	5 inches	(13 cm)	3 inches	(7.5 cm)	VL
Chionodoxa luciliae (glory-of-the-snow)*	5 inches	(13 cm)	3 inches	(7.5 cm)	VL
Puschkinia scilloides var *libanotica*	5 inches	(13 cm)	4 inches	(10 cm)	VL
Anemone blanda (windflower)	5 inches	(13 cm)	3 inches	(7.5 cm)	VL
Muscari spp. (grape hyacinth)	5 inches	(13 cm)	3 inches	(7.5 cm)	VL
Tulipa spp. (tulips)					
Kaufmanniana	8 inches	(20 cm)	6 inches	(15 cm)	VL
Fosterana	8 inches	(20 cm)	6 inches	(15 cm)	L
Single Early	8 inches	(20 cm)	6 inches	(15 cm)	L
Double Early	8 inches	(20 cm)	6 inches	(15 cm)	L
Hyacinthus (hyacinths)	8 inches	(20 cm)	6 inches	(15 cm)	L
Narcissus spp.					
Miniature daffodils	8 inches	(20 cm)	4 inches	(10 cm)	L
Trumpet daffodils	8 inches	(20 cm)	6 inches	(15 cm)	MH
Midspring					
Tulipa spp. (tulips)					
Greigii	8 inches	(20 cm)	6 inches	(15 cm)	L/MH
Triumph	8 inches	(20 cm)	5 inches	(13 cm)	MH
Darwin Hybrid*	8 inches	(20 cm)	6 inches	(15 cm)	H
Narcissus spp.*	8 inches	(20 cm)	5 inches	(13 cm)	MH*
Fritillaria imperialis	8 inches	(20 cm)	12 inches	(30 cm)	VH
Late spring					
Dutch iris*	8 inches	(20 cm)	4 inches	(10 cm)	MH
Tulipa spp. (tulips)					
Parrot*	8 inches	(20 cm)	6 inches	(15 cm)	MH
Double Late (peony-flowered)	8 inches	(20 cm)	6 inches	(15 cm)	MH
Lily-flowered	8 inches	(20 cm)	6 inches	(15 cm)	H
Rembrandt	8 inches	(20 cm)	6 inches	(15 cm)	H
Darwin	8 inches	(20 cm)	6 inches	(15 cm)	H/VH
Cottage, Single Late	8 inches	(20 cm)	6 inches	(15 cm)	H/VH
Allium giganteum	8 inches	(20 cm)	8 inches	(20 cm)	VH

Flowering height code

VL — very low, up to 6 inches (15 cm)

L — low, 6 to 12 inches (15 to 30 cm)

MH — medium-high, 12 to 20 inches (30 to 50 cm)

H — high, 20 to 28 inches (50 to 70 cm)

VH — very high, over 28 inches (70 cm)

F. acmopetala. A very striking fritillaria with two to three downward-facing bells. The flowers appear in April and are striped purple-brown and pale green. It flourishes in dappled shade in rich well-drained soil, and grows to a height of about 10 inches (25 cm).

F. assyriaca. Bears bell-shaped flowers on arched stems up to 12 inches (30 cm) in March or April. Maroon in colour, fading to yellow at the tips of the petals, this is a lovely fritillaria that needs a sunny, well-drained site. The flower has a dusty look to it and it associates well with grey-leafed plants which need similar growing conditions.

F. camschatcensis. An excellent garden plant with colours that vary from deep purple, almost black, to greyish purple. The bell-shaped flowers have bright yellow anthers and bloom in May. Up to six flowers bloom on 12-inch (30-cm) pale green stems. A partly shaded position is ideal.

F. meleagris (snake's head fritillary). These are widely available, but are worth a special mention. Curious lantern-shaped flowers with a delicate chequered pattern hang down singly or in pairs from stems that grow to a height of about 12 inches (30 cm). They will naturalize rapidly in sun or light shade, in a position where the soil does not dry out in summer. The flowers come in shades of maroon, lilac or white with greenish markings and nod gracefully above slender grey-green leaves.

F. michailowski. Honey-scented and exquisite, this little fritillaria has tiny, deep maroon bells edged in yellow. It grows to a height of no more than 6 inches (15 cm) and flowers in early spring. It will colonize an area that is hot and dry in the summer, and does well in front of Mediterranean plants that thrive in the same conditions.

F. pallidiflora. This is a good candidate for the woodland garden, as it likes cool, moist conditions. Large, primrose-yellow flowers appear in April and early May, and are carried in groups of three. Handsome glaucous leaves set off the pale yellow bells to perfection. Growing to a height of 12 inches (30 cm), the flowers are described as having a musky scent.

Narcissus species

There are thousands of daffodils to choose from, but take a close look at some of the species and you will find that what they lack in size they make up for in other qualities—fragrance, for example, an attribute rarely found in the large garden cultivars. They are equally suited to alkaline or acid soil, but require a well-drained site.

N. bulbocodium var. *conspicuus* (hoop petticoat). An excellent form with golden "hoop petticoats" on stiff stems. The leaves are thin and grasslike, and these little bulbs naturalize beautifully in short grass. It grows to a height of 6 inches (15 cm).

N. cyclamineus. The flower resembles a cyclamen with its slender tube of reflexed petals. A very dainty little bulb reaching a height of 8 inches (20 cm). The flower is a very rich yellow, and it blooms in March. Good for naturalizing under a deciduous tree or shrub.

N. poeticus (poet's narcissus or pheasant's eye). Not a tiny treasure perhaps, but a treasure nonetheless. It grows 15 to 18 inches (38 to 45 cm). It flowers quite late, April into May, and has the most delicious scent. The flowers are white, with a small yellow frilled cup rimmed in red. It naturalizes easily in the garden. *N. poeticus* var. *recurvus* (old pheasant's eye) has backward-curving petals.

N. pseudonarcissus (**the Lent lily**). Excellent for naturalizing, providing it is planted in a position that does not dry out. Lovely golden trumpets with paler yellow petals from March into April on 6- to 8-inch (15- to 20-cm) stems. Plant in deep loamy soil under deciduous trees or naturalize in grass.

N. triandrus var. *albus* (**angel's tears**). A small nodding cup with reflexed petals, it blooms in March and April. It grows no more than 4 to 6 inches (10 to 15 cm), and needs a sunny position in light, well-drained soil.

Tulipa species

The name tulip comes from the Turkish word for turban, which the flower somewhat resembles. They were among the first garden plants to be hybridized and we are all familiar with the story of tulipmania that gripped Europe in the 17th century. Here we take a look at some of the smaller-flowered species.

T. acuminata (**horned tulip**). With twisted, pale yellow petals rimmed with red, this interesting tulip grows to a height of 18 inches (45 cm). It blooms in April and appreciates summer baking.

T. clusiana var. *chrysantha* (**lady tulip**). The pointed flowers open in April and are a rich golden-yellow marked with smudges of red. Growing to a height of 6 to 8 inches (15 to 20 cm), this tulip does well in well-drained soil in full sun. With its pretty, grey-green leaves, it associates well with other plants with the same greyish colouring.

T. kaufmanniana (**water-lily tulip**). Flowering in March, with as many as five flowers per stem, this lovely little tulip requires only a sunny well-drained spot to flourish. The flowers are a creamy yellow with a darker yellow centre and open widely in full sunshine. The backs of the petals are flushed red and the flowers are enhanced by attractive, glaucous green, wavy-margined leaves. Height to 8 inches (20 cm).

T. linifolia. Bearing dazzling red flowers with a jet-black centre, this tiny tulip reaches a height of no more than 6 inches (15 cm). The foliage is a grey-green with fine red margins. It too requires excellent drainage and a sunny position, but given the right conditions will soon form a colony. Looks wonderful with Mediterranean silver-leafed plants.

T. tarda. One would think from the name that this would be a late-blooming species, but in fact it blooms in April. White with a beautiful, sunny yellow centre, it has as many as eight flowers growing from each bulb. Short-stemmed, to a height of just 6 inches (15 cm), it opens out to a star shape in full sun. It is a great tulip for naturalizing on a south-facing slope.

 # Lilies

Of all the summer-flowering bulbs, lilies are among the most dramatic. On a warm summer's evening there is nothing to compare with their heady perfume wafting in the breeze. They are such spectacular, exotic-looking flowers that it comes as a surprise to find that they are as easy to grow as most other bulbs, and require only the right conditions to bloom and multiply year after year. It is these qualities that have made them a mainstay in gardens for centuries.

Hybridists have been hard at work and two new groups of lilies have recently been introduced. The first new group to mention is a result of crossing Aurelian trumpets with Japanese Oriental lilies. They go by the rather ungainly name of Orienpets at present, but their hardiness and vigour, plus a whole new range of colours, make them a welcome addition to the garden. The second group are hybrids of the *Lilium longiflorum*, or Easter lily, which up to now has been thought of primarily as a greenhouse plant, but whose hybrids are proving reliably hardy even on the Canadian prairies. So far we have seen new introductions of *L. longiflorum* x Asiatic, *L. longiflorum* x Aurelian and *L. longiflorum* x Oriental hybrids. With these exciting new developments, the only difficulty is choosing which of these exotic and highly fragrant plants we want to grow in our gardens. Perhaps the following lists will help. But first, a bit about the species lilies, which are the parents of the more highly regarded and widely grown hybrids.

Lilium species

There is a whole new appreciation for the species lilies, partly because we have become aware that many are in danger of extinction, but mostly because of their beauty. Around 80 are recognized by botanists and they come from a very wide area all over the northern hemisphere, with a major collection coming from North America. Not all of them are suitable for cultivation in gardens but many are, and some have been grown and admired for many years.

L. candidum (Madonna lily), for example, is known to have been in cultivation as early as 1500 B.C. Featured on frescoes and vases of the Minoan civilization, it then became a Christian symbol for Renaissance artists and has remained an emblem of purity to this day. Another species that is much admired is *L. regale*, which was discovered by Ernest Wilson in 1903 and became hugely popular when introduced to the gardening community. However, there are so many others that are

worthy of our attention and would be a wonderful addition to our gardens. As interest grows, so too does the selection that is offered by garden centres and growers. Here are a few to look out for, with our own native lily, *L. columbianum*, topping the list.

L. canadense. In cultivation from the early 1600s, it is widely distributed from Quebec across to Nova Scotia and all the way down to Alabama. Varying in height from 2 to 4 feet (.6 to 1.2 m), it carries pendant, yellow-orange to red, turk's-cap flowers. Tolerant of a wide range of growing conditions, it does best in humus-rich damp soil in a sunny location.

L. candidum (Madonna lily). In cultivation for a few thousand years, its culinary use predated it being prized for its beauty alone. With large, open, pure white, heavily fragrant flowers that face outwards, it differs from all other lilies in that it needs to be shallowly planted; it should only be covered to a depth of 1 inch (2.5 cm). Also unlike most other lilies, it likes lime in the soil. After flowering it produces rosettes of leaves in late summer, which remain green all winter, while the others die back completely.

L. columbianum. The most commonly encountered species here on the west coast, it is widely distributed all the way down to California. It grows to about 4 feet (1.2 m) and has nodding, orange-yellow, turk's-cap flowers spotted red. It is easy to grow and it does well in a sunny or lightly shaded area in moist but well-drained soil.

L. formosanum. Sweetly fragrant, pure white, trumpet-shaped flowers with pinkish reverse in late summer. Growing to a height of about 6 feet (1.8 m), the old seed stalks make for great winter ornament in the garden or for use in dried flower arrangements. It is a good idea to give the bulbs some winter protection and to grow them in a well-drained site. There is a dwarf form, *L. formosanum* var. *pricei,* which has now become widely available. It grows 1 to 2 feet (30 to 60 cm) high and has proved hardier than *L. formosanum.*

L. leucanthum. Starting to become more available, it has very large, fragrant, trumpet-shaped white flowers with yellow throats that open from buds flushed green and maroon. Growing to about 6 feet (1.8 m) it requires sun or very light shade and humus-rich soil.

L. martagon. Long in cultivation, it is highly valued for its relatively early bloom and its trouble-free culture once established. A good plant for woodlands or between shrubs, it grows to between 4 and 6 feet (1.2 to 1.8 m) with distinctive, red to pink-purple, spotted turk's-cap flowers. Strongly perfumed and exceedingly lovely, it does best in humus-enriched, slightly limey soil.

L. nanum. A small but charming species, native to the western Himalayas. It grows to 1 foot (30 cm) and bears only a single bloom. The colour varies, but it is generally pale violet. Does best in full sun and needs sharp drainage.

L. nepalense. A lovely but rarely seen bi-coloured Himalayan species. Growing to a height of about 3 feet (90 cm), it has large, fragrant yellow flowers with recurved petals and deep maroon-blotched throats. This is one of the stoloniferous species (producing prostrate stems that root) and it requires full sun to partial shade in humus-rich soil in which its stolons can spread.

L. regale. A favourite for nearly a century, its large, heavily perfumed, pure-white trum-pet-shaped flowers have a yellow throat and open out from beautiful pinkish-purple buds. Growing to between 3 and 4 feet (.9 to 1.2 m), it is very amenable to cultivation and requires only a well-drained site to do well.

L. speciosum. A lovely Japanese species that is gloriously scented. Growing to a height of between 3 and 4 feet (.9 to 1.2 m), it has a large number of semipendant flowers that can vary in colour from white to crimson. It blooms in very late summer and early fall and requires a lime-free humus-rich soil.

These are but a few of the plants that are becoming more available. Check out the websites listed in the back of the book for availability of bulbs and more information.

Hybrids

The horticultural classification of lilies was an attempt to maintain some order when they began to be more widely bred. At the moment, lilies are divided into 10 categories, but as the number of interdivision hybrids increases, some reclassification will become necessary. In terms of popularity, the clear winners are the Asiatic Hybrids, followed by the trumpets and then the Orientals; we list a few in these groups that have won major awards over the years and still remain popular and readily available. We will also give a few suggestions for the two new groups of hybrids, the Orienpets and the *L. longiflorum* hybrids. First however, some information about how to grow these lilies and where to see them.

How to grow hybrids

Lilies thrive in slightly acidic conditions and need well-drained, rich soil and good air circulation. Sandy, loamy soil rich in humus is ideal, and it's a good idea to add some well-rotted compost to help aerate the soil and assist drainage. Leaf mould is ideal, and putting a layer on as a mulch will help conserve moisture and insulate the soil from excessive temperature fluctuations. Lily bulbs should be treated very carefully, because unlike other bulbs, they lack a protective outer coating and never go completely dormant. The bulbs are best acquired in fall or early spring, and should be potted up or planted outside immediately. It is a good idea to prepare the planting site before you buy the bulbs.

Lilies have an interesting root system, in that they have two sets of roots, one set growing from the base of the bulb and one set growing from the stems that emerge in summer. The roots below the bulb are able to contract and pull the lily down to the correct level if planted too shallowly. The upper roots, which lie between the bulb and the soil surface, are feeding roots. It is best to plant about 4 to 5 inches (10 to 12 cm) down in light, well-aerated soil.

Where to grow

While lilies like sun, many are quite happy growing in light shade, and since they like much the same conditions as rhododendrons, these two plants can live quite happily side by side, with the lilies providing colour when the rhododendrons have finished flowering. Lilies also suit the perennial border, as long as they are given the right conditions, and they make excellent container plants. There are many dwarf cultivars specially bred for this purpose and they mix well with other containerized plants.

Where are lilies on view and for sale?

VanDusen Gardens, Minter Gardens and Butchart Gardens all have lovely displays of lilies in the summer. Lily societies have annual shows, and members have the opportunity of buying bulbs, as well as going on field trips and garden visits to see lilies in bloom. (See "Horticultural Societies and Garden Clubs" in the Resources section for further information.)

Growers, such as B & D Lilies in Port Townsend, Washington, and The Lily Nook, in Manitoba, produce beautiful colour catalogues of their stock (see "Mail-order Gardening" in the Resources section).

Asiatic Hybrids

These are among the first to bloom and are the easiest to grow, blooming from the middle of May until July. They are unscented, very hardy, multiply freely, and come in a wide variety of colours, their flowers lasting a long time. They prefer sun or part shade, with the pinks holding their colour better if they have a little afternoon shade. This group is divided into upward-facing, outward-facing or downward-facing.

'Alpenglow' (upward-facing). 2 to 3 feet (60 to 90 cm); blush-pink flowers.

'Apricot Supreme' (outward-facing). 3 to 4 feet (.9 to 1.2 m); rich clear apricot, nicely spotted flowers.

'Connecticut King' (upward-facing). 3 feet (90 cm); a long-time favourite with clear yellow, unspotted flowers and a deeper gold centre.

'Enchantment' (upward-facing). 3 to 4 feet (.9 to 1.2 m); vivid orange-red spotted flowers; great cut flowers.

'Fireworks' (downward-facing). 3 feet (90 cm); vibrant orange-red flowers and nicely recurved petals.

'Red Velvet' (outward-facing). 4 to 5 feet (1.2 to 1.5 m); glowing rich red flowers.

'Sally' (downward-facing). 6 feet (1.8 m); orange-pink, with darker orange centres and wide recurving petals.

'Tiger Babies' (downward-facing). 3 feet (90 cm); salmon-pink flowers that are strongly spotted.

Trumpet Hybrids

These include the true trumpets and the Aurelian Hybrids. Generally tall with heavy flower heads, many need staking. They bloom in July and do well in sun or part shade. They are divided into four groups, depending on whether their flowers are trumpet-shaped, bowl-shaped, flat or have recurved petals.

'Black Dragon' (trumpet-shaped). 5 to 8 feet (1.5 to 2.4 m); the most popular and widely known of the group, with massive heads of heavily fragrant, pure white flowers with soft yellow centres and dark purple-red reverse.

'Gold Eagle' (flat). 5 to 7 feet (1.5 to 2.1 m); splendid sunburst lily with open, rich, lemon-yellow blooms and rusty-red papillae in the centre.

'Golden Splendour' (trumpet-shaped). 3 to 4 feet (.9 to 1.2 m); golden flowers with wine-purple stripe down the outside of each petal.

'Heart's Desire' (bowl-shaped). 4 to 6 feet (1.2 to 1.8 m); creamy white, fragrant flowers with tangerine gold centres.

'Lady Bowes Lyon' (recurved). 3 to 4 feet (.9 to 1.2 m); very rich red flowers with black spotted centres.

'Pink Perfection' (trumpet-shaped). 6 feet (1.8 m); huge dark pink flowers.

'White Henryi' (flat). 5 feet (1.5 m); a vigorous and disease-resistant plant with wide flat flowers, strong orange throats and rusty-red papillae.

Oriental Hybrids

Few flowers are more spectacular than those of the Oriental lilies. They are the last to bloom and the most strongly scented. They come in whites, pinks and reds and are divided into four flower types: trumpet-shaped, bowl-shaped, flat or recurved.

'Angelo' (trumpet-shaped). 3 feet (90 cm); wide, trumpet-shaped, rose-pink flowers.

'Casa Blanca' (bowl-shaped). 4 feet (1.2 m); huge, glistening, snow-white, heavily scented flowers.

'Everest' (recurved). 4 to 5 feet (1.2 to 1.5 m); lovely, shining, pure white flowers with a small number of small maroon dots.

'Journey's End' (recurved). 4 to 5 feet (1.2 to 1.5 m); an indestructible lily with rich, dark, glowing, crimson-pink flowers that are attractively spotted.

'Star Gazer' (flat). 2 to 3 feet (60 to 90 cm); one of the first up-facing Oriental lilies, with crimson flowers paling to white at the edges and attractively spotted overall; great cut flower.

Orienpets

There are no long-standing favourites in this group as they are comparatively new. Here are some that are listed in current catalogues.

'Northern Beauty'. 4 feet (1.2 m); dark red with yellow tips and margins, and a dark yellowish-green throat.

'Northern Carillon'. 4 feet (1.2 m); beautiful, large, red-purple blooms with white margins.

'Scheherazade'. 5 feet (1.8 m); deep red flowers edged in gold, fading to white at the edges and tips.

'Starburst Sensation'. 3 to 4 feet (90 cm to 1.2 m); strong unspotted purplish-red flowers with yellowish-white tips

'Victorian Lace'. 4 to 5 feet (1.2 to 1.5 m); elegant rose-red blooms edged in creamy yellow; slight fragrance.

L. *longiflorum* Hybrids

This is another recently introduced group of lilies; they are surprisingly hardy and able to withstand even prairie winters. They are also disease resistant and have very large flowers on sturdy stems. Some have a slight perfume.

'Aladdin's Sun'. 3 feet (90 cm); vivid yellow with a greenish throat; flowers are upward-facing and bowl-shaped.

'Best Seller'. 2 to 3 feet (60 to 90 cm); a dazzling glowing apricot.

'Coral Fashion'. 3 feet (90 cm); the unusual shade of coral has made this a popular choice.

'My Fair Lady'. 3 feet (90 cm); soft shell-pink.

'Royal Sunset'. 3 feet (90 cm); brilliant red with yellow-orange centres.

Planting a Large Container for Winter Pleasure

From October to mid-May, this planted container will add colour and interest to your patio, balcony or front walkway. By layering bulbs, planting an evergreen shrub as a focal point, and adding winter-flowering pansies and trailing ivy, you can create a colourful winter garden in a very small area.

Materials

- A half-barrel or other large container with drainage holes in the bottom.
- Potting soil.
- A handful of bone meal.
- Drainage rocks.
- 1 evergreen shrub, 2 1/2 to 3 1/2 feet (.8 to 1.1 m) tall. Some examples of evergreens you could try are holly, boxwood, dwarf Alberta spruce, camellia, rhododendron or azalea. (In a very cold winter, the camellia and boxwood might be damaged unless the barrel is in a well-protected spot.)
- 12 to 15 tulip bulbs (one colour looks best).
- 12 to 15 hyacinth bulbs.
- 25 crocus bulbs.
- 7 winter-flowering pansies.
- 5 small-leafed trailing ivy plants.

Method

Place the drainage rocks on the bottom of the container, and half-fill it with potting soil. Sprinkle bone meal evenly over the soil at this level. Stand the evergreen shrub in the centre and place the tulip bulbs around it, near the centre. The tulip bulbs should be planted at the deepest layer, about 10 inches (25 cm) from the top of the barrel.

Add soil until just the tip of the tulip bulbs show. Then add the hyacinth bulbs, planting them just to the outside of the tulip bulbs.

Add more soil, up to 3 to 4 inches (8 to 10 cm) from the top of the barrel. Lightly press the crocus bulbs into the soil and between the other bulb locations. Plant flowering pansies around the edge, leaving space between them for the trailing ivy. Add more soil and plant the ivy.

The pansies will flower from October to springtime, depending upon winter weather; the crocuses from February to March; the hyacinths in April; and the tulips in April and May.

If you have an outdoor electrical outlet nearby, you could hang small lights throughout the shrub for added interest around the end of December.

Aftercare

Towards the end of May, when the tulip bulbs are past their prime, take all the bulbs out and dry them. They can be dug into a bare spot in the garden, and the container can be re-planted with summer annual bedding plants.

Recommended Reading

Bulbs

Cavendish Plant Guides. *Bulbs.* Cavendish Books, North Vancouver, 1997.

Lacy, Allen. *The Little Bulbs: A Tale of Two Gardens.* Duke University Press, Durham, N.C., 1986.

Mathew, Brian. *Bulbs: The Four Seasons. A Guide to Selecting and Growing Bulbs All Year Round.* Pavilion Books, London, 1999.

McDonald, Elvin. *The 100 Best Bulbs.* Random House, Toronto, 1997.

McHoy, Peter. *Spring Bulbs.* The New Plant Library, Lorenz Books, London, 1998.

Pavord, Anna. *The Tulip.* Bloomsbury, London, 1999.

Phillips, Sue. *Gardeners' World Book of Bulbs.* Parkwest Publications, Eatontown, New Jersey, 1992.

Rix, Martyn and Roger Phillips. *The Bulb Book.* Pan Books, London, 1981.

Taylor, Patrick. *Gardening with Bulbs.* Timber Press, Portland, Oregon, 1996.

Whiteside, Katherine. *Classic Bulbs: Hidden Treasures for the Modern Garden.* Random House, Toronto, 1992.

Lilies

Austin-McRae, Edward. *Lilies: A Guide for Growers and Collectors.* Timber Press, Portland, Oregon, 1998.

Jefferson-Brown, Michael and Howland Harris. *The Gardener's Guide to Growing Lilies.* Timber Press, Portland, Oregon, 1995.

Winter container gardening

Brown, Kathy. *Kathy Brown's Seasonal Container Gardening.* Penguin Books, Markham, 1995.

Container Gardening Through the Year. Dorling Kindersley, London, 1998.

Hillier, Malcolm. *Malcolm Hillier's Container Gardening Through the Year.* Dorling Kindersley, London, 1995.

Rees, Yvonne and David Palliser. *Container Gardening: All Year Round.* Cavendish Books, North Vancouver, 1991.

Stevens, Elaine. *The Creative Container Gardener.* Whitecap Books, Vancouver, 1995.

October

Octember is a month of warm days and cool nights, misty one day and crisp and clear the next. The quality of light can be soft and quite magical. Plants reach the peak of their fall colour with translucent yellows and rich purple hues. The autumn mauves of chrysanthemums and Michaelmas daisies are complemented by the soft burgundies of trees, shrubs and climbers such as hawthorn, flowering plum, oak, smoke bush, azalea, hydrangea and Virginia creeper. Vine maples, mountain ashes and larches turn various shades of yellow and gold, and wooded hillsides throughout the province are ablaze with colour. Fall is an especially good time to appreciate trees, and this chapter highlights garden and city trees.

Fall colours in the forest are usually at their very best around Canadian Thanksgiving. The morning air is sharp, but it's often bright and sunny. Shafts of sunlight stream into the woods through the trees, reminding us of summer just past and hinting of winter yet to come. Leaves are thick on the ground, and rose hips are ripening. Among the forest undergrowth, delicate, tasty mushrooms lie in wait for the adventurous. If you pick some, do make sure they are edible before you eat them.

Back home, the pumpkin patch is ripening, ready for Hallowe'en. A surprisingly large number of bedding plants and perennials are still in bloom and will continue to flower right up to the end of the month. As more and more of them die back, the main fall clean-up begins. Although this is quite a bit of work, the more you clean up now, the less problem you'll have with pests and diseases next year.

October is an important month for moving and planting evergreens, as long as you water them in well. It's a good time for taking cuttings of deciduous shrubs, planting bulbs and buying bulbs for forcing indoors. Although you can move and plant deciduous trees and shrubs now, it is better to wait until November when you are sure the plants are dormant. Deciduous plants in pots can be planted anytime.

This month, when the garden is winding down for the winter, we also discuss the Plant Introduction Scheme of the University of British Columbia. This is an innovative and successful program instituted by the UBC Botanical Gardens to introduce new and interesting plant cultivars to the commercial market.

Garden Highlights

indicates fragrance

Bulbs

Colchicum autumnale and *Crocus* spp. (autumn crocus), *Cyclamen hederifolium* (hardy cyclamen), *Dahlia* spp., *Nerine bowdenii* (nerine).

Perennials

Anemone x *hybrida* (Japanese anemone), *Aster* spp. (Michaelmas daisy), *Chrysanthemum* spp., *Cortaderia selloana* (pampas grass), *Liriope muscari* (lily turf), *Schizostylis coccinea* (Kaffir lily), *Sedum spectabile* (stonecrop).

Climbers

Clematis orientalis, *C. tangutica*, *Parthenocissus quinquefolia* (Virginia creeper), *Vitis* spp. (grape vines).

Shrubs

Aucuba spp., *Berberis* spp. (barberry), *Cotinus coggygria* (smoke bush), *Cotoneaster* spp., *Euonymus europaeus* (spindle tree), *Fothergilla major*, *Hippophae rhamnoides* (sea buckthorn), *Pyracantha* spp. (firethorn), *Rosa moyesii* (rose), *R. rugosa* (rose), *Skimmia* spp., *Symphoricarpos* spp. (snowberry), *Viburnum carlesii*, *V. opulus* (viburnum).

Trees

Acer spp. (maple), *Crataegus* spp. (hawthorn), *Hamamelis* spp. (witch hazel), *Liriodendron tulipifera* (tulip tree), *Rhus typhina* (stag's horn sumac), *Sorbus* spp. (mountain ash).

October Checklist

Annuals, perennials and bulbs

- Continue planting spring-flowering bulbs and perennials (see the September chapter).
- As perennials fade, lift and divide them, or label those you want to move or divide in the spring.
- Clear beds of annuals by the end of the month and add to compost.
- Dig up dahlias, gladioli and tuberous begonias, label and store in a frost-free place.
- Plant peonies.

- Lift and divide clumps of nerines if necessary after they have finished flowering.
- Cut stems of perennials, clean up borders and keep well weeded. Mulch with well-rotted compost or manure.
- Plant out wallflowers and forget-me-nots that were sown earlier.
- Plant lily bulbs from now until March (see the September chapter).

Trees, shrubs and climbers

- Put sticky bands of Tanglefoot around trees to trap winter moths (see "Pests and Diseases" in the March chapter).
- Plant shrubs and trees.
- Lightly prune roses (see the June chapter). Collect and destroy old leaves. Prune ramblers now, cutting old flowering stems down to ground level.
- Feed lilacs and other shrubs that are heavy feeders with bone meal.

Fruits, vegetables and herbs

- Keep harvesting fruits and vegetables, and make final sowing of lettuce in beds or the cold frame.
- Continue taking cuttings of bush fruits, prune back fruited canes and stake the new ones.
- Gather grapes.
- Take final cuttings of herbs, such as lavender, rosemary and bay laurel. Keep the cuttings indoors for the winter. Bay laurel should always be brought in for the winter since it will not survive outside.
- Divide clumps of chives, and pot up young plants of mint, chives and parsley for indoor use.
- Cultivate and enrich soil in area you plan to sow in spring.
- Plant garlic, shallots and overwintering onions.

General garden activities

- Keep lawn free of leaves, and continue cutting it as long as it grows. Aerate and scarify if needed or not already done.
- Continue sowing new lawns.
- As leaves fall, put net over the pond and clean up pool for winter. Continue to feed fish as long as they are active. Lower pots of lilies to the bottom of the pond, cut back oxygenators and discard top growth.

 # Trees

In this part of the world, we are very conscious that we live on the edge of a temperate rain forest. Our cities were carved out of it, and massive native conifers such as Douglas fir and western red cedar still grow in the urban landscape. Every year hikers get lost in nearby mountains, often within sight of civilization. Wolves, cougars and bears live in wilderness areas bordering our cities, skunks and raccoons are regular backyard visitors, and bald eagles gather by the hundreds in the middle of winter to fish local rivers.

Fortunately for us, far-sighted city fathers set aside some land for natural parks, such as Stanley Park, Beacon Hill Park, and Pacific Spirit Park, helping to preserve a little of the wilderness within city boundaries. This action has contributed to a consciousness of the need to preserve our environment, a need expressed by many people in our community today. Our cities are some of the greenest in the world. This is a fact of which we can be justly proud, but it is also something we need to work hard to maintain.

Not only are trees vital for replenishing the oxygen in our atmosphere, they also reduce the urban stress factors of air pollution, noise, glare and heat build-up from urban construction materials. They modify the climate by helping to clean the air, capture dust to be recycled for plant food, and generally help to improve the quality of life within a city.

Street trees—an important part of the cityscape

Since their earliest beginnings, the cities of Vancouver and Victoria have had a policy to beautify city streets by planting street trees. Trees are selected on the basis of their shape, size, rooting qualities, growing habits, disease resistance, appearance, longevity and ability to tolerate street growing conditions.

In the early days of the cities' development, many large trees, such as elm, ash, maple, London plane and black locust, were planted, with little thought for the size they would eventually attain. In the 1930s many of these trees were gradually replaced with trees better suited to the city, and today almost a hundred different species and varieties of trees can be found on the streets of Vancouver and Victoria.

Appreciating our heritage trees

In order to appreciate fully the wonderful heritage of trees we have, it's worth taking a walk around your area, noting the different kinds of trees, both evergreen and deciduous, you can find. If, for example, you live in Victoria, you might want to start your walk along Circle Drive in Beacon Hill Park where the spring- and fall-flowering cherries are planted, especially in the section of the park from Chestnut Row along Northeast Drive, bounded by Douglas Street to the west.

Within this area of the park you will find giant sequoias; Japanese cryptomerias; California nutmeg, with plumlike fruit streaked with purple and a large brown seed; blue Atlas cedar, with its upright cones; weep-

ing holly, growing on a stump; two species of mountain ash; a grouping of native wild cherries; white fir; two Deodar cedars; weeping beech; incense cedar from southern Oregon; five willows; a grove of poplars; several Norway spruce; a small dawn redwood; a large hazelnut; Portuguese laurel; silver maples; a katsura tree; paper birch; a European fan palm; a green ash; a variegated holly; a red oak; Japanese maples; and one of Victoria's largest Yoshino cherries.

For more information on Victoria's trees, look for a book published by the Heritage Tree Book Society called *Trees of Greater Victoria: A Heritage*. This informative book notes trees to watch for around the city and gives maps and information for several walking tours around Victoria and the Saanich Peninsula.

In Vancouver, a Tree Walk Program has been set up for residents to learn more about the city's trees with the help of a printed guide. The booklet is called "A Self-guided Walking Tour of Vancouver Street Trees (The Alma St. and Tenth Avenue Area)." It takes walkers through seven blocks from Alma and 11th Avenue to Trutch Street and 13th Avenue. A map identifies the route and provides a key to the trees found on each street. This area was chosen because it contains a representative selection of trees found on Vancouver boulevards. The walk takes about an hour, and you can pick up a booklet at the Vancouver Board of Parks and Recreation, 2099 Beach Avenue. Phone for information at 257-8600, or check out the website at http://www.city.vancouver.bc.ca/parks/1.htm.

Every year the Park Board organizes a week of events celebrating the urban forest. Arbor Week is always held the last full week of October that begins on a Monday. Call the number listed above for more information.

There are currently more than 110,000 trees on Vancouver's streets under the care of Park Board staff, with more than 4,000 being planted annually.

You can find more detailed information about Vancouver's street trees in Gerald Straley's book *Trees of Vancouver* and Marg Meikle and Dannie McArthur's book *Garden City Vancouver* (see Further Reading for more information).

Flowering cherries and plums

The signature trees for city streets in Vancouver have been the flowering cherries and plums. Sadly, in recent years, these trees have been increasingly affected by a variety of diseases such as bacterial canker and have come under attack by pests such as borers. As a result, the number of flowering cherries and plums has been dramatically reduced, and they have been replaced by other flowering trees that are more disease resistant. Trees now commonly used are crabapples, hawthorns, styrax, magnolias and the dogwoods—*Cornus* 'Eddie's White Wonder' and *Cornus kousa*. Other trees that the Park Board are currently looking at as candidates for planting on the city's boulevards are *Cornus mas, Cladastris lutea, Davidia involucrata, Halesia carolina, Magnolia grandiflora* and many *Acer* species.

How about the home garden?

Trees are just as important a feature of the home garden as they are of the city street. They are the most prominent and permanent plants in your garden. The water and nutrients they take out of the soil, the spread of their roots, the density of their leafy canopy and the amount of shelter they provide will dictate the growing conditions for plants around them. Thus, when it comes to choos-

ing such a large and long-lasting plant, it is important to choose the right species and locate it appropriately.

Unless you have a lot of property, many evergreen trees and deciduous trees are far too big. They will rapidly cast shade over most of your garden, may damage drainage tiles and foundations, and deplete the soil of moisture and nourishment.

Far better for gardens are trees of limited height and spread that offer some special feature, such as appealing foliage, bark or flowers. A tree makes a good focal point in a planting design and can be used to screen an eyesore or a neighbouring house. Deciduous trees can be just as effective for screening as evergreens because even in winter their tracery of branches will distract the eye and act as a delicate visual screen.

Trees should always be in harmony with the house and surrounding landscape, and should not overwhelm it. They are the investment of a lifetime. If you plant a slow-growing tree, you may never see it reach full maturity. However, you will be planting a living heritage for your children and grandchildren, for other people's children, and for future generations of urban dwellers.

A list of small trees maturing at 25 feet (7.6 m) and therefore suitable for growing under power lines can be accessed at the City of Vancouver's website: http://www.city.vancouver.bc.ca/commsvcs/planning/treebylaw/treehydr.htm#hydrolist.

Trees for a small garden

The trees on the following list are suitable for a small garden. The native vine maple (*Acer circinatum*) and the hybrid flowering dogwood (*Cornus* 'Eddie's White Wonder') are also excellent; both are described in the February chapter, in the native garden section.

Acer davidii (**snake bark maple**). A small tree with attractively striated green and white bark. The shining green leaves turn brilliant orange and red in fall. Clusters of yellow-green flowers in April or May are followed by red-flushed winged seeds in autumn. It reaches a height of about 20 feet (6 m) and is tolerant of most soils in a semishaded location.

Acer griseum (**paperbark maple**). This tree is grown primarily for the beauty of its cinnamon-coloured bark. It reaches a height of 20 feet (6 m), but is slow-growing, compact, and an ideal tree for the small garden.

Acer palmatum '**Bloodgood**' (**Japanese maple**). This is an excellent Japanese maple with very deep reddish-purple leaves throughout the season that turn a vivid red in fall. It is a slow grower and does well in sun or part shade. It eventually reaches a height of 15 to 20 feet (4.6 to 6 m).

Acer palmatum '**Sango kaku**' (**coral bark maple**). Also sold as 'Senkaki', this is a wonderful small tree for winter effect, with bright coral-red bark. It has a narrow upright growth habit and grows to about 20 feet (6 m). The green palmate leaves turn apricot and golden-yellow in the fall, giving it year-round interest.

Acer shirasawanum '**Aureum**' (**golden full-moon maple**). A spectacular small tree with lime-green spring foliage that lights up the garden. However, it needs shade to prevent the leaves from getting scorched. It grows to 8 to 12 feet (2.4 to 3.7 m), and the leaves turn orange-red in autumn.

Amelanchier **spp. (Saskatoon berry, June berry, serviceberry, snowy mespilus).** These lovely large shrubs or small trees deserve to be more widely grown. Clouds of small starry flowers in spring cover the branches before the leaves are fully developed, and they are followed by small edible berries. The foliage is often richly coloured in autumn. Tolerant of most conditions, they do best in moist, well-drained soil. *A. alnifolia* grows to a height of about 15 feet (4.5 m), with delicious berries and good fall colouring. *A. canadensis* is a large suckering shrub to 20 feet (6 m) with sweet juicy berries and excellent fall colour. *A.* x *grandiflora* has very pretty young bronze leaves and an abundance of white flowers. It grows to about 20 feet (6 m). Two cultivars to look for are 'Autumn Brilliance' and 'Rubescens'.

Arbutus unedo '**Compacta**' (**strawberry tree**). This evergreen tree has small, dark green leaves and bears ivory white flowers in small clusters in the fall. The strawberrylike fruits ripen the following fall and are edible, but mealy and tasteless. It reaches a height of about 25 feet (7.6 m), but is slow-growing.

Catalpa bignonioides '**Aurea**' (**golden bean tree**). A small, slow-growing deciduous tree with very large, velvety, soft yellow leaves. White-scented foxglove-type flowers appear on mature trees in late summer, followed by long thin seed pods, which remain on the tree long after the leaves have fallen. It has a wide-spreading growth pattern and reaches a height of about 25 feet (7.6 m). The leaves keep their colour through the season and are at their brightest in full sun.

Cercidiphyllum japonicum (**katsura tree**). This handsome upright tree has small rounded leaves that turn a brilliant colour in autumn and give off a sweetly pungent scent like burnt sugar. It can reach a height of 25 to 35 feet (7.6 to 10.5 m), so it shouldn't really be listed here under small trees. However, there are two weeping forms that do meet the criteria. These are *C. japonicum* 'Pendulum' and *C. japonicum* var. *magnificum* 'Pendula'. Both are attractive forms, with the latter having larger leaves and a narrower canopy of branches. Both reach a height of about 15 feet (4.6 m).

***Cercis canadensis* 'Forest Pansy' (North American redbud).** A lovely selection with deep purple, heart-shaped leaves. It can be difficult to get established in some areas, but if the conditions are right, it makes a lovely addition to the garden. Plant where you can take advantage of the light shining through the plum-coloured leaves for a remarkable sight. It grows to a height of 20 to 25 feet (6 to 7.6 m).

***Cercis siliquastrum* (Judas tree).** This slow-growing, wide-spreading tree has rounded leaves with rich, rose-purple, pea-shaped flowers. The flowers appear in clusters on the naked stems in May, and are followed by flat, green seed pods which become tinted with red in late summer. The Judas tree does best in sun and likes to be dry and hot in summer, with perfect drainage, making it a good choice for the Gulf Islands. It reaches a mature height of 20 feet (6 m).

***Cornus alternifolia* 'Argentea'.** A large shrub or small tree with horizontally spreading branches, it has the best silver-variegated leaves—green with a creamy white margin. It grows to 25 feet (7.6 m) and does well in any type of soil in sun or light shade. It is hard to find, but worth hunting for.

***Cornus controversa* 'Variegata'.** This is a much sought-after tree, and it is easy to see why. Sometimes called the wedding cake tree, it has tiers of silver-margined leaves on slender branches. The overall effect is stunning. It reaches a height of about 25 feet (7.6 m). Be warned, it doesn't come cheap. It is hard to propagate, and the plants for sale in nurseries are grafted trees imported from Europe.

***Cornus florida* 'Rubra' (pink dogwood).** The showy blossomlike bracts of this pretty dogwood vary from blush white to deep pink. The tree's dark green leaves turn brilliant orange and scarlet in fall. It grows up to 15 feet (4.6 m), with a spread of 20 feet (6 m) or more. Among its many excellent cultivars are 'Apple Blossom' and 'Spring Song', both of which are a medium pink, and 'Cherokee Chief', which is dark pink.

***Cornus kousa* var. *chinensis* (Chinese dogwood).** This attractive, shrubby tree grows up to about 20 feet (6 m). In June it bears great quantities of large, creamy white flowerlike bracts in horizontal sprays, followed by edible, strawberrylike fruits and attractive red-tinted foliage in the fall.

***Eucalyptus gunnii* (cider gum).** Many eucalyptus will not survive in our climate. This one is said to be half-hardy, but will usually do well in a protected location. In its native Australia, it will grow to 45 feet (14 m) in height, and it can grow quite tall here, but can be kept under control with annual pruning. When the tree is young, its leaves are blue-grey to silvery, but in maturity they become blue-green or dark green. The tree will produce juvenile foliage each year if all its stems are cut back hard in late spring. It may die to the ground in a severe winter, but do not dig it up immediately, since new shoots may appear from the base.

***Gleditsia triacanthos* var. 'Inermis' (thornless honey locust).** This tree, grown mainly for its lovely ornamental pinnate leaves, is an excellent specimen tree in a small garden. Its golden yellow leaves of spring and early summer turn green later in the season. It needs moist, well-drained soil. The tree grows to about 20 to 25 feet (6 to 7.6 m).

Koelreutaria paniculata (**golden rain tree**). An attractive tree with pinnate leaves growing to a height of 15 feet (4.6 m). It bears large panicles of small yellow flowers in July and August, followed by conspicuous, bladderlike seed capsules. The foliage turns a bright yellow in fall. It should be grown in full sun.

Magnolia grandiflora '**Little Gem**' (**southern magnolia**). A slow-growing tree that reaches a mature height of about 15 feet (4.6 m). It blooms when young, and has small, glossy, leathery, mid- to dark green leaves that are rusty and furry underneath. It bears bowl-shaped, scented, creamy white flowers in July and August. It is not hardy in containers and should be protected in a harsh winter.

Magnolia x *loebneri* '**Leonard Messel**'. A chance hybrid of *M. stellata* 'Rosea' and *M. kobus*, it has the best qualities of both parents with lovely, lilac-pink star-shaped flowers that are deeper pink in bud. It grows to a height of 15 to 18 feet (4.6 to 5.5 m).

Magnolia sieboldii. This is a lovely but often overlooked magnolia. It becomes a large widespread shrub or small tree to 15 feet (4.6 m). The waxy white, cup-shaped flowers with dark, pink-purple stamens are fragrant and produced intermittently throughout spring and summer.

Magnolia stellata (**star magnolia**). This slow-growing, deciduous, shrubby tree is a delightful addition to a small garden. It grows to a maximum height of 10 to 15 feet (3 to 4.6 m), with a 10-foot (3-m) spread. In the winter, its furry buds are very attractive. In March and April, before the leaves are fully out, the buds open into fragrant, white, star-shaped flowers.

Malus **spp.** (**crabapple**). There are over 500 cultivars of crabapple, varying in size from 8 to 40 feet (2.4 to 12 m). Many attractive small cultivars are now available. Crabapples are lovely trees, produce fruits for the birds in the fall, and can survive poor drainage conditions. They can be susceptible to scab, so be sure to choose a specimen that is scab resistant. A commonly seen street tree is *M. floribunda*, which grows to a height and spread of 30 feet (9 m), too large for most city gardens. *M.* 'Louisa' is a weeping form to 15 feet (4.6 m), with pink flowers and yellow fruit. *M. tschonoskii* is a narrow upright

Tip of the Month: Tree Banding

This is the time to "band" your trees to protect them against the ravages of the winter moth, whose caterpillars feed on the leaves and buds in early spring. The male moths are brownish-grey with a wingspan of about 1 1/2 inches (4 cm). The females are wingless, and it is the female that we want to prevent from climbing the trunks of trees to lay her eggs.

Wind 2-inch (5-cm) masking tape several times around the tree trunk to make two 6-inch-wide (15-cm) bands 4 and 5 feet (1.2 and 1.5 m) above ground level. Cover the bands with a sticky product such as Tanglefoot. The female moth will become trapped on the sticky substance as she climbs the trunk. Make sure there are no gaps under the bands for the moth to crawl through.

The lower band should be replaced as it gets covered with dead moths, or when moths begin to get trapped on the upper band. Bands should be removed and destroyed the following spring.

tree to 25 feet (7.6 m), with white flowers and red-tinged yellow fruit. It is one of the best for fall colour.

***Prunus* spp.** There are more than 400 species of *Prunus*. Most of them are deciduous trees and shrubs: the ornamental almonds, peaches, plums, cherries and cherry laurels. They are among the most popular of the spring-flowering ornamentals. A number of the species have rich fall colour, and a few have attractive fruits. The important thing to remember when buying one of these trees for your garden is to find out, for sure, just how big it gets when it is mature. They can grow upwards of 40 feet (12 m), depending upon the cultivar, and many are far too big for the average city garden. Following are some interesting smaller species and cultivars.

P. 'Amanogawa' (Japanese cherry) is an attractive, columnar tree, 20 feet (6 m) high, spreading to 6 to 8 feet (1.8 to 2.4 m). It bears semidouble, slightly fragrant, soft pink flowers in late April and May. *P.* x *blireana* grows up to 18 feet (5.5 m), a flowering plum with coppery purple leaves and rose-pink double flowers. *P.* 'Shirotae', also called 'Mt. Fuji' (Japanese cherry), grows to 15 feet (4.6 m) tall, with a 20-foot (6-m) spread. A horizontally spreading form with clusters of large, white, double flowers in early spring. *P.* 'Kiku-shidare Sakura' (Cheal's weeping cherry) has a height and spread of 15 to 20 feet (4.6 to 6 m). It is a graceful tree with arching branches covered with deep pink double flowers in March or April. The young leaves are bronze-green. *P. subhirtella* 'Autumnalis' (autumn-flowering cherry) grows to 20 feet (6 m). This pretty, delicate tree flowers in late fall and continues sporadically throughout the winter.

***Pyrus salicifolia* 'Pendula' (weeping pear).** This particular cultivar rarely exceeds 15 feet (4.6 m) in height. It is grown for its ornamental white flowers in spring, and for its willowlike, silvery leaves which turn grey as they mature. The tree has a particularly attractive shape. It may be hard to find.

***Robinia pseudoacacia* 'Frisia'.** An outstanding small to medium-sized tree with rich golden-yellow leaves that create a brilliant splash of colour even on the darkest day. It can be "stooled" and treated like a shrub or left to grow to its full height of 25 feet (7.6 m). A slight drawback is that it is a suckering tree, and that can sometimes be a problem in small gardens.

Stewartia pseudocamellia. A small to medium-sized tree to 25 feet (7.6 m) and over, with a very attractive trunk and flaking bark. White flowers resembling camellias with bright yellow anthers are produced in July and August. Good autumn colouring along with the bark and flowers make the tree an attractive feature year round. It needs lime-free soil in woodland conditions.

***Styrax japonica* (Japanese snowbell).** This lovely little tree is deservedly becoming more popular. It bears masses of faintly fragrant, bell-like white flowers in June, and has delicate, light green leaves. It is ideal for placing beside a patio, since it provides open, lacy shading. It grows relatively slowly to a mature height of 25 feet (7.6 m).

The UBC Botanical Garden's Plant Introduction Scheme

In the 1980s the University of British Columbia's Botanical Garden started a Plant Introduction Scheme in conjunction with the B.C. Nursery Trades Association and the B.C. Society of Landscape Architects. Designed to introduce new and lesser-known plants into the nursery trade, the scheme has been a great success. Each year a panel of experts selects 2 or 3 plants from a list of 12 to 15 plants in the Botanical Garden's collection. The selected plants are propagated in the nursery and distributed to participating nurseries, who each contract to produce a specified number of plants prior to the release date.

These plants are tested at sites across North America, and are identified in retail nurseries by a specially designed label. Plants are now distributed across Canada and the United States and also exported to world markets. The royalties are returned to the UBC Botanical Garden to support the program. You can visit their website at http://www.hedgerows.com/UBCBotGdn/index.htm to keep abreast of the latest introductions. There is also a list of Recommended Plant Releases, which, although they were not developed by UBC, have been distributed to local B.C. growers to help diversify the plant stock in the industry.

The plants are particularly well suited to B.C., and we encourage you to look for them in your local nursery. They should be identified by a characteristic blue tag. The following plants have all been introduced through UBC Botanical Gardens.

Anagallis monelli **'Pacific Blue' (blue pimpernel).** This cultivar is a low-spreading herbaceous perennial with gentian-blue flowers from May until frost. It requires full sun and average to well-drained soils. It may not survive very cold or wet winters.

Arctostaphylos uva-ursi **'Vancouver Jade' (bearberry, kinnikinnik).** This evergreen groundcover has fragrant clusters of tiny pink flowers in early spring, and bright red fruit. It grows well in sun or light shade, and is an excellent groundcover in well-drained or sandy soil.

Aronia melanocarpa **'Autumn Magic' (eastern chokeberry, black chokeberry).** An upright deciduous shrub growing to a height of about 7 feet (2.1 m), with glossy, dark green leaves and fragrant white flowers in May. Attractive clusters of shiny black berries appear in the fall, and the foliage turns a brilliant mixture of red, orange and purple. Tolerant of most soils, it can be grown in sun or partial shade.

Artemisia stellerana **'Silver Brocade' (seashore artemisia).** 'Silver Brocade' is completely herbaceous in colder areas, but is slightly shrubby in warmer locations. It prefers average to well-drained soils and full sun or light shade. Its prostrate habit makes it suitable as a groundcover or cascading from tubs and hanging baskets.

Clematis **'Blue Ravine'.** A deciduous vine climbing to 7 to 10 feet (2.1 to 3 m), bearing an abundance of large, flat flowers in May and June, with a few later in the season. The wavy-edged flower petals are a soft violet, slightly darker along the midrib and veins, with a tuft of dark, red-purple stamens and white styles in the centre.

Clematis chiisanensis **'Lemon Bells'.** A deciduous clematis that reaches a height of 7 to 10 feet (2.1 to 3 m), it has lovely, pale yellow, nodding flowers in May and June, and produces a few more throughout the summer. The flowers have a wine-red tinge at the base of the four petals when grown in full sun; the colour is less noticeable if grown in shade. The young stems are a shiny dark purple and contrast well with bright green foliage and pale yellow flowers. The attractive seed heads extend the season of interest for many months. Pruning is generally not needed, but it can be pruned immediately after its first flowering in May or early June in order to keep it at the desired height.

Diascia rigescens (**twinspur**). Diascia is not a cultivar, but a recommended species. It is a compact, herbaceous perennial with grey-green leaves and 18-inch (45-cm) stalks of rose-pink flowers produced continually from May until frost. It flowers best in full sun and likes average to well-drained soil.

Genista pilosa '**Vancouver Gold**' (**spreading broom**). 'Vancouver Gold' is probably the best-known cultivar from the Plant Introduction Scheme. Developed from a species native to western Europe, it is a low-spreading evergreen shrub with bright yellow flowers in May. It prefers average to well-drained soils and a sunny location.

Lonicera '**Mandarin**' (**Mandarin honeysuckle**). A vigorous woody vine that grows to 20 feet (6 m) at maturity, this lovely new honeysuckle was bred by Wilf Nichols and is a cross between *L. tragophylla* and *L.* x *brownii* 'Dropmore Scarlet'. The young leaves are coppery-brown, becoming a dark glossy green when mature. The long tubular flowers are produced in May and June, and then periodically throughout the summer. They are dark reddish-orange on the outside, paler yellow-orange on the inside, with the overall effect being an intense orange set off beautifully by the foliage. Although not fragrant, it deserves a place in the garden. It grows equally well in full sun or partial shade.

Microbiota decussata (**Siberian or Russian cypress**). A coniferous shrub with cascading, fernlike branches, making it excellent for mass plantings or groundcovers. It requires well-drained soil, and in winter it takes on a coppery-brown colour.

Penstemon fruticosus '**Purple Haze**'. An evergreen or partially evergreen subshrub growing up to 8 inches (20 cm) tall and 2 feet (60 cm) wide. The plants are covered with tubular, mauve to purple flowers in late spring, forming a solid mound of colour for several weeks. The plant looks attractive most of the year.

Potentilla fruticosa '**Yellow gem**' (**shrubby cinquefoil**). 'Yellow Gem' is a low, mounded deciduous shrub spreading to over 3 feet (90 cm) across, with bright yellow flowers from May to frost. It needs full sun or light shade and average to well-drained soil. It looks equally well as a specimen, or in groups or massed plantings.

Ribes sanguineum '**White Icicle**' (**flowering currant**). The wild species of this plant is native to southwestern B.C., and this cultivar is thought to have originated in Victoria. It is a deciduous shrub growing 9 to 10 feet (2.7 to 3 m) tall with a 6-foot (1.8-m) spread, bearing drooping clusters of flowers in early spring. It is suited to mixed shrub borders and makes a good specimen plant. It grows well in full sun or light shade and likes average, well-drained soil.

Rubus calycinoides '**Emerald Carpet**' (**Taiwan creeping rubus**). This is a particularly vigorous groundcover which may need to be pruned back during the growing season. It is an excellent substitute for ivy in sunny or partially shaded areas. The flowers and fruits are usually insignificant, except in hotter, drier areas.

***Sorbus hupehensis* 'Pink Pagoda' (Hupeh mountain ash).** This deciduous tree can reach 30 to 40 feet (9 to 12 m) when mature. It provides almost year-round colour, beginning with white flower clusters in spring. It has blue-green compound leaves that become orange and red in the fall, and its fruits turn from late-summer pink to midwinter white.

***Sorbus reducta* (Chinese dwarf mountain ash).** This delightful shrub grows to 3 to 4 feet (.9 to 1.2 m), and its dark green leaves turn red or bronze in the fall. The white flowers of spring turn into pink fruit in the fall. It prefers average to well-drained soils, in full sun or light shade.

***Teucrium scorodonia* 'Crispum' (crispy wood sage).** A herbaceous perennial, growing to 18 inches (45 cm) tall. It has wide, ruffled leaves, and small, pale, yellow-green flowers. The wild plant is native to Europe and is naturalized in eastern North America.

***Viburnum plicatum* 'Summer Snowflake'.** This viburnum produces clusters of white flowers from May until frost. The leaves turn dark red to purple in the fall. It likes full sun or light shade and average, well-drained soil. It grows to about 7 feet (2.1 m), with a spread of about 5 feet (1.5 m).

Forcing Bulbs: the Unexpected Gift

With a bit of foresight in October and November, we can enjoy the beauty and fragrance of spring blossoms indoors from December through March. When looking for spring bulbs for your garden, be sure to buy a variety of bulbs for forcing indoors. Many bulbs will be labelled "good for forcing" or "precooled" and are excellent for forcing. Here are some varieties that force easily.

- Hyacinths (all).
- Paper white narcissus.
- 'Peter Pan', 'Pickwick' and 'Remembrance' crocus.
- 'King Alfred', 'Mount Hood' and 'Pink Glory' daffodils.
- 'Early Giant' grape hyacinths.
- *Iris reticulata* 'Harmony'.
- 'Bing Crosby', 'Hibernia' and 'Triumph' tulips.

Soilless forcing of hyacinths and paper whites

Hyacinths and paper whites can be brought to bloom easily with water alone. This method of forcing is very elementary, and a good project for children.

Hyacinths

Materials

- Precooled hyacinth bulbs.
- Hyacinth glasses (available at garden centres).

Method

Add water to the hyacinth glass. Place the bulb in the glass so that the water is just touching the base of the bulb. Place the container in the dark to encourage the bulb to grow roots, and top up the water occasionally so that the level of the water remains at the base of the bulb.

Within six to eight weeks the roots will be developed and the hyacinth bud will be about 1 inch (2.5 cm) high. Bring the bulb into the light, but not into direct sunlight, which might burn the shoot. It will grow rapidly and flower,

usually within two to three weeks. Plant hyacinth bulbs successively over a two-month period for continuous bloom. After blooming, discard the bulb, since it will not flower again.

Paper whites

Materials

- Precooled paper white or 'Soleil d'Or' narcissus.
- Shallow containers with no drainage holes.
- Charcoal, pebbles or sand.

Method

Place a thin layer of charcoal at the bottom of the container to keep the water sweet. Fill the pot with pebbles or sand to 1 inch (2.5 cm) below the top of the container. Add water to just below the pebble/sand surface.

Place bulbs on top and add pebbles or sand to cover one-quarter of the bulb base. Keep the water level consistent. Keep plants in low light, with the temperature between 50° and 59°F (10° to 15°C) for two to three weeks, until the roots and shoots are well established.

Bring into full light and watch them bloom. Discard the bulbs after blooming, as they will not flower again.

Forcing regular bulbs

Bulbs that are not precooled will need to have 12 to 15 weeks of temperatures ranging from 41° to 50°F (5° to 10°C) before they will break dormancy and bloom. For December blooms, plant bulbs early in September; for end of December and January blooms, plant at the beginning of October.

The bulbs contain enough food for the developing flowers and roots and do not need to be fertilized when they are forced. They do, however, need good drainage, and should be planted in clean pots. Clay pots should be soaked overnight.

Materials

- Wide, short pots with drainage holes.
- Drainage material such as pebbles.
- Potting soil composed of one-third soil, one-third sand and one-third perlite.
- Firm, healthy-looking bulbs.
- Labels.

Method

Plant crocuses, grape hyacinths and irises with tips about 1 inch (2.5 cm) below the soil surface, and 1/2 inch (1 cm) apart.

Plant daffodils and tulips with their tips just above the soil surface, placing bulbs close together but not touching. Three, five or seven bulbs per pot is a good number. Make sure to plant tulip bulbs so that the flat side is towards the outside of the pot. This way the first leaf of each plant will face outward. Label each pot with the date of planting, name of the bulbs and the date you can bring bulbs indoors.

Place pots of bulbs in a cool, 41° to 50°F (5° to 10°C), frost-free, dark spot. Irises, crocuses and grape hyacinths need 12 weeks cooling off. Daffodils and tulips need 15 weeks.

Water regularly to keep soil damp. After 12 to 15 weeks, the leaves should be well up above the soil. At this point, bring the bulbs into a cool (59°F/15°C), semidark area. After five days bring them into full light.

The bulbs cannot be forced again. When they have finished blooming, dismantle the pots, give the bulbs a dusting of bulb dust against disease, and plant in your garden.

Amaryllis

Amaryllis can easily be forced. They flower from December to June, and it takes six to eight weeks from potting to flowering.

Materials

- Amaryllis bulbs.
- One pot per bulb, with drainage holes.
- Potting soil mix, as above.

Method

Before planting, place the bulb and its dangling roots in lukewarm water for

several hours. Plant in a pot slightly larger than bulb size, with about one-third of the bulb above the rim of the pot.

Add potting soil, but do not fill the pot with too much soil, so that there is room for watering. Set the bulb gently into the soil. Water sparingly for the first few weeks until the bud and part of the stem have developed. Direct sunlight will help the plant to grow properly. When green sprouts begin to show, water the plant more generously. The flowers will last for several weeks.

After blooming, the stem can be cut close to the bulb, leaving the leaves. By late summer, stop watering completely and the leaves will die away. The following October, store the bulb in a cool dark place for 8 to 12 weeks, then bring back into the sunlight and the flowering cycle will start again.

Recommended Reading

Trees

Bartels, Andrea. *Gardening with Dwarf Trees and Shrubs.* Timber Press, Portland, Oregon, 1987.

Chaster, G.H.; D.W. Ross; and W.H. Warren. *Trees of Greater Victoria: A Heritage.* Heritage Tree Book Society, Victoria, 1988.

Grant, John A. and Carol L. *Trees and Shrubs for Coastal B.C. Gardens.* Whitecap Books, Vancouver, 1990.

Hillier Nurseries. *The Hillier Manual of Trees and Shrubs.* David & Charles, Newton Abbot, U.K. 1992.

Johns, Leslie. *Shrubs, Bushes and Small Trees.* Treasure Press, London, 1984.

Papworth, David and Noel Procktor. *Planting Trees and Shrubs For Small Places.* Cavendish Books, Vancouver, 1997.

Phillips, Roger. *A Photographic Guide to More Than 500 Trees of North America and Europe.* Random House, New York, 1978.

Squire, David. *Shrubs and Small Trees.* Colour Library Books, Goldalming, U.K., 1994.

Straley, Gerald. *Trees of Vancouver.* UBC Press, Vancouver, 1992.

Taylor's Guide to Trees. Houghton Mifflin, Boston, 1961.

Trees for Small Gardens. A Wisley Handbook. The Royal Horticultural Society with Cassell Educational, London, 1987.

Bulbs

See Recommended Reading for the September chapter.

November

*I*n November it rains. Not that it doesn't rain at other times of the year, but there is something relentless, unforgiving and chilling about the rain in November. It's easy to see why gardeners start to reach for the first of their fall picture-comic books— the mail-order catalogues—and dream of next year. Craft projects, such as making a holiday wreath, are good activities for cold and dreary evenings.

Out in the garden, between downpours and deluges, November is a great time for moving and planting. The earth is still workable, even though there may be frost on the ground, and plants have died back to their winter state. This is the best month to plant roses and evergreens, and there's time to put in the last of the spring bulbs.

This is a good time to take inventory of your garden tools and take any to be sharpened and serviced before the winter. It's also the last chance for fall clean-up. Any foliage or growth that has been attacked by disease or may harbour the eggs of insect pests should be gathered and bagged up for garbage disposal. However, most of the fallen leaves and decaying foliage should be saved for the compost pile. When you've finished tidying up, don't forget to sprinkle the seeds of annuals, such as poppies and cornflowers, where you want them to come up in the spring.

The colour of berries and fruits is increasingly welcome as flower and leaf colours fade and the garden is stripped to its bare essentials. Deciduous trees and shrubs have lost their leaves, and their naked branches sway in the wind. A few hardy plants, such as the autumn-flowering cherry, start to bloom. Evergreens come into their own, providing welcome patches of green in the brown and grey landscape.

The last of the migrating birds have headed south, but there are many others who spend their winters with us. If you have planted your garden with birds in mind, you'll be able to enjoy their cheerful presence even in this dreary month.

Garden Highlights

*indicates fragrance

Bulbs

Cyclamen hederifolium, also called *C. neopolitanum* (hardy cyclamen), *Nerine bowdenii* (nerine).

Perennials

Iris unguicularis (Algerian iris),* *Gentiana sino-ornata* (gentian), *Liriope muscarii* (lily turf), *Schizostylis coccinea* (Kaffir lily), *Serratula coccinea* (knapweed).

Climbers

Jasminum nudiflorum (winter jasmine).

Shrubs

Cornus alba 'Elegantissima' (Tatarian dogwood), *C. a.* 'Sibirica' (Siberian dogwood), *C. sericea* 'Flaviramea', also known as *C. stolonifera* 'Flaviramea' (red-osier dogwood). Also see the October list.

Trees

Acer griseum (paperbark maple), *Prunus serrulata* (Japanese flowering cherry). Also see the October list.

November Checklist

Annuals, perennials and bulbs

- Complete bulb planting.
- Dig up dahlias and other summer bulbs if not already done.
- Clean up beds and borders and mulch with compost or manure.
- Make sure cushion plants like dianthus and saxifrage don't get covered in leaves, as they will rot.
- Write for seed catalogues.
- Cut back chrysanthemums when they have finished flowering.
- Pot up geraniums (*Pelargonium* spp.) and fuchsias and store in frost-free place. Water once a month.
- Continue to edge and weed flower beds.
- Continue sowing hardy annuals such as poppies and cornflowers, and biennials such as foxgloves.

Trees, shrubs and climbers

- Plant bare-root roses as they become available (see the June chapter).
- Give roses a final deadheading and a light pruning. Apply some dolomite lime around established roses.
- Prune back newly planted trees and shrubs to compensate for root loss.

Fruits, vegetables and herbs

- Plant new berry bushes and fruit trees.
- Continue taking cuttings of bush fruits and prune to remove crossed and crowded branches.

- Dig soil in vegetable garden as areas become vacant in preparation for planting early in the year. Add manure or compost to soil.
- Plant garlic, shallots and overwintering onions.

General garden activities

- Keep raking leaves.
- Keep aerating established lawns.
- Build or repair existing garden structures (fences, arbours, trellises).
- Sharpen and oil tools and service the lawn mower.
- Keep clearing leaves from pond.
- This is a good time of year to have your soil tested and make improvements before spring planting.
- Spread dolomite lime around lime lovers, such as lilac, and over the vegetable garden (excluding the potato patch).
- Plan the vegetable garden for next year, allowing for crop rotation.

The Winter Garden

Too often, the garden in winter is as drab and uninteresting as the weather. Sodden clumps of rotting foliage mark the spots where perennials lurk, the grass is flattened and mushy, and even the laurel hedge looks as if it has seen better days. If this sounds like your garden, take heart: it doesn't have to be this way. There are a wide variety of evergreen trees and shrubs that can bring colour and form into the garden at this time of year, and even leafless deciduous trees can be interesting if they have strong colours, shapes and textures.

Winter is a time to look for subtle beauty and elegance. Things that go unnoticed during the colourful seasons of spring, summer and fall become strikingly apparent when distractions are removed. Moss on a rock, the shape of a pine tree, the designs and patterns of tree bark, seed pods still dangling from a deciduous tree: in so many ways the muted landscape expresses the resting state of the garden.

If you are looking for inspiration, visit the countryside, the seaside, and our public parks and gardens. Both UBC Botanical Garden and the Horticulture Centre of the Pacific have winter gardens and are wonderful places to see the plants that come into their own at this time of year. You'll find scenes that seem to have been created with winter in mind. This is especially true of the Oriental gardens open to the public, where harmony and tranquillity are created by arching branches of trees and the shapes of rocks. Ghostly silhouettes of these lovely forms are reflected in a nearby pond, reinforcing the calm of the season.

As early as November, the first of the winter-flowering trees, the autumn-flowering cherry (*Prunus subhirtella* 'Autumnalis'), begins to bloom. Winter-flowering plants are a special bonus in the garden—not only because they flower when very little else is in bloom, but also because when the garden is full of colour, it is often hard to concentrate on the beauty of one plant. But in winter a single plant in bloom can become the focus of the garden, changing our appreciation for the whole. It's rather like moving furniture and pictures around the house; it creates a fresh way of looking at a familiar sight.

The indoor winter garden

One of the most pleasant ways to enjoy the garden in winter is to create a greenhouse or conservatory as an extra room to the house. It can be very small, but there is no lovelier place to have tea on a rainy afternoon than in a room full of plants, surrounded by glass and light. Such a room expands your gardening possibilities enormously. It's the ideal place to overwinter tender plants and cuttings, and to start seedlings in late winter. If the temperature and humidity are right you can grow orchids and tropical plants.

You'll want to site this room in such a way that it connects with the garden outside and is a transition between house and garden. Trees and shrubs planted nearby can soften the edges of the room when seen from the outside, and yet share the feeling of its greenery when you are inside.

Garden lighting brings the winter garden into focus

Dramatic lighting in a garden is especially useful in winter. For practical purposes, it is important to guide people safely along garden paths and walkways. For aesthetic reasons, however, it can be used to highlight trees, shrubs and other features in the garden, especially ones with particularly interesting shapes and forms. This could be a clump of silver birch, the peeling bark of an arbutus tree or a garden statue. Night lighting in winter can be used to draw attention to shapes and forms that have taken a back seat the rest of the year.

Design flaws begin to show

In winter the structure of the garden has to stand on its own merits. Now that you are assessing your garden for winter interest, this is an excellent time to look again at design. After all, January is nearly here again, and that's time to plan any design and structural changes you want to make for the next season. If you start to look critically at the garden now, you will be ready in January to put pen to paper. The list of trees and shrubs for fall

and winter interest in this chapter will give you some ideas for plants you can use as part of this design, to enhance the beauty of your garden in winter.

Evergreens

Evergreens give a solid, comfortable feel to a garden. They define and divide spaces and borders, provide protection from wind, noise and neighbours, and contribute a wide variety of shapes, sizes, textures and shades of green all year round. If used unimaginatively, they can be very boring: here's where a bit of flair can make a big difference in the garden. Take a look around your neighbourhood and see how others have used evergreens. If you see ideas you like, adapt them to your own garden.

Deciduous trees and shrubs

When leaves have fallen, it is the silhouettes of deciduous trees and shrubs that first catch our attention. Contorted branches of the corkscrew hazel and graceful branches of weeping willows are much more interesting in winter than they are in summer. Stately oaks and maples in the park have a stark simplicity and grace when they are leafless, which contrasts with their rich, soft fullness when clothed in summer greenery. The furry buds of the magnolia invite you to reach out and touch. Catkins dangle in soft clusters from overhanging branches of alder and birch.

Some trees and shrubs have particularly striking bark, including many of the maples, birches and cherries. Upright twigs of shrubby dogwoods turn bright yellow or red, and look particularly dramatic when surrounded with fallen snow. Many trees and shrubs keep their berries well into winter, providing cheerful splashes of colour in the dull landscape, as you will see from the list below. There are also several plants, bulbs, trees and shrubs that flower during the cold winter months and early spring.

Fruits of the fall

Some plants combine a display of flowers in spring or summer with a secondary display of colourful fruits in winter. These trees and shrubs have conspicuous berries or fruits that add interest to the winter garden.

Arbutus menziesii (**madrone**). This lovely tree is native to the Pacific coast, and is the only native broadleaf evergreen in Canada. The arbutus has glossy green leaves and attractive, reddish-brown peeling bark, and it produces clusters of reddish-orange berries that last most of the winter months. It is a protected species, and thrives on our rocky coastline. It is very hard to obtain, hard to transplant, and grows best close to the ocean. If you are lucky enough to have one in your garden, cherish and enjoy it!

Arbutus unedo (**strawberry tree**). The European arbutus is an attractive evergreen tree, suitable for the home garden. Its trunk and branches have red shedding bark, and as the tree ages it becomes gnarled and twisted, adding to its character. Clusters of urn-shaped, white or greenish-white flowers and strawberry-like red and yellow fruits appear at the same time in fall and winter. The fruit is edible, but unfortunately it is mealy and tasteless.

Callicarpa spp. (**beautyberry**).This bush has very unusual mauve-blue or violet-magenta berries covering the branches after leaf fall and for most of the winter. *C. bodinieri* var. *giraldi* is the variety most commonly grown in this area, with a small violet fruit that lasts well into the fall.

Clerodendrum trichotomum (**glorybower**). A slow-growing deciduous shrub with clusters of fragrant white flowers in August, followed by metallic blue-green berries surrounded by scarlet calyces. It grows to a height of 10 to 15 feet (3 to 4.6 m).

Cotoneaster spp. A large genus that ranges from prostrate species to those growing to 20 feet (6 m). All of the cotoneasters are valuable for their foliage and their generous clusters of bright berries that last well into the winter months.

C. apiculatus (cranberry cotoneaster) is a deciduous shrub growing to a height of 4 feet (1.2 m). Pink flowers in spring are followed by large, cranberry-sized berries in the fall, which are retained well into winter. *C. salicifolius* var. *floccosus* is a graceful evergreen shrub with arching branches reaching a height and spread of between 12 and 15 feet (3.6 to 4.6 m). The glossy, narrow, willowlike leaves are grey-white underneath. White flowers in June are followed by dense clusters of bright red berries that persist through the winter.

Gaultheria mucronata. A low-growing evergreen shrub with small, glossy green leaves. White heathlike flowers are followed by clusters of round berries that come in various colours of pink, red or white. The berries are produced in the fall and last throughout the winter. There are many good cultivars, such as 'Rubra', red berries; 'Rosea', pink berries; and 'Alba', white berries.

Pyracantha spp. (**firethorn**). This valuable group of evergreen shrubs produces masses of colourful berries throughout the fall and winter months. Two good cultivars of *P. coccinea* are 'Fiery Cascade', which grows to 4 feet (1.2 m) and has masses of orange berries that turn red in September and October; and 'Wyattii', a bushy shrub with upright growth to 6 feet (1.8 m), and an abundance of orange-red berries in the fall and winter.

Rosa spp. (roses). Several species and hybrids are worth growing for their hips alone. Most of the species bear some form of fruit, varying in shape from round to bottle-necked or pear-shaped, in various shades of red, purple and orange. *R. canina* has orange-red hips, rich in vitamin C, that are used for rose-hip syrup and for making wine. *R. moyesii* has flask-shaped, orange-red hips and *R. glauca* (*R. rubrifolia*) has lovely, oval, reddish-purple hips. While the species are the main fruit-bearers, some hybrids also bear beautiful hips. For example, 'Frau Dagmar Hastrup' has red, tomatolike hips; 'Mme. Gregoire Staechelin' has large, orange-red hips.

Skimmia spp. These are low-growing evergreen shrubs with compact, glossy green leaves. Clusters of tiny white flowers in April and May are followed by red berries that last throughout most of the winter, as long as one male plant is planted with female plants. *S. reevesiana* is self-fertile.

Symphoricarpos spp. (snowberry). These are hardy, deciduous suckering shrubs that are useful for low hedging. They have large, white or pink berries that are very decorative for winter floral arrangements. *S. albus* reaches a height of 5 to 7 feet (1.5 to 2.1 m) and has urn-shaped pink flowers from July to September, followed by glistening white berries that last from October to February. 'Laevigatus' has large, pure white berries.

Viburnum opulus (guelder rose). A 12-foot (3.7-m) deciduous shrub with heavily scented flowers in May, followed by translucent red berries in the fall.

Winter-flowering plants and bulbs

The two winter-flowering plants we most commonly see here are the "winter roses" (*Helleborus* spp.), described in detail in the December chapter, and the beardless Algerian iris (*I. unguicularis*, also known as *I. stylosa*), which flowers from October to March. This iris has soft lavender or lilac flowers with a yellow blaze, and its cheerful presence is very welcome in the middle of winter. There are several bulbs also worth considering, notably the cyclamens, crocuses, snowdrops, winter aconites and some irises. Several of these are discussed in the September chapter, but listed here are some midwinter bloomers.

Crocus spp. The early-flowering species crocuses listed here are hard to find but worth the search if you do find them. *C. speciosus* is an easy crocus to grow. It has large, lilac-blue flowers opening in October. 'Albus' is a pure white form and 'Artobis' has pale blue flowers marked with darker lines. *C. longiflorus* is one of the most strikingly scented of the crocuses. It has 3-inch (7.5-cm) flowers, deep lilac with an orange throat. *C. imperati* blooms from late December to February. *C. chrysanthus* blooms in February, with golden-yellow flowers. *C. tomasinianus* has 3-inch (7.5-cm) flowers in February. Two good varieties are 'Barr's Purple' and 'Whitewell Purple', which are both a deeper mauve than the species.

Cyclamen hederifolium, formerly C. neapolitanum. Lovely, silver-marbled foliage and dainty, rose-coloured flowers are produced from September to October, and the foliage persists through the winter. 'Album' has pure white flowers. *C. coum* flowers from December to March and has magenta flowers with crimson bases. 'Album' is a white form, also crimson at the base, and 'Roseum' has pink flowers with a crimson base.

***Eranthis* spp. (winter aconite).** Winter aconites resemble buttercups, with tiny yellow flowers on 4-inch (10-cm) stems. They flower from February onwards, or earlier in mild winters. *E. hyemalis* is the most commonly grown.

***Galanthus* spp. (snowdrops).** *G. elwesii* is the giant snowdrop, producing flowers on stems up to 10 inches (25 cm) high. They are in full flower in January and February. *G. nivalis* is the common snowdrop, which flowers from January onwards. 'Flora Plena' is a double form.

***Iris* spp.** Iris species, with their delicately shaped flowers and rich fragrance, come in a wide choice of dwarf forms that flower in February.

I*. danfordiae* has honey-scented, clear yellow flowers in early February. The flowers open before the leaves are fully developed. They grow 3 to 4 inches (7.5 to 10 cm) tall, and most do best if lime is added to our naturally acid soil. *I. histri-* *oides* flowers in February, but in a mild winter it can begin to flower in early January. The flowers are bright blue. *I. reticulata* is an easily grown species. Its deep blue flowers with an orange blaze appear in February. There are many good hybrids of both *I. histrioides* and *I. reticulata*, such as 'Cantab', pale blue; 'Harmony', deep royal blue; and 'Pauline', deep dusky violet-pink with a white spot.

Trees and shrubs for winter and early spring interest

This list contains trees and shrubs that bloom during the winter and early spring, from mid-November to March, bringing colour to the garden during the grey days of midwinter.

***Camellia* spp.** These handsome evergreen shrubs thrive in our climate and like lime-free soil enriched with organic matter. They need to be sheltered from wind and strong summer sun, so are excellent candidates for a north-facing exposure.

C. sasanqua is a bushy shrub or small tree reaching 10 to 15 feet (3 to 4.6 m) at maturity. Its thin, oblong, dark green leaves contrast well with its flowers, which can be white, rose-pink or red, and are produced from November to February. Good cultivars include 'Yuletide', red single flowers with yellow stamens, 'Showa-no-Sakae', ice-pink with semidouble flowers, and 'White Doves', white semidouble flowers. *C. williamsii* are an outstanding group of hybrids growing to 6 to 8 feet (1.8 to 2.4 m). Once they have finished flowering they drop their blooms, unlike some other species. They flower from November to April. Good cultivars include 'Donation', semidouble free-flowering; and 'J.C. Williams', single-flowered, pale blush-pink with large golden stamens.

Tip of the Month: Heeling in Roses

Bare-root roses are shipped from nurseries or can be purchased at some local garden centres from October to March. But it is not always possible or convenient to plant the roses in their permanent spot at this time. If that is the case, the roses can be heeled in and moved to their chosen location in early spring.

To heel in roses, dig a hole or trench about 12 inches (30 cm) deep and large enough to accommodate the roots; place the roses in the trench about 3 to 6 inches (7.5 to 15 cm) apart, at an angle of 45 degrees. Replace the soil and firm down, making sure the budding union is 2 inches (5 cm) below the ground. Water well.

Chimonanthus praecox (winter sweet). This is a lovely deciduous shrub with intensely fragrant, spicy flowers of creamy yellow. It grows best in full sun and reaches 10 by 10 feet (3 by 3 m) at maturity. Although it may take some years to flower, it is worth it if you have the space. It blooms in February and March.

Cornus mas (Cornelian cherry). A bushy shrub whose naked boughs are covered with pale golden flowers in February, followed in the fall by large, reddish berries the birds like. It grows up to 12 feet (3.7 m), with a spread of up to 10 feet (3 m), but can be kept smaller by pruning.

Daphne spp. These fragrant shrubs are a bonus in any garden. *D. mezereum* (February daphne) is a deciduous shrub growing to 5 feet (1.5 m), which flowers in February. Its sweetly scented mauve-pink flowers open before the leaves unfurl. It needs well-drained soil and partial shade. *D. odora* (winter daphne) is evergreen and also grows to about 5 feet (1.5 m). It blooms in February or March and carries pale mauve flowers on crowded terminal heads. It is not always hardy, but is worth having for its exquisite scent. The hardiest form is 'Aureo-Marginata', with creamy white–margined leaves.

Erica spp. (heath). The heaths are prostrate, mat-forming shrubs which generally need a soil with a low pH, our natural condition here. Certain cultivars will flower all winter, no matter what the weather. *E. carnea*, the winter heath, and its cultivars are normally prostrate in growth, reaching little more than a foot (30 cm) in height. Once established, they can spread many feet and provide a winter-long carpet of flowers and foliage.

Garrya elliptica (silk-tassel bush). This bush has pendulous, grey-green male catkins in January and February that lengthen as spring begins. Its evergreen leaves are attractive but need protection from severe frost. The female catkins are smaller and less attractive, but are followed by round clusters of purple-green fruits. Plants of both sexes are required for fruits to be produced. Silk-tassel bush grows up to 15 feet (4.6 m) with a spread up to 12 feet (3.7 m). It should be planted in April, if possible, against a south- or west-facing wall. The male cultivar, 'James Roof', is the one most readily available in garden centres. This is an excellent plant with large leathery leaves and very long, greyish-green catkins.

Hamamelis spp. (witch hazel). This shrub thrives in our acid soil. From December to March it bears sweetly scented, spiderlike yellow, red or orange flowers on leafless branches, ideal for flower arranging. The shrubs vary in height but usually grow to a height and spread of 10 to 15 feet (3 to 4.7 m). The curiously shaped flowers can withstand the coldest winter, and an added bonus is the outstanding fall colour of yellows and oranges. Good cultivars are *H. x intermedia* 'Arnold Promise', with large, bright yellow flowers; 'Diane', one of the best red forms; and 'Copper Beauty', with large, coppery-red flowers in dense clusters. *H. mollis* (Chinese witch hazel) cultivars to look for are 'Brevipetala', with small, short, deep yellow petals borne in dense clusters; and 'Pallida', with paler yellow flowers faintly flushed with red at the centre.

Jasminum nudiflorum (winter jasmine). Although this loose, open plant grows up to 10 feet (3 m), it is not really a climber and needs to be anchored to a support. It thrives in shade and produces starlike golden flowers on leafless green stems. It should be pruned back to old wood immediately after flowering. Plant where it can be appreciated from close quarters.

Mahonia spp. These are handsome and valuable evergreen shrubs, with distinct, pinnate foliage with prickly margins. *M. aquifolium* (Oregon grape) is native to our area and bears fragrant yellow flowers in numerous dense clusters in March and April. It has a height and spread of 3 to 5 feet (.9 to 1.5 m). *M.* 'Charity' is a desirable hybrid of *M. japonica* and *M. lomariifolia* that grows up to 10 feet (3 m), with fragrant, deep yellow flowers from November to February.

Prunus spp. The flowering cherries, plums and almonds have been discussed in the October chapter. However, one that should be mentioned in this list, since it flowers from November to March, is the autumn-flowering cherry, *Prunus subhirtella* 'Autumnalis', which bears semidouble, pale pink flowers intermittently during the winter months.

Rhododendron spp. There are a number of rhododendrons that flower in winter. The following are some especially good ones. *R.* 'Cilpinense' is a dwarf plant bearing open, bell-shaped, pinkish-white flowers in late February and March. *R. dauricum* is an evergreen or semi-evergreen shrub with pink flowers on bare branches in late January or February. *R. mucronulatum* is deciduous, with rose-purple flowers freely produced on bare branches in late January or February. *R. moupinense* is evergreen, with white, red-freckled flowers in February and March. *R.* 'Olive' is a hybrid of *R. dauricum* and *R. moupinense* and

blooms in February. *R.* 'Praecox' is a purplish-lilac hybrid, sometimes evergreen, which blooms in March.

Salix spp. (pussy willow). The shrubby willow comes in quite a range of leaf shapes and colours, with variations in catkins, bark and size. *S. caprea* 'Pendula' (weeping pussy willow) is a lovely tree for the winter garden, forming a narrow column of weeping branches, clothed in silvery catkins that turn gold with pollen. *S. lanata* (woolly willow) is a much smaller, slow-growing shrub suitable for rock gardens. Rounded, midgreen leaves are covered with grey-white felt, and the stout yellow catkins appear in March. *S. gracilistyla* var. *melanostachys* (black pussy willow) is an unusual form with exquisite black catkins. Bright red stamens emerge from the catkins before the branches leaf out.

Sarcococca spp. (sweet box). This small evergreen shrub, which flowers in midwinter, has tiny blooms that give off a sweet vanillalike fragrance. Good species are *S. hookeriana* var. *humilis*, with black berries, and *S. ruscifolia* with red berries. Both are best planted in the shade of taller shrubs or trees.

Viburnum spp. *V. tinus* (laurustinus) is a popular evergreen shrub that grows up to 10 feet (3 m). It has white flowers with pink tinges on the bud, and small, deep blue berries that become black as they age. The buds start to open in November and continue throughout winter in mild spells. There are attractive dwarf varieties.
V. x *bodnantense* flowers in January and February. This lovely deciduous shrub bears very fragrant clusters of pink flowers, or white flowers tinged with pink in the bud. It grows up to 8 feet (2.4 m). The most desirable flowering form is 'Dawn'.

Garden Gear

Gardeners don't need a lot of tools to do a good job. But it helps to choose them carefully, getting the best quality you can afford. The right tools, well maintained, will increase your efficiency and make your work in the garden more enjoyable.

What to look for when buying garden tools

There is no substitute for quality. In the long run it is cheaper to buy one good piece of equipment that will last a lifetime than to be replacing poorly made tools every few years. However, it is important to know what to look for when you are going out to buy a garden fork, spade, hoe, rake or other piece of basic equipment.

First, check the metal that has been used. Tempered steel or heat-treated metal is superior to tools stamped out of sheet metal; stainless steel is even better, but it is the most expensive. Look at the handles. Solid wood handles made of straight-grain ash or elm are the best; check for knots or other flaws in the wood that could crack, and avoid painted plastic handles since they could be covering flaws in the wood. Don't be fooled by plastic handles that are made to look like wood.

Look at the place where the metal shaft joins the working end of the tool. You'll want a tool constructed out of one piece of metal, with a solid shank, rather than one that is joined at the bottom of the shaft, since the latter is weaker and won't last as long. In some tools, the wooden handle is held into its socket simply by a tight fit, and this will work loose as the tool is used. Make sure your equipment has a rivet made of solid, heavy hardware that keeps the working part of the tool attached to the handle.

Evaluate its size and weight. If the handle is too long or too short, if the tool is too heavy or too light, you will find it uncomfortable to use.

A basic gardener's kit

A basic gardener's kit includes tools for digging, planting, edging, hoeing, cultivating, weeding, raking, pruning, cutting, watering, hauling, mowing grass, general maintenance and staking and tying plants.

For digging, planting, and edging: a garden fork, shovel and spade.

For cultivating: a hoe and long-handled cultivator.

For weeding: a hand fork, trowel and dandelion weeder.

For raking: a rake, preferably two, one rigid, flat or bow-headed for beds, and the other wider, made of bamboo or metal, for lawns.

For pruning and cutting: a variety of pruning and cutting tools, including secateurs, a pruning knife, long-handled grass-edging shears, a bow saw, a pruning saw and branch loppers. A word of advice about secateurs: buy yourself a really good pair, guard them with your life, and never lend them to friends. Lending your secateurs is every bit as fatal as lending your omelette pan.

For watering: a watering can, a sprayer, a sprinkler, garden hose and soaker hose.

For hauling: a wheelbarrow.

For cutting grass: a lawn mower.

For general garden maintenance: a garden broom, stakes, twine, scissors, netting, soil-testing kit, Reemay, Tanglefoot, other organic supplies and organic fertilizers.

Maintaining and storing garden gear

It's worth taking an afternoon to sort, tidy and organize garden tools, putting up pegboards for small tools, hanging spades and forks on nails on the wall, using a large, old barrel for rakes and brooms, and setting aside one shelf for your organic fertilizers, plant pots and other bits and pieces. Here are some other useful tips.

- A rag soaked in motor oil can be used for wiping the metal parts of tools.
- Use a hand file to sharpen spades, hoes and hand pruners. For all other cutting tools, use a whetstone.
- Store all tools out of the weather, and keep them dry over the winter.
- Gas-powered equipment should be run until out of gas at the end of the season.
- Spark plugs should be disconnected, and all equipment should be cleaned thoroughly before storing for the winter.

Making a Holiday Wreath

Evergreen wreaths have become synonymous with the UBC Botanical Gardens. Handmade by Friends of the Garden from fresh greenery gathered on site or from the gardens of the volunteers, the wreaths are a sight to behold. Over 200 are made every year and are available for purchase at the Shop in the Garden which is also run and staffed by Friends of the Garden (FOGS). Buying a wreath here is a wonderful way to lend your support. Take time for a tour while you are there, and see the many interesting plants that are at their best at this time of year. Walking around the Winter Garden will give a new appreciation of what can be grown in this season.

If you want to learn how to make your own wreath, you can take a wreath-making class. These classes were started by Judy Newton and David Tarrant, and for many years they have taught both FOGS and members of the public how to create these wreaths using materials that are all around us. Check

for dates and times of classes by calling 822-9666.

For those of you who live too far away from UBC, here is a brief description of how they are made, as taught by David and Judy. Basically it is a case of overlapping and tying small bundles of fragrant cedar or pine wrapped in moss onto a wire frame and adding interesting "accent" pieces.

Materials

- A 14-inch (36-cm) wire frame; this is available at craft stores and some garden centres, but you can easily make your own.
- Garden twine (jute, not plastic).
- Roll of 3-inch-wide (7.5-cm) green plastic; this is available at craft stores, or you can use a green garbage bag cut into 3-inch (7.5-cm) strips.
- Moss.
- Branches of cedar, pine or other conifers. You can also use boxwood, salal or any broadleafed evergreen. It is difficult to give an exact amount, as a lot depends on how thick you want the wreath to be and what material you choose, but approximately one grocery bag full.
- Interesting accent pieces with berries or coloured foliage. Some suggestions are holly, skimmia, gaultheria, callicarpa, rose hips, ivy with flowers and berries, leucothoe, clematis seed heads or other seed pods or cones, coloured twigs of huckleberry or shrubby dogwoods, variegated evergreens or golden forms of conifers. Be adventurous, try anything. Again, it is hard to estimate how much you will need, but it is a good idea to cut an uneven number—say five, seven or nine pieces—of each of your chosen accent materials.

Method

First, clear a large work surface on which to arrange all your materials. To start the wreath, wrap the wire frame with the green plastic. This is done for several reasons. First, wire frames tend to rust, so the plastic will protect your door when the wreath is hung. The plastic also helps keep the moss damp by trapping in the moisture. Wrap the plastic around loosely, pushing it down into the trough as you go. The idea is to create a well in which to place your moss wrapped greenery. Don't worry if the wrapping isn't perfect; once the greenery is in, all will be well.

Next, cut the greenery and the accent pieces into approximately 6-inch (15-cm) pieces, or a bit longer if you prefer. Of course you can cut up the greenery as you go along, but you will make the wreath a lot faster if you have everything prepared beforehand. Having separate piles of each type of plant you will be using will make designing your wreath a lot easier. Don't waste any of your precious greenery; even little short pieces can be used when making the bundles.

Tie a piece of green garden twine anywhere on the outside or inside ring of the frame. Now make a bundle by grouping about six pieces of greenery together, arranging it like a small bouquet, with the nicer pieces at the front and the short stubby pieces at the back. Wrap the end of the bundle in a small amount of moss and place it in the trough of the frame. Wind the string over the frame and the moss end of the bundle and pull it taut.

Make another bundle in the same way and place it snugly over the moss of the previous bundle. Wrap the string around the frame and moss end of the bundle as before. Keep adding bundles until the frame is full. Tuck the last bundle into the frame by carefully lifting up the first bundle. As you work, check the back of the frame from time to time. The string should be evenly spaced about 1 inch (2.5 cm) apart.

Plan how you are going to use your accent pieces before you start. You can either place them evenly or randomly around the wreath. Some people like to put an accent piece in every bundle, some every second or third bundle. What you do is up to you.

When you have finished putting in all the bundles, make a loop with the string for hanging up the wreath, before cutting off the excess. At this stage you can either add a bow or leave it as it is. This type of moss wreath keeps fresh for many weeks. If it shows signs of wilting, you can put it outside in the rain or simply lay it on the ground and water it, taking care, of course, not to wet the bow if you have one.

Recommended Reading

The winter garden

Bowles, E.A. *My Garden in Autumn and Winter.* Timber Press, Portland, Oregon, 1998.

Hinkley, Daniel. *Winter Ornamentals.* Cascadia Gardening Series, Sasquatch Press, Seattle, 1993.

Lovejoy, Ann. *The Year in Bloom: Gardening for All Seasons in the Pacific Northwest.* Sasquatch Books, Seattle, 1989.

Verey, Rosemary. *The Garden in Winter.* Timber Press, Portland, Oregon, 1995.

The Winter Garden. A Wisley Handbook. The Royal Horticultural Society with Cassell Educational Limited, London, 1989.

Shrubs

See Recommended Reading in the April chapter.

Bulbs

See Recommended Reading in the September chapter.

Trees

See Recommended Reading in the October chapter.

Garden gear

Damrosch, Barbara. *The Garden Primer.* Workman Publishing, New York, 1988.

Hessayon, D.G. *The Garden Expert.* pbi Publications, Herts, England, 1986.

December

T he days are short. The nights are long. Winter solstice approaches. It's time to take a bow, congratulate yourself on a successful year completed in the garden, and relax from garden chores. Although there are a few things you can do, they can probably wait. The festive season is here, and this is the time to think about garden-related presents for your friends and family.

You'll be ahead of the crowd if you made herbal vinegars, dried flowers and potpourri in August, potted bulbs for forcing in October, or created a holiday wreath in November. But don't worry if you didn't. There's plenty of time to browse the garden stores and make up your own gift packages, using some of the ideas in this chapter.

Prune back a few holly branches and cedar boughs for inside decorations, and bring out your pots of paper whites to scent the air. Towards the end of the month or beginning of January, the Christmas rose will start to bloom: this lovely flower and its *Helleborus* relatives are featured this month.

If you have a small evergreen tree near the front door, especially if it is in a pot, plan to decorate it with lights and string it with cranberries and popcorn for the birds. The best way to feed the birds, of course, is to provide them with trees and shrubs that are laden with their favourite fruits, and some of these are highlighted in this chapter.

In preparation for next spring, you may want to make a trough garden. This month there are instructions for this charming, old-fashioned addition to a garden.

But above all, December is a time to reflect on the year that is nearly over, and to consider the benefits of being a gardener. For this we leave the final word to Elizabeth von Arnim (from *Elizabeth and her German Garden*): "I do sincerely trust that the benediction that is always awaiting me in my garden may by degrees be more deserved, and that I may grow in grace, and patience, and cheerfulness, just like the happy flowers I so much love."

Garden Highlights

indicates fragrance

Bulbs

Crocus (early species), *Cyclamen coum* (cyclamen), *Galanthus nivalis* (snowdrop).

Perennials

Helleborus niger (Christmas rose), *Iris unguicularis* (Algerian iris).*

Climbers

Jasminum nudiflorum (winter jasmine).

Shrubs

Camellia sasanqua,* *Cornus* spp. (see the October chapter), *Daphne mezereum* (February daphne),* *Erica* spp. (heath), *Fatsia japonica* (Japanese aralia), *Ilex* spp. (holly), *Mahonia* 'Charity',* *Viburnum* x *bodnantense*,* *Viburnum tinus* (laurustinus).

Trees

Prunus subhirtella 'Autumnalis' (autumn-flowering cherry). See also Garden Highlights for November.

December Checklist

Annuals, perennials and bulbs

- Protect crowns of tender plants on frosty nights.
- Divide and replant perennials, weather permitting, and firm down plants whose roots are loosened by frost.
- Start ordering flower seeds.
- Check dahlia and begonia tubers, and gladiola corms, and remove infected ones.

Trees, shrubs and climbers

- Trees and shrubs may be planted, weather permitting.
- Lightly prune hollies and evergreens, and use clippings for wreaths and seasonal decorations.
- Continue to plant roses if ground is not frozen or waterlogged (see the June chapter).
- Rake up and destroy old rose leaves to prevent overwintering of diseases.

Fruits, vegetables and herbs

- Plant fruit trees and bushes in good weather.
- Mulch herb bushes if weather turns severe.
- Plan vegetable garden and start ordering seeds.
- Begin spraying fruit trees with dormant oil and lime sulphur in mild weather.
- Check stored fruit and other produce and remove any that are rotting.
- Ventilate cold frames in mild weather.

General garden activities

- Rake leaves and debris off lawns and avoid walking on frozen grass.
- Take the opportunity to clean and sharpen tools and service the mower and any other power equipment.

The Roses of Winter

A perennial that blooms in the middle of winter is a rare sight. When it is as lovely as the "winter roses" (*Helleborus* spp.) it is a special treasure for any garden. One species or another is in bloom from early January to April, their large, nodding flowers blooming serenely through winter snow and rain.

Hellebores have been cultivated for centuries and are the subject of many legends and superstitions. In medieval times they were thought to cure madness and counteract witchcraft, and they were planted near cottage doors to prevent evil spirits from crossing the threshold.

Hellebores are ideally suited to the shady garden, thriving under deciduous shrubs and trees or on a north-facing wall in well-drained humus-enriched soil. They will also grow well in full sun if the humus content and moisture are adequate, and all benefit from an annual mulch of aged manure or compost.

Hellebores look lovely grouped together, or even better in combination with early spring bulbs such as snowdrops (*Galanthus* spp.), winter aconite (*Eranthus hyemalis*), *Cyclamen coum*, *Erythronium* spp., *Trillium* spp., and early *Narcissus* spp. and their cultivars. They also combine well with early perennials, including *Corydalis* spp., *Pulmonaria* spp., and *Arum italicum*. Later, their attractive foliage contributes to the shade garden with *Dicentra* spp., *Meconopsis* spp., ferns and hostas.

Hellebores can be propagated by division, although they are resentful of being disturbed and take some time to recover. They may also be raised quite easily by seed, sown as soon as it is ripe. The pursuit of authenticity in hellebore cultivation is not for the timid. These wonderful plants have the habit of hybridizing and seeding themselves freely, so if it is considered really essential to propagate a particular named cultivar, it should be done by division after flowering. Alternatively, pollination may be performed by hand before the flower opens.

Hellebores often harbour fungal spores, so the removal and destruction of the leaves in early January is advised. Not only can you see the flowers much better, but the old leaves tend to detract from the beauty of the flowers.

Following are some gardenworthy species, named hybrids and cultivars.

***H. argutifolius* (syn. *H. corsicus*).** Growing to 2 to 3 feet (60 to 90 cm), this easily grown plant has magnificent, large, glossy green leaves and stems that produce heads of cup-shaped, apple-green flowers from late winter into midspring. 'Pacific Frost' is a variegated version that originated in the Vancouver garden of Pam Frost.

H. foetidus. The stinking hellebore has attractive, deeply divided, dark green foliage and contrasting, bell-like, chartreuse flowers rimmed with burgundy. It blooms throughout winter and most of spring. 'Wesker Fisk' is a most beautiful cultivar with red-tinted stems and petioles. It's not always long-lived but reseeds itself freely.

***H.* x *hybridus* (formerly *H. orientalis*).** The Lenten rose, one of the most popular and beautiful hellebores in cultivation, possesses a wide spectrum of colour, ranging from pure white, yellow and pale pink to maroon and dark purple. The flowers are mostly single (although recent breeding has seen the introduction of some double forms) and can be speckled, spotted, veined or plain.

H. niger. The Christmas rose is probably the best-known hellebore. It has black roots (hence its botanical name), and the flower stalks emerge directly from the soil, bearing pure white flowers, flushing with pink as they mature. It does not like to be disturbed. 'White Magic' has pure white flowers and prominent gold stamens.

- **H.** x **sternii.** This is not the hardiest of hellebores, but it's a very beautiful plant that thrives in full sun to part shade. An outstanding foliage plant, it has coarse-toothed grey-green leaves that often have a maroon tinge. The flowers are greenish-yellow flushed with pink.

 # Gifts for Gardeners

The garden has settled back for its winter rest and leaves us little to do besides planning for next year. What better time to shop for gifts for gardeners? Whether your friends and family are gardeners or not, you will be able to find unusual and memorable presents for them, presents that will be treasured and valued for years to come.

Gifts that money can't buy

One of the most priceless gifts of all is the gift of your time, especially for the elderly, sick or handicapped. This could be an offer to help with weeding, pruning, shovelling topsoil, tree planting, or other heavy garden chores. You could make an I.O.U. booklet with vouchers for different gardening services, such as helping to make a garden plan, potting up containers with bedding plants, planting bulbs and so on.

Some people would love to have a chauffeured day trip to bulb fields and parks and gardens in the spring or a visit to a flower show or specialty nursery, together with a picnic or lunch at a favourite restaurant. Mark a calendar for them with gardening treats, so they can enjoy your gift all year.

Gifts that last all year

Memberships and subscriptions are an excellent way to give pleasure through the year. Annual membership to a botanical garden is a great idea, or you may want to give a year's membership to a specialty club or society or an annual subscription to a gardening magazine. Some garden centres are willing to sell gift certificates for plants, to be redeemed in the spring. This is a lovely gift if your friends need plants for their garden but you don't know what they want.

Gardening books

There's a good reason why books are always popular presents. They are a great way to increase knowledge about a particular area of interest, and they are inspirational too. There are so many excellent gardening books on the market now and they really need no introduction; even the smallest bookstore will have a selection.

A much wider selection of books for B.C. gardeners is available today, and they are extremely useful. Our growing conditions are so different from the rest of Canada, and even from England, although growing conditions here are often compared to those in England. If you are looking for a heart-warming stocking stuffer, *Elizabeth and her German Garden* is not to be missed (see Further Reading).

Gardening classes

There are many excellent gardening courses available, both credit and non-credit. As well as countless community centres, the botanical gardens, and community colleges, garden centres and nurseries, such as Brookswood Nursery in Langley and Happy Valley Herb Farm in Victoria, give classes and workshops.

Check the Resources section for courses, and remember to look in your local newspaper for special guest lecturers coming to your area. The gift of a course you know someone will enjoy, or tickets to hear a guest lecturer, is always a welcome present.

Going organic

Composting is such a valuable way to turn vegetative wastes into rich, dark earth that it's no surprise more and more companies and individuals are developing composters. A book on composting may be enough to get someone started, or you may want to buy one of the many composting models on the market today. Other unorthodox organic gifts might include a shredder, organic fertilizer, insecticidal soap, a soil-testing kit or bags of manure.

Tools and garden wear

Quality garden tools make marvellous gifts (see the November chapter for a basic garden tool list). There's something for every pocketbook, from stainless steel spades and forks to garden twine and plant labels. Watering cans, rubber boots, sun or rain hats, gloves, even a waterproof jacket, are gifts any gardener will welcome.

Garden furnishings

This is probably one of the most enjoyable kinds of gardening gifts to buy a friend. Sundials, garden antiques, topiary animals, terra cotta pots and garden benches are some suggestions. There are several excellent places

to look for interesting and different garden ornaments catering to every taste, from concrete frogs to twiggy furniture.

For the birds

Don't forget the birds when you are shopping. Apartment dwellers with no garden at all would still appreciate binoculars to watch the birds, a hanging window bird feeder, and bird books. Bird baths, bird feeders and bird houses come in many different shapes and sizes, and there are excellent books on attracting birds and butterflies into your garden.

Give a pot

Pots and containers come in a wide variety of shapes and sizes, made from terra cotta, stone, wood or concrete. There are some lovely hand-painted ones, and all make good containers for plants, bulbs, trees or shrubs. Some ideas include a pot of paper whites, a bonsai container with or without a plant, hyacinth glasses with hyacinths ready to bloom, a basket of cyclamen and indoor ferns, or a small tree in a cement pot.

Botanical illustrations or motifs

In our area we have many fine artists who specialize in botanical illustrations, and their works make excellent presents. Some artists' illustrations have been used to decorate canvas bags, T-shirts, trays, aprons and mugs, and many of these are very attractive. The shops at the botanical gardens are excellent places to shop for these, and you can check out their book selection while you are there.

Do it yourself

If you have friends who are handy with their hands, there are some excellent do-it-yourself possibilities. How about an Adirondack chair kit, or a pond liner or pump with instructions

---

Tip of the Month: Hellebore Protection

To prevent hellebore flowers from being splattered with mud during heavy rains, spread grit or coarse sand around the base of the plant.

on how to make a water garden? A set of outdoor garden lights is easily installed by some, and others will appreciate a dried flower arrangement with a book on how to dry their own.

Garden comics

There are so many gorgeous colour gardening catalogues on the market today that it can make your head reel. An excellent and unusual present is to order a selection of these catalogues and present them in a bag with a good bottle of wine for a winter evening's enjoyment.

The scented garden

If you made potpourri in August, it will be just right to give away in December. Present it in a pretty bowl or container, or sew it into sachets for the underwear drawer. Herbal bath oils, soaps and good hand creams are certainly appreciated by the gardener whose hands and body show signs of garden wear and tear.

The gourmet gardener

Keen vegetable gardeners will appreciate books and seeds on exotic edible gardening. Since the seed companies have started to produce interesting and unusual cultivars, many home gardeners have started to become more adventurous, and this is a chance to encourage their creativity. After all, you may benefit from their produce next summer.

For children

We often forget about children when buying gardening gifts, but many children are very interested in gardens, insects and plants, not necessarily in that order! An insect catcher and magnifying glass will give them endless hours of amusement, and most children love to grow easy and rewarding plants, such as

sunflowers and radishes. They may appreciate their own piece of outdoor furniture and their own set of gardening books. The lovely little Beatrix Potter books make nice presents, especially when accompanied by seeds for the children to grow in their own vegetable gardens.

Say it with holly

If all ideas fail you, and your friends and family live in one of the coldest parts of Canada, how about sending them a box of local holly? There are holly farms on Vancouver Island that ship around the globe. As we give thanks that we can grow this cheerful decorative shrub, it's a great time to remind ourselves that we live in one of the best spots in the world.

Feed the Birds

When planning your garden, spare a thought for the birds. Carefully selected and positioned plants, especially native plants that the birds know and like, will provide food and cover for them. Birds like variety, so the more kinds, shapes and sizes of plants you grow, the more birds you will attract. If you plan carefully, your garden can have plants that attract and feed birds year round.

Conifers are important for cover and nesting sites and provide the most thermal protection in winter. Seed cones attract birds such as crossbills, which eat the seeds, and nuthatches, chickadees, pine siskins, warblers and goldfinches, which glean the insects from the cones.

Native shrubs and climbers attractive to birds include all the berry fruits, such as blueberries, blackberries, huckleberries and salmon berries, and plants, such as Oregon grape (*Mahonia aquifolium*), elderberry

(*Sambucus* spp.), salal (*Gaultheria shallon*), Saskatoon berry (*Amelanchier* spp.), red-osier dogwood (*Cornus stolonifera*), hazelnut (*Corylus cornuta*), honeysuckle (*Lonicera* spp.), sumac (*Rhus glabra*), red-flowering currant (*Ribes sanguineum*), wild rose (*Rosa* spp.) and snowberry (*Symphoricarpos albus*). Some other bushes they like include *Cotoneaster* spp., *Pyracantha* spp., cultivated honeysuckles (*Lonicera* spp.), *Viburnum* spp. and the cultivated berry bushes.

Fruit-producing trees are essential food for birds. Trees that produce a lot of small fruits, such as mountain ash (*Sorbus sitchensis*), will attract many different species of birds. Other good trees to grow are dogwoods (*Cornus* spp.), hawthorn (*Crataegus* spp.) and crabapple (*Malus* spp.). They will be visited throughout the winter as long as their fruit remains on the tree.

Making a Trough Garden

One attractive way to display tiny plants, especially alpines, is to create a trough garden out of concrete. If the trough has good drainage and is filled with the specific soil mix the plants require, they will thrive. A good place to view trough gardens is VanDusen Botanical Garden.

Trough gardens are easy to make, and they are remarkably weatherproof; they are the perfect home for hardy alpines year round. The following instructions can be used to make a simple rectangular trough.

Materials

- Polyethylene sheeting.
- Two sturdy cardboard boxes, one 1 1/2 to 2 inches (3.8 to 5 cm) larger in length and width than the other.
- Strapping tape.
- Cement.
- Perlite.
- Peat moss.
- Half-inch (1.2-cm) mesh chicken wire.
- Three pieces of 1/2-inch (1.2-cm) diameter dowelling, each 6 inches (15 cm) long.
- A sharp knife or razor blade.
- A large rubber bucket.
- Rubber gloves.
- Measuring cup (such as an empty coffee can).
- Wire cutters.
- An old knife or scraper.

Method

Choose a good work space where a bit of mess won't be a problem (heated workshop, basement or garage), and where you can have access to water. Prepare the mould out of the cardboard boxes, fitting the smaller box, closed end up, neatly inside the other, so that there is a 1 1/2- to 2-inch (3.8- to 5-cm) gap between the sides of the boxes when nested. If it is necessary to cut the smaller box to fit, do so and tape it to the required size with strapping tape. The inner box should be 4 to 6 inches (10 to 15 cm) deep, the other one at least 3 inches (7.5 cm) higher. Wrap a couple of bands of strapping tape near the top and

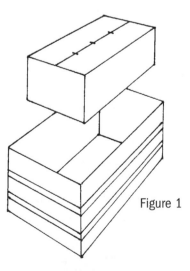

Figure 1

bottom of the outer box to keep the cardboard from buckling under the pressure of wet concrete (Fig. 1).

Now it is time to mix the cement. Good proportions are 1 part cement, 1 1/2 parts peat moss, and 1 1/2 parts perlite. Mix with enough water to reach the consistency of cream-style cottage cheese, in small enough quantities each time so that it doesn't harden before you can use each batch.

Put a 1-inch (2.5-cm) layer of the mix in the bottom of the large box. Place a piece of chicken wire, cut to size, on the concrete and force it into the concrete until it is covered. Then add another 1-inch (2.5-cm) layer of concrete mix to cover the wire completely,

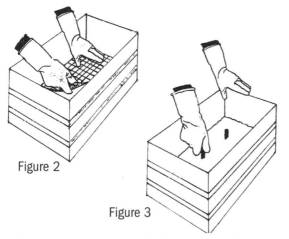

Figure 2

Figure 3

and pack it down evenly to remove all air bubbles (Fig. 2). Set the wooden dowels deep and upright in the concrete so that they will make drainage holes (Fig. 3).

Place the smaller box upside-down and centred inside the larger one and indent it slightly into the concrete. Cut a strip of chicken wire long enough to fit around the small box, and of a width equal to the height of the small box, pressing it firmly into the concrete at the bottom of the large box (Fig. 4). Wait about thirty minutes, then fill the space between the sides of the two boxes with

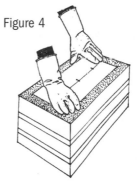

Figure 4

enough concrete to encase the wire and cover its edges. Pack the mix in by the handful and tap the box gently on the work surface in order to prevent and remove air bubbles.

Leave it to cure, undisturbed and at room temperature, for three days, then remove the outer box. Mist the outside with water lightly, and leave it for another seven days. Remove the inner box and dowels and leave it for at least another week to cure completely. Since the concrete is high in lime, which may be toxic to the plants, leave it outdoors to weather for several weeks so that the lime can be leached by rainfall.

Your trough garden is now ready to plant.

Recommended Reading

Hellebores

Rice, Graham and Elizabeth Strangman. *The Gardener's Guide to Growing Hellebores.* Timber Press, Portland, Oregon, 1993.

Feeding Birds

Merrilees, Bill. *Attracting Backyard Wildlife.* Whitecap Books, Vancouver, revised 2000.

Trough Gardens

Beckett, Kenneth and David Stevens. *The Container Garden: A Complete Illustrated Guide to Growing Plants, Flowers, Fruits and Vegetables Outdoors in Pots.* Viking Press, New York, 1983.

Foster, H. Lincoln. *Rock Gardening: A Guide to Growing Alpines and Other Wildflowers in the American Garden.* Timber Press, Portland, Oregon, 1982.

Botanical Names, Glossary, Common Pests and Diseases, and Poisonous Plants

Making Sense of Botanical Names

Botanical names are used solely to avoid the confusion that arises when several different plants have the same common name. Don't be intimidated by this new language, and don't worry too much about the pronunciation. In general, emphasis should be placed on the next-to-last syllable, but even the experts pronounce them differently. Botanical plant names follow a very simple system.

Every plant has a name made up of two (or sometimes more) parts. The first part of the name is the genus to which the plant belongs, and it is always capitalized and set in italics—for example, *Magnolia*.

The second part of the name is the specific epithet, and this helps distinguish the plant from other members of the same genus. It is also italicized, and is not usually capitalized—for example, *Magnolia grandiflora*. This identifies the particular kind of magnolia, in this case, the large-flowered magnolia. (Sometimes a capital letter is used with the specific epithet to denote that the plant is named after a person, but this convention is rarely used in most books, and not used here.) These two parts, the genus name and the specific epithet, combine to make the species name.

The third name, if there is one, can get quite complicated. It gives more information about the plant. For example, plants that are bred, selected and cultivated, called cultivars, are given names that are neither italicized or underlined but are enclosed in single quotation marks, and each word begins with a capital letter. Thus, *Magnolia grandiflora* 'Little Gem' is a cultivar.

When a plant is a cross between two natural species it is termed a hybrid and a multiplication sign is placed before the specific name. For example, *Magnolia* x *soulangeana* is a cross between *M. denudata* and *M. liliflora*. If the parents are not known, the x may be dropped, and just the cultivar name used, for example, *Mahonia* 'Charity'.

Some plant species have naturally occurring, distinct subgroups, and these are given the designation of either variety or subspecies (var. and ssp.). Examples of these are *Sarcococca hookerana* var.

humilis and *Hydrangea anomala* ssp. *petiolaris*. The abbreviation ssp. is plural for species; thus *Helleborus* spp. means all the members of the species *Helleborus*.

Some Latin for gardeners

Many plant names tell about aspects of the plants. With a little knowledge of Latin, it becomes easier to remember names because they describe the plants. (Adapted from "Garden Variety Latin" by Christine Allen in *Gardens West*, February 1991.)

Colour

alba	white
atropurpurea	dark purple
aurea	golden
caerulea	blue
candida	shiny or glossy white
cardinalis	crimson
coccinea	scarlet
cyanus	bright blue
flava	clear yellow
fulva	tawny yellow
glauca	grey or bluish-grey
incana	grey or white
lacta	milky white
lutea	clear yellow
purpurea	purple
rosea	pink
rubella	rosy-red
rubra	red
sanguinea	blood-red
sempervirens	evergreen
virens	green

Flowers

flora	flower
grandiflora	large-flowered
multiflora	many-flowered
parviflora	small-flowered
semperflorens	always flowering

Flower beauty

amabilis	wonderful
blanda	attractive
formosa	beautiful
pulcherrima	prettiest
speciosa	showy or splendid
spectabilis	spectacular

Blooming times

aestivum	summer-flowering
autumnale	autumn-flowering
praecox	early
verna	spring-flowering

Leaves

aesculifolia	chestnutlike leaf
angustifolia	narrow-leafed
cordifolia	heart-shaped leaf
folia	leaf
hederifolium	ivylike leaf
latifolia	broad-leafed
longifolia	long-leafed
millefolia	thousand leaves
pinguifolia	thick-leafed
quercifolia	oaklike leaf
sagittifolia	arrow-shaped leaf
salicifolia	willowlike leaf

Leaf and flower shape

campanulata	bell-shaped
flabellata	fan-shaped
nebulosa	cloudlike
umbellata	umbrella-shaped

Growth habits

contorta	twisted
fruticosa	bushy
nana	small
pendula	weeping
pumila	small
reptans	creeping
tenax	clinging

Texture

lanata	woolly, soft, hairy
pungens	stinging
subhirtella	prickly

Smell

citriodora	lemon-scented
foetida	stinking
graveolens	strong-smelling
odora	sweet-smelling

Where they grow

gypsophila	lime-loving
maritima	by the sea
nemerosa	in shady places

Who discovered them

douglasii	David Douglas
drummondii	James Drummond
hookeri	William or Joseph Hooker
lewisia	Meriwether Lewis
linnaea	Carolus Linnaeus

Where they come from

californica	California
cambrica	Wales
canadensis	Canada
chinensis	China
japonica	Japan
sinensis	China

Glossary

Acid soil: Soil with a pH below 7.0. The more acid the soil, the lower the pH number on a scale from 1 to 14, where 7.0 is neutral. In areas with heavy rainfall, as is the case here, the soil is more typically acidic than in areas with less rain.

Aerial roots: Roots formed above ground. Climbers such as ivy and climbing hydrangea cling to walls with aerial roots.

Alkaline soil: Soil with a higher basic, or lime, content, the opposite of acid soil. It has a pH of more than 7.0.

Annual: A plant whose life span is complete in one season.

Basal leaves: The lowest leaves of a plant, arising at or near soil level, often different in shape from those on the stem.

Bedding plants: Plants that are put in place for one season only. These may be annuals, biennials or tender perennials, or even tender shrubs, such as fuchsia.

Biennial: A plant that completes its life cycle in two growing seasons, forming foliage the first year, then flowering, seeding and dying in the second season. Some may self-seed, giving the impression they are perennial.

Bone meal: Organic fertilizer made of ground-up animal bones. It is a good source of phosphorus.

Cloche: A bell-shaped glass jar developed in France for protection of early crops. Now rarely seen in its original form, the name is used for any protective covering that acts as a mini-greenhouse.

Compost: A mix of fresh and dried organic materials, broken down into a nutrient-rich humus. It renews and conditions the soil, helps retain moisture and provides food for the plants.

Cutting: Any part of a plant removed from its parent and treated so that it produces roots, and in time a completely new plant. Cuttings may originate from roots, stems or leaves of the original plant.

Deadheading: Removing faded or dying flowers from a plant to improve appearance and prevent the flowers from forming seeds.

Deciduous: A plant that loses all of its leaves at one time of the year, usually late fall. The opposite of evergreen.

Division: The deliberate separating of a clump-forming plant into two or more different plants.

Dormancy: The resting state of a plant.

Drift: Poetic term used to describe a natural-looking patch of one plant, for example daffodils or snowdrops.

Dwarf and semidwarf rootstock: Size-controlling or dwarfing rootstocks developed and classified in East Malling, England, and given specific Malling or "M" numbers, denoting the maximum size to which the tree will grow. The classification is used worldwide for apple trees. For instance, "M" 27 means that the tree will not grow larger than 8 feet (2.4 m).

Espalier: A method of training fruit trees that form fruit on spurs, such as apples or pears, by selecting lateral branches to grow horizontally in pairs on either side of the main stem.

Evergreen: A plant that keeps its leaves all year. The opposite of deciduous.

Grafting: The uniting of a stem or bud of one plant onto the root of another, to form a new plant.

Groundcover: Low-growing, usually evergreen plants that provide a spreading cover over the soil.

Hardening off: A process of acclimatizing a plant to a lower temperature. A cold frame can be used for this purpose.

Hardiness: The ability to withstand frost. A hardy plant can live year-round without protection, a half-hardy or tender plant needs protection during the coldest months.

Heel cutting: An offshoot pulled from a parent plant. The heel is a small piece of the outside of the old stem. This type of cutting is the most easily rooted.

Heeling in: The temporary covering of a plant's roots with soil to keep them moist until it can be planted in a permanent position.

Herbaceous perennial: Any perennial that dies back to the ground in fall or winter, returning in the spring.

Humus: The end product of decaying organic matter. Humus improves the texture of the soil by increasing its water retention. The microorganisms in humus help break down chemicals in the soil into forms that can be used by plants.

Hybrid: The offspring of two or more plants that have been crossbred. They are denoted with the sign X, as in *Viburnum* X *bodnantense*.

Lateral: A shoot or branch that grows away from the main stem.

Leader: The uppermost, ideally central, shoot of a shrub or tree.

Leaf mould: Fallen leaves that have decayed and become crumbly. The best mould is made from beech, oak or other small leaves. It can be dug in to enrich the soil or used as a mulch.

Mulch: A material that is spread around plants, but should not touch the stem. It keeps the soil moist, cuts down on the development of weeds and enriches the soil. Good mulches are weed-free compost, leaf mould and composted manure.

Peat moss: This is made of partially decayed mosses. It has little or no food value, but is valuable in retaining water and improving the physical structure of soils. Soak it well before using it.

Perennial: A plant that lives for more than two years. The term is usually applied to herbaceous plants.

Propagation: Any method by which the number of plants is increased, either by sexual or asexual means. Sexual propagation is by means of seed; asexual methods include layering, root division, cuttings, grafting and tissue culture.

Softwood: The twigs or shoots of the current year's growth.

Standard: Any plant grown into a small, treelike form, with a single trunk and a round top of flowers or leaves.

Subshrub: A small evergreen perennial plant with a woody stem and leafy tips, such as lavender or santolina. The soft leafy tips are often pruned back every year.

Sucker: A shoot arising from the roots, or an underground stem of a plant. If a delicate variety of a plant has been grafted onto a more vigorous one, such as a delicate specimen rose grafted onto a hardy rose stock, these suckers are usually vigorous and undesirable.

Top-dress: Applying manure or compost to the surface of the soil around the plant without digging it in.

Common Pests and Diseases

Plant Health Care

By keeping plants healthy we can avoid most problems. Less than a third of plant problems are caused by diseases or pests. It is environmental and cultural factors, such as winter damage, drought stress or overwatering, that create the majority of problems. When we focus on total health care, we recognize that all things are interrelated and work with nature to maintain a healthy balance.

An ounce of prevention

- Identify the plants you have. Read up on their particular needs and problems so that you can look after them well.
- Study your garden to understand its soil, drainage, climate (sun, wind, rain, temperature) and animal (deer, rodent, pet) exposures in order to plan your personal design. Choose the "right plants for the right place." The plants you buy should be suited to the sites you choose for them. Plants under stress are much more susceptible to pests and disease.
- Buy only healthy plants and good-quality seeds and bulbs. Look for disease-resistant cultivars and select a diversity of species to limit the impact of infestations.
- Provide a habitat for naturally occurring beneficial organisms by planting a variety of nectar- and pollen-producing flowering plants.
- Prepare the ground properly when planting or sowing. Improve soil conditions by using organic matter and mulches, practice correct planting methods, and pay careful attention to watering, fertilizing and pruning (too much is as bad as too little of these).
- Do not overcrowd your plants. Ensure that trees and shrubs have adequate circulation by removing overcrowded and crossing branches. Prune out dead and diseased branches.
- Watch for signs of plant stress (yellow or wilted leaves, dead twigs) and developing pest problems. Do regular and frequent monitoring and take care of problems early, before damage is severe.
- Keep the garden tidy and weed free. Rotting plants can be a source of infection and will attract pests. Clean up and destroy all infected plant material.

- If a plant is not thriving, is diseased or is continually attacked by pests, get rid of it and plant something else.
- Ask yourself: "What will happen if I take no action?" A certain amount of damage is normal. Is this pest life-threatening, or is it really just an aesthetic problem? By accepting some imperfection, we let the garden's natural beneficials work to maintain a healthy balance.
- Consider the least toxic approach to control. Hand picking or pruning out problems, or trapping or hosing off insects with a strong spray of water can be most effective.

Common problems in our area

Aphids

This is a well-known group of pests found in colonies on stems and the undersides of leaves. They damage leaves and shoots by sucking the sap, which reduces vigour and distorts leaves, causing flower malformation. They also drop sticky honeydew onto leaves below as they feed. In our damp weather, unsightly black sooty molds then grow on this honeydew.
Control: Knock aphids off with a strong spray of water; a couple of sprays within a week should do it. Succulent soft plant growth attracts aphid attack, so don't overfertilize with nitrogen. Floating row cover like Reemay will keep aphids from vegetables such as celery. Dormant oil will control overwintering aphid eggs on fruit trees.

Black knot on plum

These wartlike growths appear on plum trees. The growths start off as soft green swellings, turning black and hard as they mature.
Control: There is really no cure for this, and it will eventually kill the tree. However, to lengthen the life of the tree, prune out and destroy affected twigs and branches each year before March 1. Spraying the infected trees with lime sulphur at the dormant stage, and spraying with sulphur 90% wp, according to label directions, when trees are in full bloom and during petal fall, may help stop spreading of the disease.

Black spot on roses

This is a common fungal disease of roses. Look for circular black spots on leaves. The leaves turn yellow and fall prematurely.

Control: Pick off diseased leaves, and rake up and destroy all fallen leaves. Encourage vigour by giving good general care through the growing season. For recommended rose treatment program, see the monthly checklists.

Blight on native dogwood

This fungal disease appears as brown blotches on the leaves. Premature defoliation occurs, and a characteristic symptom is dead leaves remaining on the branches during winter.
Control: Unfortunately, no really reliable cure is available. Rake up and destroy fallen leaves, and remove dead or diseased branches. The best solution is to replace it with a tree that is resistant to the disease. *Cornus* 'Eddie's White Wonder' and *Cornus kousa* are two such examples.

Carrot rust fly

Eggs of the carrot rust fly are laid in soil near the plants and the hatching maggots feed on roots of parsley, carrots, dill and celery. The leaves take on a rusty appearance, and the plants become stunted and the roots deformed.
Control: If carrot rust fly is a problem, remove maggot-infested carrots and destroy. Keep the vegetable garden free of other members of the carrot family that act as alternative hosts, such as dill, parsley and weeds like Queen Anne's lace. Rotate for several years with crops other than those of the carrot family. Then seed the crop very early (mid-March) under a protective covering of a floating row cover, such as Reemay. Try planting carrots in September for harvest in March. West Coast Seeds sells the cultivar 'Merida' for this. Also try cultivars, such as 'Fly Away', that are described as being somewhat resistant.

Cutworms

These fleshy, soft-bodied caterpillars curl up when disturbed, and may be found in the soil near damaged plants. Some of these pests climb plants at night to feed on the foliage and then return to the soil during the day.
Control: Protect newly planted transplants by placing collars around their stems. Use 8- to 10-cm-long cardboard or plastic tubes, or tin cans. Press them a couple of inches (several centimetres) into the ground. Hoe around affected plants and pick up and destroy caterpillars brought to the surface. Late planting should avoid the primary damage of cutworms.

Moss in lawns

Moss is a recurring problem in this high rainfall area, and may be due to poor drainage, high acidity, poor fertility or heavy shade.
Control: The best way to control it is to have a healthy, vigorous lawn. First of all, aerate the lawn in early spring with a fork or aerator. Top-dress it with coarse sand to improve drainage. Lime should be applied twice a year, in spring and late fall. If the grass is thin, or there are bare patches, overseed with a top-quality grass seed. If the lawn is in a shady area, use shady lawn mixture. Fertilize the lawn with an organic fertilizer to encourage it to outcompete the moss.

Pear trellis rust

This is a fungus that infects pears and junipers. The first sign on a pear is a bright orange spot on the leaf, which then enlarges and produces grey, hairlike projections resembling trellises. Spores are released and are capable of infecting nearby junipers. On the juniper the infection becomes obvious in wet weather in April and May. The branches release a jellylike orange mass of spores which are capable of infecting nearby pear trees.
Control: Buy junipers bearing a disease-free certification tag. Plant junipers and pears as far away from one another as possible. To minimize damage on pear trees, remove infected junipers before April 1 and destroy. Observe pear trees during the summer, pick off infected leaves as they are seen and destroy.

Powdery mildew

Powdery mildew is another common fungus, and it causes a grey or white powdery growth on leaves and shoots. Roses are particularly affected by it.
Control: Rake up and destroy all infected leaves. Good air circulation and light penetration are important in reducing mildew, but perhaps the best solution is to replace susceptible plants with disease-resistant cultivars.

Root weevils

These pests attack many types of plants, but are perhaps most notorious for making lacework of rhododendron leaves. They feed on the edge of the leaves, giving them a notched appearance. There are five or six species ranging from brown to grey, in sizes up to nearly 1/2 inch (1 cm) long.

Control: Remove accumulated leaves and other debris and place short pieces of board or corrugated cardboard among plants. Weevils hide under these and can be collected and destroyed every few days. Other methods to try are wrapping strips of steel wool, or tape covered with Tanglefoot, around the base of the trunk to trap them. However, this is only effective if the shrub has a central stem and doesn't have lower branches touching the ground. You can also cover the ground under the plants with newspaper, then go out at night and shake the plant—the weevils will fall onto the paper and you can roll it up and dispose of it.

Scab on apple and pear

Scab is a disease of apple and pear trees in coastal areas. Leaves develop sooty brown or black spots, turn yellow, then drop prematurely. Fruit is stunted and malformed, with corky brown spots and cracks.
Control: Dry spring and summer weather reduces scab problems. Many cultivars show good resistance to scab, such as 'King', 'Jonagold', 'Spartan', 'Transparent' and 'Tydeman's Red', so keep this in mind if you are looking for new fruit trees.

Sooty mould

This black fungal growth does no harm to the plant, but is very unsightly. It grows on the honeydew secreted by sap-sucking insects, especially aphids.
Control: The mould itself can be washed off with a soap and water solution. Control is aimed at the insects producing the secretions. The insects may be on the plant itself or on overhanging trees.

Slugs and snails

For people living on the west coast, these pests need no introduction. They damage the foliage of most garden plants, especially young, tender shoots.
Control: Removing rotted vegetation that serves as a hiding place will help to control them. Good traps to try are half-grapefruit shells which the slugs crawl into, and saucers of stale beer in which they will drown. You can hand-pick and destroy a lot of slugs last thing at night, with the help of a flashlight, or first thing in the morning.

Spider mites

These are tiny, eight-legged, spiderlike insects that suck the sap from leaves, fruits and roots of many vegetables, annuals, perennials, trees and shrubs. Leaves may become discoloured or curled and may be covered with webs.

Control: A forceful spray of water on the leaves in the early morning, repeated for three days, will help to deter these pests. Insecticidal soap is an effective control. Frequent light watering of the soil will help limit attacks during hot weather. Their natural predators are green lacewings and ladybugs.

Tent caterpillars

Check your trees regularly for signs of the cobweblike tents of these pests.
Control: During the dormant season, inspect branches for eggs. Prune off affected branches and destroy. In January or February spray trees with dormant oil and lime sulphur, which will smother any remaining eggs. If webs form, cut them off and destroy the tent.

White fly

These are tiny, white, mothlike insects that fly away in large groups when the plant is disturbed. The adults and their transparent, green, immature forms suck plant juices, causing discoloured foliage and weakening growth.
Control: Use yellow sticky traps to spot infestations early in the season. If you have a problem, spray every three days for several weeks with soap solution.

Winter moth (Bruce spanworm)

These bright green caterpillars are a major problem. They are nearly an inch (2.5 cm) long, with whitish stripes on each side of their bodies. They attack a wide variety of trees and shrubs, beginning in April to late May. They feed on the leaves and buds, often "sewing" the leaves together. Young worms are carried on the wind, and can drift a considerable distance on silken threads, so protected trees can become infested from neglected trees in the neighbouring area. The male moths are brownish-grey and have a wingspan of about 1 1/2 inches (4 cm). The females are wingless.
Control: Encircle trunks of trees with two sticky bands covered with Tanglefoot in late October, at heights of 12 and 24 inches (30 and 60 cm) above the ground. This will trap the females as they crawl up the trees to lay their eggs. The lower band should be replaced when it becomes dry or filled with moths, or when moths begin to be trapped on the upper band. Remove the bands in February and destroy.

Poisonous Plants

Plants are not only our basic source of food, they are also our basic source of medicines, and some of them can be poisonous. Although it is difficult to get accurate statistics on plant poisonings, the possible danger to health cannot be ignored. The seriousness of plant poisoning will depend upon the amount swallowed and the toxicity of the plant chemical involved.

Children under one year of age who are mobile and teething often go after indoor house plants, and common ones to cause problems are dieffenbachia, poinsettia and philodendron. Two-year-olds are attracted to berries. Holly and mistletoe are both toxic, as is the kernel of the yew tree fruit, daphne berries and Jerusalem cherry berries.

Four- to five-year-olds like pods. Laburnum, black acacia and castor beans are three to watch out for here. Above this age, children usually know enough not to eat unknown plants.

The seriousness of plant poisoning will usually depend upon the amount swallowed. For some plants, even a small amount can be dangerous. Poisonous plants may cause stomach and intestinal irritation, poisoning of the system, mouth and throat lining irritation, and skin irritation.

There are some important points to remember about plants.
- Learn about the plants in your area that could cause harm.
- Don't eat wild plants, including mushrooms, unless you are positive of their identity and safety.
- Don't brew homemade medicines from plants.
- Teach children how to recognize the most common poisonous plants, not to eat unknown plants, and not to play with plants.
- Keep plant seeds, bulbs and fruit well away from small children.

If a child chews on or swallows part of a plant that you think is poisonous, induce vomiting in the victim. Phone **911** and seek medical help right away. Even a simple skin irritation may deserve medical attention. Take a sample of the plant along to aid in the determination of needed treatment.

Poison control centres can be reached at the following numbers.

Vancouver	(604) 682-5050
Victoria	1 (888) 567-8911

Monthly Special Events

The gardening community in our area is very active, and there are garden-related events throughout the year. Check your local community paper, the gardening sections in the *Vancouver Sun, Province* or *Times-Colonist,* and the website http://www.hedgerows.com for additional events and plant sales in your area. Most gardening clubs have annual sales and these are a good way to find desirable specialty plants (see "Horticultural Societies and Garden Clubs" in Resources). Below we provide a month-by-month list of some of the most popular events that take place at the same time each year.

January special events

Master Gardener Program begins. For more information see the listing in Resources under "Education and Information."

February special events

BC Home and Garden Show, Southex Exhibitions, B.C. Place Stadium, Vancouver, B.C. **Tel:** (604) 433-5121, **Fax:** (604) 434-6853. **Website:** http://www.southex.com

A four-day event held at the end of February that brings new ideas, expert advice and a wide selection of home-related products for remodelling, gardening, decorating and home building.

Northwest Flower and Garden Show, held at Washington State Convention Centre in downtown Seattle. For information contact Northwest Flower and Garden Show, 1515 NW 51st St., Seattle, WA 98107. **Tel:** (206) 244-1700. **Fax:** (206) 784-545.

This annual show is held for four days in mid-February. The 5-acre (2-ha) site contains fully landscaped garden displays, commercial display and information booths, amateur competitions for gardening and floral design, and free lectures and seminars by internationally renowned experts.

Victoria Orchid Society's annual show and sale, Da Vinci Centre, 195 Bay St., Victoria, B.C.

This is an American Orchid Society judged show, and in addition to the massive orchid displays, plants are for sale, brought in by growers from across Canada and the United States. There are workshops on propagating and potting, an information booth, education table and video shows. It is held on a weekend in February or March. The date varies, so watch for local advertisements.

Seedy Saturdays

Several communities have a seed sale in February. This is an opportunity to buy organically grown and heritage seeds from organic and/or biodynamic growers. Check your local paper or phone for dates and times, if not listed below.

VanDusen Seedy Saturday, 5251 Oak St., Vancouver, B.C. **Tel:** (604) 878-9274.

Always held on the last Saturday of February. Heritage seed potatoes and ecological homes for bees are some of the many additional items featured at this sale.

Salt Spring Seedy Saturday, Mahon Hall, Salt Spring Island, B.C. **Tel:** (250) 537-5511.

Victoria Seedy Saturday, James Bay Community Centre, Victoria, B.C. **Tel:** (250) 595-5911.

Courtenay Seedy Saturday, Florence Filberg Hall, Courtenay, B.C. **Tel:** (250) 337-2223.

March special events

Horticulture Centre of the Pacific spring sale, 505 Quayle Rd., Victoria, B.C. **Tel:** (250) 497-6162. **Website:** http://www.islandnet.com/~hcp

Every spring this horticultural teaching centre sells hardy, field-grown perennials and greenhouse plants to the general public. Proceeds go towards the further development of their community teaching garden.

Vancouver Orchid Society's display and sale, Croatian Cultural Centre, 3250 Commercial Drive, Vancouver, B.C. Now held towards the end of March; check listings for exact date.

This annual show and sale is an impressive sight. Hundreds of varieties of orchids are displayed, and professional and amateur experts are on hand to discuss the plants.

VanDusen Gardens annual manure sale, 5251 Oak St., Vancouver, B.C. **Tel:** (604) 878-9274.

Well-aged steer manure is for sale in the VanDusen parking lot. Watch for notices in local newspapers or phone the gardens for the exact date. The manure is excellent; each bag weighs about 40 pounds (18 kg). Pre-orders are taken.

VanDusen Gardens rose pruning demonstration, see address above.

The Vancouver Rose Society holds a public demonstration of rose pruning at VanDusen

Gardens. Admission is free for this demonstration, so come and learn how to prune your roses and enjoy a walk around this beautiful botanic garden.

VanDusen Gardens Spring Garden Forum, see address above.

This one-day lecture series is organized by the VanDusen garden guides. Lectures given by garden experts cover a variety of gardening subjects. Other attractions include a seed and plant sale and a Master Gardeners' clinic. Numbers are limited; preregistration is necessary.

April special events

Alpine Garden Club spring show, held in mid-April at VanDusen Gardens, 5251 Oak St., Vancouver, B.C. Contact Dana Cromie. **Tel:** (604) 733-7566.

This judged show is very big, with over 60 categories, including primulas (the B.C. Primula Group have joined the Alpine Garden Club). It is a great chance to look at a wide variety of plants. Nothing is for sale at this show. The Alpine Garden Club hold their spring sale a few weeks later on the North Shore. (For the exact time and location check local listings. This is a popular sale and a good opportunity to ask questions of Alpine Garden Club members.)

Bowen Island Garden Club plant sale, Old General Store, Snug Cove, Bowen Island, B.C.

The sale takes place on the last Saturday of the month and is advertised locally.

Bradner Spring Flower Show, Bradner Community Hall, 5535 Bradner Rd., Bradner, B.C. **Tel:** (604) 856-3558.

This annual three-day event is put on by the Bradner Community Club and dates back to 1928. Over 400 varieties of locally grown daffodils and narcissi are the focal point of the show. Colours of these flowers include pink, white, cream and various shades of yellow. Tulips, irises and orchids are also featured. Local daffodil growers will take your bulb orders and deliver the bulbs to you in the fall. Take a notebook and jot down unusual varieties you may want to include in your own garden. Takes place on the second weekend in April.

Chilliwack Garden Club's spring show and plant sale, Cottonwood Mall, Chilliwack. For exact dates call the club (see listing in Resources under "Horticultural Societies and Garden Clubs") or Chilliwack Chamber of Commerce. **Tel:** (604) 858-8121. **Toll free:** 1-800-567-9535.

A large display of spring flowers brightens up the Cottonwood Mall for one weekend in April followed by a sale the next. All plants are grown by members of the club and you will find annuals, perennials and shrubs. Money goes towards scholarships for agriculture students attending Fraser Valley College. This is a good opportunity to pick up some interesting plants, get your gardening questions answered and support the agriculture students all at the same time.

Comox Valley Horticultural Society's spring sale, Florence Filberg Hall, Courtenay, B.C.

This sale is held one Saturday in April or early May and is an opportunity to buy interesting plants, see demonstrations and get information on all aspects of gardening.

Evergreen Garden Club's spring flower show and sale, Ladner Community Centre, 4734 - 51st St., Ladner, B.C.

Annual judged event of a wide variety of spring-flowering bulbs and flowers. This popular show is open to outside entries and has a children's section and floral displays. English-style afternoon tea is served.

Mount Arrowsmith Rhododendron Society's show and sale, Qualicum Civic Centre, 747 Jones St., Qualicum Beach, B.C.

This event is held in mid-April. It includes a flower (truss) show and plant sale of early to midseason-blooming species. Experts are on hand to answer questions, and if you are interested, this is a good time to become a member of the society.

Saltspring Island Garden Club spring sale.

A good selection of perennials from the gardens of club members are for sale. The date and location vary each year, but the event is advertised locally.

Skagit Valley Tulip Festival, Mount Vernon, Washington. For more information, contact the Mount Vernon Chamber of Commerce, P.O. Box 1007, Mount Vernon, Washington, 98273. **Tel:** (360) 428-5959. **Website:** http://www.tulipfestival.org

The tulip festival runs for three weeks in April. Acres of tulip fields are in full bloom and many growers open their fields to the public. The towns of La Conner and Mount Vernon celebrate the arrival of spring flowers with st. fairs and other scheduled events. Write for a descriptive brochure of events, exact dates and locations. This is a leisurely day trip from Vancouver, or a weekend if you are from Vancouver Island. Approximate blooming dates for daffodils are March 15 to April 15; for tulips, April 1 to May 10.

University of Victoria Finnerty Garden tour. Check newspapers for location and meeting point. Contact Betty Kennedy. **Tel:** (250) 592-2070. **Website:** http://victoria.tc.ca/Environment/UVicGdnFriends

Tours of the garden are led by knowledgeable volunteers. This is a good opportunity to view this lovely garden and to learn more about the volunteer group called "Friends of University of Victoria Finnerty Gardens," who raise funds for, and are actively involved in, its design and development.

Vancouver Dahlia Society's annual sale, held at VanDusen Gardens Floral Hall, 5251 Oak St., Vancouver, B.C. **Tel:** (604) 878-9274.

Over 200 varieties of dahlia tubers are offered for sale by members of the dahlia society in mid-April. Bring a list of dahlias you have been looking for, and you are sure to find them here. If you have any questions regarding dahlias, take this opportunity to ask the experts.

Vancouver Rhododendron Society's early show and sale, David Lam Centre, UBC Botanical Gardens, Vancouver, B.C. **Tel:** UBC Botanical Gardens at (604) 822-3928.

The date for this event varies. Although entries are judged, it is less formal than the show held in May. It offers a chance to see and buy earlier-blooming species rhododendrons, and to ask questions of experts.

VanDusen Gardens annual plant sale, 5251 Oak St., Vancouver, B.C. **Tel:** (604) 878-9274.

Always held on the last Sunday in April, this is the plant sale of the year for Vancouverites. Thousands of people come, rain or shine, and walk away with boxes and barrowloads of treasures. Garden volunteers donate countless hours to prepare for the event and to work on the day. It's a chance to pick up rare and unusual varieties of plants and specialty items. It pays to be there early. The sale is well advertised.

Victoria Chrysanthemum Society's plant sale, St. Matthias Church Hall, 600 Richmond Rd., Victoria, B.C.

Members grow and sell plants at this time. This is an excellent opportunity to obtain interesting cultivars and to talk to the experts.

Victoria Rhododendron Society's show and sale. **Website:** http://victoria.tc.ca/Recreation/RhodoSoc

This is a judged show with a huge assortment of prize-winning rhododendrons on display. The show has been expanded to include camellias and magnolias. Rhododendron experts are on hand to answer questions and to help you select appropriate plants to buy for your own garden. The date varies between April and May each year, and the location also changes. Watch for local advertisements.

White Rock & District Garden Club spring show, Seaview Pentecostal Assembly Hall, 14633 - 16th Ave., South Surrey, B.C. **Tel:** (604) 541-1511.

This show is usually held on the third Saturday in April and is a judged show of seasonal flowers in bloom, potted house plants, and flower arrangements. Outside entries are welcome.

May special events

Alpine Garden Club plant sale. See entry under April.

Burnaby Rhododendron Festival, Shadbolt Centre of the Arts, 6450 Deer Lake Ave., Burnaby, B.C. **Tel:** (604) 205-3004.

Sponsored by the Burnaby Rhododendron and Gardens Society, this festival is held on the first Sunday in May and features nature and garden tours, slide shows, garden talks, demonstrations, children's activities, food and music.

Canadian Geranium and Pelargonium Society's spring show and sale, St. Helen's Catholic Church, 3871 Pandora St., Vancouver, B.C.

Usually held on Mother's Day. Check local listings. There are over 9,000 varieties of geraniums and pelargoniums and many are on display here. An excellent opportunity to buy unusual and hard-to-find ones.

Denman Island Garden Society's annual sale, Community Hall, Denman Island, B.C.

Annuals, perennials and shrubs provided by local growers are on sale. This informal event offers the opportunity to chat with other keen gardeners over a strawberry tea.

Greater Victoria Geranium and Fuchsia Society's annual sale, held at Hillside Centre, 1644 Hillside Ave., Victoria, B.C. **Tel:** (250) 595-7154.

For two days in May, an excellent selection of geraniums and fuchsias are offered for sale by members of the Geranium and Fuchsia Society. This is a good opportunity to ask questions regarding taking cuttings and overwintering plants. The sale is advertised locally.

Horticulture Centre of the Pacific's spring plant sale, 505 Quayle Rd., Victoria, B.C. **Tel:** (250) 479-6162. **Website:** http://www.islandnet.com/~hcp

The spring plant sale includes mature fuchsia baskets in a full colour range, shrubs and many unusual annuals and perennials. This is a good opportunity to become a member of the Horticultural Centre. As a member you receive first-hand information on times and dates of plant sales. Proceeds from the sale are used to further the centre's development as a teaching centre.

Mayfair Perennial Society plant sale and fair, 3776 West 28th Ave., Vancouver, B.C.

Held the last Saturday in May. Proceeds fund grass-roots projects in a village in India.

Nanaimo Rhododendron Society's annual show and sale, Centennial Bldg., Beban Park, Nanaimo, B.C.

This annual event is held the Saturday before Mother's Day. The show offers a display of midseason rhododendrons; there are many interesting rhododendrons for sale as well as a selection of companion plants. Experts are on hand to answer questions.

North Island Rhododendron Society's show and sale, Exhibition Grounds, Courtenay, B.C.

This event offers the visitor a wonderful display and sale of rhododendrons and many companion plants provided by local growers. Experts are on hand to answer your questions.

Simon Fraser University plant sale, between Strand Hall and East Parking Lot, SFU, Burnaby, B.C. **Tel:** (604) 291-4636. **Website:** http://www.sfu.ca

Held just before the May long weekend. For information check local listings.

South Surrey Garden Club Annual sale, St. Mark's Anglican Church, 12953 - 20th Ave., Surrey, B.C.

Strawberry Tea at the Glades, 561 - 172nd St., Surrey, B.C. Contact Jim or Elfried Dewolf. **Tel:** (604) 538-0928.

A Mother's Day fundraiser for the Peace Arch Hospital, this is an opportunity to "come for tea" and/or tour this beautiful 35-year-old, 5-acre (2-ha) rhododendron and azalea haven.

UBC Botanical Garden perennial plant sale, 6804 Southwest Marine Drive, Vancouver. **Tel:** (604) 822-3928.

Perennial plants are offered for sale in the garden. The plants are grown from seeds collected in the garden, from division of plant material grown in the garden, and from generous donations from the

Friends of the Garden (F.O.G.S.), who have taken plants from their own gardens. This is an excellent opportunity to find unusual perennials.

University of Victoria Garden Friends plant sale, McKinnon Gym, University of Victoria, **Website:** http://victoria.tc.ca/Environment/UVicGdnFriends.

This plant sale, held on the first Sunday in May, includes flowering shrubs, many varieties of rhododendrons, perennials, bedding plants, specialty items such as alpine and rock garden plants, and many other interesting surprises. This event is well advertised locally. Plant sale shoppers are advised to arrive early and bring their own boxes to carry plants home.

Vancouver African Violet Club's annual show and sale, held at VanDusen Gardens Floral Hall, 5251 Oak St., Vancouver, B.C.

A judged show, held in early May, with an excellent display of rare and unusual African violets and other perennials. From the tiniest miniatures to plants with huge blooms, this is an opportunity to see the new varieties and talk to the experts.

Vancouver Bonsai Association's annual show, held at VanDusen Gardens Floral Hall, 5251 Oak St., Vancouver, B.C. **Tel:** (604) 261-6060.

It is hard not to appreciate this fascinating gardening art. The dwarfed trees and shrubs look magnificently cared for in their bonsai pots. Bonsai is very popular and this two-day show is an excellent introduction for prospective bonsai gardeners.

Vancouver Island Bonsai Club's annual show, held at Hillside Centre, 1644 Hillside Ave., Victoria, B.C. **Tel:** (250) 595-7154.

This is a great opportunity to meet the club members and to see a wonderful display of all the different forms of this ancient art.

Vancouver Rhododendron Society show and sale, held at VanDusen Gardens Floral Hall, see address above.

This annual two-day event features displays of rare and unusual rhododendrons and azaleas. Exotic species and beautiful hybrids are also offered for sale. This is a good time to become a member of the Vancouver Rhododendron Society, and also to go and look at the spectacular rhododendrons in the gardens that line the Rhododendron Walk.

Victoria Conservatory of Music's annual private garden tour. Preregistration and ticket purchase necessary. Tickets may be purchased at many Victoria bookstores, but check local listings for details.

In May or June a selection of gardens in the greater Victoria area and the Saanich peninsula are open to the public for the weekend. Tour the gardens, and become inspired by fine Canadian gardens. This event is a fund-raiser for the Victoria Conservatory of Music, and is advertised in the local papers.

June special events

Fraser Pacific Rose Society Annual show, Dogwood Pavilion, 624 Poirier St., Coquitlam, B.C.

A large rose show, held the first week of June.

Vancouver Rose Society's show and sale. Tel: (604) 878-9274.

Held about the third week of June, this is advertised as the largest flower show in Canada. Over 500 cultivars of roses are displayed by rose growers and miniature roses are offered for sale. Every gardener has a favourite rose and you are sure to find yours here. Questions about roses can be answered by rose experts, and you can become a member of the Rose Society.

VanDusen Flower and Garden Show, 5251 Oak St., Vancouver, B.C. **Tel:** (604) 878-9274.

Held the first weekend in June, this show gets better all the time. Over 200 garden exhibits share space on the Great Lawn at VanDusen Gardens. The exhibit gardens are themed to explore different concepts in gardening each year.

VanDusen Private Garden Tour. Call VanDusen Gardens, (604) 878-9274, for tickets, dates and times. Modelled after the Victoria Conservatory of Music's annual private garden tour, this event is usually held in June and provides an opportunity for interested gardeners to tour selected gardens in the Vancouver area. Ticket sales are limited, so call early.

Various private garden tours. Private garden tours are also held on Bowen Island (contact the *Undercurrent* newspaper at (604) 947-2442), Burnaby (contact Burnaby Parks and Recreation at (604) 294-7128); the North Shore (contact the City of North Vancouver at (604) 985-7761; the District of West Vancouver at (604) 925-7000; or the District of North Vancouver at (604) 987-7131); the Eastside (contact (604) 254-4212); and Maple Ridge (contact Nancy at (604) 462-9394).

Victoria Flower and Garden Festival.

An annual event since 1994, this international flower and garden festival is held over a three-day period in June or July. There are exhibitor booths, display gardens and special lectures and presentations by international speakers and local gardening experts. Held at various locations, so check local newspapers.

July special events

B.C. Fuchsia and Begonia Society's annual flower show, VanDusen Gardens Floral Hall, 5251 Oak St., Vancouver, B.C.

Their annual show offers a chance to see the finest varieties growing in the Pacific Northwest, including new hybrid introductions, and to ask experts about their care.

August special events

Richmond Garden Club annual horticultural show, Richmond Arena, 7551 Minoru Gate, Richmond, B.C.

Held one weekend in August, this show includes many interesting displays by local commercial nurseries and amateur specialty garden clubs. Outside entries are welcome for a nominal entry fee. Experts are on hand to answer gardeners' questions. The event is advertised locally.

Victoria Gladiolus and Dahlia Society's show, Hillside Mall, 1644 Hillside Ave., Victoria, B.C. **Tel:** (250) 595-7154.

This is a judged show with over 600 displays of choice cultivars of gladioli and dahlias. It is held the third weekend in August.

White Rock and District Garden Club summer garden show, First United Church, Centre St. at Bonavista, White Rock, B.C.

This event is advertised locally, so watch for announcements. It is usually held around the middle of the month. It is a judged show with exhibits in many different categories, including vegetables, herbs and floral arrangements. You can submit your own entry or just come and enjoy the show.

September special events

Aldergrove Agricultural Assoc. annual fall fair, Aldergrove Arena, 2882 - 272nd St., Aldergrove, B.C.

This fair is held on the weekend following Labour Day. It is a judged fair with hundreds of displays in different categories including gladioli, dahlias, chrysanthemums, roses, vegetables and decorative house plants. There are novice, expert and junior (under 17 years) categories.

Alpine Garden Club of B.C. fall plant sale, VanDusen Gardens Floral Hall, 5251 Oak St., Vancouver, B.C.

This sale is held the second weekend in September and is a very popular event. An excellent assortment of unusual and interesting plants are for sale, including native and woodland plants, primroses, bulbs and groundcovers.

Point Grey Chrysanthemum Association early show, VanDusen Gardens Floral Hall, 5251 Oak St., Vancouver, B.C.

If you are interested in chrysanthemums, this judged show of early-flowering blooms is for you. An excellent opportunity to identify your favourites for next year.

South Burnaby Garden Club fall fair, Bonsor Complex, 6550 Bonsor Ave., Burnaby, B.C.

This judged horticultural fair is usually held the weekend after Labour Day, and includes a wide variety of categories. Arrange ahead to enter, or just come to enjoy.

Tree-mendous Compost Sale, parking lot at VanDusen Gardens, 5251 Oak St., Vancouver, B.C. **Tel:** (604) 878-9274.

A great way to replenish the soil in your garden. Usually held the last Saturday of September.

UBC Botanical Garden indoor plant sale, 6804 Southwest Marine Drive, Vancouver, B.C.

Usually held one week after the UBC fall term starts. Watch for signs and ads.

Vancouver Dahlia Society annual show, VanDusen Gardens Floral Hall, 5251 Oak St., Vancouver, B.C.

Judged show with wonderful displays of dahlias. It's a great opportunity to ask questions of local dahlia experts.

Victoria Chrysanthemum Society's show, Hillside Mall, 1644 Hillside Ave., Victoria, B.C. **Tel:** (250) 595-7154.

This is a great opportunity to see a huge variety of chrysanthemums and to meet the people who grow them. It is a judged event, and at the end of the show the plants are auctioned off. The date changes from year to year, so check local newspapers for details.

White Rock and District Chrysanthemum Society's annual show, St. Mark's Anglican Church Hall, 12953- 20th Ave., Surrey, B.C.

A judged show of cut blooms of early-flowering chrysanthemums. Several categories are open to non-club members. Usually held around the middle of the month. Watch for advertisements.

October special events

Botanical paintings sale, VanDusen Gardens Floral Hall, 5251 Oak St., Vancouver, B.C. **Tel:** (604) 878-9274.

Exhibition and sale of botanical paintings by local botanical artists. Watch for advertisements.

Fraser Valley Orchid Society's show and sale, White Rock Town Centre, 15150 Russell Ave., White Rock, B.C.

Held during the last weekend in October, this judged show has excellent displays of all types of species and hybrid orchids, and is attended by growers from as far afield as Alberta and Washington State. Experts are on hand to answer questions and there are many plants for sale.

Horticultural Centre of the Pacific's fall plant sale, 505 Quayle Rd., Victoria, B.C. **Tel:** (250) 479-6162. **Website:** http://www.islandnet.com/~hcp

Lots of interesting plants at this plant sale. This is a good opportunity to explore the gardens and to find out about the advantages of membership. Watch for advertisements, as this event is sometimes held in September.

Saltspring Island Garden Club fall bulb sale.

This popular annual event is an opportunity to buy fall-blooming plants grown by members. Date and location vary, so watch for advertisements in local papers.

UBC Botanical Garden Applefest, 6804 Southwest Marine Drive, Vancouver, B.C. **Tel:** (604) 822-9666.

Sample and buy some of the hundreds of heritage apple varieties available at this annual celebration of the apple harvest. A very popular event, Applefest is held the weekend after Thanksgiving.

Vancouver African Violet Club's floral display and open house, VanDusen Gardens Floral Hall, 5251 Oak St., Vancouver, B.C.

This is a good opportunity to take another look at these wonderful house plants and see all the new varieties that are now available. Experts are on hand to answer all your questions, and afternoon tea is served.

November special events

Point Grey Chrysanthemum Association late show, VanDusen Gardens Floral Hall, 5251 Oak St., Vancouver, B.C.

This is a judged show held on the first weekend in November. It features many varieties of later-blooming chrysanthemums, and experts are on hand to answer your questions.

December special events

UBC Botanical Garden Spectacular Wreath Sale, 6804 Southwest Marine Drive, Vancouver, B.C. **Tel:** (604) 822-9668.

Gorgeous wreaths are made by volunteers with material from the gardens and are on sale at the garden shop throughout December.

Vancouver's Festival of Lights

Every year from early December to early January, the city of Vancouver is lit with hundreds of thousands of festive outdoor lights. Probably the most magical of these are in three of our public parks and gardens: VanDusen Gardens, Park and Tilford Gardens, and the Stanley Park Miniature Railway ride. For a special treat, take friends and family and enjoy seeing these gardens in a very different way.

Victoria's Festival of Lights

The City of Victoria's seasonal light display begins, of course, at the Legislature Buildings. Buchart Gardens also puts on a lovely display in their grounds, and strolling carollers add to the festive scene.

Watercolours West, VanDusen Gardens Floral Hall, 5251 Oak St., Vancouver, B.C. **Tel:** (604) 878-9274.

One weekend in early December, there is a sale of artwork by local botanical artists. Confirm dates with VanDusen Gardens.

Resources

Parks and Gardens

Local parks and gardens can be an inspiration for novice and experienced gardeners alike, especially for those who are new to the area. The range and diversity of plants that can be grown in Canada's Pacific Northwest is enormous, and our local parks and gardens are some of the best places to see them.

There are, of course, many more parks and gardens in our area than we have included below. We have selected only those that we feel are particularly useful for gardeners, usually because their plants are well labelled, and/or there are people around to answer questions. Your list of favourites may include some others too.

In addition, our many provincial parks are excellent places to look at native plants in their natural habitat, and this would include Pacific Spirit Park and Stanley Park in Vancouver, Thetis Island Park in the Gulf Islands and Cathedral Grove Park on Vancouver Island. It's a good idea to make a note of the parks and gardens in your area and visit them regularly, at different times of the year. Take a notebook to jot down the names of any plants you particularly like, so that you can incorporate planting ideas into your own garden.

Vancouver and the Lower Mainland

Arthur Erickson Garden, 4195 West 14th Ave., Vancouver, B.C. **Tel:** (604) 738-4195. **Admission:** There is an admission charge. Wheelchair accessible.

Arthur Erickson, well-known architect of many Vancouver and international buildings, has designed a very special garden surrounding his private home in the West Point Grey area of Vancouver. The Arthur Erickson House and Garden Foundation was founded in 1996 to preserve the property. Guided tours can be arranged to view the garden.

The visitor enters into a world of wild grasses, bamboos, shrubs, trees, water and all the wildlife that goes along with a garden. The garden design creates a feeling of space and privacy on a city-sized lot.

Camosun Bog, Pacific Spirit Regional Park, 19th and Camosun, Vancouver, B.C.

The 2,000-year-old bog, situated in Pacific Spirit Regional Park, has been the focus of a restoration project for several years. Over the past 60 years,

development in the area surrounding the bog has encouraged the encroachment of non-bog species trees and shrubs, threatening the bog. Since Camosun bog is the only one of its kind in the Lower Mainland, its preservation is considered very important by many, especially as a living study site for researchers at UBC and British Columbian school students. Besides the very important sphagnum moss, the bog contains many plants, such as sundews, which are specially adapted to a bog environment. This won't help you much with your garden, unless you have some boggy ground around a water garden, but it's fascinating to visit.

Darts Hill Garden, 1660 - 168th St., Surrey, B.C. **Tel:** The Friends of Dart's Hill Garden, (604) 501-5665. **Admission:** There is an admission charge. Not open to the public: limited tours are available for horticultural groups.

Started by Francisca Dart and her husband, the 7 1/2-acre (3-ha) garden has now matured into a magnificent plant collector's paradise, with magnolias, witch hazels, rhododendrons, azaleas, mulberry trees, unusual willows, maples and many more trees and shrubs, as well as perennials. There are hundreds of unusual and interesting plants to study and admire. Francisca is a fine plantsperson and to see her garden is a privilege.

Davidson Arboretum, Riverview Hospital Site, 500 Lougheed Hwy., Coquitlam, B.C. **Tel:** (604) 524-7120. **Admission:** Free; plan of the site available at the Volunteer Centre and from the kiosk on Pine Terrace, at the south end of the grounds. **Hours:** Open all the time.

Dr. Sun Yat-Sen Classical Chinese Garden, 578 Carrall St., Vancouver, B.C. **Tel:** (604) 662-3207. **Admission:** There is an admission charge. **Hours:** May 1 to Sept. 30: 10:00 a.m. to 7:30 p.m.; winter: 10:00 a.m. to 4:30 p.m.

The garden site was slated to become part of a freeway that would have divided Vancouver's Chinatown in two, thus destroying its character. Concerned citizens organized themselves and convinced the federal and municipal governments to commit the land as a centre for Chinese culture, including a classical Chinese garden. It was named after the venerable Dr. Sun Yat-Sen, and is the first authentic Suzhou-style garden built outside China. The garden covers an area of 2 1/2 acres (1 ha). It is an intricate, harmonious blend of courtyards, pavilions, walkways, rocks, water and plants.

As in any classic Chinese garden, plants were chosen for their symbolic meaning or their physical qualities, rather than for their horticultural interest. Flowers are not emphasized. Plantings used are appreciated for their different qualities and the subtle changes each season brings. Three plants that appear in all classical Chinese gardens are the "three friends of winter"—pine, bamboo and winter-flowering plum. The pine symbolizes strength, the bamboo suggests resilience, and the plum represents renewal and hope.

The garden was designed and built in a similar way to the gardens of 12th-century China. Materials were imported from China and assembled by a team of 52 artisans from Suzhou, using the same kinds of tools as were used by the craftsmen who created the Ming dynasty gardens.

Guided tours of the gardens are offered, and there are special lectures and cultural events throughout the year. There is also a delightful gift shop.

The Glades, 561 - 172nd St., Surrey, B.C. **Tel:** (604) 538-0928. **Admission:** There is an admission charge. **Hours:** Open on Mother's Day from 10:00 a.m. to 4:00 p.m.

Owners Jim and Elfriede DeWolf open their garden annually on Mother's Day for a tour of the garden and tea. The proceeds go toward the Peace Arch Hospital. The 5-acre (2-ha) garden has over 1,600 mature rhododendrons and azaleas in a woodland garden setting. There is also a large collection of trees and shrubs, home to many birds and other wildlife.

Minter Gardens, 52892 Bunker Rd., Rosedale, B.C. **Tel:** (604) 794-7191 and (604) 792-3799. **Admission:** There is an admission charge. **Hours:** Vary. April 1 to October 31, 9:00 a.m. to dusk. Phone first to confirm. Wheelchair accessible.

The 27-acre (11-ha) site sits at the foot of 7,000-foot (2,134-m) Mount Cheam, next to the Trans-Canada Highway at the Harrison Hot Springs Exit (Exit #135), a 1 1/2-hour drive from Vancouver. The garden was created by local garden writer and radio personality Brian Minter and his family. It has 10 different gardens, with the surrounding mountains reflected in the lovely lake garden. The gardens include an 18th-century-style garden, a large rose garden, a fragrance garden, and good collections of

cactuses and ferns. The summer display of annuals is spectacular. Concrete pathways provide easy access to all parts of the site.

Nitobe Memorial Garden, University of British Columbia, located behind the Asian Centre, southwest corner of the campus. **Tel:** (604) 822-3928. **Admission:** There is an admission charge. **Hours:** 10:00 a.m. to at least 3:00 p.m. (up to 8.00 p.m. midsummer) year round, Monday to Friday. Open weekends from mid-March to mid-October.

This classical Japanese Garden is situated on 2 1/2 acres (1 hectare) of the UBC campus, next to the Asian Centre. It was opened in 1960 and dedicated to the memory of Dr. Inazo Nitobe, a Japanese educator, scholar, publicist and diplomat. The garden was designed by Professor Kannosuke Mori, a distinguished Japanese landscape architect. Extensive work was done to refurbish the garden and teahouse in 1993.

Japanese gardens are meant to interpret nature, rather than reproduce it. The pathways through the garden are thus intended to give visitors "vistas of lakes, waterfalls, mountains and forests." The large pond in the centre has live fish, and there is a teahouse and garden where formal tea ceremonies are sometimes performed.

Nitobe includes many native plants, such as hemlock, Douglas fir, vine maple, huckleberry, salal, Oregon grape, kinnikinnik and false box. Ornamental flowering cherry trees, Japanese maples, azaleas and irises were imported from Japan. The many rocks in the garden were brought from various locations in the Lower Mainland. The artistic placement and use of the rock is a study in itself. This lovely enclosed garden creates a feeling of peacefulness and solitude. It is well worth a visit.

Park and Tilford Gardens, 333 Brooksbank Ave., North Vancouver, B.C. **Tel:** (604) 984-8200. **E-mail:** parktilford@morguard.com. **Admission:** Free. **Hours:** 9:30 a.m. to dusk year round.

In 1967 Park and Tilford Distillers commissioned a garden on a 3-acre (1.2-ha) site next to the distillery as a Centennial Year community beautification project. The garden changed hands in 1988 and was refurbished. It includes a rose garden, display garden, herb garden, greenhouse with a collection of tropical plants, a small Oriental garden, and a native woodland garden. Landscape horticulture students from Capilano College gain practical experience at the garden and contribute to its upkeep.

Fifty thousand Christmas lights decorate the garden in December, making it a good stop on your Christmas lights tour. The garden is adjacent to the Park and Tilford Shopping Centre.

Queen Elizabeth Park and Bloedel Conservatory, 33rd Ave. and Cambie, Vancouver, B.C. **Tel:** (604) 257-8570 or (604) 257-8584. **Admission:** There is an admission charge. **Hours:** Call for hours.

The top of the garden is situated 500 feet (152 m) above sea level, with a superb view of the city, mountains and ocean. Pathways lead down into the ornamental gardens, past many native shrubs and trees. The garden sites were formerly two stone quarries, set aside by the city for a park in 1912, although development did not begin until 1948. Spring-flowering bulbs are replaced in the last week of May by colourful summer bedding plants, including geraniums, petunias, marigolds, verbenas and fuschias. In June the Rose Garden is in full bloom, and is a popular site for wedding photography.

The Bloedel Conservatory, originally planned as a 1967 centennial project, was opened in December 1969. The semispherical triodetic dome structure is climatically controlled and houses a variety of tropical plants and birds, and seasonal floral displays throughout the year. Nearby is a superb Henry Moore bronze sculpture *Knife Edge—Two Pieces*, unveiled when the Conservatory opened in 1969.

The park also has tennis courts, a pitch and putt, and a restaurant with a panoramic city view.

Stanley Park, 1000-acre (405-ha) park located in the heart of Vancouver, B.C. **Tel:** (604) 257-8400.

Stanley Park is Canada's best-known urban park and a landmark in Vancouver. The majority of the park is a mature forest crisscrossed with trails, providing a natural habitat for native plants, small animals and birds. Although the native plants are not labelled, this is a good place to become familiar with the look and feel of a west coast forest.

Only the eastern fringe of the park has been developed to any extent, with several distinct garden and recreation areas. The arboured rose garden, surrounded by excellent perennial borders and colourful beds of annuals, may be the most frequently visited.

The Ted and Mary Grieg Rhododendron Collection, located in the area surrounding the pitch and putt golf course, is well worth a visit in spring and late summer. In 1966 the Griegs sold their entire collection of 7,000 plants and several thousand seedlings to the Parks Board for a fraction of their actual value. In 1979 and 1980, 2,000 species rhododendrons from this collection were removed and replanted in the developing VanDusen Gardens. The collection of hybrid rhododendrons was largely intact. Of particular interest are the more than 60 *Rhododendron auriculatum* hybrids, which bloom in July and August, and the excellent springtime display of over 300 azaleas.

Public education and entertainment facilities are all located in the south end of the park and include an aquarium, miniature railway, children's farmyard, children's play area, bowling greens, cricket pitch, tennis courts, restaurants, outdoor theatre, carriage rides, nature house and Parks Board facilities.

University of British Columbia Botanical Garden, 6804 Southwest Marine Drive, Vancouver, B.C. **Tel:** (604) 822-9666. Hortline, for plant information: (604) 822-5858 on Tuesday and Wednesday from 12 noon to 3:00 p.m. Shop-in-the-Garden: (604) 822-4529. **Admission:** There is an admission charge. **Hours:** Change with the season. Open daily.

UBC Botanical Garden combines teaching, research and public service. The gardens cover 110 acres (45 ha) of land on the UBC campus. The main gardens are located on the south side of the campus. Here visitors can see many plants imported from around the world, as well as an 8-acre (3-ha) B.C. Native Garden. It includes a typical west coast forest, a dryland area similar to the area around Kamloops and Cache Creek, a marsh planting and a peat-bed planting. The collection includes one-third of the trees and flowering plants native to B.C. Bark mulch trails through this area are named after botany pioneers in B.C.

The starting point for the gardens is on the south side of Southwest Marine Drive, through the David Lam Asian Garden. Below the trees in this 30-acre (12-ha) garden is an extensive and unusual collection of many tree and shrub species, including rhododendrons, azaleas, magnolias, Asiatic dogwoods and rare Oriental species plants. The garden has the largest collection of woody Asian plants on the North American continent.

The E.H. Lohbrunner Alpine Garden, situated next to the Native Garden, is the largest alpine garden in North America. Over 2000 tonnes of volcanic rock and light limestone were gathered from B.C.'s interior. This rock forms the base of the garden, which houses over 12,000 alpine plants. The rock garden is laid out in pathways that lead visitors through different altitudes of various continents.

The main garden also has a replica of a medieval garden, containing hundreds of medicinal plants and ornamental herbs. Nearby is a vegetable and fruit garden, which includes a wide variety of espaliered fruit trees and also shows different methods of composting.

The UBC Botanical Garden has a strong research and development component, and its Plant Introduction Scheme provides new varieties for the market each year (see the October chapter for more information). The Shop-in-the-Garden, located at the entrance to the garden, sells a wide variety of plants, pots, books and garden necessities. In the same complex is a multipurpose reception hall for conferences, seminars and receptions.

Associated with the garden is a hard-working group of volunteers, the Friends of the Garden (F.O.G.S.). They help in various areas of the garden, run the shop, grow plants from seed to sell in the shop, harvest seed from the garden, act as guides and run a plant information line, the Hortline.

VanDusen Botanical Display Garden, 5251 Oak St., Vancouver, B.C. **Tel:** (604) 878-9274. **Admission:** There is an admission charge. **Hours:** Change with the season. Open daily except December 25. Wheelchair accessible.

VanDusen Gardens consists of 55 acres (22 ha) situated on the grounds of the former Shaughnessy Golf Course. The gardens incorporate many theme gardens, such as a perennial garden, rose beds, and herb and vegetable gardens. The plants are also grouped in settings according to their families, traditional uses and habitat. The collections of hollies, bamboos, magnolias and rhododendrons are examples of plant groupings according to family. The Rhododendron Walk in May attracts people from far and wide. The holly collection in winter is also interesting for many visitors from across Canada who cannot grow holly in their area.

The newest theme garden is the Canadian Heritage Garden. This developing garden is to include endangered plants, wild plants recorded by naturalists and explorers in the 17th century in this country, and plants bred specifically to withstand harsh Canadian climatic conditions. The object of the garden is to display examples of plants that grow all over Canada, as well as to educate visitors on the conservation and preservation of native plants.

VanDusen Gardens offers visitors a variety of interesting things to see throughout the year.

- Children can have lots of fun finding their way through the cedar maze.
- The garden holds an annual plant sale on the last Sunday in April.
- VanDusen Flower and Garden Show is held the first weekend in June. Over 200 beautiful garden displays are erected within a spectacular setting.
- Education programs are open to the public.
- Volunteer guides give walking tours year round.
- Electric carts are available with a driver for those who cannot walk easily (reservations should be made for this service).
- Seeds from plants in the garden are available for sale.
- There is a large gift shop and a restaurant, open for lunch and dinner.
- There is an extensive library, open 10:00 a.m. to 3:00 p.m., Tuesday to Friday.
- The gardens operate an in-depth education program, the Master Gardeners' Program.
- Festival of lights in December.
- Gardeners' questions are answered at a series of garden clinics run by Master Gardeners at various locations throughout the Lower Mainland in spring and summer. Phone for hours. The Master Gardeners also run a Plant Information Phoneline at (604) 257-8662 on Mondays, Wednesdays and Thursdays from 1:00 to 3:00 p.m.

Victoria Area

Beacon Hill Park, Downtown Victoria, off Douglas St. in South Victoria, B.C. **Admission:** Free. **Hours:** Always open.

Beacon Hill Park is a 134-acre (54-ha) preserve dating back to 1858 when Governor James Douglas, head of the Hudson's Bay Company, reserved the area for public use. In 1882 the government of British Columbia gave the park to the city of Victoria in trust for the use, recreation and enjoyment of the public, and it has been preserved as such ever since.

In 1889, 2,000 trees and shrubs were planted, Goodacre and Fountain Lakes were developed and the stone bridge constructed. Other lakes and streams were built in 1932 near the rose garden. Early settlers sowed broom on the hill and scattered Garry oak acorns over the bare areas, adding to the natural oaks, some of which are over 350 years old. In the spring, masses of daffodils and blue camas cover the meadows.

The site runs along the southern shoreline of the island, with an outstanding view of the U.S. Olympic

Peninsula. The Vancouver Island Rock and Alpine Garden Society maintains an alpine garden within the park. Twenty-five thousand annuals are planted each spring to offer visitors colour and beauty all summer long. Some of the rhododendrons by Fountain Lake were among those 2,000 trees and shrubs planted in 1889.

Butchart Gardens, 800 Benvenuto Ave., Brentwood Bay, Vancouver Island, B.C. **Tel:** (250) 652-4422 or (250) 652-5256 for recorded information. **E-mail:** email@butchartgardens.com. **Website:** http://www.butchartgardens.com. **Admission:** Charges vary with the season. **Hours:** Open every day of the year including holidays at 9:00 a.m.; closing times vary with the season. Phone ahead for information.

Butchart Gardens is located 14 miles (22 km) north of Victoria on Tod Inlet. Originally, the garden site was a rock quarry owned by Robert Pimm Butchart. Over the years the quarry grew to enormous proportions and was eventually abandoned. The result was nature at its ugliest. An abandoned quarry from which the Butcharts made a fortune could have been the end of the story.

Unhappy with the local eyesore, however, the Butcharts decided to try their hand at landscaping it; over many years, the old quarry was transformed into the beginning of what has become a magnificent show garden. Topsoil by the ton was hauled into the quarry by horse and buggy, and Jenny Butchart herself swung down the 50-foot (15-m) face of the rock wall in a suspended bucket, tucking vine shoots and plants into the crevices. This was the beginning of the Butchart's pet project.

The 130-acre (53-ha) garden is still owned by the family and is now an island landmark. Thousands of visitors come each year to see the well-maintained and colourful plantings. Guided tours are available, in addition to free mini guide booklets, restaurant and coffee shops, and gift shops where you can buy seeds from the gardens.

Government House Gardens, 1401 Rockland Ave., Victoria, B.C. **Admission:** Free. **Hours:** Open every day from sun-up to sun-down, year round.

Government House is the official residence of the Lieutenant-Governor of British Columbia. While the house is generally not open to the general public other than by invitation, the grounds are open all year. They cover 35 acres (14 ha), with a series of old and new gardens and open grass areas. The front 10

acres (4 ha) of the garden include an English country garden, a sunken rose garden in an Edwardian setting, a mixed flower garden, a rock outcropping with pathways and a duck pond, a newly built Victorian rose garden and a rhododendron garden.

The revitalization of the gardens was initiated by David Lam when he was Lieutenant-Governor of B.C., and a volunteer organization called Friends of Government Gardens was formed to help restore and enhance certain areas within the gardens. Work is underway on the south slope where volunteers are removing invasive broom, ivy and brambles. The aim is to encourage the return of native plants, such as camas lilies, shooting stars and erythroniums under a canopy of Garry oak. Membership is open to any individual or group interested in the preservation of these grounds for all to use and enjoy. New members are welcome.

Hatley Park, the public gardens of Royal Roads University, 2000 block Sooke Rd., Colwood, B.C. **Website:** http://www.royalroads.ca. **Admission:** Fee for parking only. **Hours:** Sunrise to sunset.

Designed by Samuel Maclure for James Dunsmuir, a former premier of B.C., Hatley Castle was built between 1908 and 1910 and the gardens completed two years later. The gardens include a formal Italian garden complete with loggia, a tranquil Japanese garden, and a rose garden. There are two fine perennial borders, a hot-coloured one in red, orange and yellow, and a cooler one in white and pastels. Hatley Park was home to Royal Roads Military College from 1940 to 1995 and is now the site of an independent university.

Horticulture Centre of the Pacific, 505 Quayle Rd., Victoria, B.C. **Tel/Fax:** (250) 479-6162. **E-mail:** hortcentre@bigfoot.com. **Website:** http://www.islandnet.com/~hcp. **Admission:** There is an admission charge. Call for information on guided tours, lectures and special events. **Hours:** April to September, 8:00 a.m. to 8:00 p.m., October to March, 9:00 a.m. to 4:30 p.m.

The Horticulture Centre of the Pacific was created in 1979. Over the years, with the active support of local garden clubs, the Victoria Horticultural Society and members of the Horticultural Centre, it has developed into a series of demonstration gardens. A featured attraction is the Doris Page Winter Garden, a joint project of the Victoria Horticultural Society and volunteers from the HCP Society. The winter garden is at its best from November to April and is an inspiration to those who feel that the gardening year only starts in the spring. The HCP also has demonstration gardens for heather, rhododendrons, herbs and drought-tolerant plants, lilies, fuchsias, ornamental grasses and roses, to name a few. More recent developments are the Takata Japanese Garden and the establishment of an internationally recognized trial garden for dahlias (see the August chapter).

The HCP is home to a training school for students in the Landscape Horticulture Certificate Program, so there are usually trainees as well as volunteers on hand to help with questions about the garden. The Society maintains over 15 acres (6 ha) of demonstration and teaching gardens. It also has stewardship of about 90 acres (36 ha) of undeveloped land, which includes areas of wetlands, pockets of Garry oak habitat and other areas of sensitive plant material native to this part of the island. These areas are being carefully restored with volunteers hard at work removing invasive non-native plants such as Scotch broom and Himalayan blackberry bushes.

As well as free admission to the gardens, members of HCP Society receive six newsletters a year, reduced fees for workshops and lectures, and discounts on plant sales.

The Native Plant Gardens, Royal British Columbia Museum, 675 Belleville St., Victoria, B.C. **Admission:** Free. **Hours:** Always open. Guided tours are offered in the summer. Check with the museum for times. An informative brochure is available at the information desk inside the main entrance.

The Native Plant Gardens were established in 1968 as a living exhibit to provide a representative sample of plants native to British Columbia. The gardens surrounding the Museum and Provincial Archives Building contain plants from the three major vegetation zones, coast forest, dry interior and alpine. This includes a wetland garden, sand dune garden, Oregon grape bed and a camas bed. The camas bed contains *Camassia quamash*, which can still be seen in great numbers in Victoria's Beacon Hill Park and Uplands Park in spring, and the larger *Camas leichtlinii*. Like other collections in the museum, these living plants provide raw material for research and give visitors the opportunity to see many of the trees and shrubs that are part of B.C.'s landscape. To learn more about the plants, take a guided tour and visit the Museum Shop. The shop has a variety of books about B.C.'s native plants, including information on aboriginal plant use.

Novitiate Garden, St. Ann's Academy, Academy Close (between Blanshard and Quadra streets), Victoria, B.C. **Admission:** Free. **Hours:** During daylight hours.

The grounds of this 1871 heritage building have recently been restored. Of particular interest to the gardener is the Novitiate Garden, located at the back of the academy, adjoining the east side of the chapel. It was used originally as a quiet place for rest and reflection by the convent novices, with a kitchen garden and a summer house. A replica of the summer house has now been built, and under the leadership of Lynne Milnes, the garden has been redesigned after extensive research of the archives. There is now a herb garden and a border full of shrubs and perennials. Many of the plants would have been familiar to the novices of the day. Featured are many symbolic plants. For instance, the vows taken by each novice on entering the order of St. Ann are represented by basil (poverty), veronica (chastity) and sunflower (obedience). Other symbols to look out for are yew (faith), iris (hope) and white lilies (charity).

Point Ellice House, 2616 Pleasant St., Victoria, B.C. **Tel:** (250) 380-6506. **Fax:** (250) 388-7565. **Website:** http://www.heritage.gov.bc.ca/point/tour.htm. **Admission:** There is an admission charge. **Hours:** 10:00 a.m. to 5:00 p.m. mid-May to mid-September.

Point Ellice House was built in 1890 by the O'Reilly family, and the surrounding garden is being restored as an authentic Victorian-era garden—the only authentic Victorian garden west of Manitoba.

The house and garden were acquired by the province in 1974. The garden was well documented from its beginnings by the O'Reillys, and many of the original plants are still there. Undergrowth has been removed to reveal rose gardens, old dahlias, jasmine and ilex bushes. Family diaries reveal where brick pathways and gravel walks used to be. Hundred-foot (30-m) trees bordering the grounds were planted years ago as 5-foot (1.5-m) hedges.

As gardeners, we often inherit other people's plant choices and garden designs. This restored Victorian garden is an inspiration for all gardeners and may give you ideas for restoring your own.

Ross Bay and other memorable cemeteries. For information on guided tours, call The Old Cemeteries Society at (250) 598-8870. **E-mail:** oldcem@oldcem.bc.ca. **Website:** http://www.oldcem.bc.ca or call the administration of the individual churches.

Cemeteries may sound like odd places to look at plants, but Vancouver Island has a few special cemeteries worthy of botanical note. One is worth visiting for its trees, and the other three for the native lilies.

The Ross Bay Cemetery was laid out in 1872, and like many Victoria cemeteries, was conceived as an arboretum. It is the oldest formal landscape planting in the province and has been maintained according to the original planting plan. The cemetery is located on Dallas Rd. at Memorial Crescent and contains the largest collection of *Pinus* spp. and *Prunus* spp. in B.C. Although the cemetery is worth a visit at any time, the flowering trees are an exceptional sight in the spring. Tours of the site are given every first and third Sunday of the month at 2:00 p.m. year round, except in January, and topics include the trees themselves and the floral symbolism of the grave markers.

Three other cemeteries to visit in the spring are the Church of St. Mary the Virgin, 4125 Metchosin Rd., near the corner of Happy Valley Rd., (250) 474-4119; St. Peter's Anglican Church, 5800 Church Rd., Quamichan, just outside Duncan, (250) 746-6262; and St. Stephen's Anglican Church, 7921 St. Stephen's Rd., Saanichton, just off Mount Newton Cross Rd., (250) 652-4311. All the churches date from the 1860s. The churchyard of St. Mary the Virgin is full of erythroniums, which form a white carpet in April. A tour is given in April. St. Stephen's Anglican Church sits in a beautiful setting in Mount Newton Valley, nestled among farms and mature trees, and is also ablaze with erythroniums and other lilies in the spring. St. Peter's Anglican Church is purple with camas lilies (*Camassia* spp.) in April, and the churchyard is also graced with Garry oaks. The gardeners don't mow the churchyard until July.

Saxe Point Park, Fraser St., Esquimalt, B.C. **Admission:** Free. **Hours:** Always open.

This garden is situated on 19 acres (8 ha) of waterfront in the warmest spot in Canada, and its microclimate enables some tender plants to survive here that cannot survive anywhere else in the country. A lot of the site is completely untouched, with stands of native fir trees. There are several viewpoints of the ocean from which seals, whales and migratory birds can be seen. It has an excellent spring bulb display, as well as perennial beds and flowering shrubs.

Towner Crest, 10629 Derrick Rd., R.R. #1, Sidney, B.C. **Tel:** (250) 656-1039. **Admission:** Free. **Hours:** By appointment only; phone ahead.

This private garden, owned and operated by Nick and Evelyn Weesjes, comprises 7 acres (2.8 ha) of woodland, all hand-cleared to retain as much as possible of the natural setting. The garden offers an extensive collection of species and hybrid rhododendrons and azaleas, and native plants such as primroses, trilliums, ferns and huckleberries, under a canopy of Douglas fir, arbutus, flowering cherry and maple trees.

The time to visit is during April when the species rhododendrons and flowering cherries are at their peak, or in May, for the hybrid rhododendrons.

University of Victoria, Finnerty Gardens. The entrance to the gardens is near the University Chapel, on the southwest edge of the campus. The gardens encompass an area north of Cedar Hill Cross Rd. and west of Henderson Rd. By car, take the Ring Rd. to parking lot 6, where some metered parking is available. Parking is free after 6:00 p.m. weekdays and on weekends and holidays. **Website:** http://victoria.tc.ca/Environment/UVicGdnFriends. **Admission:** Free. **Hours:** Always open.

The garden was started in the mid-1970s with the donation of a private collection of rhododendrons. The garden now features an extensive rhododendron collection of over 1,000 species and hybrids, as well as many other flowering trees, shrubs and perennials. A volunteer group, the Friends of University of Victoria Finnerty Gardens, offers guided tours one weekend in April (see Monthly Special Events listing for details).

Specialty Nurseries, General Nurseries and Garden Centres

Just as interesting as parks and gardens to visit are the many nurseries and garden centres in our area. Many specialty growers sell directly to the public, and large garden centres carry an impressive variety of plants. In the past ten years there has been a substantial increase both in the numbers of local growers and the variety of plants available, all catering to an increasingly large number of knowledgeable gardeners.

Our list is not exhaustive. Some small businesses did not want to be included here since they are already working to capacity. Others we did not include because they did not fit our criteria. We chose to list those we felt were of particular interest, either for the plants they grow or the range of items they carry.

The following key will help to locate the right nursery or garden centre for the particular plants you want. Detailed descriptions of the individual nurseries and centres begin on p. 233.

> LM = Lower Mainland
> VI = Vancouver Island
> GI/SI = Gulf Islands and Sunshine Coast

Alpines
VI   Alpine Meadows Nursery
LM   Hansi's Nursery

Aquatic Plants
VI   Cannor Nursery and Florist
     GardenWorks
VI   Hillier Water Gardens and Nurseries
LM   Jones Garden Centre
VI   Long Lake Nursery and Florist
LM   Mandeville Garden Centre
VI   Ponds 'n' Stuff
VI   Pacific Ponds
LM   Southlands Nursery Gardens

Bamboo
GI/SC The Bamboo Ranch

Bonsai
GI/SC Shikoku Bonsai
VI   Stone Tree Nursery

Dahlias
GI/SC Dahlias Galore
LM   Ferncliff Gardens

Daylilies
LM   Beachwood Daylilies and Perennials
LM   Erikson's Daylily Gardens
LM   Ferncliff Gardens
VI   Kilmalu Farms Daylily Nursery

Fruit Trees
LM   Cannor Nursery
VI   Le Coteau Farms and Garden Centre
LM   Mrs. Valle Lunzman
LM   Bert Vos
LM   Derry Walsh

Fuchsia
LM   Chestnut Greenhouses
LM   P. & J. Greenhouses
GI/SC Wheelbarrow Nursery

General Garden Centres
LM   Art Knapp Plantland
VI   Brentwood Bay Nurseries
VI   Cannor Nursery and Florist
VI   Cedar Hill Nurseries and Garden
       Centre
LM   David Hunter Garden Centres
VI   B. Dinter Nursery
VI   Elk Lake Garden Centre
GI/SC Foxglove Farm and Garden Supply
LM   GardenWorks
VI   GardenWorks
VI   Green Thumb Garden Centre
VI   Long Lake Nursery and Florist
LM   Mandeville Garden Centre
LM   Maple Leaf Garden Shops
VI   Marigold Nursery
LM   Minter Country Garden World
LM   Murray Nurseries
LM   Nurseryland
VI   Oakridge Nursery and Garden Centre
VI   Snapdragon Nursery
LM   Southlands Nursery Gardens
LM   West Van Florist

Hanging Baskets
(most garden centres carry a good selection.)
LM   Amsterdam Greenhouses and Garden
       Centre
LM   Keefer Farms and Greenhouses

Hedging
(most garden centres carry a good selection.)
LM   Cedar Rim Nursery
LM   Holland Nursery

Hellebores
LM   GardenWorks
LM   Jenray Nursery
LM   Southlands Nursery Gardens

Herbs
LM   Easy Acres Herb Farm
VI   The Garden Path
VI   Happy Valley Lavender and Herb Farm
VI   Hazelwood Farm
LM   Lowland Herb Farm
VI   Ravenhill Herb Farm

Hostas
LM   Made in the Shade Nursery
LM   Meadow Farms Garden Nursery
LM   The Perennial Gardens

Mushrooms
LM   Marvellous Mushrooms

Orchids
LM   Brookside Orchid Garden
VI   Kingfisher Orchids
VI   Orchids North
VI   Orchid Species Specialist
VI   Poul Hansen Orchids
LM   Southlands Nursery Gardens
LM   Valley Orchid Partners

Native Plants
GI/SC   Fraser's Thimble Farms
VI   C.E. Jones Nursery
LM   The Perennial Gardens
VI   Streamside Native Plants

Ornamental Grasses
LM   Meadowsweet Farms Garden Nursery
LM   The Perennial Gardens
GI/SC   The Plant Farm
LM   Rainforest Nurseries

Perennials
VI   Alpine Meadows Nursery
VI   Blue Haven Specialty
VI   Brentwood Bay Nurseries
VI   Cannor Nursery and Florist
LM   Cardinal Gardens Nursery
VI   Cedar Hill Nurseries and Garden
        Centre
GI/SC   Cusheon Creek Nursery
LM   Earthrise Garden Store
LM   Elizabeth's Cottage Perennials
VI   For Wild Birds and Gardeners
GI/SC   Foxglove Farm and Garden Supply
GI/SC   Fragrant Flora
GI/SC   Fraser's Thimble Farms
LM   Free Spirit Nursery
VI   The Garden Path
LM   GardenWorks
VI   GardenWorks
LM   Glad's Nursery
LM   Hansi's Nursery
LM   Made in the Shade Nursery
L   Meadowsweet Farms Garden Nursery
LM   The Perennial Gardens
LM   Petals and Butterflies
LM   Phoenix Perennials
GI/SC   The Plant Farm
LM   Rainforest Nurseries
VI   Russell Farms

LM   Shop-in-the-Garden and Plant Centre
VI   Snapdragon Nursery
LM   Southlands Nursery Gardens
LM   Southside Gardens
VI   Whitegate Farm

Rhododendrons and Azaleas
VI   Cedar Hill Nurseries and Garden
        Centre
LM   Cedar Rim Nursery
LM   Clay's Nursery
VI   Firwood Nursery
VI   Green Thumb Garden Centre
VI   Haida Gold Gardens
VI   Rhodo Mania
LM   Wrenhaven Nursery

Roses
VI   Brentwood Bay Nurseries
LM   Como Lake Garden Centre
LM   Earthrise Garden Store
VI   Elk Lake Garden Centre
GI/SC   Foxglove Farm and Garden Supply
LM   Killara Farm
LM   Mandeville Garden Centre
LM   Murray Nurseries Ltd.
VI   Oakridge Nursery and Garden Centre
GI/SC   Old Rose Nursery
LM   Select Roses
LM   Southlands Nursery Gardens
VI   Whitegate Farm

Shrubs
VI   Cannor Nursery and Florist
VI   Cedar Hill Nurseries and Garden
        Centre
GI/SC   Cusheon Creek Nursery
VI   Danica Nurseries
GI/SC   Foxglove Farm and Garden Supply
GI/SC   Fragrant Flora
LM   GardenWorks
VI   GardenWorks
LM   Glad's Nursery
VI   Marigold Nursery
VI   Meadow Oak Nursery
VI   Russell Farms
VI   Stone Tree Nursery
GI/SC   Wheelbarrow Nursery
GI/SC   Willow Farm Nursery

Trees
LM   Bill's Little Tree Farm
VI   Cannor Nursery and Florist

VI	Cedar Hill Nurseries and Garden Centre
LM	Cedar Rim Nursery
LM	Como Lake Garden Centre
GI/SC	Cusheon Creek Nursery
VI	Danica Nurseries
GI/SC	Fragrant Flora
LM	GardenWorks
VI	GardenWorks
LM	Glad's Nursery
LM	Jones Garden Centre
VI	Marigold Nursery
VI	Meadow Oak Nursery
VI	Russell Farms
LM	Turner Trees
GI/SC	Wheelbarrow Nursery
GI/SC	Willow Farm Nursery

Vancouver and the Lower Mainland

Amsterdam Greenhouses and Garden Centre, 19100 Dewdney Trunk Rd., Pitt Meadows, B.C., V3Y 1Z1. **Tel:** (604) 465-6073. **Hours:** 9:00 a.m. to 6:00 p.m. daily; 9:00 a.m. to 9:00 p.m. weekdays during the summer.

Specialties include fuchsias: standards, baskets and starters, and moss baskets. They have an expanded water garden section with a good selection of water plants, grasses and unusual annuals. A garden-theme gift shop features local artists; monthly workshops on seasonal gardening topics and projects are held in their large greenhouse.

Art Knapp Plantland. Website: http://www.artknapp.com.

This chain of family-owned nursery/garden centres is located throughout B.C. and carries a good selection of nursery stock.
Abbotsford, 31888 Marshall Rd.
Tel: (604) 864-0202 Fax: (604) 864-0204
Burnaby, 4362 East Hastings St.
Tel: (604) 299-1777 Fax: (604) 299-0707
Langley, 22454 - 48th Ave.
Tel: (604) 533-0388 Fax: (604) 533-8238
Port Coquitlam, 300 Dominion Ave.
Tel: (604) 942-7518 Fax: (604) 942-1859
Port Moody, 3150 Saint John St.
Tel: (604) 461-0004 Fax: (604) 461-0708
Richmond, 10840 No. 5 Rd.
Tel: (604) 271-9581 Fax: (604) 271-4151
South Surrey, 4391 King George Hwy.
Tel: (604) 596-9201 Fax: (604) 596-9240

Country Rambles in the Lower Mainland
Grab a map and a picnic and venture into the countryside for a day-long exploration. There are display gardens, nurseries, specialty outlets, agricultural fairs, farmers' markets and walking trails to discover.

Langley
Get the latest Guide to Farm Gate Sales in Langley at the Langley Chamber of Commerce InfoCentre at #1 – 5761 Glover Rd., or phone (604) 530-6656. Tour the "Golden Square" of Nurseries: start at Made in the Shade Nursery; move on to Erikson's Daylily Gardens (open daily in July, weekends April through June, or by appointment); continue on to Select Roses and finish at Meadowsweet Nursery. Free Spirit Nursery and Rainforest Nurseries are other must-visits in the neighbourhood. For tea, stop in at Tuscan Gardens and stroll through their lavender/echinacea gardens. You can include Westridge Farms if you phone ahead— the vistas and fields of grasses are quite wonderful (buy bread at the Austrian Bakery just before you turn down their lane).

Maple Ridge/Mission
Start at Cardinal Gardens and Ferncliff Gardens in Mission; rest at Cistos Pub at Hatzic Bench in Mission for lunch; go on to Hansi's Nursery on 112th Ave. (across from Whonnock Lake recreation area); then visit Bill's Little Tree Farm and The Perennial Gardens (formerly Rainforest Gardens) on 224th St. in Maple Ridge. The heritage gardens at Haney House on the Fraser River at 224th St. in Maple Ridge is worth a visit, and a walk along the dikes will add even more to your day.

Abbotsford
If you come on the Saturday before Thanksgiving you can join the community Cranberry Harvest Festival at Tilsonberry Farm, a 100-acre (40-ha) cranberry farm in the Glen Valley, a 15-minute drive east of Fort Langley. The flooded fields are a sea of pink surrounded by hills of red and gold. Check with the Abbotsford Chamber of Commerce for local walks and Saturday farm and antique actions. Tilsonberry Farms is at 8201 Dyke Rd.; phone (604) 856-2582 or check their web page at http://www.tilsonberry.bc.ca for details and directions.

Art Knapp Plantland (cont.)
Surrey, 16287 Fraser Hwy.
Tel: (604) 597-9701 Fax: (604) 597-9784
Vancouver, 1401 Hornby St.
Tel: (604) 662-3303 Fax: (604) 662-8268
Vancouver, 1896 Victoria Dr.
Tel: (604) 253-1696 Fax: (604) 253-1548

Check hours of operation at individual locations. All stores are independently owned, although some buying is done collectively. Good selection of nursery stock.

Art's Nursery Ltd., 8940 - 192nd St., Surrey, B.C. **Tel:** (604) 882-1201. **Fax:** (604) 882-5969. **E-mail:** arts@direct.ca. **Hours:** Open every day; exact hours change with the seasons.

A wholesale/retail nursery where you can shop 10 acres (4 ha) of landscape nursery stock that includes trees, shrubs and seasonals.

Beachwood Daylilies and Perennials, 7075 - 264th St., Aldergrove, B.C. **Tel:** (604) 856-8806. **E-mail:** sian_krannitz@beachwooddaylily.com. **Website:** http://www.beachwooddaylily.com. **Hours:** 10:00 a.m. to 4:00 p.m. Friday, Saturday and Sunday in July, and open by appointment at other times. Catalogue available.

Founded by Edward Woch in 1992 and purchased by Sian and Norm Krannitz in 1998, this family nursery includes a daylily display garden and a mail-order business. Their collection includes over 600 varieties and they are creating a display bed of Stout Medal Award winners to show off varieties that do well in our particular northern climate.

Bill's Little Tree Farm, 13554 - 224th St., Maple Ridge, B.C., V4R 2P8. **Tel:** (604) 461-0669. **Hours:** Wednesday to Saturday inclusive, 11:00 a.m. to 5:00 p.m.

Bill Browne's specialty is growing uncommon trees from seed he collected in the Pacific Northwest or southern Ontario. He selects small trees with unique shapes, leaf colour and form. You can roam through the hundreds of field-growing trees. Tree list includes interesting small maples.

Bradner Bulb Co., 6775 Bradner Rd., Mt. Lehman, B.C., V0X 1V0. **Tel:** (604) 856-4923. **Hours:** Display garden is open in the month of April.

Daffodils, tulips and narcissi, both home-grown and imported. Plant/price list available on request.

Brookside Orchid Garden, 23779 - 32nd Ave., Langley, B.C., V2Z 2J2. **Tel:** (604) 533-8286.

E-mail: info@brooksideorchids.com. **Website:** http://www.brooksideorchids.com. **Hours:** Tuesday to Saturday 9:00 a.m. to 5:00 p.m., Sunday 11:00 a.m. to 4:00 p.m.

This retail orchid shop is at the site of one of the largest breeders and growers of orchids in western Canada. Visit their shop or website to browse through their selection of orchids, or learn about their special event shows, tour days and monthly classes.

Brookswood Nursery and Garden Centre, 3497 - 205th St., Langley, B.C., V2Z 2C9. **Tel:** (604) 530-8029 or (604) 530-3457 (residence). **Hours:** 10:00 a.m. to 5:00 p.m. daily, but can vary with the season, so call ahead.

This 21-year-old nursery and garden centre is part of a working poultry farm. The owner, Lucille, offers horticultural classes on pruning, bonsai and container gardening in her greenhouse. She sells bonsai plants, pottery for bonsai from around the globe, and supplies, tools and books about bonsai, as well as flowering shrubs, hedging, annuals and perennials.

Cannor Nursery, 48255 Chilliwack Central Rd., R.R. #1, Chilliwack, B.C., V2P 6H3. **Tel:** (604) 795-5914. **Website:** http://www.weluvgardening.com. **Hours:** Varies with season but generally 9:00 a.m. to 5:30 p.m. daily.

Cannor Nursery has an excellent selection of fruit trees, both dwarf and semidwarf. They also sell a full line of nursery stock, including bulbs and seeds. Check their website for updates on what's new, calendar of events and newsletter articles.

Cardinal Gardens Nursery, 13050 Cardinal St., Mission, B.C., V2V 5X4. **Tel:** (604) 820-0845. **Hours:** Please call ahead for visits. Open March to September.

Thirteen acres (5 ha) of display gardens, specializing in perennials. Catalogue available with mail-order purchase.

Cedar Rim Nursery, 7024 Glover Rd., Langley, B.C., V2Y 2R1. **Tel:** (604) 888-2466. **E-mail:** cedarrim@uniserve.com. **Website:** http://www.cedar-rim-nursery.com.

This nursery has a wide variety of rhododendrons, cedars, deciduous trees and shrubs, hedging material, tropical plants and pond supplies.

Chestnut Greenhouses, 17974 - 40th Ave., Surrey, B.C., V4P 1M5. **Tel:** (604) 574-5798. **Hours:** 9:00 a.m. to 5:00 p.m. daily.

They sell specialty geraniums and fuchsias. Other potted plants are available. Send S.A.S.E. for fuchsia list.

Clay's Nursery, 3666 - 224th St., Langley, B.C., V4P 1M5. **Tel:** (604) 530-5188. **Hours:** Varies with the season; please phone ahead.

This nursery is noted for is azaleas, rhododendrons and kalmias. The nursery sells both wholesale and retail. A catalogue is available on request.

Como Lake Garden Centre, 1649 Como Lake Rd., Coquitlam, B.C., V3J 3P7. **Tel:** (604) 939-0539. **Hours:** Call ahead for hours.

This nursery has a good selection of roses and Japanese maples. They also have perennials, bedding plants, garden supplies and fresh flowers.

David Hunter Garden Centres
Vancouver, 2084 West Broadway
Tel: (604) 733-1531 Fax: (604) 733-5811
Surrey, 15175 - 72nd Ave.
Tel: (604) 590-2431 Fax: (604) 590-1281
Hours: 9:00 a.m. to 5:30 p.m. Monday to Saturday; 9:00 a.m. to 5:00 p.m. Sunday.

These garden centres carry a complete line of nursery stock and giftware, and they have an interest in unusual perennials. Check individual locations for in-store demonstrations and seminars.

Earthrise Garden Store, 2954 West 4th Ave., Vancouver, B.C., V6K 1R4. **Tel/Fax:** (604) 736-8404. **Hours:** 10:00 a.m. to 5:30 p.m. Monday, Wednesday, Thursday, Friday and Saturday; 1:00 p.m. to 5:00 p.m. Sunday. Times subject to change in winter.

This friendly little garden centre is always worth a visit. Here you will find English roses, unusual clematis and other climbers, interesting perennials and trees and shrubs suitable for a city lot. There is a good selection of garden books and ornaments, as well as seeds (including Bolton's sweet peas) and fresh flowers every Thursday. The proprietors will do plant searches for customers and also offer garden design and consultation.

Easy Acres Herb Farm, 12063 - 64th Ave., Surrey, B.C., V3W 1W5. **Tel:** (604) 596-8485. **Hours:** 9:00 a.m. to 5:00 p.m. daily.

This farm, started in 1986, has a large variety of both summer and winter herbs and now supplies most garden centres in western Canada. The plants are retailed at Granville Market every day from the last weekend in February to the first weekend in July. Potted herbs only are sold.

Elizabeth's Cottage Perennials, 24980 - 56th Ave., Langley, B.C., V4W 1B1. **Tel/Fax:** (604) 856-5279. **E-mail:** esds@uniserve.com. **Hours:** April to June, 10:00 a.m. to 3:00 p.m. Wednesday to Sunday.

This small garden nursery of .5 acre (.2 ha) specializes in old-fashioned cottage garden plants, particularly perennials and companion plants for roses. Plant list is available.

Erikson's Daylily Gardens, 24642 - 51st Ave., Langley, B.C. **Tel:** (604) 856-5758. **E-mail:** pamela1@istar.ca. **Website:** http://www.plantlovers.com. **Hours:** Weekends April to June, daily through July for peak bloomtime, and other times on request. Catalogue and mail order available.

This 1-acre (.4-ha) wholesale/retail nursery and display garden offers over 1,400 varieties of daylilies, as well as a selection of Asiatic, Oriental and trumpet lilies.

Ferncliff Gardens, 8394 McTaggart St., Mission, B.C., V2V 6S6. **Tel:** (604) 826-2447. **Fax:** (604) 862-4316. **Hours:** 9:00 a.m. to 4:30 p.m. Monday to Saturday; open daily August and September. Closed weekends October 15 to March 15.

Ferncliff Gardens was started 80 years ago by the present owner's grandfather. The mail-order catalogue features many of the most outstanding dahlias, irises, daylilies and peonies available. Plants are grown locally; some are locally hybridized. You can order anytime, but note the shipping dates: dahlias and gladiolas are shipped mid-March to end of May; irises are shipped mid-July to mid-September; peonies are shipped early September to mid-October; daylilies are shipped August 15 to through October. Visitors are welcome to view the fields in bloom, especially from August 5 to October 5 when the dahlias are at their best.

Free Spirit Nursery Inc., 20405 - 32nd Ave., Langley, B.C., V2Z 2C7. **Tel:** (604) 533-7373. **Fax:** (604) 530-3776. **Website:** http://www.plantlovers.com. **Hours:** April to October, 10:00 a.m. to 4:00 p.m. every Thursday, Friday and Saturday. Closed July.

Free Spirit Nursery specializes in garden-worthy perennials from around the globe. Of particular interest are unique collections of *Digitalis*, *Epimedium*, *Monarda*, *Salvia* and *Thalictrum*. By using established design concepts, this retail nursery is aesthetically pleasing as an open classroom filled with useful information.

A plant list and additional mail-order information are available at the nursery for a small fee.

GardenWorks
E-mail: emailservice@gardenworks.ca. **Website:** http://www.gardenworks.ca.
Burnaby, 6250 Lougheed Hwy.
Tel: (604) 299-0621
Langley, 20530 Walnut Grove
Tel: (604) 881-6003
Mission, 32270 Lougheed Hwy.
Tel: (604) 826-9112
North Vancouver, 3147 Woodbine Dr.
Tel: (604) 980-6340
North Vancouver, 705 West 3rd St.
Tel: (604) 988-8082
South Surrey, 2124 - 128th St.
Tel: (604) 535-8853
Vancouver, 8697 Granville St.
Tel: (604) 266-9313

These are all full-service garden centres and carry nursery stock of excellent quality and selection. They publish a quarterly newsletter and offer classes and workshops. Check individual locations for hours of business.

Glad's Nursery, 23859 - 14A Ave., Langley, B.C., V2Z 2Y5. **Tel/Fax:** (604) 530-5298.

Five acres (2 ha) of parklike setting display this nursery's stock of trees, shrubs and perennials. You can choose and dig your own dwarf conifers, rhododendrons and kalmias, or select container plants. Call ahead for hours of opening.

Hansi's Nursery, 27810 - 112th Ave., Maple Ridge, B.C., V2W 1P9. **Tel:** (604) 462-8799. **Fax:** (604) 462-8042. **E-mail:** Hansisnursery@sprint.ca. **Hours:** 9:00 a.m. to 5:00 p.m. Friday, Saturday and Sunday, March to October. Closed August.

This 5-acre (2-ha) nursery includes a demonstration garden, alpines, perennials, trees and shrubs. Many of her treasures are grown from seed imported from all over the world, and Hansi's knowledge, enthusiasm and expertise are very infectious.

Holland Nursery, 16170 - 84th Ave., Surrey, B.C., V3S 2P1. **Tel:** (604) 572-7666. **Hours:** Varies with the season; call ahead. Closed January.

This is a good year-round garden centre, specializing in hedging material, in particular a large variety of cedar hedging.

Jenray Gardens Nursery, 19429 - 62A Ave., Surrey, B.C. **Tel:** (604) 530-8226.

Hellebores, many grown from seed acquired from the gurus of the hellebore world, are a specialty and a passion in this home-based nursery.

Display garden open in March and April. Call ahead for hours.

Jones Garden Centre, 16880 Westminster Hwy., Richmond, B.C., V6V 1A8. **Tel:** (604) 278-8671. **Hours:** 9:00 a.m. to 5:30 p.m. April to October; 8:00 a.m. to 5:30 p.m. November to March.

This location supplies the retail market with a wide variety of nursery stock. Specializing in large specimen trees and free-standing water gardens, they also carry a good selection of ceramic containers. A newsletter is available at the nursery, and courses are given in both Mandarin and Cantonese.

Keefer Farms and Greenhouses, 17080 Cambie Rd., Richmond, B.C., V6V 1A8. **Tel:** (604) 278-8943. **Hours:** 9:00 a.m. to 8:00 p.m. from May 1 to end of June (depending on seasonal conditions and supplies).

This is a small family business that supplies beautiful hanging baskets and containers. A great stop for Mother's Day.

Killara Farm, 21733 - 8th Ave., Langley, B.C. **Tel:** (604) 532-9831. **Hours:** By appointment.

Roses are a specialty at this charming little farm. The half-acre (.2-ha) display garden features over 100 varieties of old garden roses and shrub roses raised on their own roots.

Lowland Herb Farm, 5685 Lickman Rd., R.R. #3, Sardis, B.C., V2R 4B5. **Tel:** (604) 858-4216. **Hours:** 10:00 a.m. to 6:00 p.m. mid-March to September. Call ahead.

This biodynamic wholesale/retail herb farm was a pioneer in organic herb growing in this area. There is a comprehensive selection of herbs.

Mrs. Valle Lunzman, 4549 - 220th St., Langley, B.C., V3A 8E2. **Tel:** (604) 530-8440.

This is a hobby rather than a business, and Mrs. Lunzman is generous in sharing her expertise with those who share her interest in fruit trees. She has more than 35 varieties of apples and has given demonstrations on grafting to Master Gardeners for a number of years. Order for scionwoods should be made before February for grafting wood and before August for budding wood.

Made in the Shade Nursery, 4586 Saddlehorn Cres., Langley, B.C., V2Z 1J7. **Tel:** (604) 856-2010. **Fax:** (604) 856-0049. **E-mail:** Goody@intergate.bc.ca. **Website:** http://www.plantlovers.com. **Hours:** 10:00 a.m. to 4:00 p.m. Thursday to Saturday, March to October. Call for an appointment at other times.

This charming home-based nursery is set among 2.5 acres (1 ha) of woodland. You can view many varieties of ferns, hostas, pulmonarias, tiarellas and other sought-after shade-loving plants in their growing environment. A catalogue and mail-order service are available.

Mandeville Garden Centre, 4746 Marine Drive, Burnaby, B.C., V5J 3G6. **Tel:** (604) 434-4111. **Fax:** (604) 434-0240. **Hours:** 9:00 a.m. to 7:00 p.m. Monday to Friday; 9:00 a.m. to 6:00 p.m. Saturday and Sunday. Holidays may vary; some extended hours in December.

This large garden centre carries a diverse and interesting selection of plant material, in addition to an organic produce market, garden accessories, gift shop, floral service and café. A bi-monthly newsletter advises of courses and workshops.

Maple Leaf Garden Shops
North Vancouver, 1343 Lynn Valley Rd.
Tel: (604) 985-1784
West Vancouver, 2558 Haywood Ave.
Tel: (604) 922-2613 Fax: (604) 926-9735

Wide selection of nursery stock, including shrubs, trees and perennials. Check individual locations for hours of operation.

Marvellous Mushrooms—Western Biologicals Ltd., P.O. Box 283, Aldergrove, B.C., V4W 2T8. **Tel:** (604) 856-3339. **E-mail:** western@prismet.bc.ca. For hours, appointment and free brochure, call ahead.

They offer mushroom-growing kits, mushroom spawn and Asian pear varieties, as well as mushroom cultivation and plant tissue cultivation courses.

Meadowsweet Farms Garden Nursery, 19656 - 16th Ave., South Langley, B.C.,V2Z 1K1. **Tel:** (604) 530-2611. **E-mail:** meadowsweet@pacificgroup.net. **Hours:** 9:00 a.m. to 5:00 p.m. seven days a week March to October.

A favourite of the gardening cognoscenti, this nursery offers a very good selection of perennnials and unusual plants, including one of the biggest selections of hostas and ornamental grasses available. Their recent move has allowed the inclusion of more display beds. A catalogue is available.

Minter Country Garden Centre Ltd., 10015 Young Rd., North Chilliwack, B.C., V2P 4V4. **Tel:** (604) 792-6612. **E-mail:** brianm@minter.org. **Website:** http://www.minter.org. **Hours:** Open year-round, but extended hours during gardening season; call for exact times.

Brian Minter, the well-known garden writer, lecturer and guest garden expert on CBC, is the owner of this diverse garden centre. Here you can purchase many of the perennials and annual bedding plants you may have admired in Minter Gardens. The centre specializes in new introductions from around the world and carries a good selection of small fruits. If you are looking for something out of the ordinary or new, you may just find it here. It is well worth a drive to Chilliwack.

Minter Country Garden World, 45675 Knight Rd., Sardis, B.C., V2R 1B1. **Tel:** (604) 858-6162. **E-mail:** brianm@minter.org. **Website:** http://www.minter.org. **Hours:** See above.

This is a smaller operation, also owned by Brian Minter, offering a florist service, flowering plants and tropicals. There is a good selection of annuals, perennials, bulbs, vines, fertilizers and soil.

Murray Nurseries Ltd., 3140 West 57th Ave., Vancouver, B.C., V6N 3X6. **Tel:** (604) 261-2151. **Fax:** (604) 266-8514. **Hours:** April to July 9:00 a.m. to 6:00 p.m.; August to March 9:00 a.m. to 5:30 p.m.

This family-owned business has been serving Vancouver gardeners since 1916. Situated in the heart of Southlands equestrian area, they carry a full line of nursery stock and supplies, including a good selection of roses.

Nurseryland
Garibaldi Plants, 38917 Progress Way, Squamish, B.C. Tel: (604) 892-3892.
Gibbs Garden Centre and Florist, 7950 - 200th St., Langley, B.C. Tel: (604) 888-2121.
Harris Nursery and Florist, 5456 - 12th Ave., Tsawwassen, B.C. Tel: (604) 943-2984.
Homestead Nurseries, 33973 Cyril St., Abbotsford, B.C. Tel: (604) 854-6601.
Triple Tree Nursery and Florist, 20503 Lougheed Hwy., Maple Ridge, B.C. Tel: (604) 465-9313.

These independently owned, well-established garden centres carry a full line of nursery stock. Check hours of operation at individual locations.

P. & J. Greenhouses, 20265 - 82nd Ave., R.R. #11, Langley, B.C., V2Y 2A9. **Tel:** (604) 888-3274. **Fax:** (604) 888-3211. **Hours:** Call ahead to check.

A very wide selection of fuchsias and pelargoniums is available here.

The Perennial Gardens, 13139 - 224th St., Maple Ridge, B.C., V4R 2P6. **Tel:** (604) 467-4218. **Fax:** (604) 467-3181. **E-mail:** info@perennialgardener.com. **Website:** http://www.perennialgardener.com. **Hours:** March 8 to July 29, 10:00 a.m. to 5:00 p.m. Wednesday to Saturday. Closed August. September 1 to October 28, 10:00 a.m. to 4:00 p.m. Wednesday to Saturday.

Formerly Rainforest Gardens, this excellent nursery includes a display garden featuring over 2,000 different species and cultivars. Specialties include hardy geraniums, hostas, ferns, astilbe, phlox, B.C. flora, a good selection of alpines, and drought-tolerant, shade-loving and general-use perennials. A large portion of this nursery's business is mail-order, for which there is a catalogue available. A $4.00 subscription covers two years with two issues per year.

Petals and Butterflies, 121 - 210th St., Langley, B.C., V2Z 2G6. **Tel:** (604) 530-9205. **Hours:** 9:30 a.m. to 4:30 p.m. Thursday to Saturday, April to June, September and October.

This delightful, small home-based nursery, operated by Gwen Odermatt, specializes in perennials that provide colour and nectar that attracts butterflies and hummingbirds. It also carries some interesting shrubs.

Phoenix Perennials Nursery, 3380 No. 6 Rd., Richmond, B.C., V6V 1P3. **Tel/Fax:** (604) 270-4133. **E-mail:** Nursery@phoenixperennials.com. **Website:** http://www.phoenixperennials.com. **Hours:** March to November, 10:00 a.m. to 4:00 p.m. Wednesday to Saturday; also open Sundays in May and June, 10:00 a.m. to 4:00 p.m.

This working wholesale/retail nursery offers a broad selection of new and unusual plant material, specializing in perennials, flowering shrubs and vines. Call ahead for information on education seminars. A catalogue is available. Landscape design is a specialty.

Potters Garden Centre and Florist, 20811 Fraser Hwy., Langley, B.C., V3A 4G7. **Tel:** (604) 534-3813; (604) 533-1551 for florist. **Fax:** (604) 530-8406. **Hours:** Daily 9:00 a.m. to 6:00 p.m.

This large outdoor nursery specializes in roses and perennials. There are also indoor tropicals, gardening tools, books, bird houses and a full-service florist. They offer courses and produce a monthly newsletter.

Rainforest Nurseries, 1470 - 227th St., Langley, B.C., V2Z 1K6. **Tel/Fax:** (604) 530-3499. **Website:** http://www.plantlovers.com. **Hours:** 8:00 a.m. to 5:00 p.m. every day, February to November.

This nursery, situated on 5 acres (2 ha), offers an extensive collection of perennials, grasses, shrubs, trees and selected annuals, ranging from old favourites to the latest botanical "must-have." There is an impressive display garden, and planters, trellises and garden furniture are also available. Catalogue and free public seminars are offered.

Select Roses, 22771 - 38th Ave., Langley, B.C. **Tel:** (604) 530-5786. **E-mail:** bjalbert@uniserve.com. **Website:** http://www.plantlovers.com. **Hours:** 10:00 a.m. to 5:00 p.m. early March to September 15. Closed Tuesdays.

A family cottage nursery specializing in Canadian-grown garden roses. They grow a large selection of miniature roses and a good selection of full-sized roses. See over 700 blooming roses displayed from June to September.

Shop-in-the-Garden and Plant Centre, UBC Botanical Garden, 6804 Southwest Marine Drive, Vancouver, B.C., V6T 1Z4. **Tel:** (604) 822-4529. **Website:** http://www.hedgerows.com. **Hours:** daily 10:00 a.m. to 6:00 p.m.

The Shop-in-the-Garden is run by volunteers and all proceeds support UBC Botanical Garden. You will find a choice selection of perennials and shrubs as well as books, tools and accessories. Unusual seeds from the garden are available online from http://www.eseeds.com.

Southlands Nursery Gardens, 6550 Balaclava St., Vancouver, B.C., V6N 1L9. **Tel:** (604) 261-6411. **E-mail:** tomhobbs@direct.ca. **Website:** http://www.plantlovers.com. **Hours:** Daily 9:00 a.m. to 5:30 p.m. in winter and extended hours during spring and summer.

This attractive, 2-acre (.8-ha) nursery is located in the Southlands equestrian area. It is stocked with the latest in interesting and unusual outdoor plants, terra cotta pots, and indoor tropicals—including many orchids offered by the proprietor, Thomas Hobbs.

Southside Gardens, 3250 West 55th Ave., Vancouver, B.C. **Tel:** (604) 261-7665. **Hours:** 9:00 a.m. to 5:00 p.m.

A family-run garden centre in the Southlands area that sells many varieties of native plants, groundcovers and perennials. After Mother's Day, they stock unusual annuals.

Turner Trees, 1437 - 212th St., Langley, B.C. **Tel:** (604) 532-9262. **Hours:** Call ahead.

This 5-acre (2-ha) display garden specializes in unusual trees and shrubs, particularly pine species and cultivars. Mr. Turner will do plant searches for perennials, trees and shrubs for customers during his annual trip to Washington and Oregon nurseries. Plant list is available.

Tuscan Farm Gardens, 24453 - 60th Ave., Langley, B.C., V2Z 2G5. **Tel:** (604) 530-1997. **Fax:** (604) 532-0350. **E-mail:** heather@tuscanfarmgardens.com. **Website:** http://www.plantlovers.com. **Hours:** Call ahead for current hours of operation and entrance fee to the walking trails.

This family enterprise "working farm" includes fields of echinacea and lavender, a bed and breakfast, a tea shop with in-house products, walking trails and also a small plant shop with echinacea and lavender for sale.

Valley Orchid Partners, 12621 Woolridge Rd., Pitt Meadows, B.C., V3Y 1Z1. **Tel:** (604) 465-8664 or (604) 465-8374. **Hours:** Visits by appointment.

Come to view and select from many different species and hybrid orchids growing in their greenhouse. They also sell orchid how-to books and supplies. A catalogue is available by phone.

VanDusen Botanical Garden Shop, 5251 Oak St. (at 37th), Vancouver, B.C. **Tel:** (604) 878-9274. **Hours:** The shop is located at the garden entrance and is open daily from 10:00 a.m. Evening closures are seasonal; confirm with office.

The garden's gift and plant shop offers an attractive display of interesting plants, garden books and accessories.

Bert Vos, 5518 - 183rd Ave., Surrey, B.C., V3S 4N9. **Tel:** (604) 576-1933. **Hours:** Phone ahead for appointment.

Bert Vos specializes in tree fruits with four different varieties of apple rootstock that are dwarf or semidwarf. Of particular interest to those who wish to grow organically are four varieties that show good resistance to scab: 'Prima', 'Liberty', 'Redfree' and 'Jonafree'. There are many other varieties, including a number from Europe.

Derry Walsh, Aldergrove, B.C. **Tel/Fax:** (604) 856-9316. **E-mail:** wchase@interchange.ubc.ca. **Website:** http://www.interchange.ubc.ca/wchase/HTML.

Derry's specialties include dwarf apple trees (heritage and modern), fruit tree rootstocks (dwarf and semidwarf), apples (Elstar, Fiesta and Jonagold), llamas, llama manure, native bee condominiums and

nesting straws. She sells at VanDusen Garden Seedy Saturday in February, the VanDusen Plant Sale at the end of April and the University of B.C. Apple Festival in October. You can make an appointment with Derry by phone, fax or e-mail, and you can see her stuff on her educational website.

West Coast Seeds Demonstration Garden, 6511 Dyke Rd., Richmond, B.C., V7E 3R4. **Tel:** (604) 482-8800. **E-mail:** info@westcoastseeds.com. **Website:** http://www.westcoastseeds.com. **Hours:** Dawn to dusk year round.

This organic demonstration garden is located at London Heritage Farm in historic Steveston. Take a self-directed tour or call ahead for a guide. All the plants are labelled, and you can taste and sample as you go. The garden is best from July to September.

West Van Florist, 1821 Marine Drive, West Vancouver, B.C., V7V 1J7. **Tel:** (604) 922-4171. **Hours:** Monday to Saturday 9:00 a.m. to 6:00 p.m.; 10:00 a.m. to 5:00 p.m. Sunday.

A small general garden centre with an excellent selection of perennials and a good selection of bedding plants and shrubs.

Willow Creek Nursery, 6540 - 256th St., Aldergrove, B.C., V4W 1T8. **Tel:** (604) 856-6998. **Hours:** April to June 9:00 a.m. to 6:00 p.m. Phone ahead for appointment at other times.

Willow Creek turned from a hobby to a business a few years ago. They specialize in bedding plants, including vegetables and herbs. There is a selection of ready-made hanging baskets, and you can order custom moss baskets by calling the above number. Try some herb baskets for your culinary needs. Baskets and containers can also be refilled to order, provided that they are brought out early in the season.

Wrenhaven Nursery, 16651 - 20th Ave., Surrey, B.C., V4P 2R3. **Tel:** (604) 536-7283. **Hours:** Midweek 9:00 a.m. to 6:00 p.m. except Tuesday (closed); weekends 10:00 a.m. to 6:00 p.m. Note that closing hours vary seasonally.

Begun in 1965 as C. and T. Azalea Nursery, Wrenhaven specializes in field-grown rhododendrons, azaleas and bonsai. You can walk through their parklike acreage and select from a large and interesting assortment of species and hybrid varieties.

Yoshizawa Nurseries, 9062 - 140th St., Surrey, B.C., V3V 5Y9. **Tel:** (604) 951-0068. **Hours:** 8:30 a.m. to 5:00 p.m. Monday to Friday; weekends in spring and summer. Call ahead to check.

This family business has been operating for 18 years. The nursery and garden centre occupy about 10 acres (4 ha) and sell both wholesale and retail. They propagate their own stock, which is then container- or field-grown. They have a large selection of semidwarf fruit trees and specialize in grafting different varieties onto one rootstock. Also available are ornamental trees, Japanese maples, shrubs, rhododendrons, azaleas, perennials, annuals and hanging baskets. Bonsai and bonsai containers are available around Christmas time.

Victoria and Vancouver Island

Alpine Meadows Nursery, 1965 - 6th St. East, Courtenay, B.C., V9N 6W6. **Tel:** (250)338-5267. **Hours:** By appointment.

Specializes in alpines and choice perennials such as lewisias and gentians.

Blue Haven Specialty, 2881 Church Way, R.R. #2, Mill Bay, B.C.,V0R 2P0. **Tel/Fax:** (250) 743-3876. **E-mail:** plants@bluehavennursery.com. **Website:** http://bluehavennursery.com. **Hours:** Call ahead for opening hours but generally open the third week in February until the middle of October.

This nursery specializes in meconopsis, primula and other rare and unusual perennials. An extensive catalogue is posted on their website.

Brentwood Bay Nurseries, 1395 Benvenuto Ave., Brentwood Bay, B.C., V8M 1J5. **Tel:** (250) 652-1507. **Fax:** (250) 652-2761. **E-mail:** bbnplants@home.com. **Website:** http://www.coast-net.com/~plants/index.html#toc.

This small specialist nursery is the place to go if you are looking for the unusual or hard-to-find perennials. They also have a very large selection of roses, mainly old roses, English roses, modern shrub roses and climbers. Plant lists are available.

Cannor Nursery and Florist.
Website: http://www.weluvgardening.com.
Parksville, 609 East Island Hwy.
Tel: (250) 248-0093 Fax: (250) 248-0284
Victoria, 4660 Elk Lake Drive
Tel: (250) 658-5414 Fax: (250) 658-5052

Most of the nursery stock is grown at their nursery in Chilliwack. They have a large selection of field-grown trees, including hedging cedar and a number of shade and fruit trees. They also have a wide variety of water plants, and carry all the necessary pool/pond supplies. Check individual locations for hours of business.

Cedar Hill Nurseries and Garden Centre, 1550 Church Ave., Victoria, B.C., V8P 2H1. **Tel:** (250) 477-2658. **Hours:** Monday to Saturday 9:00 a.m. to 5:30 p.m.; Sunday 10:00 a.m. to 5:00 p.m.

They have a good selection of rhododendrons, winter-flowering shrubs, spring bulbs and other interesting plants.

Danica Nurseries, 6705 Pat Bay Hwy., Victoria, B.C., V8Y 1T9. **Tel:** (250) 652-2718. **Fax:** (250) 652-5665. **E-mail:** danicanurseries@home.com. **Hours:** 9:00 a.m. to 5:00 p.m. daily. Extended hours in spring.

This nursery, specializing in ornamental shrubs, grows 95 percent of their own stock.

B. Dinter Nursery, 2205 Phipps Rd., R.R. #7, Duncan, B.C., V9L 6L2. **Tel:** (250) 748-2023 or (250) 748-0544. **E-mail:** bdinter@cowichan.com. **Website:** http://www.cowichan.com/dinternursery. **Hours:** 8:00 a.m. to 6:00 p.m. daily.

One of the Nurseryland group of garden centres with a good selection of nursery stock.

Elk Lake Garden Centre, 5450 Pat Bay Hwy., Victoria, B.C., V8Y 1T1. **Tel:** (250) 658-8812. **Hours:** 9:00 a.m. to 5:30 p.m. daily.

In this garden centre the focus is on "instant colour" in the form of annuals, bedding plants, hanging baskets and a wide selection of plants for containers. There is a limited selection of shrubs, clematis, rhododendrons, perennials and bare-root roses.

Firwood Nursery, 5631 Batu Rd., Victoria, B.C., V8Z 6K5. **Tel:** (250) 658-5102. **E-mail:** itodd@pinc.com. **Hours:** Phone ahead to visit this lovely woodland garden and nursery.

Firwood propagates and grows an interesting selection of rhododendrons. Currently they offer more than 200 species and 400 hybrid varieties. Most are grown from cuttings from their own stock plants; some are grown from tissue culture liners; some are imported from a leading Washington grower, and a few are grown from seed. Please note that this is a small nursery, so there is a limited number of plants of each variety. Catalogue available on request.

For Wild Birds and Gardeners, 4596 West Saanich Rd., Victoria, B.C., V8Z 3G4. **Tel:** (250) 881-7515. **Fax:** (250) 881-8550. **Hours:** Monday to Friday 11:00 a.m. to 5:30 p.m., Saturday 10:30 a.m. to 5:30 p.m., Sunday 12 noon to 5:30 p.m.

Here you will find plants that attract wild birds and butterflies. Penstemons, salvias, kniphofias, hardy fuchsias, mimulus, lobelia, phygelius and monarda are some of the many choice and unusual plants that they propagate. They also sell rare perennials and grasses.

The Garden Path, 395 Conway Rd., Victoria, B.C., V8R 3X1. **Tel:** (250) 881-1555. **Fax:** (250) 881-1304. **Website:** http://www.earthfuture.com/gardenpath. **Hours:** April, May and June, open daily 10:00 a.m. to 5:00 p.m.

This organic plant nursery specializes in heritage plants and seeds and has a wonderful selection of heirloom vegetables, herbs and perennials. It has recently moved to its new location on 2 1/2 acres (1 ha), and you are invited to view the demonstration gardens. Phone or check the website for information on workshops and plant sales.

GardenWorks
Website: http://www.gardenworks.ca.
Colwood, 1859 Old Island Hwy.
Tel: (250) 478-2027 Fax: (250) 478-5796
Saanich, 4290 Blenkinsop Rd.
Tel: (250) 721-2140 Fax: (250) 721-2821
Victoria, 1916 Oak Bay Ave.
Tel: (250) 595-4200 Fax: (250) 595-4644
Check hours of operation at individual locations. Good general nursery stock.

Green Thumb Garden Centre, 6261 Hammond Bay Rd., Nanaimo, B.C., V9S 5N7. **Tel:** (250) 758-0944. **Fax:** (250) 758-1987. **Hours:** 9:00 a.m. to 5:30 p.m. March 1 to October 31; 9:00 a.m. to 5:00 p.m. November 1 to February 28.

This garden centre propagates and grows their own rhododendrons, which are mostly hybrids, as well as bringing in locally grown trees, roses, perennials and annuals. They will fill special orders for hanging baskets and "refill" for their regulars. They carry evergreens in larger sizes, especially pines and some spruce.

Haida Gold Gardens, 769 Chaster Rd., Courtenay, B.C., V9N 5P2. **Tel:** (250) 338-8345. **Hours:** Please call ahead for appointment.

This is another hobby nursery run by a rhododendron enthusiast. A wide variety of rhododendron hybrids and species are propagated and grown and can be viewed in the display garden.

Happy Valley Lavender and Herb Farm, 3505 Happy Valley Rd., Victoria, B.C., V9C 2Y2. **Tel/Fax:** (250) 474-5767. **Hours:** Friday, Saturday and Sunday the second weekend in July or by appointment.

The focus here is on lavender and all its related products. They grow over a thousand lavender plants

in eight different varieties. Potted plants, as well as dried lavender, are for sale.

Hazelwood Farm, 13576 Adshead Rd., R.R. #1, Ladysmith, B.C., V9G 1H6. **Tel:** (250) 245-8007. **Fax:** (250) 245-2775. **E-mail:** hazelwood@ultranet.ca. **Website:** http://www.ultranet.ca/hazelwood. **Hours:** April to September daily 11:00 a.m. to 5:00 p.m.; October to December, Friday to Sunday 11:00 a.m. to 5:00 p.m. or by appointment.

Located 4 miles (6 km) north of Ladysmith, half a mile (.8 km) from the Island Highway off Cedar Rd. (look for signs). Hazelwood specializes in culinary, medicinal and ornamental herbs. They have a wide selection of scented geraniums and now sell approximately 400 varieties of herb plants. Their gift shop is stocked with numerous products made from the herbs they grow. There are two gardens open to the public: the production garden where they grow and harvest herbs and a large formal display garden. Herbal-related classes in soapmaking, skin care, gardening and cooking are held at the farm each year.

Hillier Water Gardens and Nurseries, 985 Howard Rd. off the Alberni Highway, Qualicum Beach, B.C., V9K 1W4. **Tel:** (250) 752-6109. **Fax:** (250) 752-1890. **Hours:** Open every day except Wednesday from 9:30 a.m. to 4:30 p.m. (later in the summer). Closed January and February.

This nursery sells everything for the water garden and specializes in the unusual. Approximately 30 ponds house an enormous selection of aquatic, bog and poolside plants. The nursery also carries a good variety of ferns, ornamental grasses and groundcovers. Pool liners and accessories, such as underwater lights, pumps, fountains and ornaments are available, and there is a selection of water-gardening books. Plant list is available.

C.E. Jones Nursery, "The Native Plant Place," Kanishay Rd., North Saanich, B.C. **Tel:** (250) 655-1374. **Fax:** (250) 655-1356. **Hours:** Call ahead but generally open seven days a week in April, May, June, September and October.

This nursery does not have a st. number but is located off West Saanich Rd. near Deep Cove. As the name suggests, it deals only in native plants and has a huge selection of trees, shrubs, perennials and groundcovers.

Kilmalu Farms Daylily Nursery, 624 Kilmalu Rd., R.R. #2, Mill Bay, B.C., V0R 2P0. **Tel/Fax:** (250) 743-5446. **E-mail:** kilmalu@coastnet.com. **Hours:** July during peak bloom, but please phone ahead.

Primarily a mail-order nursery but open for visitors during bloom season in July. This is an excellent opportunity to see the daylilies and make your choice, rather than reading descriptions in the catalogue. There is a good selection, ranging from the tried and true to the latest introductions. An informative catalogue is available.

Kingfisher Orchids, 615 Cromar Rd., Sidney, B.C., V8L 5M5. **Tel:** (250) 656-3094. **Fax:** (250) 656-3025. **Hours:** Greenhouses open Sunday by appointment.

Kingfisher sells orchids and supplies, and has a good collection of *Phalaenopsis* species.

Le Coteau Farms and Garden Centre, 304 Walton Place, R.R. #3, Victoria, B.C., V8X 3X1. **Tel/Fax:** (250) 658-5888. **E-mail:** farms@lecoteau.bc.ca. **Website:** http://www.lecoteau.bc.ca/farms.

A family business for 40 years on a farm of about 25 acres (10 ha), their specialty is fruit trees. They also have a good selection of shrubs, perennials, climbers, annuals and herbs.

Long Lake Nurseries and Florist, 4900 Island Highway North, Nanaimo, B.C., V9T 1W6. **Tel:** (250) 758-5012. **Hours:** 9:00 a.m. to 5:00 p.m. daily.

Long Lake has 2 acres (.8 ha) of retail space and carries perennials, shrubs (including some hard-to-find hybrid rhododendrons), and a large selection of heathers. Herbs are also available. For water gardens they have a supply of garden pool liners, pumps, accessories and aquatic plants.

Marigold NurseryLtd., 7874 Lockside Drive, Saanichton, B.C., V8M 2B9. **Tel:** (250) 652-3312. **Fax:** (250) 652-1330. **E-mail:** marigold@bengal.net.

Their specialty is annuals, but they also have a good general nursery stock.

Meadow Oak Nursery, 1070 Wain Rd., Sidney, B.C., V8L 5V1. **Tel:** (250) 655-1756. **Fax:** (250) 655-1786. **Hours:** Open seven days a week 9:00 a.m. to 5:00 p.m. February to mid-December, with longer opening hours in the spring.

This nursery specializes in flowering and ornamental shade trees. They have a wide selection of trees and shrubs with many unusual and hard-to-find varieties. They also have many perennials and annuals, which they propagate and grow.

Oakridge Nursery and Garden Centre, 3537 Cowichan Valley (Hwy. 18), Duncan, B.C., V9L 5Z4. **Tel:** (250) 746-5846. **E-mail:** roses@oakridge.com. **Website:** http://www.oakridgenursery.com. **Hours:** February 15 to April 1, Thursday to Monday

9:30 a.m. to 5:30 p.m.; April 1 to July 13, daily 9:30 a.m. to 5:30 p.m.; July 14 to October 31, Thursday to Monday 9:30 a.m. to 5:30 p.m. Off-season by appointment only.

This garden centre specializes in hardy, disease-resistant roses suited to our west coast climate. Medilland roses are grafted and unwaxed and sold bare root or in 2 1/2-gallon pots, depending on the season. They also have a selection of perennials, annuals, shrubs and clematis.

Orchids North, 7005 Brentwood Drive, R.R. #1, Brentwood Bay, B.C., V0S 1A0. **Tel/Fax:** (250) 652-6133. **Hours:** Call ahead.

Specialty growers and importers of orchids, both species and hybrids, they will ship orders across Canada.

Orchid Species Specialist, 3880 Telegraph Rd., R.R. #2, Cobble Hill, B.C., V0R 1L0. **Tel:** (250) 743-5134. **Hours:** By appointment.

They have greenhouse supplies, osmunda, firbark and treefern fibre, sphagnum pellets and orchid plants and will ship across Canada.

Pacific Ponds, 8370 East Saanich Rd., Saanichton, B.C. **Tel:** (250) 652-5028. **E-mail:** ponds-r-us@home.com. **Website:** http://www.hookedonwatergardens.com. **Hours:** March 1 to October 30, 10:00 a.m. to 5:00 p.m. daily. Closed on Mondays.

Here you will find everything you need for the water garden, from plants, liners, pumps and filters to fish, snails and tadpoles. The nursery, situated on a large property, has pond, stream and waterfall displays. There are four greenhouses full of water plants, with tropical water lilies and lotus a specialty. Pacific Ponds is a full-service pond company and does construction as well as pond maintenance. Plant catalogue available.

Ponds'n' Stuff, 3525 James Heights, Victoria, B.C., V8P 3R6. **Tel:** (250) 389-1125. **Hours:** Open by appointment.

This nursery carries an interesting selection of water plants. They sell butyl rubber pond liners, pumps and fountains, and offer consultation and design services.

Poul Hansen Orchids, 4980 Echo Drive, R.R. #7, Victoria, B.C., V8X 3X3. **Tel/Fax:** (250) 479-3272. **E-mail:** adele.poulhansen@telus.net. **Hours:** By appointment.

This well-known *Miltonia* grower has a good selection of plants and will ship across Canada. No catalogue available.

Ravenhill Herb Farm, 1330 Mt. Newton Crossroad, Saanichton, B.C., V8M 1S1. **Tel:** (250) 652-4024. **Fax:** (250) 544-1185. **E-mail:** andnoel@pacificcoast.net. **Website:** http://www.slugsandsalal.com. **Hours:** Sunday 12:00 noon to 5:00 p.m., from April to August.

There are many interesting culinary herbs plus some standard rosemary and bay trees. They host an annual craft fair in their barn at the end of November, which is advertised in the local papers.

Rhodo Mania, 3582 - 17th Ave., Port Alberni, B.C., V9Y 5E9. **Tel/Fax:** (250) 723-6677. **Hours:** Please call ahead for appointment.

This hobby nursery specializes in rhododendrons, with many interesting and rare varieties imported from the U.S.

Russell Farms, 1370 Wain Rd., North Saanich (take Wain Rd./Deep Cove exit off Pat Bay Highway). **Tel:** (250) 656-0384. **E-mail:** russellnursery@telus.net. **Hours:** Open March through December, closed Mondays, except for holidays.

A family-owned and -operated nursery, specializing in shade and ornamental trees, with a very good selection of Japanese maples. They also have a wide selection of interesting shrubs, perennials, climbers, annuals and herbs. There is a small display garden in which to view some of the perennials and ornamental grasses that are available at the nursery.

Snapdragon Nursery, 2360 Beacon Ave., Sidney, B.C. **Tel:** (250) 656-5199. **Fax:** (250) 656-8916. **Hours:** 9:30 a.m. to 5:30 p.m., 7 days a week; extended hours during spring.

A family-owned business started in 1989, specializing in growing a large selection of uncommon varieties of bedding plants. They carry a complete line of nursery stock, perennials, water plants and house plants and make unusual baskets and colour bowls.

Stone Tree Nursery, 2271 Lake Trail Rd., Courtenay, B.C., V9N 9C3. **Tel/Fax:** (250) 338-9785. **Hours:** March to December, Wednesday to Saturday 10:00 a.m. to 5:00 p.m., or by appointment.

This home-based business has become one of Vancouver Island's largest suppliers of bonsai and related products. They offer choice selections of trees, shrubs and perennials along with water garden supplies, garden pottery and seasonal cut flowers. The nursery, situated on a 1-acre (.4-ha) site, has display gardens in which to view the plants for sale.

Streamside Native Plants, 3300 Fraser Rd., R.R. #6, Site 695, C6, Courtenay, B.C., **Tel/Fax:** (250) 338-7509. **E-mail:** barport@mars.ark.com. **Website:** http://mars.ark.com/~barport/streamside.htm. **Hours:** Thursday, Friday and Saturday from mid-March to July and during September, 10:00 a.m. to 5:00 p.m., or phone ahead for an appointment.

This nursery specializes in the propagation of woody shrubs and perennials from the Comox Valley and northern Vancouver Island genetic stock. Although primarily growing for restoration projects, they also propagate a wide selection of native shade- and sun-loving perennials, groundcovers, ferns and shrubs.

Whitegate Farm, 3700 Kingburn Rd., R.R. #1, Cobble Hill, B.C., V0R 1L0. **Tel:** (250) 743-7106. **Hours:** Open April to October, Wednesday to Saturday, 12 noon to 6:00 p.m., or anytime by appointment.

This nursery specializes in fragrant plants and has a wonderful selection of peonies, lilies, scented geraniums, clematis, sweet peas, herbs and roses, with an emphasis on unusual perennials. Fresh-cut flowers are also available, as well as some dried flowers.

The Gulf Islands and the Sunshine Coast

The Bamboo Ranch, 185 Thomas Rd., Salt Spring Island, B.C., V8K 1R2. **Tel:** (250) 537-1808. **E-mail:** bamboo@saltspring.com. **Hours:** By appointment only.

Over 50 varieties of bamboo are available, from dwarf to giant timber. Phone ahead for an appointment. Price list available on request.

Cusheon Creek Nursery, 175 Stewart Rd., Salt Spring Island, B.C., V8K 2C4. **Tel:** (250) 537-9334. **Fax:** (250) 537-9354. **E-mail:** cusheoncreek@saltspring.com. **Website:** http://www.theamateursdigest.com/cusheon.htm. **Hours:** March 1 to October 31, Thursday and Friday 10:00 a.m. to 5:00 p.m., Saturday 12 noon to 5:00 p.m.; November 1 to February 28, by appointment only.

The nursery specializes in drought-resistant plants and carries a wide variety of unusual trees, shrubs and perennials, and many species of cacti and succulents. The owners do almost all their own propagating, largely growing from seed.

Dahlias Galore, located at 5245 Selma Park Rd., Selma Park, Sechelt. Mailing address: R.R. #1, Legion Site C22, Sechelt, B.C., V0N 3A0. **Tel/Fax:** (604) 885-4841. **Hours:** August 1 to October 15, open Monday to Saturday 9:00 a.m. to 6:00 p.m., Sunday viewing only 1:00 to 6:00 p.m.

Tubers and cut flower sales. The large field of blooming dahlias in summer is quite a sight to behold—great for choosing the variety you want. Order in the fall for spring shipment.

Foxglove Farm and Garden Supply, 104 Atkins Rd., Salt Spring Island, B.C., V8K 2R5. **Tel:** (250) 537-5531. **Hours:** Monday to Saturday 9:00 a.m. to 5:30 p.m.

Foxglove has been in business for nearly 25 years, selling bulbs, perennials, old roses, shrubs and seeds. It also sells banana and ginger plants.

Fragrant Flora, 3741 Sunshine Coast Hwy., R.R. #22, Roberts Creek, B.C., V0N 2W2. **Tel/Fax:** (604) 885-6142. **E-mail:** fragrantflora@sunshine.net. **Hours:** Open March 15 to July 15 and September 1 to October 31, Thursday to Sunday from 12 noon to 5:00 p.m.; otherwise by appointment.

This nursery specializes in trees, shrubs, climbers and perennials that are scented and/or attractive to butterflies and hummingbirds. It's located in a tranquil forest setting. Mail order and a detailed catalogue are available.

Fraser's Thimble Farms, 175 Arbutus Rd., Salt Spring Island, B.C., V8K 1A3. **Tel/Fax:** (250) 537-5788. **E-mail:** thimble@saltspring.com. **Website:** http://www.thimblefarms.com. **Hours:** March 1 to June 30 daily 10:00 a.m. to 4:30 p.m. Closed Mondays from July 1 to February 28 and occasionally for weeks at a time in August, around midwinter and late February. Best to phone ahead in off-season.

A family business and the oldest nursery on the Gulf Islands, Fraser's Thimble Farms occupies 2 1/2 acres (1 ha) and stocks a wide variety of perennials, shrubs and trees. They specialize in North American and Pacific Northwest native, rare and unusual plants, and carry over 500 species, including ferns, hardy orchids, grasses, arisaemas and trilliums. Collector's list available, or check the website.

Old Rose Nursery, 1020 Central Rd., Hornby Island, B.C., V0R 1Z0. **Tel:** (250) 335-2603 or (250) 335-2602. **E-mail:** oldrose@mars.ark.com. **Website:** http://www.oldrosenursery.com. **Hours:** vary with the season, so please call ahead.

Old Rose sells wholesale to nurseries throughout Vancouver Island, sells retail from the nursery, and ships to destinations in western Canada in spring and fall. They specialize in old-fashioned and heritage roses, growing the roses from cuttings and propagating many hundreds of different kinds. Catalogue is $4.00 by request or available for view on their website: there is a January list for spring sales and an August list for fall sales. Shipping and delivery can be arranged.

The Plant Farm, 177 Vesuvius Bay Rd., Salt Spring Island, B.C., V8K 1K3. **Tel/Fax:** (250) 537-5995. **Hours:** February 15 to November 15, Thursday to Monday, 10:00 a.m. to 4:00 p.m.

Over 3 acres (1.2 ha) of display gardens with an emphasis on low-maintenance plants, including bamboo, rhododendrons, grasses, hostas, daylilies and beardless iris. A catalogue is available for $3.00 and they will ship anywhere in Canada, spring and fall.

Shikoku Bonsai, R.R. #24, 2530 Miles Rd., Roberts Creek, B.C., V0N 2W4. **Tel:** (604) 886-3915. **Fax:** (604) 886-0284. **Hours:** Open most Sundays, 12 noon to 4:00 p.m., and Monday to Saturday by appointment.

Shikoku grow all their plants from seed or cuttings and have an inventory of over 12,000 trees. Owner Gerald Rainville is internationally known for his bonsai cultivation. They ship Canada-wide.

Wheelbarrow Nursery, 2280 South Rd., Gabriola Island, B.C. **Tel:** (250) 247-8728. **Fax:** (250) 247-8726. **Hours:** Daily 9:00 a.m. to 5:00 p.m. from March to October. Winter hours are flexible; call ahead.

A delightful nursery set in the owner's garden in the middle of the forest. The garden has a big pond with giant gunnera, unusual trees and a collection of remarkable 35- to 40-year-old fuchsias. There's also a large selection of ornamental trees, flowering shrubs and evergreens. It's worth a visit if you are on the island, even if you're not in the market for plants.

Willow Farm Nursery, 6739 Norwest Bay Rd., Box 787, Sechelt, B.C., V0N 3A0. **Tel:** (604) 885-3989. **Fax:** (604) 740-9913. **Hours:** Closed Tuesdays. Otherwise open daily, 10:00 a.m. to 6:00 p.m., February 15 to December 24.

This nursery specializes in trees and shrubs, particularly Japanese maples, some perennials and ferns.

Mail-order Gardening

There are hundreds of glossy mail-order catalogues to tempt gardeners and kindle enthusiasm. Some are free, while others have to be purchased. Here is a list to get you started, with an emphasis on Canadian-based catalogues. In addition, garden magazines usually give extensive lists in their midwinter issues, and the Internet is a treasure trove of addresses, one of the most comprehensive of which is http://www.icangarden.com/catalogue/seedalph.htm.

Abundant Life Seed Foundation, Box 772, Port Townsend, WA 98368. **Tel:** (360) 385-5660. **Fax:** (360) 385-7455. **E-mail:** abundant@olypen.com. **Website:** http://csf.colorado.edu/perma/abundant.

Non-profit organization specializing in open-pollinated, heirloom seeds; 62 pages.

Aimers, 126 Catharine St. North, Hamilton, ON L8R 1J4. **Tel:** (905) 529-2601. **Fax:** (905) 528-1635. **E-mail:** bill.aimers@odyssey.on.ca.

A wide selection of unique flower varieties including individual wildflowers and mixes for across the country; $2, refundable; 42 pages; photos, botanical names.

Artemis Gardens, 30182 Harris Rd., Abbotsford, BC V4X 1Y9. **Tel:** (604) 856-0189. **Fax:** (604) 856-0393. **E-mail:** daylilies@artemisgardens.com. **Website:** http://artemisgardens.com.

Over 700 varieties of field-grown daylilies.

Aurora Farm, 3492 Phillips Rd., Creston, BC V0B 1G2. **Tel/Fax:** (250) 428-4404. **E-mail:** aurora@kootenay.com. **Website:** http://www.kootenay.com/~aurora.

Open-pollinated and heirloom herb, flower and vegetable seeds; $3.

Blue Haven Specialty, 2881 Church Way, R.R. #2, Mill Bay, BC V0R 2P0. **Tel/Fax:** (250) 743-3876. **E-mail:** plants@bluehavennursery.com. **Website:** http://bluehavennursery.com.

This nursery specializes in meconopsis, primulas and other rare and unusual perennials. An extensive catalogue is posted on their website.

Bluestem Ornamental Grasses, 1949 Fife Rd., Christina Lake, BC V0H 1E3. **Tel/Fax:** (250) 447-6363.

Ornamental grasses, willows and native plant seed; $2; 30 pages, photos.

Boltons Seeds, Robert Bolton and Son, the Sweet Pea Specialists, Birdbrook, near Halstead, Essex, England, C09, 4BQ. Sweet pea seeds.

Brentwood Bay Nurseries Ltd., 1395 Benvenuto Ave., Brentwood Bay, BC V8M 1J5. **Tel:** (250) 652-1507. **Fax:** (250) 652-2761. **E-mail:** plants@coastnet.com.

Perennials, shrubs, vines, grasses and roses. Rose list, 25 pages; perennial list, 50 pages. Each list $2, refundable; botanical names.

The Butchart Gardens Ltd., Box 4010, Victoria, BC, V8X 3X4. **Tel:** (250) 652-4422. **Fax:** (250) 652-1475. **E-mail:** email@butchartgardens.bc.ca. **Website:** http://www.butchartgardens.com/seed/index.html.

Seeds for annuals and perennials, including collections for window boxes, and children's, cottage and rock gardens. Free.

Campbell Craig Delphiniums, 14219 Middle-bench Rd., Oyama, BC, V4V 2B9. **Tel:** (250) 548-9271. **Fax:** (250) 548-4134. **Website:** http://www.members.cnx.net/camcraig/delphiniums.

Delphinium plants grown from hand-pollinated seed. SASE for list; germination instructions.

The Cedar Creek Seed Company, 254 East 1st St., North Vancouver, BC, V7L 1B3. **Tel:** 604) 984-6594. **Fax:** (604) 984-6558. **E-mail:** cedarcrk@infinet.net.

Wildflower mixes and more than 90 individual varieties, including wild perennial sunflower, wild perennial sweet pea and rose angel. Free; 6 pages.

Chiltern Seeds, Bortree Stile, Ulverston, Cumbria, England LA12 7PB. **Tel:** 011-44-229/581137. **E-mail:** chilternseeds@compuserve.com. **Website:** http://www.chilternseeds.co.uk.

More than 4,000 seeds for unusual perennials, annuals and trees; $4 Cdn.; botanical names.

Choice & Lovely Seeds, Box 1830, Sechelt, BC V0N 3A0.

Rare and common perennials and native plants; meconopsis, lobelias, primulas, verbascums and alceas; plants for wildlife, fragrance and foliage interest. $3/2 years; botanical names.

Cottage Trail Gardens, 2507 - 36th Ave., Vernon, BC V1T 2V6. **Tel:** (250) 558-7791.

Hardy perennials, helianthemum, thymes and other perennials. $2; 15 pages; botanical names.

Cruickshank's Inc., 780 Birchmount Rd., Unit 16, Scarborough, ON M1K 5H4. **Tel:** (800) 665-5605. **Fax:** (416) 750-8522. **Website:** http://www.cruickshanks.com.

Bulbs, irises, poppies, peonies, lilies, gladioli, tuberous begonias and dahlias. Gardening tools and accessories. Three catalogues yearly; $3/year; photos, botanical names.

Cusheon Creek Nursery, 175 Stewart Rd., Salt Spring Island, BC V8K 2G4. **Tel:** (250) 537-9334. **Fax:** (250) 537-9354. **E-mail:** cusheoncreek@saltspring.com.

Drought-resistant species, indoor cacti, hardy succulents, alpines; unusual perennials, trees and shrubs. Free plant list.

Dahlias Galore, R.R. #1, Legion Site, C22, Sechelt, BC V0N 3A0. **Tel:** (604) 885-9820. **Fax:** (604) 885-4841.

Dahlias and Japanese iris. Free list with SASE.

Dominion Seed House, Box 2500, Georgetown, ON L7G 5L6. **Orders:** (800) 784-3037. **Fax:** (800) 282-5746. **Website:** http://www.dominion-seed-house.com.

Flower and vegetable seeds; bulbs, garden accessories; plants. Free; 130 pages, two catalogues per year; photos; botanical names.

Erikson's Daylily Gardens, 24642 - 51st Ave., Langley, BC V2Z 1H9. **Tel:** (604) 856-5758. **E-mail:** pamela@istar.ca. **Website:** http://www.plantlovers.com.

Retail catalogue and wholesale lists of over 1,400 daylilies. $3; good information and photos.

e-seeds.com. **Tel:** (877) 373-3376 or (604) 222-2402. **Fax:** (604) 222-9718. **Website:** http://www.eseeds.com.

Internet sales of seeds, plants, bulbs, gifts, tools and art, from international suppliers. Descriptions of plants include botanical and common names, cultivation, propagation, history and folklore.

Ferncliff Gardens, 8394 McTaggart St., Mission, BC V2V 6S6. **Tel:** (604) 826-2447. **Fax:** (604) 826-4316.

More than 200 dahlias, irises, peonies and daylilies.

Fraser's Thimble Farms, 175 Arbutus Rd., Salt Spring Island, BC V8K 1A3. **Tel/Fax:** (250) 537-5788. **Website:** http://www.thimblefarms.com.

Hard to find, nursery-grown, Pacific northwest native plants, ferns, unusual perennials, shrubs and trees. Catalogue $3; fall bulb list (available midsummer) $2.

Free Spirit Nursery, 20405 - 32nd Ave., Langley, BC V2Z 2C7. **Tel:** (604) 533-7373. **Fax:** (604) 530-3776. **Website:** http://www.plantlovers.com.

Ornamental grasses, perennials, vines and specialty shrubs. Assortment list for $1.50 in SASE .

Garden Crazy, 128 St. Laurent, Beauharnois, PQ J6S 6G3. **Tel:** (888) 442-7299. **Fax:** (888) 442-7298. **Website:** http://www.gardencrazy.com.

Online garden centre with seeds, bulbs, perennials, herbs, planters, books, hoses and reels, glass greenhouse kits, water gardening supplies, fertilizers, beneficial insects, bird houses, bird feeders, specialty bird food, wind chimes, weather vanes, fountains, statuary and more.

Garden Import, Box 760, Thornhill, ON L3T 4A5. **Tel:** (905) 731-1950 or (800) 339-8314. **Fax:** (905) 881-3499. **Website:** http://www.gardenimport.com.

Unusual perennials, flowering shrubs, David Austin roses, Evison clematis, hostas, summer-flowering bulbs, Sutton seeds. $5 for 2 years (4 issues), refundable; 90 pages, photos, botanical names.

The Heather Farm, Box 2206, Sardis, BC, V2R 1A6. **Tel:** (604) 823-4884.

More than 200 varieties of heaths and heathers. Free list with SASE; 4 pages, detailed descriptions.

Heronswood Nursery, 7530 NE 288th St., Kingston, WA 98346-9502. **Tel:** (360) 297-4172. **Fax:** (360) 297-8231. **Website:** http://www.heronswood.com.

New and hard-to-find conifers, shrubs, trees, vines, perennials and grasses. $5 US; 300 pages, 2,600 listings.

Hole's Greenhouse and Gardens Ltd., 101 Bellerose Drive, St. Albert, AB T8N 8N8. **Tel:** (888) 884-6537. **Fax:** (403) 459-6042.

Perennials, annuals, roses, seeds, fruit and shade trees, garden accessories. Free; photos.

Holt Geraniums, 34465 Hallert Rd., Abbotsford, BC V3G 1R3. **Tel:** (604) 859-3207. **Website:** http://www.holtgeraniums.com.

More than 1000 varieties of pelargoniums; $2; photos.

Hortico Inc., 723 Robson Rd., R.R. #1, Waterdown, ON L0R 2H1. **Tel:** (905) 689-9323. **Fax:** (905) 689-6566. **E-mail:** office@hortico.com. **Website:** http://www.hortico.com.

Perennials, roses and shrubs. Botanical names, rose catalogue, photos; $3; 45 pages.

Island Seed Co., Box 4278, Depot 3, Victoria, BC V8X 3X8. **Tel:** (250) 744-3677. **Fax:** (250) 479-0221.

Seeds for culinary herbs, heirloom vegetables and old-fashioned flower seeds; emphasis on heritage, disease resistance. $2, refundable.

Kilmalu Farms Daylily Nursery, 624 Kilmalu Rd., R.R. #2, Mill Bay, BC V0R 2P0. **Tel/Fax:** (250) 743-5446. **E-mail:** daylilies@kilmalu.com.

A good selection of daylilies ranging from the tried and true to the latest introductions. An informative catalogue is available.

Lee Valley Tools Ltd., P.O. Box 6295, Station J, Ottawa, ON K2A 1T4. **Tel:** (800) 267-8767. **E-mail**: customerservice@leevalley.com. **Website:** http://www.leevalley.com.

Excellent selection of garden tools and supplies, including do-it-yourself kits for benches, chairs, etc.

McFayden Seed Co. Ltd., 30 - 9th St., Suite 200, Brandon, MB R7A 6N4. **Tel:** (800) 205-7111. **Fax:** (204) 725-1888.

Seeds, hardy perennials, bulbs, roses, trees, shrubs and garden products. Free; photos.

Mason Hogue Gardens, 3520 Durham Rd., 1 (Brock Rd.), R.R. #4, Uxbridge, ON L9P 1R4.

Perennials, including hardy geraniums, drought-tolerant plants, unusual container plants. $2; 50 pages; botanical names.

Meadowsweet Farms Garden Nursery, 19656 - 16th Ave., South Langley, BC V2Z 1K1. **Tel:** (604) 530-2611. **Fax:** (604) 530-9996. **E-mail:** meadowsweet@pacificgroup.net. **Website:** http://www.plantlovers.com.

Large selection of perennials, hostas and ornamental grasses; $3.

Nature's Garden Seed Co., Box 32105, 3749 Shelbourne St., Victoria, BC V8P 5S2. **Tel:** (250) 595-2062. **Fax:** (250) 595-7195. **E-mail:** naturesgarden@bc.sympatico.ca. **Website:** http://www.naturesgardenseed.com.

Native flower, shrub and tree seeds; butterfly and hummingbird native plant mix, children's vegetable gardening book with seeds; botanical T-shirts. $1, refundable; 12 pages.

P. & J. Greenhouse, 20265 - 82nd Ave., R.R. #11, Langley, BC V2Y 2A9. **Tel:** (604) 888-3274. **Fax:** (604) 888-3211.

Over 1,500 varieties of geraniums; other plants from around the world. $3; fuchsia catalogue, $2.

The Perennial Gardens Inc., 13139 - 224th St., Maple Ridge, BC V4R 2P6. **Tel:** (604) 467-4218. **Fax:** (604) 467-3181. **Website:** http://www.perennialgardener.com.

Spring catalogue: hostas, geraniums, primulas, ferns, ornamental grasses, astilbe and a large selection of unusual herbaceous perennials. Fall catalogue: hemerocallis, iris, ranunculus, bulbs and other perennials. $4 for 2 years.

P.K. Growers, 22646 - 48th Ave., Langley, BC V2Z 2T6. **Tel:** (604) 530-2035. **Fax:** (604) 530-2022. **E-mail:** pfitness@uniserve.com. **Website:** http://www.plantlovers.com.

Fuchsias, including trailers, uprights, species and hardies; pelargoniums, including regals, angels, stellars and scenteds. $2, refundable.

The Plant Farm, 177 Vesuvius Bay Rd., Salt Spring Island, BC V8K 1K3. **Tel/Fax:** (250) 537-5995.

Bamboo, hostas, roses, rhododendrons (including hardy Finnish), heathers, ornamental grasses, beardless iris, perennial geraniums and daylilies. $3 for 2 years.

Rainforest Nursery, 1470 - 227th St., Langley, BC V2Z 1K6. **Tel:** (604) 530-3499. **Fax:** (604) 530-3480. **Website:** http://www.plantlovers.com.

Grasses, perennials, shrubs, annuals, bog and marginal plants; $5.

Salt Spring Seeds, Box 444, Ganges P.O., Salt Spring Island, BC V8K 2W1. **Tel:** (250) 537-5269. **Website:** http://www.saltspring.com/ssseeds.

Beans, grains, tomatoes, lettuce, garlic, amaranth, quinoa; all certified organic. $2; 20 pages, growing instructions.

Scents of Time Gardens, 11948 - 207th St., Suite 204, Maple Ridge, BC V2X 1X7. **Website:** http://www.members.tripod.com/~scents_of_time_gardn.

Authentic, original varieties of heritage seeds for flowers, vegetables and herbs, including 17 types of fragrant antique sweetpeas. Catalogue $10 for 2 years; list $4 for 2 years.

Seeds of Diversity Canada, Box 36, Station Q, Toronto, ON M4T 2L7. **Tel:** (905) 623-0353. **Website:** http://www.seeds.ca.

Seed exchange for heirloom, rare and non-hybrid vegetables, fruits, flowers, grains and herbs. Magazine 3 times per year and annual seed listing with $25 membership.

Seeds of Victoria, 395 Conway Rd., Victoria, BC V8X 3X1. **Tel:** (250) 881-1555. **Fax:** (250) 881-1305.

Organic vegetable, flower and herb seeds collected from the Garden Path nursery garden in Victoria; also heritage plants, old-fashioned flowers and open-pollinated, heirloom vegetables; $2.

Stokes Seeds Ltd., 39 James St., Box 10, St. Catharines, ON L2R 6R6. **Tel:** (905) 688-4300. **Fax:** (888) 834-3334. **Website:** http://www.stokeseeds.com.

Flower, herb and vegetable seeds. Free; 112 pages, photos, growing instructions.

Thompson & Morgan Inc., Dept. PR99, Box 1308, Jackson, NJ 08527. **Tel:** (800) 274-7333. **Fax:** (888) 466-4769. **Website:** http://www. thompson-morgan.com.

Traditional seed varieties; also known for their rare and unusual varieties, many of which aren't obtainable elsewhere. More than 2,000 flower and vegetable varieties. Free; photos.

Tropic To Tropic Plants, 1170 - 53A St., South Delta, BC V4M 3E3. **Tel:** (604) 943-6562. **Fax:** (604) 948-1996.

More than 100 exotic varieties for Zone 8; also bamboos, eucalyptus, flowering ginger, bananas, cannas, passion fruit, vines and silk trees. $3, refundable; 6 pages; botanical names.

Vesey's Seeds Ltd., York, PEI C0A 1P0. **Tel:** (800) 363-7333. **Fax:** (800) 686-0329. **Website:** http://www.veseys.com.

Vegetable, herb and flower seeds for short seasons. Free; photos. Also fall-planted bulb catalogue for Canadian customers only; free.

West Coast Seeds Ltd., 8475 Ontario St., Suite 206, Vancouver, BC V5X 3E8. **Tel:** (604) 482-8800. **Fax:** (604) 482-8822. **Website:** http://www.westcoastseeds.com.

Vegetable, herb and flower seeds, including European, Oriental and heritage varieties. Free catalogue and organic gardening guide; 96 pages, photos, botanical names.

Western Biologicals Ltd., Box 283, Aldergrove, BC V4W 2T8. **Tel:** (604) 856-3339. **Website:** http://www.catscan.com.

Mushroom spawn and rare or medicinal herbs, including stevia. $3; 40 pages, cultivation information.

Whitegate Farm Nursery, 3700 Kingburn Rd., R.R. #1, Cobble Hill, BC V0R 1L0. **Tel/Fax:** (250) 743-7106.

Specializes in peonies, perennials, shrubs and bulbs noted for fragrance, and cut flowers. SASE with two 46¢ stamps; 15 pages, botanical names.

William Dam Seeds, Box 8400, Dundas, ON L9H 6M1. **Tel:** (905) 628-6641. **Fax:** (905) 627-1729. **E-mail:** willdam@sympatico.ca.

Untreated seeds; more than 900 varieties of vegetables, flowers and herbs. Free; 80 pages, photos.

Mail-order plant materials from abroad

If you are trying to locate a source of a particular plant, check out *Gardening by Mail* by Barbara Barton and Ginny Hunt (see Further Reading.).

How to import plants

Importing plants from the United States used to be a long process of filling out import permits and waiting for inspectors to check the plants once they arrived in Canada. Often, at the end of the process the result was the arrival of a weary, unhealthy-looking plant. The laws have changed and non-restricted plant material no longer requires an import permit. A Physosanitary Certificate issued by a state inspector and attached to your plant order is all that is required. This shortens the shipping time and means that the plant shipment can arrive by mail to your door.

If you are interested in importing plants, contact Agriculture Canada at 1-888-732-6222 to ensure the plant material you want to import has no restrictions. The change in rules makes it possible for Canadian visitors going to the Northwest Flower & Garden Show to bring back bare-rooted peonies, irises, lilies, and daylilies from the show.

For information regarding importing plants from other countries, contact your local Agriculture Canada office.

Horticultural Societies and Garden Clubs

Joining a garden club is a great way to share information, plants and ideas with other garden enthusiasts. Novices will find mentors to guide them, and the experienced will find a network of like enthusiasts to expand their knowledge. Seed exchanges, bulletins, plant shows, sales and tours are all part of the membership. Local garden societies and clubs are keen to welcome new members and we urge you to check out the ones that interest you.

With this edition we include contact names and telephone numbers only where necessary since often these are quickly out of date, whereas times and places tend to remain the same. The Internet is a good source for the most up-to-date information on societies and clubs. Good sites to check for

B.C. clubs are http://www.hedgerows.com, http://www.icangarden.com, and http://www.plantlovers.com. If you still have difficulty locating a particular club or society, try the B.C. Council of Garden Clubs.

Vancouver and the Lower Mainland

B.C. Council of Garden Clubs. Contact: Lorna Herchenson, (604) 929-5382; Peter Greenaway, (604) 524-1529 or (604) 619-2703 (cell phone).

This is an umbrella organization for about 150 garden clubs in the province. It provides a bimonthly bulletin for affiliated clubs and individual members, a list of potential garden speakers, a list of judges for horticultural events, and an up-to-date directory for member clubs. It also publishes a judging standards manual for non-specialized shows.

Aldergrove Daylily Society. Contact: Pam Erickson. **Tel:** (604) 856-5758.
Website: http://www.plantlovers.com.

Meet in members' homes from February to November, 7:30 p.m., third Thursday of the month.

Alpine Garden Club of B.C.
Website: http://www.hedgerows.com.

Meet at VanDusen Botanical Garden, 5251 Oak St., Vancouver, 7:30 p.m., second Wednesday of the month, September through June.

B.C. Bonsai Federation. Umbrella organization for most of the bonsai societies in B.C. **Website:** http://www.icangarden.com.

Meet at Japanese Gardeners Association, 4289 Slocan St., Vancouver, six times a year.

B.C. Bonsai Society.

Meet at Japan Bonsai, 16164 - 24th Ave., Surrey, 7:30 p.m., third Tuesday of the month except January and February.

B.C. Floral Art Society.

Meet at Elks Hall, 6884 Jubilee Ave., Burnaby, 10:00 a.m., second Monday of the month.

B.C. Fuchsia and Begonia Society. Contact: Lorna Herchenson. **Tel:** (604) 929-5382. **Website:** http://www.hedgerows.com.

Meet at St. Helen's Catholic Church gymnasium, 3971 Pandora St., Burnaby, 8:00 p.m., first Monday of the month except December.

B.C. Guild of Flower Arrangers.

Meet at VanDusen Botanical Garden, 5251 Oak St., 10:00 a.m., fourth Monday of the month, except August and December.

B.C. Lily Society. Contact: John Taylor. **Tel:** (604) 589-0623. **Website:** http://www.hedgerows.com.

No regularly scheduled meetings. Call or check website for meetings and special events.

B.C. Primula Group.
Website: http://www.hedgerows.com.

Meet at VanDusen Botanical Garden, 5251 Oak St., 7:30 p.m., third Wednesday in January, March, May, September and November.

Burnaby Cactus and Succulent Club. Contact: Pat Campbell. **Tel:** (604) 921-7042.

Meet at Bonsor Recreational Complex, 6650 Bonsor Ave., Burnaby, 12:30 p.m., fourth Wednesday of the month from September through May, except in December.

Burns Bog Conservation Society.
Website: http://www.burnsbog.paconline.net/.

Burns Bog, in Delta, is the largest undeveloped urban land mass in Canada. It is home to an amazing variety of plants and animals, including some rare and endangered species. The society aims to preserve the bog for "all life in perpetuity."

Butterfly Garden Resource Group.
Tel: (604) 530-4983.

Meet at the Campbell Valley Regional Park Visitors Centre, 8th Ave. and 204th St., first Tuesday of the month except December and January. Call ahead for details.

Canada Koi Club of B.C. Contact: Richard Adema. **Tel:** (604) 596-0211. **E-mail:** radema@sprint.ca.

Meet the second Sunday of the month at members' homes. Call or e-mail for information.

Canadian Geranium and Pelargonium Society.
Website: http://www.hedgerows.com.

Meet at St. Helen's Catholic Church gymnasium, 3971 Pandora St., Burnaby, 8:00 p.m., second Monday of the month.

Canadian Herb Society.
Website: http://www.herbsociety.ca.

Meet at VanDusen Botanical Garden, 5251 Oak St., 7:00 p.m., second Monday of the month from September to May. Date occasionally changes. Phone ahead to confirm.

Capilano Flower Arranging Club.

Meet at Delbrook Recreation Centre, 600 West Queens Rd., North Vancouver, 7:30 p.m., second Wednesday of the month from September to June.

Capilano Garden Club.
Meet at Canyon Heights Christian Assembly, Capilano Rd. and Mount Royal Boulevard, North Vancouver, 7:30 p.m., second Monday of the month except July and August.

Chilliwack Garden Club (formerly Chilliwack Horticultural Society).
Website: http://www.hedgerows.com.
Meet at Elks Hall, 46185 - 4th Ave., Chilliwack, 8:00 p.m., second Tuesday of the month (except January, July and August).

Chinese Penjing Society of Canada.
Meet at the Chinese Cultural Centre, 50 East Pender St., Vancouver, 7:00 p.m., third Sunday of the month.

Deep Cove Gardening Club. Contact: Lorna Herchenson. **Tel:** (604) 929-5382.
Meet at Seycove Community Secondary School, 1204 Caledonia Ave., North Vancouver, 7:30 p.m., last Thursday of the month except July, August and December.

Delbrook Garden Club. Contact: Judy Gunn. **Tel:** (604) 922-1433.
Meet in members' homes, 7:30 p.m., fourth Monday of the month except December, July and August. Membership limited.

Delta Diggers Garden Club.
Website: http://www.hedgerows.com.
Meet at Royal Heights United Church, 9316 - 116th St., North Delta, 7:30 p.m., third Thursday of the month except January and December.

Desert Plant Society of Vancouver. Contact: Pat Campbell. **Tel:** (604) 921-7042.
Meet at VanDusen Botanical Garden, 5251 Oak St., Vancouver. Dates and times are variable. Phone for details.

Dunbar Garden Club.
Website: http://www.hedgerows.com.
Meet at the Dunbar Community Centre, 4747 Dunbar St., Vancouver, 7:30 p.m., fourth Tuesday of the month.

Evergreen Garden Club.
Meet at the Phoenix Hall, 6062 - 16th Ave., Tsawwassen, 7:30 p.m., third Wednesday of the month except July and December.

Fraser Pacific Rose Society.
Website: http://www.hedgerows.com.

Meet at Dogwood Pavilion, 624 Poirier St., Coquitlam, 7:30 p.m., last Tuesday of the month except December.

Fraser South Rhododendron Society.
Website: http://www.hedgerows.com.
Meet at St. Andrew's Anglican Church Hall, 20955 Old Yale Rd., Langley, 8:00 p.m., third Wednesday of the month except July and August.

Fraser Valley Dahlia Society.
Website: http://www.hedgerows.com.
Meet at Central Heights Church, 1661 McCallum Rd., Abbotsford, 8:00 p.m., fourth Tuesday of the month, March through October.

Fraser Valley Gladiolus Society. Contact: Doug Lockwood. **Tel:** (604) 946-2532.
Time and location varies.

Fraser Valley Herb Society.
Website: http://www.hedgerows.com.
Meet at Flowers from a Country Garden, 3309 - 232nd Ave., Langley, 7:30 p.m., fourth Tuesday of the month except July, August and December.

Fraser Valley Heritage Tree Society. **Website:** http://www.freeyellow.com/members/fvhtreesociety/.
Meet at Kwantlen University College, Langley Campus, 8:00 p.m., second Thursday of the month, September to May.

Fraser Valley Koi and Water Garden Club.
Website: http://www.hedgerows.com.
Check the website for meeting times. Meetings rotate around the Fraser Valley at members' homes.

Fraser Valley Orchid Society. **Website:** http://www.chebucto.ns.ca/Recreation/OrchidSNS/fvos.html.
Meet at Langley Civic Centre, 20699 - 42nd Ave., Langley, at 8:00 p.m., first Wednesday of the month except July and August.

Fraser Valley Rhododendron Society.
Website: http://www.hedgerows.com.
Meet at St. Andrews Presbyterian Church, 22279 - 116th Ave., Maple Ridge, at 7:30 p.m., fourth Monday of the month from September to May.

The Honourable David C. Lam Gardening Society.
A club formed to help new immigrants learn about local gardening ways.
Meet at VanDusen Botanical Garden, 5251 Oak St., 7:00 p.m., first Tuesday of the month.

Japanese Gardeners Association Bonsai Club.
Website: http://www.icangarden.com.
Meet at West Coast Gardeners Coop of B.C., 4289 Slocan St., Vancouver, 7:30 p.m., on the fourth Friday of the month.

Langley Garden Club.
Website: http://www.hedgerows.com.
Meet at Sharon United Church Hall, 21562 Old Yale Rd., Langley, 7:00 p.m., first Friday of every month except January.

Lynn Valley Garden Club.
Website: http://www.hedgerows.com.
Meet at Lynn Valley United Church, 3201 Mountain Highway, North Vancouver, 7:30 p.m., third Thursday of the month except July and August.

Maple Ridge Garden Club.
Website: http://www.hedgerows.com.
Meet at Centennial Centre, 11940 - 224th St., Maple Ridge, 6:45 p.m., third Wednesday of the month, except December.

Mission Garden Club.
Website: http://www.hedgerows.com.
Meet at the Mission Library on 2nd Ave., 7:00 p.m., second Thursday of each month, except July, August and December.

Native Plant Society of B.C. (NPSBC).
E-mail: Npsbc@hotmail.com.
No monthly meetings. Members receive newsletter. Lots of local events.

New Westminster Horticultural Society.
Website: http://www.hedgerows.com.
Meet in Centennial Community Centre, 65 East 6th Ave., New Westminster, 8:00 p.m., second Tuesday of each month except January.

North Surrey Horticultural Society.
Meet at Southside Community Centre, 12642 - 100th Ave., Surrey, 8:00 p.m., second Tuesday of the month from March to November.

Pacific Northwest Palm and Exotic Plant Society.
Website: http://www.icangarden.com.
Meet at VanDusen Botanical Garden, 5251 Oak St., Vancouver, 7:30 p.m., last Monday in March, May, July, September and November.

Peace Arch Rhododendron Society.
Website: http://www.hedgerows.com.
Meet at St. John's Presbyterian Church, 1480 George St., White Rock, 7:30 p.m., third Monday of the month from September to June.

Pinegrove Garden Club.
Meet at the Seniors Centre, Matsqui Recreation Centre, 3106 Clearbrook Rd., Clearbrook, 7:30 p.m., fourth Tuesday of the month except December.

Poco Garden Club.
Website: http://www.hedgerows.com.
Meet at Trinity United Church Hall, Prairie Ave. and Shaughnessy St., Port Coquitlam, 7:30 p.m., third Tuesday of the month, except July, August and September.

Point Grey Chrysanthemum Club.
Website: http://www.hedgerows.com.
Meet at VanDusen Botanical Garden, 5251 Oak St., Vancouver, 8:00 p.m., second Thursday of the month except July and December.

Richmond Garden Club.
Website: http://www.hedgerows.com.
Meet at Minoru Sports Pavilion, 7191 Granville Ave., Richmond, 7:30 p.m., fourth Wednesday of the month except August and December.

Riverview Horticultural Centre Society.
Tel: (604) 290-9910 for recorded information on guided tours.
Riverview is the site of an exceptional arboretum and the Society aims to preserve it.

South Burnaby Garden Club.
Meet at Bonsor Recreation Complex, 6550 Bonsor Ave., Burnaby, 7:30 p.m., first Tuesday of the month, except January, September and December.

South Surrey Garden Club.
Website: http://www.hedgerows.com.
Meet at St. Mark's Anglican Church, 12953 - 20th Ave., Surrey, 7:30 p.m., fourth Wednesday of the month, except December.

Squamish Gardeners.
Meet at Squamish Public Library on 2nd at Main, 7:30 p.m., third Monday except December.

Sun Yat-Sen Penjing Club.
Meet at the Dr. Sun Yat-Sen Classical Chinese Garden, 578 Carrall St., Vancouver, 7:00 p.m., second Tuesday of the month. In the winter, club members meet at each other's homes.

Taguchi Bonsai Club.
Website: http://www.icangarden.com.
Meet at VanDusen Botanical Garden, 5251 Oak St., Vancouver, 7:30 p.m., third Monday of the month except January, July, August and December.

Taiwanese Canadian Bonsai Club.
Website: http://www.icangarden.com.
Meet at the Taiwanese Canadian Cultural Society, 101 - 1200 West 3rd Ave., Vancouver, 7:30 p.m., second Saturday of the month.

Upper Lonsdale Garden Club.
Meet at St. Martin's Church, 195 Windsor St., North Vancouver, 7:30 p.m., second Thursday of the month, except December.

Valley Fuchsia and Geranium Club.
Website: http://www.hedgerows.com and http://www.icangarden.com.
Meet at St. Andrews Anglican Church, 20955 Old Yale Rd., Langley, 7:30 p.m., fourth Tuesday of the month, except July, August and December.

Vancouver African Violet Club.
Meet at VanDusen Botanical Garden, 5251 Oak St., Vancouver, 1:30 p.m., third Sunday of the month except July, August and December.

Vancouver Bonsai Association.
Website: http://www.icangarden.com.
Meet at VanDusen Botanical Garden, 5251 Oak St., Vancouver, one Saturday morning a month from February to October. Call VanDusen to confirm dates.

Vancouver Dahlia Society.
Website: http://www.hedgerows.com.
Meet at VanDusen Botanical Garden, 5251 Oak St., Vancouver, 7:30 p.m., third Wednesday of the month except November and December.

Vancouver Hardy Plant Group. Contact: Beverly Merryfield. **Tel:** (604) 921-6266.
For perennial enthusiasts. No formal meetings; speakers and newsletter. Call for information.

Vancouver Ikebana Association. Contact: Sachiko Sumida. **Tel:** (604) 274-0289.
Umbrella association for Japanese flower arranging, with five additional clubs as listed here. Call for dates and locations.
• Ikenobo Ikebana Society of Vancouver. Contact: Sachiko Sumida. **Tel:** (604) 274-0289.
• Kado-Sumi Ryu. Contact: Kaz Takahashi. **Tel:** (604) 734-5400.
• Ohara Ryu. Contact: Kay Komori. **Tel:** (604) 266-5231.
• Sangetsu Ryu. Contact: Joan Fairs. **Tel:** (604) 524-3523.
• Sogetsu Ryu. Contact: Kiyoko Boycott. **Tel:** (604) 275-6215.

Vancouver Mycological (Mushroom) Society.
Website: http://www.icangarden.com.
Meet at VanDusen Botanical Garden, 5251 Oak St., Vancouver, 7:30 p.m., first Tuesday of the month except January, July, August and December.

Vancouver Natural History Society.
Tel: (604) 737-3074.
Birding, conservation, botany and general groups meet under the umbrella of the society. Call for more details.

Vancouver Orchid Society.
Website: http://www.hedgerows.com.
Meet at VanDusen Botanical Garden, 5251 Oak St., Vancouver, 7:00 p.m., fourth Wednesday of the month except July and August.

Vancouver Rhododendron Society.
Website: http://www.hedgerows.com.
Meet at VanDusen Botanical Garden, 5251 Oak St., Vancouver, 7:30 p.m., third Thursday of the month, except July and August.

Vancouver Rose Society.
Website: http://www.hedgerows.com.
Meet at VanDusen Botanical Garden, 5251 Oak St., Vancouver, 7:30 p.m., third Tuesday of the month except August and December.

Vancouver Sumi Bonsai Club (also known as Vancouver Japanese Bonsai Club).
Website: http://www.icangarden.com.
Meet at VanDusen Botanical Garden, 5251 Oak St., Vancouver, 7:30 p.m., second Wednesday of the month except January, July and August.

Wakayama Kenji Jai Bonsai Club.
Meet at the Steveston Japanese Cultural Centre, 411 Moncton Rd., Steveston, 7:30 p.m., on the second and fourth Tuesdays of the month.

Water Garden Club of B.C.
Website: http://www.hedgerows.com.
Meets at East Delta Hall, 104th St. and No. 10 Highway, Delta, 7:30 p.m., first Wednesday of the month except January, July and August.

West Coast Bonsai Society.
Meet at VanDusen Botanical Garden, 5251 Oak St., Vancouver, 7:30 p.m., first Friday of the month, except in January and July.

West Vancouver Garden Club.
Meet at St. David's United Church, 1525 Taylor Way, West Vancouver, 7:30 p.m., first Tuesday of the month except July and August.

White Rock and District Chrysanthemum Society.
Website: http://www.hedgerows.com.

Meet at St. John's Presbyterian Church, 1480 George St., White Rock, 7:30 p.m., first Tuesday of the month except November and December.

White Rock and District Garden Club.
Website: http://www.hedgerows.com.

Meet at Seaview Pentecostal Fellowship Hall, 14633 - 16th Ave., Surrey, 2:00 p.m., second Tuesday of the month.

Wild Thymes Herbal Guild.
Website: http://www.hedgerows.com.

Meet at Park and Tilford Gardens, 333 Brooksbank Ave., North Vancouver, 7:30 p.m., second Wednesday of the month except December.

Victoria and Vancouver Island

Baynes Sound Garden Club. **Website:** http://mars.ark.com/~lazdan/garden.html.

Meet at the Old Age Pensioners' Hall, on Ship's Point Rd. in Fanny Bay, 7:30 p.m., first Thursday of the month except December and January.

B.C. Fruit Testers Association.
Website: http://www.bcfta.bc.ca/index.shtml.

Box 48123, 3575 Douglas St., Victoria, B.C., V8Z 7H5. Members receive a quarterly publication called the "Cider Press."

Central Vancouver Island Orchid Society.
Website: http://www.hedgerows.com.

Meet at Maffeo Auditorium, Community Services Building, 285 Prideaux St., Nanaimo, 12 noon, on the Saturday before the last Wednesday of the month except July and August.

Comox Valley Horticultural Society.

Meet at the Florence Filberg Centre, 411 Anderton Rd., Courtenay, 7:30 p.m., third Monday of the month.

Cowichan Valley Rhododendron Society.
Website: http://www.hedgerows.com.

Meet at Fellowship Hall, First Christian Reformed Church, 930 Trunk Rd., Duncan, 7:00 p.m., first Wednesday of the month, September to May.

Eaglecrest Garden Club.

Meet at the Qualicum Civic Centre, 747 Jones St., Qualicum Beach, 7:30 p.m., third Wednesday of the month except December and January.

Esquimalt Garden Club.
Website: http://www.icangarden.com.

Meet at the Municipal Nursery, 1100 Craigflower Rd., 7:30 p.m., the second Wednesday of the month except November, December and August.

Friends of the University of Victoria Finnerty Gardens. Contact: Betty Kennedy.
Tel: (250) 592-2070. **Website:** http://victoria.tc.ca/Environment/UVicGdnFriends.

No monthly meetings, but there is a quarterly newsletter. New members welcome.

Gordon Head Garden Club.

Meet at Gordon Head United Church Hall, 4201 Tyndall Ave., Victoria, 7:30 p.m., first Monday of the month except July, August and January.

Greater Victoria Geranium and Fuchsia Society.

Meet at the Garth Homer Centre, 813 Darwin Ave., Victoria, 7:30 p.m., fourth Monday of the month, for most of the year and at various locations in the summer.

Heritage Tree Society.

Meet at Pacific Forestry Centre, 506 Burnside Rd., Victoria, 7:00 p.m., third Thursday of the month except July and August.

Horticultural Centre of the Pacific. **Tel:** (250) 479-6162. **E-mail:** hortcentre@bigfoot.com.
Website: http://www.islandnet.com/~hcp.

Located at 505 Quayle Rd., Victoria, B.C. Members receive free admission to the gardens, newsletters and reduced fees for workshops and lectures.

Metchosin Garden Club.

Meet at the New Hall, St. Mary's Church, 4125 Metchosin Rd., Victoria, 7:30 p.m., the second Tuesday of the month except December and January.

Mill Bay Garden Club.

Meet at Mill Bay Community Centre, Mill Bay/Shawnigan Lake Rd., Mill Bay, 7:30 p.m., fourth Tuesday of the month except July, August and December.

Mount Arrowsmith Rhododendron Society.
Website: http://www.hedgerows.com.

Meet at Qualicum Civic Centre, 747 Jones St., Qualicum Beach, 7:30 p.m., the second Wednesday of the month except June, July, August and December.

Nanaimo Horticultural Society.
Meet at Brechin United Church Hall, 1998 Estevan Rd., Nanaimo, 7:30 p.m., second Wednesday of the month except August.

Nanaimo Rhododendron Society.
Website: http://www.hedgerows.com and http://www.icangarden.com.
Meet at Beban Park Recreational Centre, 2300 Bowen Rd., Nanaimo, 7:30 p.m., on the second Thursday of the month from September to May.

Nanoose Amateur Gardeners Ideas and Exchanges.
Meet at Nanoose Library Centre on Nanoose Rd. (off the N.W. Bay Rd.), 1:30 p.m., first Friday of the month.

North Island Rhododendron Society.
Meet at Comox United Church, 250 Beach St., Comox, 7:30 p.m., second Tuesday of the month.

Oak Bay Garden Club. For information contact The Monterey Seniors' Centre, 1442 Monterey Ave., Victoria, B.C., V8S 4W1. **Tel:** (250) 370-7300.
Meet at Windsor Park Pavilion, 2451 Windsor Rd., Oak Bay, Victoria, 2:00 p.m., third Wednesday of the month except July, August and December.

Peninsula Garden Club.
Meet at Silverthreads, Resthaven Drive, Sidney, 7:30 p.m., second Thursday of the month. A "New Gardeners" forum starts at 6:30 p.m.

Peninsular Rose Club.
E-mail: peninsular@nurserysite.com. **Website:** http://www.nurserysite.com/clubs/peninsular.
Meet at Elk Lake Baptist Church, 5363 Pat Bay Highway, 7:30 p.m., third Tuesday of the month except December and January.

Saltair Garden Club.
Meet at the United Church Hall, corner of 3rd and High streets, Ladysmith, 7:30 p.m., third Thursday of the month.

Sooke Garden Club.
Meet at the Royal Canadian Legion Hall, 6726 Eustace St., Sooke, 7:30 p.m., fourth Wednesday of the month.

Valley Garden Club.
Meet at St. John's Anglican Church Hall, 486 Jubilee Ave., Duncan, 7:30 p.m., second Wednesday of the month except July and August.

Vancouver Island Bonsai Club.
Website: http://www.icangarden.com and http://www.absbonsai.org/clubsca.html.

Meet at Garth Homer Centre, 813 Darwin Ave., Victoria, 7:30 p.m., second Wednesday of the month.

Vancouver Island Rock and Alpine Garden Society.
Website: http://victoria.tc.ca/Recreation/VIRAGS.
Meet at St. David's Church by the Sea, 5182 Cordova Bay Rd., Victoria, 8:00 p.m., fourth Tuesday of the month except July, August and December.

Victoria Cactus and Succulent Society.
Meet at the Language Institute, 4680 Elk Lake Drive, Victoria, 7:30 p.m., last Wednesday of the month except July, August and December.

Victoria Chrysanthemum Society.
Meet at St. Matthias Church Hall, 600 Richmond Ave., Victoria, 7:30 p.m., fourth Thursday of the month except June, July, September and December.

Victoria and District Heather Society. Contact: Mary Helmcken. **Tel:** (250) 592-7820.
Meet in various locations, 2:00 p.m., second Monday of the month.

Victoria Flower Arrangers' Guild.
Meet at Garth Homer Centre, 813 Darwin Ave., Victoria, 7:30 p.m., second Wednesday of the month.

Victoria Gladiolus and Dahlia Society.
Meet at St. Michael's Church Hall, West Sannich Rd., Victoria, 7:30 p.m., first Thursday of the month except January and September.

Victoria Horticultural Society.
Website: http://victoria.tc.ca/Recreation/VHS.
Mailing address: Box 5081, Station B, Victoria, B.C., V8R 6N3.
Meet at Garth Homer Centre, 813 Darwin Ave., Victoria, 7:30 p.m., the first Tuesday of every month. Pre-meeting workshop starts at 6:30 p.m. V.H.S. offers a number of special-interest groups that include hardy plants, native plants, vegetables, water gardens and a new-gardeners group. Contact numbers and a list of activities for each group is listed in "Gardenry," the monthly newsletter.

Victoria Orchid Society.
Website: http://www.members.home.net/bearman1.
Meet at Garth Homer Centre, 813 Darwin Ave., Victoria, 7:30 p.m., the Tuesday before the fourth Wednesday of the month except July and August.

Victoria Rhododendron Society.
Website: http://victoria.tc.ca/recreation/rhodosoc.
Meet at Garth Homer Centre, 813 Darwin Ave., Victoria, 7:30 p.m., first Thursday of the month except July, August and December.

View Royal Garden Club.

Meet at All Saints' Parish Hall, corner of Stewart and Palliser streets, Victoria, 7:30 p.m., fourth Thursday of the month except July and December.

Western Garden Club.

Meet at Colwood Community Hall, 2219 Sooke Rd., Victoria, 8:00 p.m., second Tuesday of the month except June, July and August.

The Gulf Islands and the Sunshine Coast

Bowen Island Garden Club.
Website: http://www.hedgerows.com.

Meet at the Old General Store, Bowen Island, 7:30 p.m., the second Monday of the month except July, August and December.

Denman Island Garden Club.

Meet at the United Church Hall, 7:30 p.m., third Wednesday of the month.

Galiano Garden Club.

Meet at North Galiano Community Hall, 2:00 p.m., second Wednesday of the month except December and January.

Gibson's Garden Club.

Meet at St. Bartholomew's Church Hall, North Rd. and Highway 101, 7:30 p.m., third Thursday of the month except January, July, August and December.

Pender Island Garden Club.

Meet at the Pender Island Public Library meeting room, 1:30 p.m., second Thursday of the month except July and August.

Powell River Garden Club.

Meet at The Inn at Westview, 7050 Alberni at Joyce, Powell River, 7:30 p.m., third Tuesday of the month except July and August.

Salt Spring Island Garden Club.

Meet at Royal Canadian Legion Hall on the Lower Ganges Rd., 7:00 p.m., fourth Wednesday of the month except July, August, December and January.

Sechelt Garden Club.

Meet at St. Hilda's Parish Hall, Sechelt, 7:30 p.m., first Wednesday of the month, except July, August and January.

Education and Information

Gardening courses

Many gardening courses are given throughout the year by schools, community colleges, specialty garden societies and clubs, and botanical gardens. Often they are taught by well-known local landscape architects, designers and horticultural experts. They are an excellent opportunity to find out more about your favourite garden topic and meet local experts.

Schools and community centres

A good place to start is with local community centres and school boards. Many of these offer evening classes and workshops on everything from pruning to garden design.

Community colleges

Several different colleges offer one- to two-year certificate courses in horticulture/agriculture, with specialties in such areas as integrated pest management, greenhouse technology, agriculture technology, ornamental horticulture, landscape architecture, landscape maintenance, turf management and nursery management. Also available are non-credit courses for day or evening sessions.

B..C. Horticulture Centre, Kwantlen University College, 20901 Langley Bypass, Langley, B.C.
Tel: (604) 599-3254. **Fax:** (604) 599-3242.
E-mail: tricia@Kwantlen.bc.ca.

Horticulture Citation Programs for entry-level horticulture workers. Students in this program are doing part-time studies only. There are six areas of specialization: landscape maintenance, parks arboriculture, turfgrass, greenhouse production, retail horticulture and landscape design.

The Horticulture Certificate Program is a 10-month, full-time program with three specializations: greenhouse vegetable production, landscape maintenance and garden centre retail technician.

The Horticulture Apprenticeship Program includes 24 weeks of schooling and four years of employment-based training. Specializations are landscape horticulture, production horticulture and arboriculture urban forestry.

The Horticulture Technology Program is 18 months of full-time study. Specializations are landscape, greenhouse and nursery production, turf management and general horticulture.

In the Commercial Florist Program, students study full-time for 8 months.

Camosun College, Interurban Campus, 4461 Interurban Rd., Victoria, B.C. **Tel:** (250) 370-3841. **Fax:** (250) 370-3750. **Website:** http://www.camosun.bc.ca.

Horticultural Technician Program. This 10-month program is offered through Camosun's Interurban Campus starting in July of each year, but classes are actually held at the campus of Royal Roads University. The program offers courses in botany, plant identification, arboriculture and integrated pest management and is transferable to B.C. Horticulture Centre's two-year diploma program.

Capilano College, 2055 Purcell Way, North Vancouver, B.C. **Tel:** (604) 984-4960. **Fax:** (604) 990-7835. **E-mail:** rwelsh@capcollege.bc.ca.

Landscape Horticulture Program. This is an eight-month certificate program. Classes are held Monday to Friday from 8:30 a.m. to 4:30 p.m. Main study areas include basic landscape design, landscape installation, greenhouse production, irrigation and drainage, pest control, turf management, plant nutrition and other landscape-related subjects.

Malaspina College, 900 - 5th St., Nanaimo, B.C. **Tel:** (250) 753-3245. **Fax:** (250) 755-8725. **Website:** http://www.mala.bc.ca.

A 12-month Horticultural Technician Program, which includes a 2-month practicum. Approximately 50% of this program is spent in actual "hands-on" training on and off campus. The program is taught at the G.R. Paine Horticultural Training Centre, situated on 32 acres (13 ha) minutes from the Malaspina Campus. Milner Gardens, a 45-acre (18-ha) estate in Qualicum Beach also offers the students an opportunity to work in an established seaside garden. The program covers plant propagation, landscape design, plant identification, pruning techniques and environmentally responsible greenhouse, nursery and landscape practices.

Continuing education

North Shore Continuing Education. Contact: Nel Grond, program manager. **Tel:** (604) 523-0255.

Certificate in Residential Landscape Design. This is a part-time evening certificate program organized through the North and West Vancouver School Board. To successfully complete this program, seven courses must be taken. Emphasis is on drafting and drawing, hardscaping and plant identification.

University of British Columbia, Continuing Studies, 2075 Westbrook Mall, UBC Campus, Vancouver, B.C. **Tel:** (604) 822-1462. **Fax:** (604) 822-1499. **E-mail:** gardendesign@cce.ubc.ca. **Website:** http://www.cstudies.ubc.ca/garden.

Certificate in Garden Design. This course was conceived by Ron Rule, a local landscape architect. Including practical training in drafting, horticulture, construction and maintenance, this course is for professional and amateur gardeners who would like to learn more about designing small residential gardens in the Pacific Northwest. Participants must complete six courses within a six-month period to obtain a certificate. Enrollment is limited and this program is offered yearly, starting in spring. Classes are held on evenings and weekends except for two one-week intensives.

Botanical gardens

Horticulture Centre of the Pacific, 505 Quayle Rd., Victoria, B.C., V8X 3X1. **Tel/Fax:** (250) 479-6162. **E-mail:** hortcentre@bigfoot.com. **Website:** http://www.islandnet.com/~hcp.

The Master Gardener Program is modelled on the VanDusen course, but is longer and more intense, combining levels 1 and 2. It is administered in conjunction with VanDusen, which keeps track of the HCP MG members and their clinic and volunteer hours. The course starts in February and is divided into 30 3-hour sessions. Like other Master Gardening programs it covers botany, plant identification, pests and diseases, soils, integrated pest management, fruit and vegetables, pruning, lawns and weed identification. Students are required to pass an exam on completing the course and volunteer hours in the community to gain certification and maintain membership. Master Gardeners may choose to volunteer in a variety of areas, such as setting up clinics at local gardening centres, helping at major events, or answering questions on plant information lines.

The Landscape Horticulturist Trades Qualification Preparation Program was developed for those who have work experience in the industry but lack a formal horticulture education. It prepares participants for the provincial Trades Qualifications exam. Participants in this course take most of the same courses as the Master Gardeners and both groups take many of the same courses together at the same time.

Landscape Horticulture Certificate Program. This is a 42-week, full-time certificate program starting in February and finishing in December. Students spend approximately 15 hours a week in the classroom and the same amount of time each week learning practical aspects of identification, care and culture of plants. With 100 acres (40 ha) of coastal Douglas fir habitat and wetland, and many demonstration gardens from fruit and vegetables to rhododendrons and dahlias, there is ample opportunity to work with a wide variety of plants that have very different cultural requirements.

UBC Botanical Garden, 6804 Southwest Marine Drive, Vancouver, B.C. **Tel:** (604) 822-4804.

There is a broad selection of courses on such topics as garden design, vegetable gardening and planning a perennial border, as well as workshops ranging from how to make a hanging basket to how to prune a tree. There are usually about 20 classes offered in each of the winter, spring and summer sessions.

The courses are listed in the calendar of the Centre for Continuing Education, among their non-credit courses. Copies are available at your local library, or can be obtained by calling 822-1444.

The Friends of the Garden (F.O.G.S.) also have regular lectures. (For information on F.O.G.S. see UBC Botanical Gardens under "Public Parks and Gardens," in the Resources section.)

VanDusen Botanical Garden, 5251 Oak St., Vancouver, B.C. **Tel:** (604) 878-9274.

The garden offers a family-oriented education program with excellent courses for adults and children throughout the year. Topics are varied, including a wide range of gardening subjects, botanical painting, flower arranging, and lots of practical workshops. Information on upcoming programs is available in the *Vancouver Botanical Garden* Bulletin, published quarterly in January, April, June and September. The *Bulletin* is mailed to members of the Vancouver Botanical Gardens Association, and can also be picked up at VanDusen Gardens.

They also offer an in-depth course, the Master Gardener Program, a 10-week course of one-day sessions on a wide range of topics.

Plant and garden information lines

Most garden and specialty garden stores are happy to answer your questions. However, sometimes you may have difficult questions they may not have the time

or resources to answer. That's the time to place a call to one of the following numbers.

Horticulture Centre of the Pacific's Information Line. Tel: (250) 479-6162.

Questions can be phoned in at any time during office hours. The questions are forwarded to a "plant doctor," who then calls back directly with the answer.

UBC Botanical Garden's Plant Information Hort Line. Tel: (604) 822-5858, Tuesday and Wednesday 12:00 noon to 3:30 p.m.

This information line is provided by volunteers from the Friends of the Garden (F.O.G.S.).

VanDusen Botanical Gardens Plant Information Line. Tel: (604) 878-9274, Monday, Wednesday and Thursday from 1:00 to 3:00 p.m.

This information line is provided by volunteers from the VanDusen Master Gardener's Program. The Master Gardeners also run regular clinics at VanDusen Gardens on weekends during the growing season, and at various garden centres, specialty stores and selected locations throughout the area. These provide an opportunity for gardeners to bring samples of troubled plants for diagnosis and advice. For exact times and numbers of clinics, call the number above.

Newspaper, television and radio gardening advice

Gardening has become so popular that just about every newspaper and radio station, as well as many television stations, have regular gardening columnists and feature various gardeners and garden celebrities during the year. For instance, David Tarrant and Des Kennedy write regular newspaper columns (*Vancouver Sun/Globe and Mail*) and have their own spots on CBC television (*The Canadian Gardener/Midday*). Helen Chestnut, like her father before her, is a weekly columnist (*Vancouver Province/Victoria Times-Colonist*), and the *Vancouver Sun* carries regular feature articles by *Sun* editor Steve Whysall, plus a weekly column of readers' gardening questions, answered by VanDusen Master Gardeners. Regular radio gardeners include Brian Minter (CBC *Almanac*), Dagmar Hungerford (CBC *Saturday*), Betty Murray (AM 1040, Vancouver), Len Rowclisse (CFAX, Victoria), and Wim Vander Zalm (CKNW, Vancouver).

Compost Education and Demonstration Gardens

Over 30 per cent of the household waste generated in our region is organic material, rich in nutrients that can easily be turned into compost to nourish the soil. To learn more about the benefits of composting, it is well worth paying a visit to your local compost demonstration garden. Many of the gardens have people on hand to answer questions, and there are signs explaining the composting process. Some of the gardens also offer workshops and/or tours for school children and community groups.

In Vancouver, for further information on composting call the Compost Hotline at (604) 736-2250. It is operated by City Farmer. In Victoria, call (250) 386-WORM (386-9676), to get advice and information on all aspects of composting. For more information and home pages for many of the compost demonstration gardens see: http://www.compost.org. Also http://www.oldgrowth.org/compost/misc.html, and http://www.gvrd.bc.ca/waste.bro/swcomp2.html.

Vancouver and the Lower Mainland

Crescent Beach Compost Demonstration Garden, 2916 McBride Ave. (garden off McKenzie at Sullivan), Crescent Beach, B.C. **Tel/Fax:** (604) 535-4158. **Hours:** Open daily for self-service; staffed on Sundays from 10:00 a.m. to 3:00 p.m. April to October. Call for workshop schedule.

Earthwise Garden (formerly Delta Society Compost Demonstration Garden), 7046 Brown St., Delta, B.C. **Tel:** (604) 946-9828. **Fax:** (604) 946-3823. **E-mail:** preith@drsociety.bc.ca. **Hours:** Open daily 9:00 a.m. to 5:30 p.m., except statutory holidays. Staff on hand weekday mornings to answer gardening and composting questions. From May to August the garden is staffed from 9:00 a.m. to 3:00 p.m., Monday to Saturday.

This 1-acre (.4-ha), waterwise demonstration garden features a woodland garden, butterfly and hummingbird gardens, native plant garden and dry garden. It focuses on sustainable landscape design. Public education programs include composting, waterwise gardening, and backyard wildlife habitats. Volunteer programs, allotment gardens, school tours and workshops. Phone for details.

GVRD Compost Demonstration Garden, 4856 Still Creek Ave. (just off Douglas Rd.), Burnaby, B.C.

Tel: (604) 299-0659 (garden) and (604) 436-6803 (Nov. to Feb.). **Fax:** (604) 436-6811. **Website:** http://www.gvrd.bc.ca. **Hours:** Staffed from 10:00 a.m. to 3:00 p.m., Tuesday to Saturday. Group tour bookings can be made for Mondays from mid-March to the end of October. Call (604) 946-9828 for workshop information. Service available for all member municipalities.

Kwantlen College Garden, 12666 - 72nd Ave., Surrey, B.C. **Tel/Fax:** (604) 535-4138. **Hours:** Staffed on Saturdays from 10:00 a.m. to 3:00 p.m. Call for workshop schedule.

Park and Tilford Gardens, 333 Brooksbank, North Vancouver, B.C., V7J 3S8. **Tel:** (604) 984-9730. **Hours:** Self-guided tours from 9:30 a.m. to dusk. Staffed mid-May to October from 8:30 a.m. to 4:00 p.m., Monday to Friday, and on weekends from 10:00 a.m. to 6:00 p.m. Call for workshop information.

Port Haney Compost Education and Urban Organic Garden, 11739 - 223rd St., Maple Ridge, B.C. **Tel:** (604) 463-5545. **Hours:** April to October, Wednesday to Sunday, from 10:00 a.m. to 4:00 p.m. Call for workshop information.

Richmond Compost Demonstration Garden, 6080 River Rd., Richmond, B.C. **Tel:** (604) 276-4010 or (604) 270-3257. **Hours:** Not staffed, but call for tours and workshop information. This garden was moved in spring 2000 from its old location at the recycling yard and now includes a waterwise demonstration garden as well as a compost demonstration garden and allotments. All organic.

Township of Langley Compost Demonstration Garden, 4914 - 221st St., Langley, B.C. **Tel:** (604) 533-6054. **Hours:** Staffed from May to August 31 from Tuesday to Saturday, 8:30 a.m. to 4:30 p.m. Self-guided tours possible daily from dawn to dusk. Call for workshop information.

Vancouver Compost Demonstration Garden, 2150 Maple St., Vancouver, B.C., V6J 3T3. **Tel:** (604) 736-2250 (the compost hot-line, a seven-day-a-week service). **Website:** http://www.cityfarmer.org. **Hours:** April to November, Wednesday to Saturday from 9:00 a.m. to 4:00 p.m. From December to March the garden is staffed Friday and Saturday from 9:00 a.m. to 4:00 p.m.

This model organic garden was the site of the first compost garden in western Canada. City Farmer, a non-profit urban agriculture group that has been involved in organic urban gardening since 1978, started the garden and operates it for the City of Vancouver. City Farmer has initiated school classroom gardening programs and gardening for people with disabilities, and is involved in the development of compost demonstration gardens and community allotment gardens. The group organizes workshops and lectures on urban food production, maintains a good-sized resource library, and operates an excellent and informative website. Call for hours of workshops and tours.

West Vancouver Compost Demonstration Garden, 15th and Argyle (beachside), West Vancouver, B.C. **Tel:** (604) 984-9730. **Hours:** Not staffed; open dawn to dusk for self-guided tours. Call for workshop information.

Victoria and Vancouver Island

The Hive (corner of Holland Rd. and Blueridge Ave., near the Victoria General Hospital). **Contact:** Lifecycles (below). **Tel:** (250) 386-5800.

This demonstration garden was created out of a degraded piece of land and now serves as a demonstration site for organic food growing, water conservation, pest control, soil building and garden design. The Hive was created to be an accessible and inviting place where everyone can learn the basics of organic gardening. Bees have been chosen as theme guides as "they are vital to pollination and growth of plants, and give us insight into the many interactions that exist in a healthy, balanced garden ecosystem."

Everything that is grown on the site is donated to the Mustard Seed Food Bank. The site is open Saturdays for free guided tours. There is also a Children's Garden, which is open for school tours during the week. Call Lifecycles to find out about upcoming workshops, training programs, special events or volunteering opportunities.

Lifecycles, 527 Michigan St., Victoria, B.C., V8V 1S1. **Tel:** (250) 386-5800. **Fax:** (250) 386-3449. **E-mail:** lifecycles@coastnet.com. **Website:** http://www.coastnet.com/~lifecycles.

Lifecycles offers programs and services to promote interest in organic gardening, including allotment and community gardens, and linking people willing to share their land with people who want a place to garden. This predominantly youth-driven organization is geared towards building community connections through gardening projects.

Projects include Common Harvest, where organic farmers provide produce for subscribers either weekly or biweekly. The project guarantees local growers a market and gives local consumers the opportunity to buy organic food grown by local farmers. Grow-a-Row is a project that encourages farmers and gardeners to donate a row of their harvest to local food distributing agencies. The Sharing Backyards Program is linking people who live in apartments or rental properties and have no access to land to neighbours who have land to share. Many partnerships are between students and seniors who need help with their gardens, but who have a wealth of knowledge to share. Another interesting initiative is the Victoria Fruit Tree Project, in which permission is sought from landowners and tenants to harvest fruit that would otherwise go to waste.

Victoria Compost Education Centre, 1216 North Park St., Victoria, B.C., V8T 1C9. **Tel:** (250) 386-9676. **Fax:** (250) 386-9678. **E-mail:** compost@ampsc.com. **Website:** http://www.compost.bc.ca. **Hours:** 10:00 a.m. to 4:00 p.m., Wednesday to Saturday.

The Compost Education Centre is a not-for-profit organization providing compost and water conservation education to the residents of Greater Victoria. The centre operates a Compost Hotline, demonstration gardens including native plant, organic veggie, waterwise and permaculture (permanent agriculture) garden beds, a compost bin demonstration area and the first publicly accessible straw-bale building. A "Master Composter" training program is offered to those interested in volunteering at the centre and helping with school programs, slide presentations, group tours or gardening. The Victoria Compost Education Centre is funded by the Capital Regional District, the City of Victoria and the Fernwood Community Association.

Gulf Islands

Hornby Island. At the Recycling Depot and Freestore. Contact the Recycling Depot Manager, Hornby Island, B.C., V0R 1Z0.

Allotment (Community) Gardens

Allotment or community gardens are a great way for apartment-dwellers to stay in touch with the earth. These gardens are very popular. Most are organized as associations, with a coordinator to assign plots, collect rent, and keep an eye on the garden. Annual charges vary, with a nominal initial fee, and include exclusive use of a plot of land, use of water, and usually some communal equipment. The contacts for the gardens change fairly often, so it is probably best to go to the garden and ask someone there who to call. Many community gardens have notice boards with this information. You can also call city planning departments for current contacts. Some gardens have big waiting lists, but others are eager to accept new members.

Of special note is the program "Plant a Row for the Hungry." This program is a Garden Writers Association of America initiative, and it has spread across North America over the past few years. Simply, seed companies provide the seed, garden centres distribute them, individuals make a commitment to plant the seeds and donate a portion of their harvest to the local food bank. Check out your local garden centre for information, or phone 1-800-665-6340.

Vancouver and the Lower Mainland

Arbutus Victory Garden, 6600 block East Boulevard, near 50th Ave., Vancouver, beside the railroad tracks on the CPR right of way. Eight plots, each with a 50-foot (15-m) frontage.

Burnaby and Region Allotment Gardens Association (BARAGA), Meadow Ave., off Marine Drive, Burnaby. Five-acre (2-ha) site, 372 plots. Contact Burnaby Parks and Recreation at (604) 294-7450.

Burquitlam Community Organic Garden, 515 Ebert Ave. (corner of Whiting Way, near the Lougheed Mall), Coquitlam. New garden covering three city lots, with 60 plots, all organic. The garden is run by the Burquitlam Community Organic Garden Society, and members are eligible to rent the plots. For more information contact the City of Coquitlam Parks and Leisure at (604) 927-3000.

City of Richmond River Road Community Garden, 6080 River Rd. (foot of No. 2 Rd. Bridge), Richmond. This organic garden has 45 plots and is a collaboration between the community and the Richmond Environmental Youth Corps. Waterwise and compost demonstration gardens on site. Phone the City of Richmond Parks Department at (604) 244-1208.

Colony Farm Community Garden Society, located in Colony Farm Regional Park, off the Lougheed Highway, Coquitlam. This 7-acre (2.8-ha) site currently has 280 developed plots, all organic, and is

developing more. The site includes raised beds for people who cannot bend over or are in wheelchairs. Contact the GVRD for more information, at (604) 520-6442.

Cottonwood Community Garden, 103 - 700 East Pender St. (south end of Strathcona Park, near Prior St. and Hawks Ave.), Vancouver. Operated by Strathcona Community Garden Society. Contact Vancouver Parks and Recreation at (604) 257-8400.

Cypress Community Garden, located next to the Arbutus rail line on 6th Ave., between Cypress and Burrard streets in Vancouver. Has 67 plots and a lovely communal flower garden at one end of the garden. They are starting a wildlife garden. Applications for plots are taken at the SPEC office, 6th and Maple.

Dunsmuir Gardens, Camp Alexandra, Crescent Beach, Surrey. One hundred plots. Contact Surrey Parks and Recreation at (604) 501-5050.

Earthwise Garden (formerly Delta Recycling Society Community Garden), 7046 Brown St., Delta. One-acre (.4-ha) garden with a focus on ecological and waterwise gardening, and 26 plots; see entry under "Compost Education and Demonstration Garden." above. Call (604) 946-9828.

Elizabeth Rogers Community Garden, northeast corner of Jonathan Rogers Park, 7th and Manitoba, Vancouver. Operated by Urban Diggers Society, there are 55 plots. Call Vancouver Parks and Recreation at (604) 257-8400.

Fraser St. Neighbourhood Garden (formerly Mount Pleasant Community Garden), 8th and Fraser St., Vancouver. Operated by Urban Diggers Society, there are 55 plots. Call Vancouver Parks and Recreation at (604) 257-8400.

Gardeners by the Bay, 1050 Beach Ave., Vancouver. Located in the West End, behind the Aquatic Centre.

Heights Neighbourhood Garden, 3897 Pender St., East Vancouver; 43 plots.

Kitsilano Community Garden, on 6th between Maple and Arbutus streets, Vancouver. About 30 plots, operated by Kitsilano Community Garden members. Call Vancouver Parks and Recreation at (604) 257-8400.

Langley Family Services Community Garden, 5339 - 207th St., Langley. There are 10 plots and three raised beds that are wheelchair-accessible. Call (604) 534-7921.

Lord Roberts Community School Garden, on Cardero at Pendrell, in Vancouver's West End. Cooperative project between the community and the school children.

Maple Community Garden, between Maple and Cypress streets, next to the railway tracks on 6th Ave. in Vancouver. There are 75 plots. Applications are taken at the SPEC office, 6th and Maple.

McSpadden Park,, south of 4th Ave. and west of Victoria Drive, East Vancouver. There are 18 plots. Call Vancouver Parks and Recreation at (604) 257-8400.

Mission Soap Box Community Garden, 10th and Taulbut, Mission. There are 11 plots.

Mole Hill/Nelson Park, located in Vancouver's West End, in the city block between Pendrell, Comox, Bute and Thurlow streets. Operated by Mole Hill Living Heritage Society.

Moodyville Garden Association, 1st St. between Lonsdale and St. George, North Vancouver. Contact the City of North Vancouver Parks Department at (604) 983-6318; the area is zoned for development and planners are looking to relocate.

Navvy Jack Gardens, 2000 block Bellevue Ave., West Vancouver. Private garden with 26 plots, used by nearby residents. For information call West Vancouver Parks and Recreation at (604) 925-7200.

Richmond Allotment Gardens Association, 10711 Palmberg Rd., north of Steveston Highway, Richmond. There are 130 plots.

Robson Park Community Garden, St. George and West 14th St. in Vancouver, northwest corner. Operated by Urban Diggers Society, there are 40 plots. Call Vancouver Parks and Recreation at (604) 257-8400.

SFU Community Garden, beside Naheeno Park, Burnaby Mountain. There are 99 plots. Contact SFU housing at (604) 291-3526.

Stoney Creek Community Garden, 2898 Neptune Crescent, Burnaby. There are 100 plots.

Strathcona Community Garden, south of Prior St. and west of Hawks Ave., East Vancouver. Over 100 large plots, operated by Strathcona Community Garden Association. Call Vancouver Parks and Recreation at (604) 257-8400.

Sunrise Rotary Community Garden, Walnut Grove Community Park, 212 block off 88th Ave., Langley. Contact Jane D'Silva, horticultural therapist at Sunrise Rotary Club of Langley, (604) 888-3376. There are 42 plots; 2 are wheelchair-accessible.

UBC Community Garden, Acadia family housing complex, UBC. There are 84 plots. Contact Acadia Park Commons Block at (604) 822-3172.

West Vancouver Argyle Ave. Allotment Gardens, at 1460 and 1534 Argyle Ave., West Vancouver. Each site has 28 plots, administered by West Vancouver Parks and Recreation. Call (604) 925-7200.

Victoria area

Agnes St. Garden Association, 600-block of Agnes St. (corner of Glanford and Agnes St. in Victoria), 32 plots. Contact: A list of phone numbers is posted on the notice board at the gardens, or call the Capital Regional District at (250) 360-3000.

Capital City Allotment Garden, 641 Kent Rd., Victoria (off Glanford Rd. at the end of the cul de sac), 134 plots. Contact: A list of phone numbers is posted on the notice board at the garden, or call the Capital Regional District at (250) 360-3000.

Craigflower Community Garden, off Admirals Rd. at the corner of Craigflower Rd., Victoria. On the grounds of Craigflower Manor, this is a new project and only a small number of plots are available at present. Look for a notice board with contact numbers.

Earth Bound Community Gardens, 2500 block of Garden St., Victoria. (off Bay St.), 35 plots. Contact the Fernwood Community Association. **Tel:** (250) 384-7441. **E-mail:** fca@islandnet.com.

Fernwood Allotment Gardens, 1216 North Park St., Victoria (corner of Chambers St. and North Park Ave.). The allotment gardens share the same site as the Victoria Compost Education Centre, with 34 plots. Contact the Fernwood Community Association at (250) 384-7411. **E-mail:** fca@islandnet.com. **Website:** http://www.islandnet.com/~fca. Or contact the Compost Education Centre at (250) 386-9676. **Fax:** (250) 386-9678.

Gordon Head Allotment Gardens, 4100-block of Gordon Head Rd., Victoria (at Feltham Rd.), 195 plots. Contact: Check the notice board for a list of phone numbers, or call the Capital Regional District at (250) 360-3000.

James Bay Allotment Gardens, 100-block of Montreal St., Victoria (between Niagara and Simcoe streets), 53 plots. Contact: Check the notice board for contact numbers.

Michigan St. Community Gardens, 500-block Michigan St., Victoria (Michigan and Menzies). Contact: Lifecycles at (250) 383-5800. **E-mail:** lifecycles@coastnet.com.

Oak Bay Allotment Garden, 1700-block of Monteith Ave., Victoria (Monteith and Cranmore), 13 plots. Contact: Oak Bay Municipal Hall at (250) 598-3311.

University of Victoria Community Allotment Gardens, Sinclair and Finnerty, roughly 15 plots. Contact: Check the notice board for contact numbers.

This small allotment garden is used primarily by students with families living on campus and by university staff. It is also available for members of the surrounding community, with the understanding that part of the mandate is to raise food for local food banks. Some of the beds are set aside for this purpose.

Soil: Testing and Supplies

Soil testing

How healthy is your soil? If you're not sure, the most important first step is to test it, either yourself or by using a reputable soil laboratory.

The following laboratories in B.C. will test home gardeners' soil samples. The average cost is $35 to $40 per test, and testing takes about a week. Call first for instructions on how best to take samples, and for current costs of analysis. For soil-testing laboratories in your neighbourhood, check the Yellow Pages under "Laboratories."

MB Research Analytical and Testing Services, 10115 McDonald Park Rd., Sidney, B.C. **Tel:** (250) 656-1334. **Website:** http://www.mblabs.com.

Comprehensive and detailed analysis of soil samples and recommendations as necessary.

Pacific Soil Analysis, 5 - 11720 Voyager Way, Richmond, B.C. **Tel:** (604) 273-8226.

Comprehensive and detailed analysis of soil samples and recommendations as necessary.

Soilcon Laboratories, 275 - 11780 River Rd., Richmond, B.C. **Tel:** (604) 278-5535. **Website:** http://www.intouch.bc.ca.soilcon.

This is primarily a research laboratory, and soil testing helps fund their research. Comprehensive and detailed analysis and recommendations as necessary.

Topsoil

Topsoil quality varies considerably. Bad topsoil, loaded with weeds, such as horsetail and morning glory, will give you nothing but trouble. It is important to buy from a reputable dealer and to confirm their source. Local municipalities can tell you the location of sites where soil removal is permitted and give you the names of permit holders. Landscape supply companies are also reliable sources for topsoil.

Soil amendments

See the March chapter for information on organic gardening and soil amendments. Soil that has not received any help in a long time will most likely need one or more of the following.

Sand. Lightens heavy soil with a high clay content, helps drainage. Easily available through concrete supply companies, listed in the Yellow Pages.

Well-rotted manure. Provides necessary organic matter and some nutrients, helps break up soil and retain moisture. Aged steer manure, chicken manure and other farm animal manures are often sold through groups and school fundraisers. Mushroom manure is available through local mushroom growers. Often local newspapers list manure sales under the heading "Garden Supplies."

Compost. All gardeners should be making this. See the March chapter for information on how to compost and how to make your own composter; for supplies, see "Compost Education and Demonstration Gardens" above.

Street leaf and yard trimmings made into compost is available from the City of Vancouver. It is sold by the bag annually at VanDusen Gardens, but for larger amounts, call (604) 946-2688 or fax (604) 946-2873. Or e-mail paul_henderson@city.vancouver.bc.ca. The compost is made from 40,000 tonnes of yard trimmings a year from residential drop-offs and the pick-up program.

Organic and biological supplies

More and more garden stores, nurseries, grocery stores and hardware stores are beginning to carry environmentally friendly products, such as insecticidal soaps, Tanglefoot, floating groundcovers such as Reemay, organic fertilizers, dormant oil, natural source soil amendments, insect traps, and other organic products. Ask first in your local store for the products you need.

If you are unable to find what you want locally, some of the specialty garden stores listed under "Specialty Nurseries and Garden Centres" above carry a good range.

Further Reading

Each chapter includes a list of books that relate specifically to topics covered in that month. The following is a list of books by local B.C. authors to look for and also some books by authors elsewhere in Canada and the United States.

Local

Allen, Christine. *Gardens of Vancouver.* Raincoast Books, Vancouver, 1999.

Allen, Christine. *Roses for the Pacific Northwest.* Steller Press, Vancouver, 1999.

Bradbury, Elspeth and Judy Maddocks. *The Garden Letters.* Polestar Press, Vancouver, 1995.

Bradbury, Elspeth and Judy Maddocks. *The Real Garden Road Trip.* Polestar Press, Vancouver, 1997.

Clearview Horticultural Products. *The Concise Guide to Clematis in North America,* 1996.

Croft, Philip. *Nature Diary of a Quiet Pedestrian.* Harbour Publishing, Madeira Park, B.C., 1986.

Grant, John and Carol. *Trees and Shrubs for Coastal BC Gardens.* Whitecap Books, Vancouver, 1990.

Hobbs, Thomas. *Shocking Beauty.* Raincoast Books, Vancouver, 1997.

Kennedy, Des. *Crazy about Gardening.* Whitecap Books, Vancouver, 1994.

Kramer, Pat. *Gardens of British Columbia.* Altitude Publishing, Canmore, Alberta, 1998.

Meikle, Marg and Dannie McArthur. *Garden City: Vancouver.* Polestar Press, Vancouver, 1999.

Merilees, Bill. *Attracting Backyard Wildlife.* Whitecap Books, Vancouver, 1989.

Milnes, Lynne. *In a Victoria Garden.* Orca Book Publishers, Victoria, 1995.

Minter, Brian. *Brian Minter's New Gardening Guide.* Whitecap Books, Vancouver, 1998.

Newton, Judy. *Gardening in Vancouver.* Lone Pine Publishing, Edmonton, 1992.

Noble, Phoebe. *My Experience Growing Hardy Geraniums.* Trio Investments, 1994.

Pettinger, April. *Native Plants in the Coastal Garden: A Guide for Gardeners in British Columbia and the Pacific Northwest.* Whitecap Books, Vancouver, 1996.

Richardson, Nöel. *In a Country Garden: Life at Ravenhill Farm.* Whitecap Books, Vancouver, 1996.

Richardson, Nöel and Jenny Cameron. *Herbal Celebrations: Another Visit to Ravenhill Farm.* Whitecap Books, Vancouver, 2000.

Sommer, Ramona. *Island Gardening.* Orca Book Publishers, Victoria, 1994.

Stevens, Elaine. *The Creative Container Gardener.* Whitecap Books, Vancouver, 1995.

Straley, Gerald B. *Trees of Vancouver.* UBC Press, Vancouver, 1992.

Stubbs, Betty. *From Golf Course to Garden: A History of VanDusen Botanical Display Gardens.* VanDusen Botanical Garden Assoc. Vancouver, 1985.

Tarrant, David. *David Tarrant's Canadian Gardens.* Whitecap Books, Vancouver, 1994.

Tarrant, David. *Pacific Gardening Guide.* Whitecap Books, Vancouver, 1999.

Tarrant, David. *A Year in Your Garden.* Whitecap Books, Vancouver, 1989.

Tarrant, David and Richard Bird. *Hostas.* Whitecap Books, Vancouver, 1999.

Tarrant, David and Jenny Hendy. *New Perennials.* Whitecap Books, Vancouver, 1999.

U.B.C. Guide to Gardening in British Columbia. U.B.C. Botanical Garden, Vancouver, 1990.

Victoria Horticultural Society. *Gardening Victoria: Tips and Techniques from the Victoria Horticultural Society.* Gardenisle Publishing, Victoria, 1995.

Wales, Paddy. *Journeys Through the Garden: Inspiration for Gardeners in B.C. and the Pacific Northwest.* Whitecap Books, Vancouver, 1998.

Whysall, Steve. *100 Best Plants for the Coastal Garden.* Whitecap Books, Vancouver, 1998.

Whysall, Steve. *The Blooming Great Gardening Book.* Whitecap Books, Vancouver, 2000.

Willis, A.R. *The Pacific Gardener.* Whitecap Books, Vancouver, 1995.

Yeoman, Andrew. *West Coast Kitchen Garden: Growing Herbs and Vegetables.* Whitecap Books, Vancouver, 1995.

Canada

Arthurs, Penny. *Canadian Gardening's Small-Space Gardening*. Penguin Books, Toronto, 1997.

Cullen, Mark. *Canadian Garden Design: Ideas and Inspiration for your Garden*. Penguin Books, Toronto, 1999.

Harrap, David. *Roses for Northern Gardeners*. Lone Pine Publishing, Edmonton, 1998.

Harris, Marjorie. *The Canadian Gardener's Guide to Foliage & Garden Design*. Random House, Toronto, 1993.

Harris, Marjorie. *Favourite Garden Tips*. HarperCollins, Toronto, 1994.

Harris, Marjorie. *Seasons of my Garden*. HarperCollins, Toronto, 1999.

Hole, Lois. *Lois Hole: Herbs & Edible Flowers*. Penguin Books, Toronto, 2000.

Hole, Lois. *Lois Hole's Rose Favourites*. Lone Pine Publishing, Edmonton, 1997.

Hole, Lois. *Lois Hole's Tomato Favourites*. Lone Pine Publishing, Edmonton, 1996.

Johnson, Lorraine. *Grow Wild! Native Plant Gardening in Canada*. Random House, Toronto, 1998.

Lima, Patrick. *The Art of Perennial Gardening: Creative Ways with Hardy Flowers*. Firefly Books, Willowdale, Ontario, 1998.

Primeau, Liz. *Canadian Gardening's Great Ideas for the Garden*. Penguin Books, Toronto, 1996.

United States

Barton, Barbara and Ginny Hunt. *Gardening by Mail*. Houghton Mifflin, New York, 1997.

Druse, Ken. *The Collector's Garden*. Clarkson Potter, New York, 1996.

Druse, Ken. *The Natural Shade Garden*. Clarkson Potter, New York, 1992.

Hinkley, Daniel. *The Explorer's Garden*. Timber Press, Portland, Oregon, 1999.

Kruckeberg, Arthur. *Gardening with Native Plants of the Pacific Northwest: An Illustrated Guide*. University of Washington, Seattle, 1982.

Lovejoy, Ann. *Cascadia*. Sasquatch Books, Seattle, 1997.

Lovejoy, Ann. *Naturalistic Gardening*. Sasquatch Books, Seattle, 1998.

Sunset Western Garden Book. Editors of Sunset Books & Magazines, Menlo Park, California, 1995.

Recommended Websites

Although nothing compares to curling up with a good book, the Internet is a great source of information for gardeners. Check out some of these sites, but keep in mind that while this information was correct at the time of printing, things change rapidly on the Internet. Websites that are here today can vanish without trace.

Alpines
http://www.alpinegardensoc.demon.co.uk (The Alpine Garden Society)
http://www.nargs.org (North American Rock Garden Society)

Aquatic Plants
http://www.azgardens.com/gallery2.htm (Aquatic Plants)
http://www.blueiriswatergardens.com (Blue Iris Water Gardens)

Bamboo
http://www.bamboo.org/abs (American Bamboo Society)
http://www.bodley.ox.ac.uk/users/djh/ebs (European Bamboo Society)

Begonias
http://www.geocities.com/RainForest/4369 (Canadian Begonia Society)

Birds
http://www.bcadventure.com/adventure/wilderness/birds (Birds of B.C.)
http://www.birding.bc.ca (Bird Watching in B.C.)
http://www.songbirdproject.org (Song Bird Project)

Bonsai
http://www.absbonsai.org/abs_home.html (American Bonsai Society)
http://www.bonsai-bci.com (Bonsai Clubs Int'l.)

Books
http://chapters.ca (Chapters books)
http://whitecap.ca (Whitecap Books, Vancouver)
http://www.amazon.com (online bookstore)
http://www.bolen.bc.ca (Bolen Books, Victoria)
http://www.bookwire.com (online bookstore)
http://www.gardenbook.com (online bookstore)
http://www.sidneybooktown.com (bookstores in Sidney, Vancouver Island)
http://www.timberpress.com (Timber Press Portland, Oregon)

Botanical Artists
http://huntbot.andrew.cmu.edu/ASBA (American Society of Botanical Artists)

Botanical Gardens
http://www.city.vancouver.bc.ca/parks/ parks&gardens/vandusen/default.shtml (VanDusen Gardens)
http://www.hedgerows.com/UBCBotGdn/index.htm (UBC Botanical Gardens)
http://www.islandnet.com/~hcp (Horticulture Centre of the Pacific)

Botany
http://www.botany.net/ (Internet Directory for Botany)
http://www.helsinki.fi/kmus/botcons.html (Internet Directory for Botany)
http://www.herbaria.harvard.edu/china (Flora of China)

Bulbs
http://www.asis.com/~nwilson (species and miniature narcissus)
http://www.bulbsociety.com (The International Bulb Society)
http://www.bloomingbulb.com (Blooming Bulb Company)
http://www.cyclamen.org (The Cyclamen Society)
http://www.dutchbulbs.com (Van Bourgondien Bulbs)
http://www.mc.edu/~adswww (American Daffodil Society)
http://www.mmews.demon.co.uk (Jacques Amand)
http://www.rareplants.co.uk (Paul Christian—rare plants; unable to ship to Canada, but excellent information and photo resource)

Butterflies
http://webmesc.mesc.nbs.gov/butterfly/ north_america/north_america.html (North American Butterflies)
http://www.chebucto.ns.ca/Environment/NHR/ lepidoptera.html (Butterflies of the World)

Camellias
http://www.med-rz.uni-sb.de/med_fak/physiol2/ camellia/home.htm (American Camellia Society)
http://www.peach.public.lib.ga.us/ACS (American Camellia Society—Massee Lane Garden)

Clematis
http://www.clematis.org (American Clematis Society)
http://www.dialspace.dial.pipex.com/clematis (International Clematis Society)

http://www.howells98.freeserve.co.uk/index.html (Dr. John Howells on Clematis)

Composting
http://www.cityfarmer.org (City Farmer, Vancouver)
http://www.crd.bc.ca (Capital Regional District, Vancouver Island)
http://www.gvrd.bc.ca (Greater Vancouver Regional District—click on index, then composting)
http://www.oldgrowth.org/compost (compost resource page)
http://www.smartgardening.com (composting information)

Dahlias
http://www.dahlia.com/quebec/index.html (Quebec dahlia web site)
http://www.dahlia.org (American Dahlia Society)
http://www.mountain-inter.net/~wholland (Wayne Hollands's Dahlia Page)

Daylilies
http://www.casarocca.com (Italian Specialty Nursery)
http://www.connect.no./garden/daylilies/HE (Hemerocallis Europa)
http://www.daylilies.com/daylilies (Daylilies Growing Along the Information Highway)
http://www.daylilies.org (American Daylily Society)
http://www.daylily.com (The Daylily Exchange)
http://www.primenet.com/~tjfehr/daylily.html (Friends of the Daylilies)

Delphiniums
http://www.delphinium.demon.co.uk (The Delphinium Society)

Ferns
http://www.hardyferns.org (The Hardy Fern Foundation)
http://www.inetworld.net/sdfern (Fern Resource Hub—San Diego Fern Society)
http://www.visuallink.net/fern (American Fern Society)

Fruit Trees
http://coopext.cahe.wsu.edu/infopub/eb1640/ eb1640.html#kiwi (Washington State University)
http://www.appleluscious.com (Apple Luscious Apple Orchards, Salt Spring Island)
http://www.bcfta.bc.ca (BC Fruit Testers Association)

General
http://carver.pinc.com/home/gardenmall (a resource for Victoria gardeners)
http://gardening.wsu.edu/ (Washington State University)

General (cont.)

http://hg.women.com/homeandgarden/refer/resor/ 00plen11.htm (Homearts Plant Encyclopedia)

http://www.ahs.org (American Horticultural Society)

http://www.gardencrazy.com (general gardening website)

http://www.gardenguides.com (general gardening website)

http://www.gardeningbc.com (B.C. Resources)

http://www.gardening-online.co.uk/home.html (U.K. gardening website)

http://www.gardennet.com (general gardening website)

http://www.gardenweb.com (general gardening website)

http://www.gardenworld.co.uk/links/links.html (U.K resources)

http://www.hedgerows.com (Hedgerows Garden Tapestry)

http://www.icangarden.com (Canadian gardening internet resources)

http://www.interlog.com/~bcook/ogw/ogw2.htm (Over The Garden Wall—money-saving ideas)

http://www.nwgardening.com/gardenlinks.html (Seattle-based gardening website)

http://www.oxalis.co.uk (British gardening online)

http://www.plantlovers.com (Vancouver, B.C. website)

http://www.prairienet.org/ag/garden (Garden Gate— general gardening website)

http://www.rhs.org.uk (The Royal Horticultural Society)

http://www.slugsandsalal.com (Gardening in the Pacific Northwest)

http://www.suite101.com/category.cfm/gardening (general gardening website)

http://www.tpoint.net/neighbor (Gardening Launch Pad)

http://www.vg.com (Time Life—Virtual Garden)

Grasses

http://www.hostas.com/grasses (Hosta and Ornamental Grasses Enthusiasts)

http://www.smgrowers.com/ (wholesale grower in Santa Barbara—good links)

Herbs

http://hortweb.cas.psu.edu/vegcrops/herbs.html (Dept. of Horticulture, Pennsylvania State Univ.)

http://www.athomewithherbs.com (At Home with Herbs TV Show)

http://www.bibliomania.com/NonFiction/Culpeper/ Herbal (Culpeper—The Complete Herbal)

http://www.cpgarden.demon.co.uk (Chelsea Physic Garden)

http://www.richters.com (Richters)

http://www.tuscanfarmgardens.com/ (Tuscan Farm Gardens)

http://www.ultranet.ca/hazelwood/index.htm (Hazelwood Herb Farm)

Hostas

http://www.hosta.org (American Hosta Society)

Importing Plants

http://www.cfiaacia.agr.ca/english/plant/oper/ oper_e.html (Canadian Food Inspection Agency site)

Integrated Pest Management

http://pupux1.env.gov.bc.ca/~ipmis/ipmis.html (B.C. government)

http://www.nysaes.cornell.edu/ent/biocontrol/ index.html (Cornell University)

Irises

http://easyweb.easynet.co.uk/~ianblack/japiris/ index.html (Japanese Irises)

http://www.irises.com (Society for Japanese Irises)

http://www.irises.org (American Iris Society)

http://www.pacificcoastiris.org (Society for Pacific Coast Native Iris)

http://www.telp.com/asi (Aril Society International)

Lilies

http://www.bdlilies.com (B&D Lilies)

http://www.heronswood.com (Heronswood Nursery)

http://www.lilies.com (Cobeco Lilies)

http://www.mnews.demon.co.uk (Jacques Amand)

http://www.lilynook.mb.ca (The Lily Nook)

http://www.oxford.net/~lilium/nals/index.html (American Lily Society)

Magazines

http://www.ab.sympatico.ca/mags/cangardening (Canadian Gardening)

http://www.bhglive.com/gardening/index.html (Better Homes and Gardens)

http://www.coastalgrower.com (Coastal Grower— Gardening in the Pacific Northwest)

http://www.garden.com (Garden Escape Magazine)

http://www.gardengatemag.com (Garden Gate)

http://www.gardenmag.com (The Virtual Gardener)

http://www.growingedge.com (information for inside and outside growers)

http://www.hortmag.com (Horticulture Magazine)

http://www.organicgardening.com (Rodale—Organic Gardening)

Magazines (cont.)

http://www.rebeccasgarden.com/magazine/index.html (Rebecca's Garden)

http://www.taunton.com/fg/index.htm (Fine Gardening)

http://www.tropicalgardening.com (Online Tropical Gardening Magazine)

http://www.watergardening.com (Water Gardening Magazine)

Master Gardeners

http://whatcom.wsu.edu/ag/homehort/mg/mgarden.htm (Washington State)

http://www.hcs.ohio-state.edu/mg/mg.html (Ohio)

Native Plants

http://rbcm1.rbcm.gov.bc.ca/nh_papers/nativeplants/index.html (Royal BC Museum)

http://www.bcadventure.com/adventure/wilderness/wildflowers (Wildflowers of British Columbia)

http://www.epa.gov/glnpo/greenacres/wildones/ (Natural Landscaping)3

http://www.nps.gov/plants/index.htm (Native Plant Conservation)4

http://www.orst.edu/instruct/for241/ (native trees of the Pacific Northwest)

http://www.tardigrade.org/natives/ (Pacific Northwest Native plants)

http://www.wnps.org (Washington Native Plant Society)

Orchids

http://retirees.uwaterloo.ca/~jerry/orchids/ (an orchid enthusiast)

http://www.chebucto.ns.ca/Recreation/OrchidSNS/wcanada.html (Canadian Orchid Sites)

Organic Supplies

http://www.tvorganics.com (Terra Viva Organics)

Plant Information

http://www.sierra.com/sierrahome/gardening/encyc (plant database)

Rhododendrons and Azaleas

http://www.azaleas.org (Azalea Society of America)

http://www.exbury.co.uk (Exbury Gardens)

http://www.halcyon.com/rsf (Rhododendron Species Foundation)

http://www.whidbey.net/meerkerk/gardens.html (Meerkerk Gardens—Washington State)

http://www.rhododendron.org (American Rhododendron Society)

Roses

http://www.ars.org (American Rose Society)

http://www.classicroses.co.uk (Peter Beales, U.K.)

http://www.country-lane.com (Country Lane Gardens)

http://www.everyrose.com (The Rose Reference Database)

http://www.helpmefind.com/sites/rrr/sltlist.html (Rose Database)

http://www.mc.edu/~nettles/rofaq/rofaq-top.html (The Rose Page)

http://www.meilland.com/indexeng.htm (Meilland Roses, France)

http://www.mirror.org/groups/crs (The Canadian Rose Society)

http://www.pickeringnurseries.com (Pickering Roses, Ontario)

http://www.rosarian.com (rose resource and information page)

http://www.roses.co.uk (Harkness Roses, U.K.)

http://www.weeksroses.com (Weeks Roses, California)

http://www3.sympatico.ca/mor-pol/ (Quebec Rose Society)

Seeds

http://csf.colorado.edu/perma/abundant (The Abundant Life Seed Foundation)

http://heirloomtomatoes.net/Varieties.html (Heirloom Tomato Seeds)

http://members.aol.com/pasiflora1 (Passiflora and Brugmansia Seeds)

http://www.burpee.com (Burpee Seeds)

http://www.eseeds.com (seeds from mail-order supply companies worldwide)

http://www.evergreenseeds.com (Oriental Vegetable Seeds)

http://www.heirloomseeds.com (Heirloom Seeds—heritage fruit and vegetable seeds)

http://www.richters.com (Richters)

http://www.seedcatalog.com (The Garden Path Nursery—seed catalogue)

http://www.seedsearch.demon.co.uk (Seed Search Comprehensive Directory of Growers)

http://www.seedsofdistinction.com (Seeds of Distinction—unusual seeds)

http://www.shepherdseeds.com (Shepherd's Seeds)
http://www.silverhillseeds.co.za (South African Seeds)

http://www.thompson-morgan.com (Thompson and Morgan)

http://www.veseys.com (Vesey's Seeds)

Seeds (cont.)

http://www.virtualseeds.com (Virtual Seeds Company)

http://www.westcoastseeds.com (West Coast Seeds)

Specialty Nurseries, Garden Centres and Garden Stores

http://bluehavennursery.com (Blue Haven Nursery, Mill Bay)

http://mars.ark.com/~barport/streamside.htm (Streamside Native Plants, Courtenay)

http://oberon.ark.com/~innersea (Inner Coast Nursery—heritage fruit trees)

http://www.brecks.com (Brecks Nursery)

http://www.coastnet.com/~plants/index.html#toc (Brentwood Bay Nursery, Saanich)

http://www.cowichan.com/dinternursery (Dinter Nursery, Duncan)

http://www.digthis.com (Dig This)

http://www.earthfuture.com/gardenpath (The Garden Path)

http://www.gardenworks.ca (Garden Works)

http://www.heronswood.com (Heronswood Nursery, Washington State)

http://www.jacksonandperkins.com (Jackson and Perkins)

http://www.lecoteau.bc.ca/farms (Le Coteau Farms and Garden Centre, Saanich)

http://www.oakridgenursery.com (Oakridge Nursery, Duncan)

http://www.perennialgardener.com (The Perennial Gardens, Maple Ridge)

http://www.phoenixperennials.com/index.htm (Phoenix Perennials, Richmond)

http://www.plantdel.com (Plant Delights Nursery, North Carolina)

http://www.plantlovers.com/ (Erickson's Day Lilies, Langley)

http://www.southlandsnursery.com (Southlands Nursery, Vancouver)

http://www.thimblefarms.com (Fraser's Thimble Farms, Salt Spring Island)

http://www.weluvgardening.com (Cannor Nurseries)

Succulents

http:www.houseleeks.freeserve.co.uk

TV Shows

http://www.canadiangardening.com (Canadian Gardening)

http://www.canadianhouseandhome.com (with link to Gardening Life)

http://www.gardenersworld.beeb.com (BBC Gardeners' World)

http://www.tv.cbc.ca/canadiangardener (Canadian Gardener)

Violets

http://www.sweetviolets.com

Virtual Tours of Gardens, Public and Private

http://urbangarden.com (Urban Garden—Vancouver, BC)

http://www.alfresco.demon.co.uk (an English country garden)

http://www.butchartgardens.com (Butchart Gardens3

http://www.cix.co.uk/~museumgh (Museum of Garden History)

http://www.clubi.ie/dillongarden (Helen Dillon's Dublin garden)

http://www.clubi.ie/garden-club/index.html (Ireland's Online Gardening Resource)

http://www.discovervancouver.com/features/chinatown/chinatown.shmtl (Dr. Sun Yat-Sen Garden)

http://www.minter.org (Minter Gardens)

http://www.royalroads.ca (Hatley Park)

Water Gardening

http://www.hookedonwatergardens.com (Pacific Ponds)

http://www.pondlady.com (The Pond Lady)

Index